AF673674

From Fatigues to Civvies

Memoirs of a Paratrooper

Lt. Gen. V.K. Nayar

MANOHAR
2013

First published 2013

ISBN 978-93-5098-007-1

Published by
Ajay Kumar Jain *for*
Manohar Publishers & Distributors
4753/23 Ansari Road, Daryaganj
New Delhi 110 002

Typeset by
Ajay Arts
New Delhi-110002

Printed by
Salasar Imaging Systems
Delhi-110035

In loving memory

of my wife

SAJNI NAYAR

Contents

Illustrations

Foreword

During my long association with the Armed Forces I have had the opportunity of reading many books written by former army officers. I consider Lt. Gen. Nayar's autobiography of particular significance as, unlike other writings of this genre, it contains a meaningful analysis of issues relating to national security management and telling comments on the internal management and morale of the Indian Army.

The author was commissioned in the Corps of Signals in end 1951 and, after a great deal of struggle, he succeeded in achieving his uncompromising ambition to serve in the Infantry and that too only in the Paras. His experiences during the early years of service enhanced his determination to do and support only that which was right and, throughout his career, he refused to bend or compromise in any manner.

In 1961 the author was deputed on a Special Mission to Barahoti and virtually directed to 'forestall the Chinese' (this followed the Chinese threat earlier to Indian officials not to return to Barahoti and Longju). It is significant that the Eastern Command had refused to carry out the task later given to a young Captain. Needless to say, there was a glaring lack of clarity about the Chinese issue in the politico-military establishment and it is, therefore, not surprising that the consequential bungling paved the way to the 1962 debacle. His experiences in J&K during the 1965 War and, later, his involvement with the counter-insurgency operations in Mizoram, sensitized the author to the enormous damages which accrue if there is any deficiency in the planning and execution of military operations.

The author's comments on his experiences while in command of 2 Para and, subsequently, while serving in the Para Brigade bring out the difficulties which he had to face for refusing to compromise regimental traditions and for resisting the implementation of unjust orders. He tells us of his struggle, for nearly a decade, to successfully oppose the raising of 3 MLI when 2 Para (erstwhile 3 MLI) was already in existence. It is equally worrisome to read that he had to put up a fight for the unit to return to the Para Brigade, which he subsequently trained to achieve the highest levels of airborne efficiency. 2 Para brought the Army invaluable dividends in the 1971 operations in Bangladesh.

On the commencement of the 1971 War, the author, then serving in the College of Combat, was attached to the Operations Branch of the HQ Western Command. Later, he was given command of an independent Brigade Group in the desert where he worked alongside Maj. Gen. Sundarjee (later Army Chief). He has high regard for Gen. Sundarjee's intellectual capacity but disregards the latter's obsession with mechanized warfare and bemoans his senior's inability to recognize the harsh realities. In this context, the author asserts that those placed in positions of high authority must learn to live up to their roles.

On promotion to General Officer's rank, the author was given the prestigious command of 8 Mountain Division, to deal with insurgencies in Manipur and Nagaland. He achieved marked success in improving the internal security situation in both the states and in Manipur he earned significant credit for capturing Bisheshwar Singh, the PLA Chairman. It could be said that the author's success was due to his policy of giving no quarter in dealing ruthlessly with the insurgents and, side by side, imposing severe penalties for the failure of command by any of his officers. On the non-combat horizon, his serious concern to promote the well-being of all the people in the area of his responsibility and working feverishly to resolve their problems won admiration for him, even from the leaders of the insurgent groups.

In 1983, while functioning in the Military Operations Directorate, he was closely involved with the planning and launching of Operation Meghdoot in Siachen. About the same time, Operation Blue Star was about to happen. With regard to this venture, the author, was quite openly opposed to the Army's involvement, and blames the Army HQ for failing to understand the environment then prevailing in Punjab and the consequences of Army's involvement in such a political issue. In this context, he maintains that Operation Blue Star was 'ill conceived and executed in a bull-headed fashion to achieve military success with total disregard to the damage and casualties suffered'. While exposing some of the myths which have got related to this Operation, the author is sharply critical of both Generals Vaidya and Sundarjee.

After taking over as Corps Commander in Punjab the author maintained his stand regarding the non-involvement of the Army and sustained his posture even after Sant Longowal's murder and even later, throughout his tenure as the Western Army Commander. His analysis of the developments consequent to Mrs. Gandhi's assassination and the subsequent governmental reaction of viewing all members of a certain community with suspicion, even those in the Army, and his comments on the events in Punjab during 1985-90, merit serious consideration.

During his tenure as Corps Commander and, thereafter, as Army Commander in the Western Theatre he devoted a great deal of attention to raise the operational preparedness of his Command and, side by side, launched various initiatives to win back the confidence of the people of this trouble-torn state. Closely associated with the planning of the phased exercises titled 'Brass Tacks', the author has made some very insightful comments on the defence and security organization structures and civil-military relations and stressed the need for developing a strategic culture.

In 1993 the author was appointed Governor of Manipur when the state was being torn apart by insurgencies and ethnic clashes. In view of his earlier experience of dealing with insurgencies in this region he lost no time in establishing a firm grip on the prevalent situation. While reporting his appraisal to the President of India, the governor attributed the disturbed situation to a deeply entrenched politico-insurgent nexus and had the courage to even name the ministers and other persons involved in unlawful activities. Within a month of occupying the Raj Bhavan, the governor was given additional charge of Nagaland. Through sustained efforts he brought the law and order situation under control and, side by side, speeded up the implementation of developmental schemes and programmes. Thus, within a year of the President's Rule, there was evidence of development and progress in both the states.

When the suspended Manipur Legislative Assembly had just a few weeks left of its residual tenure, the Government of India, rejecting the governor's advice, decided to install a popular government there. Notwithstanding his clear opposition to New Delhi's aforesaid decision, the governor proceeded to implement the Centre's directive in a transparent and orderly manner. While restoring the elected government, the governor had announced a time frame, agreed to by the political parties, within which the new chief minister would be required to test his strength in the House. When this crucial date was approaching, the Governor was asked to extend the earlier decided time frame. He refused to do so despite calls from the Union Home Minister and other highly placed personalities. Instead of retracting from his decision in the matter, and thus ensuring his continued stay in the Raj Bhavan, the governor considered it fit and honourable to tender his resignation, to preserve the image and integrity of the constitutional position held by him. Needless to say, his successor advanced the date for the trial of strength of the chief minister by another two weeks, even beyond the extended time frame demanded from his predecessor.

After his premature departure from the Manipur Raj Bhavan the author lost no time in getting involved in matters in which he had been interested all his life. He made useful contributions to the Centre for Policy Research, United Service Institution of India and the Centre for North East Studies and Policy. In between, he served as a member of the Government of India's Task Force on Internal Security (2000).

This volume also contains the author's critical comments on certain other issues, which include the IPKF Operations in Sri Lanka; the problems faced in the north-east region; J&K; terrorism; left wing extremism; conflict resolution and management; and the role of intelligence in a counter-insurgency and terrorism environment. The author has drawn pointed attention to the unfortunate consequences arising from the lack of timely political management of conflict situations in our country.

The author has also recorded his pained comments on the declining image of the Indian Army in the recent years, which he attributes to the dilution of standards and systemic failure to manage the officer cadre. In this context, he has stressed the need to restore professionalism and ethical values, and reinstate the traditional balance between 'style and substance'. In the context of the declining standards, both professional and ethical, the author has recalled the hallowed motto of 'Service before Self' inscribed on the entry to Chetwode Hall at the Indian Military Academy and stressed the imperative need to abide by it.

This book should be of considerable interest to serving and retired Defence Service officers, senior functionaries in the national security establishment, parliamentarians, and all those who have interest in the preservation of the country's unity and integrity.

Raj Bhavan, Srinagar N.N. VOHRA
18 October 2012

Preface

Twenty-three years of retirement is a bit more than half of the life I served in the Army and has been equally fulfilling and rewarding, as old friendships continued and new ones were forged. Old memories revived and new ones of cheer and sorrow added. I have always gained from sharing with others. This is a narration of events, memories and reflections of what I and others I knew experienced, which I now wish to share.

The idea to put down my memories in writing occurred to me on a number of occasions, mostly instigated by friends and well wishers, who were a part of it, but it remained a moot point. It was first seriously suggested by my colleagues of the Zakhama days and later by those during my tenure in the Military Operations Directorate. After I resigned as Governor, Shri N.N. Vohra, who was the then Home Secretary, when I went to Manipur and Nagaland, insisted that I should record my experience of those turbulent days as it will be of immense value. The feeling that these may be useful also came during discussions at the Centre for Policy Research and United Service Institution of India and on a number of other occasions. Bharat Karnad even said that study, research and other serious writings I was doing were useful but it would be of greater help if I shared my experience. I often thought about it but never got down to it. It was probably the loneliness after my wife's passing away and to fill the void that I decided to do it.

I am blessed with a good memory which has helped me to put it together, along with some old writings and jottings. The narrative naturally centres around army and professional happenings but the focus is on individuals and the humane part.

Noida, 2013 Lt. Gen. V.K. Nayar

Acknowledgements

After retirement I was fortunate to have been associated with the United Service Institution, the Centre for Policy Research and Centre for North East Studies and Policy, and had the opportunity to interact with a large number of academics and professionals from all fields. I benefited from all of them.

I was also lucky to have served alongside some of the best professionals and human beings in the Services as well as outside it. The experience and learning from these people always stood me well and influenced my thinking and actions. I am thankful to my many friends and colleagues who helped me to make this effort. I am particularly grateful to Shri N.N. Vohra, presently the Governor of Jammu & Kashmir, my army colleagues Lieutenant Generals Mathew Thomas and Satish Nambiar, Chaman Lal from the police, Sanjoy Hazarika and Bharat Karnad from academia and my former Aide-de-Camp S. Ravi whose coaxing and encouragement helped me to undertake this. I am thankful to Col. V.K. Singh of the United Service Institution of India who helped me by going through the initial drafts and Ashok Kumar who did most of the typing.

Most of all I am grateful to God and the Army who provided me with the best opportunities in life.

LT. GEN. V.K. NAYAR

Abbreviations

ARMY

Ranks

2/Lt	-	Second Lieutenant
Brig	-	Brigadier
Capt	-	Captain
Col	-	Colonel
FM	-	Field Marshal
Gen	-	General
Hav	-	Havildar
Hav Maj	-	Havildar Major
JCO	-	Junior Commissioned Officer
L/Hav	-	Lance Havildar
L/Nk	-	Lance Naik
Lt	-	Lieutenant
Lt Col	-	Lieutenant Colonel
Lt Gen	-	Lieutenant General
Maj	-	Major
Maj Gen	-	Major General
Nb Sub	-	Naib Subedar
NCE's	-	Non-Combatants Enrolled
Nk	-	Naik
Sep/OR	-	Sepoy or Other Rank
Sub	-	Subedar
Sub Maj	-	Subedar Major

Unit/Formations

Bde	-	Brigade
Bn	-	Battalion
Comd	-	Command
Coy	-	Company
Div	-	Division

Arms and Services

Armd Corps	-	Armoured Corps
Arty	-	Regiment of Artillery
ASC	-	Army Service Corps
EME	-	Corps of Electrical and Mechanical Engineers
Engrs	-	Corps of Engineers
Inf	-	Infantry
MES	-	Military Engineering Service
Ordinance	-	Army Ordnance Corps
Signals	-	Corps of Signals

Appointments

2IC	-	Second-in-Command
AAG	-	Assistant Adjutant General
AAQMG	-	Assistant Adjutant and Quarter Master General
AG	-	Adjutant General
AQMG	-	Assistant Quarter Master General
Army Cdr	-	Army Commander
Bde Cdr	-	Brigade Commander
BGS	-	Brigadier General Staff
BM	-	Brigade Major
Brig i/c Adm	-	Brigadier incharge Administration
CE	-	Chief Engineer
CGS	-	Chief of the General Staff (old appointment)
CO	-	Commanding Officer
COAS	-	Chief of the Army Staff
Col GS	-	Colonel General Staff
Corps Cdr	-	Corps Commander
COS	-	Chief of Staff
DAAQMG	-	Deputy Assistant Adjutant and Quarter Master General
DCOAS	-	Deputy Chief of the Army Staff
DGMI	-	Director General of Military Intelligence
DGMO	-	Director General of Military Operations
DGMT	-	Director General of Military Training
Dy Bde Cdr	-	Deputy Brigade Commander
Dy GOC	-	Deputy General Officer Commanding
E-in-C	-	Engineer-in-Chief
GOC	-	General Officer Commanding
GOC-in-C	-	General Officer Commanding-in-Chief

GSO-1, 2, 3	-	General Staff Officer Grade 1, 2, 3
Maj Gen i/c Adm	-	Major General incharge Administration
MGGS	-	Maj Gen General Staff
MGO	-	Master General of Ordnance
MS	-	Military Secretary
OC	-	Officer Commanding
PSO	-	Principal Staff Officer
QMG	-	Quarter Master General
VCOAS	-	Vice Chief of the Army Staff

Decorations

AC	-	Ashok Chakra
AVSM	-	Ati Vishisht Seva Medal
UYSM	-	Uttam Yudh Seva Medal
KC	-	Kirti Chakra
MVC	-	Mahavir Chakra
VrC	-	Vir Chakra
VSM	-	Vishisht Seva Medal
YSM	-	Yudh Seva Medal
SC	-	Shaurya Chakra
SM	-	Sena Medal
PVC	-	Param Vir Chakra
PVSM	-	Param Vishisht Seva Medal
SYSM	-	Sarvottam Yudh Seva Medal

Old British Decorations and Other Services

DSO	-	Distinguished Service Order
MC	-	Military Cross
KC	-	Kings Cross
GM	-	George Medal
VC	-	Victoria Cross

Ministries and other Government Organizations

CBI	-	Central Bureau of Investigation
I & B	-	Ministry of Information and Broadcasting
IB	-	Intelligence Bureau
MEA	-	Ministry of External Affairs
MHA	-	Ministry of Home Affairs
MOD	-	Ministry of Defence
NIA	-	National Intelligence Authority
RAW	-	Research and Analysis Wing

Other Services

AOC-in-C	-	Air Officer Commanding-in-Chief
CAS	-	Chief of Air Staff
CDS	-	Chief of Defence Staff
CNS	-	Chief of Naval Staff
FOC-in-C	-	Flag Officer Commanding-in-Chief
Gp Capt	-	Group Captain

Others

Para	-	Parachute
Cdo	-	Commando
Air OP	-	Air Observation Post
TA	-	Territorial Army
IMA	-	Indian Military Academy
IPKF	-	Indian Peace Keeping Force (in Sri Lanka)
NDA	-	National Defence Academy
HQ	-	Headquarters
OTS	-	Officers Training School
RR	-	Rashtriya Rifles
SS	-	Short Service
SSB	-	Services Selection Board
ISI	-	Inter Services Intelligence of Pakistan
J & K	-	Jammu & Kashmir
LOC	-	Line of Control
Pak	-	Pakistan
POK	-	Pakistan Occupied Kashmir

POLICE AND CENTRAL ARMED POLICE FORCES

Organizations

AR	-	Assam Rifles
BSF	-	Border Security Force
CPF	-	Central Police Force
CRPF	-	Central Reserve Police Force
ITBP	-	Indo-Tibetan Border Police
NSG	-	National Security Guard
PMF	-	Para Military Forces

Appointments

ADGP	-	Additional Director General of Police
AIG	-	Additional Inspector General of Police

Comdt - Commandant
DGAR - Director General of Assam Rifles
DGP - Director General of Police
DIG - Deputy Inspector General of Police
DIGAR - Deputy Inspector General of Assam Rifles
Dy Comdt - Deputy Commandant
IG - Inspector General of Police
IGAR - Inspector General of Assam Rifles
Inspt - Inspector
SHO - Station House Office
SP - Superintendent of Police
SSP - Senior Superintendent of Police
Sub-Inspt - Sub-Inspector

TERRORIST/INSURGENT/MILITANT ORGANIZATIONS

Punjab

KCF - Khalistan Commando Force

J & K

HUM - Hizb-ul-Mujahideen
JKLF - Jammu & Kashmir Liberation Front
LET - Lashkar-e-Taiba

Sri Lanka

LTTE - Liberation Tigers of Tamil Eelam
JVP - Janatha Vimukti Peramuna

North East

HPC - Hmar People's Convention
IBRF - Indo Burma Revolutionary Front
KCP - Kangleipak Communist Party
KDF - Kuki Defence Force
KNA - Kuki National Army
KNF - Kuki National Front
LWE - Left Wing Extremists
ME - Meitei Extremists
MNF - Mizo National Front
NFG - Naga Federal Government
NNC - Naga National Council
NSCN - National Socialist Council of Nagaland

NSCN(IM)	-	National Socialist Council of Nagaland (Issak Muivah)
NSCN(K)	-	National Socialist Council of Nagaland (Khaplang)
PLA	-	Peoples Liberation Army
PREPAK	-	Peoples Liberation Army of Kangleipak
PULF	-	Peoples United Liberation Force
RGM	-	Revolutionary Government of Manipur
RJC	-	Revolutionary Joint Committee
SS	-	Self Styled
ULFA	-	United Liberation Front of Assam
UNLF	-	United National Liberation Front

CHAPTER 1

Beginning of the Beginning

I was born in a middle-class family belonging to Batala in Gurdaspur district of Punjab, with the only distinction of owning a small *haveli* known as 'Nayar-de-Haveli', which I visited only once in my childhood. My father was a middle level officer in the accounts department of the erstwhile North-Western Railway housed in Pili Kothi near Fatehpuri in old Delhi. I am the eldest of eight siblings of four brothers and four sisters. My youngest brother died in infancy. We lived in Ram Nagar area of Paharganj and I did my early schooling in Turkman Gate Municipal School till class four. My father moved to Shimla on deputation to a newly created joint office of civil and military if I remember correctly, known as the Central Provisions Office, Eastern Supply Group Council to organize and provide logistic support to the Eastern theatre of war in Burma (Myanmar), this was my only remote connection with the Services before I joined the Army. In Shimla I joined Sir Harcourt Butler School at Jakhu, which no longer exists and a Kendriya Vidyalaya has come up in its place in a new building after the old one was destroyed in a fire. Both summer and winters in Shimla those days were most enjoyable for its different charm and serenity where nature dominated the environment in its full glory unlike the present day when it has become a concrete jungle.

I recount one of the most vivid and horrifying experiences of childhood, which on hindsight appears most comical and shows my lack of awareness then. I was in class six and on one of the school holidays, while we brothers and sisters were playing together, my second sister came and told me that she had swallowed a one paisa coin and started crying. At a total loss and fearful of danger to her life, I picked her up on my back and carried her from Phagli Government quarters where we lived to Rippon Hospital, a distance of over 5 km uphill. I told the doctor in emergency to save my sister. The doctor having listened to our story smiled and told me not to worry and that she would be alright with the medicine he was giving and to look for the coin next morning after ablutions. I was happy and relieved and bought her sweets and made her walk back part of the way.

At the end of the Second World War in 1945 my father's deputation came to an end and on return to Delhi I joined the Delhi branch of Sir Harcourt Butler Higher Secondary School on Mandir Marg, next to the present Birla Mandir on the erstwhile Reading Road. It was at that time considered as one of the best schools in India with a good record both in academics and sports, with its students obtaining distinction and securing top positions in the higher secondary examinations. I had played football and hockey for my school in Shimla and on joining the school in Delhi in winter found cricket to be the most popular game. To get into the school cricket team I joined a local club on Babar Road close to our residence on Rouse Avenue. Our guide at the club (you could not really call him a coach) was the elder brother of one of my friends (Prem Nath Sharma) who represented Delhi in the Ranji Trophy as an opening bowler. A few weeks after joining I asked him as to what was the quickest and surest way to get into the team. He told me to become a wicket keeper as there were few of them and there was less competition. I practised and was selected for the school team. Later I was selected as a reserve wicket keeper for the combined schools eleven. I improved my batting and opened the innings for my school and later for the college team and also played a few matches for the university before joining the army. In the Army I played for IMA and later the Command in inter-services tournament.

I passed my higher secondary examination in 1949, just managing a first division because of my weak mathematics and joined pre-medical to be a doctor in keeping with my mother's wishes, who belonged to a family of doctors. Life at school and for a year at college was simple, eventless and centred around studies and sports. After a full day of studies, games and cycling from place to place we just had the strength to finish our homework, sit around with the family, eat and go off to sleep. Social activities were confined to family gatherings, picnics with friends and classmates and occasional visits to the cinema. One looked forward to family and religious events more as a get together to meet relatives, where every elder male was a Taya or Chacha and lady a Mausi or a Bua. Unlike nowadays, children's results caused no tension to parents and their interest was confined to that you passed and were promoted to the next class. Parental interest and involvement increased when one finished school and college education was decided to meet the requirement of the profession they wanted you to join in keeping with your capability. Guidance was firm and well directed with few dissensions from either side.

At the college a few of my friends told me that they were appearing for the entrance examination for the Indian Military Academy. More out of fun and to keep them company I also filled out the form. The examination centre was in University of Delhi. When we reached there, we were overawed by the seniority and mature looks of most of the candidates. We thought we had no chance. Some of them even looked down on us because of our small stature and boyish looks. We must have done well as two of us were called for interview at the Services Selection Board at Meerut. Before sitting for the examination when I had asked my father's permission to appear he showed little interest. But when I got the call for appearing before the selection board, he told me that depending on the result, the decision would be mine as he could hardly guide me. He also told me that his experience of working with the British service officers in Shimla during his deputation was healthy and he liked them for their uprightness.

The president of the Services Selection Board was Col. M.S. Pathania, later a Major General. Like most others we were totally raw to the Service environment. We were kept on the run and there was no time to think, we just put our heads down and did what was demanded of us. I distinctly remember that one of the candidates from the Royal Indian Military College commonly called Rimcolians shouted a lot to us during his command task and drove us as if his life depended on it. We found it both annoying and amusing. Later when I was made the group leader and given a different task, I thought about it and explained to everyone as to how it was to be done and who was to do what. One or two persons gave some suggestions, we discussed it and were able to do the task well and in time. I must have done well as I and my colleague Pawitter Singh (late Lt. Col. Pawitter Singh, SM) from the Royal Indian Military College joined the 8th Regular Course at the Indian Military Academy in January 1950 and we became good friends.

INDIAN MILITARY ACADEMY

Two years at the Indian Military Academy were as eventful as any other course before or after. However, we were subjected to more ragging and hammering than others as we were easier to monitor due to our small numbers. Two things are etched in my memory, which are worth mentioning. First, that most of the officer instructors had war experience, they were physically brave and active and a high proportion of them were decorated. They looked and behaved in a confident manner but never made an effort to impress us. They were always with us on all training, did not pretend to be extra intelligent or have the last word. Secondly, there was emphasis on physical ability, capability to stand stress, think rationally and be decisive. You were made to implement your decisions and learn from others. The emphasis was on making rather then breaking people. We were driven to the brink and helped to enhance our capacity. The junior staff was a mixture of British and Indian; the process of Indianization had started. They were professionally as good as the British but lacked their sense of humour and the knack to motivate the cadets. I think as a nation we lack the ability to laugh at ourselves and tend to be tense and dry. Games and sports were given prime importance in the army.

Having completed two terms of six months each, in the third term emphasis shifted to advance military and leadership training. There were a number of exercises and camps, where cadets were given leadership role in rotation. Camp Chindits was the toughest, based on an idea similar to Maj. Gen. O.C. Wingate, DSO's expedition in Burma during the Second World War. Gen. Wingate died in an air crash on 24 March 1944 during the War. We were in the fifth and final day of the Chindit's endurance march, going along a dry riverbed was very tough. Moreover it was hot, sultry and we were stretched to the limit of our endurance. We were rationed one water bottle per day, thirst sapped our energy and the sizzling heat of the riverbed resulted in mirages. With our tongues literally hanging out we ultimately reached the camp, where we learnt that Daniel one of our toughest cadets and a good sportsman from Naushera Company had died of exhaustion just short of the camp as he was not permitted a sip of water. We were most downhearted and upset. It further added to our misery when we were told that we would not be able to attend his funeral as the camp had still not finished and there were other people to attend to it in an appropriate manner. It taught us self-discipline, mental resilience, emotional control, to carry the weak and above all that even the strongest may weaken in given circumstances. This may sound harsh, inhuman, criminal and may be unacceptable today. Lt. Col. S.K. Korla, DSO, MC (later Major General and awarded a PVSM), our company commander told us after the incident that our team had to win the Chindit's race back to the Indian Military Academy. He put the weakest amongst us as the leader. Given a chance, this 'weakling' drove us to the finish point and victory.

During the watermanship camp in the third term, the final event was for everyone to cross the Roorkee canal. The weak and the non-swimmers were paired with good swimmers; I was one of the weak ones. To help us keep afloat we were asked to pick one of the floating aids. I picked a sealed 18 kg empty ghee tin. The canal was over 200 ft wide with a fast current of 8 to 10 knots. In spite of my partner being a very strong swimmer we were hurled down the canal and crossed it 2 km downstream but cross it we did. I have never hugged anything so hard in my life as I did the ghee tin. While crossing the canal I swore to perfect my swimming, which I did before passing out of the Indian Military Academy.

I passed out in the middle of the course but enjoyed the physical and the mental challenges and battles and always tried to be with the physically toughest and hated the clever and slippery types, who were not sincere and took them on. It cost me some uncalled for beating in boxing, I was a total novice but had the satisfaction of having lasted on my feet. During our time very few opted for technical arms or services, most preferred combat arms. A number of cadets who had some knowledge or army background opted for Armoured Corps or Artillery and the remainder of the majority for the Infantry. I did the same with Infantry as my choice. The Advisory Board recommended me but my academic background of being in higher mathematics and science came in the way and Army Headquarters sent me along with a few more on the Infantry panel to the Signals as it was short of officers.

A RELUCTANT SPARROW

During the young officer's course at the School of Signals at MHOW, I was a reluctant and belligerent student. As time passed I became more adamant and my desire to return to Infantry increased, which drew firm and blunt admonishment from the staff. What annoyed me most was the sound of the Morse code which required a blank mind to understand and I was always thinking of my predicament. Some time in the middle of the course a senior Signals officer posted on the faculty of the Senior Command Wing in the Infantry School heard about me during one his visits to the bar in the school mess. He was kind enough to come to me and told me that what I was doing will not help me to go back to the Infantry, instead if I failed I would probably be sent to one of the services like the Ordnance or Army Service Corps. That really put the fear of god in me and I worked so hard that I almost topped the course.

During my tenure with the 17 Para Field Regiment, Brig. Raj Batra, Chief Signal Officer of Eastern Command visited the signal section in the regiment which I was commanding. After seeing everything he told me that he was happy with my performance but had some advice to give. He told me, it is not good enough to be efficient but one should also look efficient. I am not sure if I imbibed his advice fully. Those days the signal section provided the control, CO's and 2IC's sets and acted as the control of the regimental net. During one of our practice camps being held at the Tughlakabad ranges near Delhi, we had an Air OP allotted to us, who happened to be Bobby Sihota, an old officer of the regiment. In one instance when the guns were still moving into a new gun area, the Air OP came up on the wireless net and asked if the regiment was ready on the regimental grid. Thinking that he was still on the ground at Palam airfield, the Adjutant Capt. Gurbachan Singh told Nk. Sheikh Imam, the control operator, to report ready. As soon as control confirmed to Air OP call sign 6 that the regiment was ready, 6 responded by giving the grid reference of a target and ordered ranging on it. We were mistaken, the Air OP was not at Palam but flying in the fold of the hilly range in front of us. Both me and Gurbachan were non-plussed as what to do. Nk. Sheikh Imam came up with the cry 6 for 6 strength 2, renet Charlie Mike Zebra (you can't be heard properly so we will realign you on the wireless net), he did that till the guns were ready when he reported ready on regimental grid. We thereafter ranged onto the target and engaged it. I got a ticking off from the CO for failure of communications but the initiative of Sheikh Imam saved the day for the regiment. When the CO heard the truth from Gurbachan he personally thanked Sheikh Imam for his quick reaction and thinking, while we two officers were confused. Brig. P.P. Kumramangalam the brigade commander (later COAS) and Director Artillery Brig. Lichfield were present. Brig. Kumaramangalam was very keen that I convert to the Gunners but I persisted with my dream to return to the Infantry.

I served in the Signals for seven and a half years, most of it in the Para Brigade. I am sure that if I was not in this formation, I would not have got my transfer back to Infantry. The struggle was long and at times arduous. My pleas and requests fell on deaf ears. I was in the middle of the eighth year of my service when I decided that enough was enough and if my request was not accepted I would quit. I could not afford to do so earlier as I had not completed the minimum period before you could quit if permitted without paying the cost of your training, which I could not afford. I therefore put in another application for my transfer to Infantry, with the plea that if my request was not accepted than I should be released from service. As on earlier occasions, I received a curt reply that my request had been considered and rejected. I was in a quandary as what to do, when fate smiled. General Maxwell Taylor, the American COAS, came on a visit to India. Being an airborne chief he was to visit the Para Brigade and of course see the Taj Mahal and other monuments. I was ordered to be his local ADC during the visit. As per the protocol Lt. Gen. S.P.P. Thorat, KC, DSO, the Eastern Army

Commander was to receive him. On seeing Lt. Gen. Thorat I saw my chance and requested the Brigade Commander, Brig. D.G.R. Rajwade, if I could speak to the Army Commander about my case and ask why it has been rejected. The Commander was reluctant and told me that it was a very formal occasion as such it will not be proper. When I told him that I could not miss the opportunity, he was annoyed but knowing my determination and with the Brigade Major Jogi Mandher, pleading my case, he relented. He spoke to the Army Commander for me to see him informally during lunch at Fatehpur Sikri dak bungalow. The brigade commander started the ball rolling by telling him the background of my case, he ended up by saying that he had recommended the case for my transfer to infantry as I deserved it. The Army Commander said that it was rejected on the recommendations of the Chief Signal Officer. Gen. Thorat was also told by him that I was not technically inclined and was lazy. Hearing this I lost my cool and told the Army Commander that if I was lined up with ten other officers and the Chief Signal Officer was asked to point out Tubby Nayar he won't be able to recognize me and he knows nothing about me. Just as the Army Commander was about to lose his temper at my outburst, the brigade commander interjected and told him that I had done well on all professional courses and he would not have recommended my case if I did not fully deserve it. That seemed to have done the trick as I learnt later on. Orders were issued by HQ Eastern Command that my case for transfer to Infantry has been recommended and forwarded to Army Headquarters and the officer was not to move till his case was decided. A few months passed but nothing further was heard. On checking I learnt that the Signals Directorate had decided to forget about it and not to reply to the MS letter asking for my release from the Signals. They even posted me out to the Armoured Division Signal Regiment, which was overturned on HQ Eastern Command's directions. I went to Delhi and with great difficulty managed to call on Brig. A.C. Ayaippa, Director and Signal Officer-in-Chief and after a few drinks and some heated argument I extracted a promise from him that in spite of all the opposition in the directorate he will release me. He fulfilled his promise. Fearing that things may go wrong again I visited the Infantry Directorate and requested the staff officer to request Brig. Harbaksh Singh, the then Director, if I could see him. Without any ceremony after a cup of tea I was ushered in. Brigadier Harbaksh Singh recognized me as one of his old cadets as he was our Deputy Commandant at the Indian Military Academy. After listening to me, he told me that the Infantry was a big ocean and one more good or bad fish would not make any difference and I was most welcome. He had spoken straight as a soldier and I was encouraged and felt happy and confident.

BACK TO INFANTRY

The orders transferring me to Infantry came a few months later, posting me to 2 J&K Rifles, in spite of the fact that I continued to be a para volunteer and had opted for 2 Para. I was quite happy and was preparing to join my new unit but the Officiating Commander Col. Onkar Deva would not have it and told me that I could not move. I was in a fix but luckily orders came saying 'for 2 J&K read 2 Para'. I joined 2 Para in May 1958. I can never thank enough all the wonderful people who helped me to achieve my heartfelt desire. I owe a debt of gratitude to Lt. Gen. Thorat, Maj. Gen. D.G.R. Rajwade, Jogi Mandher and Samir Sinha, and most of all to my friends who helped and encouraged me when I was down in the dumps. When I was thanking Jogi Mandher, who was one of my biggest supporters, he told me that I probably deserved it and told me that the only way I can thank people who helped me was by not letting them down. I have always been conscious of it and never forgotten it.

My service with the Signals was most enjoyable and rewarding and I made a lot of friends in the Corps. Even people who were opposed to my transfer were supportive and helpful in my efforts for transfer. Their support and involvement can be gauged from the fact that when the orders for my transfer came I was officiating and as such could not leave till relieved. In spite of knowing this, my 2IC Capt. later Maj. Gen. B.P. Murgai without my knowledge organized a special durbar and sent Sub. Gandharv Singh, the Senior Junior Commissioned Officer, to call me to the lines on the pretext that something has happened and I must come immediately. I rushed to the lines and enroute asked the subedar as to what has happened, but he would not say anything except that I should see for myself. On reaching the lines I found the entire Company assembled there and after reporting to me Murgai immediately went into a brief discourse of my desire and struggle for transfer to the Infantry and that they did not at all like it but were happy for me. This was followed by Gandharv Singh offering me a new maroon beret with a Para Regiment badge along with badges of rank and the lanyard on a silver salver and asked me to wear them. I told them that I could not do it as I was still their OC but they would not listen. Ultimately I submitted to their wishes. I walked out of the lines as a Para Regiment Officer. I went straight to Brig. Rajwade's office and informed him about what had happened. He smiled and told me to keep it on. I was touched by the whole incident. It ended with an infantry officer commanding the Para Brigade Signal Company. It was a good end and held the hope and promise of a wonderful new beginning.

On the day I joined 2 Para the whole battalion was watching the inter-company volleyball match, so I joined the Battalion Headquarter squad on physical training. The JCO head clerk Sub. Sharma after taking my permission marched off the squad for a road walk and run and I joined them. After a few kilometres, looking at me he asked the squad to step out, his intention was quite clear that even a head clerk had the audacity to test a newcomer. I decided to settle the issue with this lot immediately. So when the JCO asked permission to change to a walk I told them that we should step out more to a faster run. I broke out into a really fast run till the squad was stretched over 1 km. When we returned to the lines and the squad was dismissed, the JCO came to me and told me that I was 'fit for' and welcomed me to the battalion.

Those were the days of test exercises which were set by the formation headquarters to test a unit's battle-worthiness. My battalion was to undergo one shortly after I joined it. 'C' Company Commander Maj. S.S. Grewal was away from the battalion, so for the test exercise an officiating company commander had to be appointed. Amongst the available officers in the order of seniority it was me, K.S. Pannu and Mulkraj, all captains. Since I had just joined, the CO quite rightly said that although I was the seniormost but in the interest of the unit either Pannu or Mulkraj should command 'C' Company. He asked me if I had any objections. I told the CO that I was happy to do what was best for the battalion and moreover at present I was least equipped for it. I thought that I had done the right thing and that was the end of the matter. But the 2IC Maj. Ujjal Gupta interrupted and said 'C' Company was mine by right and if I was to learn my job I should start right now, never mind the mistakes. I commanded the company in the test exercise. It was a night withdrawal exercise. I had Sub. Rethal as my senior JCO and 7 Platoon Commanders, he was a wonderfully aggressive person and a master at arms in physical training with a rudimentary idea of tactics. The other two platoon commanders were Peter Atre and R.P. Limaye, both newly commissioned officers and as raw as me. The stage was set for disaster and it was a hilarious one. I lost two of the platoons at night and could establish contact with them only in the early hours of the morning and managed to reach the next position just before daylight. Only the 2IC and the Adjutant knew about it and after firing me they told me to go on with the digging. We dug so hard that we were ahead of other companies when the brigade commander and the CO came for inspection. In this Sub. Rethal was a great asset both in shouting and lending a helping hand. After the exercise 2IC Ujjal Gupta took my training in hand. I was made a section and a platoon commander for a month each and did a fortnight each with the specialist platoons. I was sent on Junior Command course and was told that I was as good as anyone else in the battalion. One could not ask for a better start. I felt lucky to be in 2 Para and resolved to always do my best for the paltan. I took over Bravo Company after a few months.

During the summer of 1959 the company was ordered to move to Delhi for Internal Security duties under Delhi Area. On arrival at Delhi we were guided to the Wazirabad Water Works. I thought that it was only our location till I was told that we were there because there was no water flowing into the inlet channel and we were to help to restore the flow. I thought that it should be the job of engineers, after all what could the Infantry do. I was discussing this with my senior JCO Sub. Shankar Bodhe, MC, who was a firm believer that you had to have infantry presence to resolve any crisis. Just then with all sirens blaring, the GOC of Delhi Area, Maj. Gen. U.C. Dubey, himself an engineer arrived and ordered a D4 dozer to be put in the inlet channel. But it went a few yards and got stuck. It was followed by a D7 dozer but that also got stuck resulting into further discussion. Bodhe sahib was a keen listener to the entire discussion, I purposely kept away as I had still to find a solution to the problem in my mind. Just then we again heard sirens and the Officiating COAS and GOC-in-C Western Command, Lt. Gen. Kulwant Singh, arrived and got into a discussion with the GOC. Suddenly Bodhe sahib marched up to the Chief and after saluting him asked him as to how he was, Gen. Kulwant Singh shook his hand and asked him as to how the battalion was and what was he doing in Delhi. He knew the battalion well as it had served with distinction under him. Seeing this I picked up courage and went forward and saluted him. He went back to the GOC and re-started the discussion. After a while Bodhe sahib again interrupted them and said to no one in particular but his loud voice was heard by all, 'when in our fields silt deposits and water stops flowing, we walk up and down in the channel, the silt is disturbed and flows away and water starts flowing'. Having said this he ordered the company to enter the channel and start marching up and down in platoon columns and both of us joined the company. Everyone was intrigued and sat on the bank watching us. After four hours the silt started shifting and water started to trickle in and by evening the dozers started to operate. The news was conveyed to the GOC and the Chief and there was jubilation all around. Lt. Col. (later Lt. Gen.) J.F.R. Jacob then GSO-1 of the Area sent a barrel of rum to the company. We had a good beat up. The next day we were told that we could return to the unit. Men wanted to stay on for a couple of days to see Delhi, I agreed. But when I learnt that troops were required for the industrial exhibition I ordered the company to pack up and we moved the same afternoon. It was a narrow escape as orders were issued for us to stay on for the same duties. It had rained a lot and the DR (messenger) was caught by the floods at Palwal while we pushed our vehicles through the water to safety. I was taken to task by the CO but we were saved from months of fatigue duties. I learnt that you cannot do without Infantry as they use common sense apart from knowledge and our biggest asset is our men who live close to the nature. I have always respected their views and judgement.

Infantry thrives on crisis and surmounts situations with initiative and innovation.

We had senior stalwart company commanders in Cedric Francis, R. MacMillan Smith and S.T. Appachanna, they commanded respect and were admired and were loved for their humane and kind nature. I did not serve with Cedric Francis but had heard a lot about him. He was serious and quiet by nature but was always there for the men and junior officers. I met him after retirement in Delhi and it is always a pleasure to meet him in Para get togethers. What all three of them did not know about men was not worth knowing. Mac Smith was an extrovert, with a disposition marked by joy, happiness and humour. A good sportsman, who excelled in hockey, he was originally from 4 Rajputana Rifles (Outrams) and a veteran paratrooper.[1] He wore thick glasses and always saw the brighter side of things and circumvented his short sightedness and night blindness with innovative humour. During a parachute jumping refresher course at the Paratrooper Training School at Kheria, I once crossed Mac without recognizing him, although he was dressed in the familiar OG field dress with a para smock denison (jacket) under a helmet. I heard a familiar voice saying 'Happy Landings Tubby'. Turning back I saw Mac's smiling face covered with sticking plaster. Before I could react, he said, 'Surprised! the sticky plaster is to keep the specs in place and to prevent them from dropping off'. Without these he could not see the ground approaching. In spite of a number of concussions and often hard landings he continued jumping. His landings were marked by loud 'F . . . s', still all in one piece. He joked that people get wounded in battle but he lands in the battle as a walking wounded. During night exercises, he was blind as a bat; Mohinder Kumar Mal, his batman (orderly), guided him to the objective with Mac wielding his stick as a feeler. Once on the objective, he would ask Mal to get a report from the platoons and one heard the familiar, 'All Stations Kilo3, report progress'. As soon as reports were heard on the wireless, Mac would order Mal to fire the very light success signal. He was all over the trenches, even inside them at times at night, but would not give up. Similarly, his turning out of the guard at night was a ritual we all loved to watch from a distance. On the day he had to turn out the guard, a cycle rickshaw was called half an hour earlier from the local cycle rickshaw stand as Mac could not cycle at night and Mrs Smith (Kay) had to accompany him. Mac fully dressed in uniform was helped into the rickshaw by Kay and then both of them would proceed to the Quarter Guard. About 10 yards short of the Quarter Guard, Kay would help him to get down and then align him to the front of the Quarter Guard. Mac would then march the distance to the marked stone, turn left, take five steps to the stone and take position. The guard would turn out and the guard commander would report, 'Guard is ready for the grand round'. Mac would recognize the NCO from his voice irrespective of which company he belonged to. After taking the report, he would order the guard to stand down, do an about turn, take five paces turn right and start marching, till he was in Kay's arms. She would guide him into the rickshaw and they would return home. A precision night exercise at its very best.

One of the most memorable and hilarious recollections is of Mac during a cricket match that the Parachute Brigade played with the Agra University team. Agra University batted first. Batting second we required 7 runs to win with 8 wickets down and 1 over left. I was batting at 60 when the eighth wicket fell. Mac walked in as the next batsman and I walked up to him and told him to watch the bowler's hand as he was mixing his leg breaks with the odd straight ball. Mac's reaction totally stunned me, he replied 'Tubby, never mind his hand if I can see the bowler then he is in for trouble'. Mac missed the first ball and I was a bit apprehensive but he hit the next one for a 4, the next one for 2 runs, missed one and scored 4 of the fifth ball and we won. I learnt that Mac as Staff Captain in the Sri division during the J&K operations in 1949, one night after a binge set fire to the mess building as he did not like its décor. Luckily he did not succeed. Next morning he was marched before Maj. Gen. K.S. Thimayya DSO the Divisional Commander, who asked him why he had tried to set fire to the mess. He coolly replied since the war had just finished he was celebrating and felt quite pinkish and did not like the dark building. Maj. Gen. Thimayya told Mac, to prevent him from feeling pinkish again, he would be the night duty officer for the next one month and in addition he would turn out each night four guards in the Badami Bagh cantonment. Such were the loving exploits of Mac.

He migrated to Australia after a stint at the Bombay Gymkhana Club after his retirement in the late 1960s.

Major S.T. Appachanna popularly known as Appachu amongst his contemporaries, was a quiet intellectual with a philosophical bent of mind and a soft gentle demeanor, who at times appeared detached and absentminded. A very caring person, whom men respected and loved. He took every opportunity to inculcate sophisticated thoughts and feelings amongst the younger officers and always used correct and civil language, a welcome change from army parlance. After the battalion was inducted into J&K, a field area, we often found him admiring the serene beauty of the Kashmir Valley. In Baramulla our mess and officer's tented accommodation were located on the banks of the Jhelum River, which was a source of great inspiration and joy for Appachu. Once after turning out the guard at about 2 a.m. at night I returned to my tent when I heard some soft rumblings beyond from the riverbank. I went there to enquire and found Appachu sitting there totally absorbed watching the full moon, its silvery light falling on the slow rippling river. He told me to sit down and watch the beauty of nature. I sat quietly with him for about half an hour, enjoying every bit of it, and then excused myself. Just as I was leaving, he told me 'Tubby, I thought you were better and could sit and stare at the beautiful things but you are the same'. All that I could do was to apologize and escape with some lame excuse. Although I had enjoyed the scene, I could not match his depth of appreciation of the beauty of nature.

The other popular character of the battalion was Capt. E.A. Thayagraj popularly known as Tiger. I had heard of him after joining the battalion and had met him briefly at Lucknow as the GSO-3 of the Para Brigade, before I joined the battalion. My first encounter with him was when the battalion moved to Baramulla in 1959. He was then a Ground Liaison Officer with the Air Force in Srinagar and I was a student at the Winter Warfare School in Gulmarg. We had come to Srinagar on Republic Day and we decided to call on Tiger and Rama his wife. After a few beers at his home we went to the Air Force mess and more celebrations and beer. After a fairly prolonged indulgence at the mess we returned to Tiger's house for lunch in his open Willy's jeep. The beer had made me feel a bit hot in spite of the freezing temperatures of minus 2°, so I took off my balaclava and opened the zip of my smock denison (para jacket) and felt wonderful as the cold air hit my head and open neck. The drive from Badami Bagh to Ram Munshi Bagh was short but proved to be my undoing and by the time we reached Tiger's house my head was in a spin and I felt terrible. As soon as I got down from the jeep, I rushed to the toilet and threw up. After washing up and cleaning the sink, when I came out Rama gave me a hot cup of coffee. It really felt wonderful. Tiger tucked me into bed and I was dead to the world. When I woke up it was dark and I found Tiger's two daughters Lata and Pushpa sitting on a chair and keeping vigil. As I stirred the girls told me 'Tubby uncle tum out ho gaye the' (Tubby uncle, you were drunk and out) and then they opened a tiffin box and offered me hot *idlis* and *vadas*. They also told me that mum and dad had gone to a party in the Air Force mess. This close encounter with the Tigers remained a point of hilarious reference for the rest of my life.

There are a lot of stories of Tiger's sense of humour of which I would like to confine to some witnessed by me and other officers of the battalion. Tiger got married to Rama in 1953 when he was with the brigade headquarters. One day Matthew Thomas, his course mate from the battalion, went to visit them. When he reached the house Rama told him that Tiger was having a bath and would join soon. Suddenly hearing Matthew's voice Tiger came out of the bathroom stark naked dripping with water. More than Matthew it was Rama who was more shocked and admonished him 'what are you doing?'. Tiger replied, 'cannot keep a friend waiting'.

On his return from Lebanon after a stint as an UN observer, having visited all the hot spots of Beirut and Cairo, Tiger decided to do a 'Chuchita' (belly dancing act) for the bachelors of the battalion. It was so real and hilarious that the ladies of the battalion demanded an encore show for themselves. We were all living in the Carriappa colony in Agra and three of the wives were expecting and would go out for walks as advised by the gynaecologist. One day when my wife, Jean Thomas and Champa Bahl were out for a walk, Tiger dressed as a pregnant woman in a *ghunghat* joined them and enquired in a feminine voice if they felt scratchy on the stomach. The ladies shared their confidence and asked for her experience (Tiger's), till much later they discovered it was Tiger.

Tiger teased the ladies till my wife started giving it back to him. Similarly, during a party in the mess after it had gone on for some time, Ujjal Gupta our bachelor CO, saw some ladies murmuring to each other. He felt there was something amiss. Of all the bachelors Ujjal or Uncle as we called him, trusted Capt. N.S. Uthaya (Uthy) the most, so he asked him to find out from the ladies, if anything was amiss. After talking to the ladies Uthy returned with a smile on his face and told uncle, 'Sir, it is better that you don't know, I feel it is one of Tiger's pranks'. We learnt later that just after the party had started Tiger slipped into the ladies bathroom and put some Eno's fruit salt nicely rolled into toilet paper and gently placed it inside the commode. As the first lady went inside to use the toilet, Eno's fruit salt on exposure to water threw up a bubbly fizz resulting in a scare and her rushing out of the toilet. This was the cause of their agitation.

Ujjal Gupta was the 2IC of the Battalion when I joined. He was widely respected by the officers and men. A shy and quiet person with a stinging sense of humour, he had been with the battalion during the Second World War and there was a deep bond amongst the veterans. Uncle would often quote indirectly to us while talking to Sub. Maj. Shankar Bodhe, MC as to how in spite of a war scenario officers always behaved as an officer and a gentleman. Younger officers held uncle in awe and to a few like Uthy he was a role model. A bachelor who was so shy of ladies that he would look at the walls and the ceiling while talking to them. He took over the Battalion from Lt. Col. Kuldeep Singh before we moved to J&K and left it after we returned from Goa. He commanded a brigade in 1965 operations and fell foul of Lt. Gen. Harbaksh Singh for being upright. He was an instructor at the Defence Services Staff College when I did the course in 1963.

1959 was to be an eventful year. The battalion received orders to move to J&K after a gap of ten years. The battalion arrived in Baramulla in October with winter cooling fast to reach below freezing point in December till March 1960. Living in wooden and brick huts, wood and cement bunkers and houseboats and dongas was a first experience for me and other new officers and men. In January there was a change in command with Ujjal Gupta as CO and Samir Sinha as the new 2IC. They were to take the unit through momentous events in the next few years. I took a mixed company for winter warfare training to Gulmarg and four of us qualified as instructors, little knowing that for Mulkraj, B.P. Singh and A.S. (Tari) Cheema it was to be their gateway to further achievements in mountaineering and Cheema was to finally stand on the pinnacle of Everest. For me it was to open a new world of adventure and professional opportunities. While the battalion was busy with operational duties they had to in addition deal with the mutinous troops of J&K militia and of the Assam Regiment. These were sad experiences. In mid-1961, J&K Militia units were agitated over disparities in terms and conditions of service between Militia and regular Indian Army in areas of pay, rations and leave, etc. 12 J&K Militia had maximum of 90 persons who revolted and were arrested. The ring leaders were tried by the CO in a Summary Court Martial and dismissed. Later J&K Militia were made regular and served outside of J&K and performed well. I had the honour to have 9 J&K Militia serve under me in 340 Independent Infantry Brigade group, the first one to serve outside J&K in 1975. Strange are the ways of Army Headquarters, first time outside J&K, they send them furthest to Trivandram (Thiruvanthapuram), to the strangest of environment changes. Almost at the same time 2 Assam located at Srinagar airfield staged virtually a mutiny under a hot-headed, arrogant officiating Sub. Major. The Commanding Officer, an equally adamant and hot-headed officer, precipitated the situation. Brigadier S.K. Kolra, DSO, MC sent by the GOC succeeded in getting the mutinous troops to lay down their arms. After surrender 2 Assam personal were moved to a camp in 2 Para location, the ring leaders, 2 JCOs and 27 ORs were segregated. 2 Assam was moved to Delhi by air for disciplinary proceeding under 2 Para escort. The battalion was specially picked by the GOC Maj. Gen. A.S. Pathania, MVC, MC for the difficult task due to his trust and faith in all ranks of the unit. Maj. S.C. Sinha the second-in-command of 2 Para was specially selected to help the 2 Assam officers, JCO and men in overcoming the aftermath as he had served for a while in the Assam Regiment and understood the JCO and men.

I joined the Winter Warfare School as Chief Instructor in December 1960. At that time it was only a 15 Corps local school managed in a very ad hoc fashion. Life surrounded by snow covered peaks was peaceful and calm and as Chief Instructor I was my own master. I had an excellent and the wildest lot on my team of instructors in Narender 'Bull' Kumar from Kumaon, J.C. Joshi (Big Joe) from the Sikhs, S.C. Vig from Guards and BP and Limaye from my battalion. The administrative head was Maj. D.S. Bath from the Assam Regiment. We lovingly called him 'Wilky' for his advice on skiing, which he never learnt. We even named a slope after him. There was lots of fun including bare body skiing down from Beta to Gulmarg in moonlight, thank god there were no serious mishaps. I always kept my fingers crossed. Our energy when not consumed by climbing and skiing in snow covered mountains of Beta, Khilemang and Aparwat was at its most destructive fury at the lower altitudes of Srinagar, which often resulted in me as the Chief Instructor being hauled up and admonished by various echelons of Division and Corps Headquarters depending on the damage inflicted by our pranks. The finest and the most destructive was that of uprooting, using picks, from a frozen road all the signs on the Residency Road in Srinagar as we did not like their bleak look under the overcast winter sky. These were put on various ski trails in Gulmarg, the one on top of Aparwat (the highest peak) read 'Silence Zone, no horns please'. Natural consequences followed, with the Chief Instructor being hauled up, Srinagar being put out of bounds for the rest of our stay at Gulmarg and to pay part of the cost of the signposts amounting to Rs. 2,000.

OPERATION TRISHUL : SPECIAL MISSION TO BARAHOTI

We had finished the first set of basic and advance courses and were enjoying the interlude with the weather warming up. The next lot of courses started in March with the usual protocol and fanfare and apart from others it had Tari Cheema from the battalion. We had done a couple of weeks when I was called to Delhi, I had no inkling of the purpose. My guess was that it was probably to present and discuss the paper I had written on the school being made an Army Institution. But I was totally wrong. I was first summoned to Srinagar to meet the GOC, Maj. Gen. A.S. Pathania, at his home, it being a Sunday. I skied down from Gulmarg to our rear base at Tangmarg and drove in the biting cold to the GOC's residence in Srinagar for the breakfast meeting. After a warm breakfast with him and Brig. P.S. Bhagat, VC, the then DMI, set me off to Delhi for a mission of which I was warned but not told. Delhi was mystifying and confusing. What intrigued me most was the fuss of having to meet the GOC, being flown in an Air Force aircraft specially sent for me, being received by Maj. Sahdev Saighal, GSO2 (MO2) and ordered to stay at the Queen Victoria Road mess rather than at my home in Delhi.

I was rushed from MO Directorate to the all powerful Chief of General Staff Lt. Gen. B.M. Kaul's office. During the briefing MOD and MEA were represented by H.C. Sareen and Jagat S. Mehta, both joint secretaries. After the briefing I gathered that I had to go to Barahoti to forestall the Chinese as a consequence of them surrounding our revenue parties in Barahoti and Longju the previous year and permitting them to leave with a warning not to return next year. A quarter inch map was thrust into my hand and I was told to plan. I was able to locate Barahoti on the map. When I asked as to what was my task in military terms, I was told to shut up and get out. Outside Gen. Kaul's office I met Lt. Col. E.A. Vas, the then officiating BGS of Eastern Command, who consoled me and told me that his command had refused the task and they (Army Headquarters) were looking for a person with no 'Mai Baap', so the axe fell on me, a lowly Captain, a mere Chief Instructor at High Altitude and Winter Warfare School. The Ides of March had set in. It was the month of April and there was no habitation beyond Joshimath, the belief was that the mission was doomed as a mountaineering expedition under Brig. Gian Singh, the Principal of HMI, had failed to cross Chorhoti Pass at 18,800 ft in the months of June/July a few years earlier due to its sharp face and drop and wind swept slopes.

After discussion with Maj. Saighal, my task became clear to me. It was to forestall the Chinese in Barahoti and establish the Indian Revenue party there before 1 May 1961. I was asked to pick my team and told that I could take the whole of the Winter Warfare School. I decided on a platoon from my own battalion and picked Cheema as the other officer. There were other senior officers available but I insisted on him. I also took Capt. Kumar under me to do the route opening and marking beyond the base camp. He was required for a short period of a fortnight only. He was in any case headed for the area for the Neelkanth expedition. I picked Capt. T. Ao, a Naga doctor with mountaineering experience, and Bala Krishna and Om Prakash of the last Everest expedition as the Signals detachment. It was a wonderful set of people and each one did us proud.

The story of a small force from 2 Para (Maratha's) long foray from Gulmarg to Barahoti in the central sector has been recorded in the official history. History is factual and impersonal but events leave a deep impression on the actual participants. I wish to share mine to honour my team and the memory of those not with us anymore. Barahoti is a small trading post and a grazing area in Uttarakhand then part of Uttar Pradesh. It is 29 miles north-east of the pilgrim centre of Badrinath as the crow flies and is 3 miles south of the Indo-Tibet border. Situated at a height of 15,000 ft, it is under snow for over nine months in a year and is one of the so-called disputed areas according to the Chinese. Indian revenue officials had been going to Barahoti since time immemorial when snows melted and traders from Tibet and India gathered for barter trade and grazing. These officials had collected taxes from both the Indian and Tibetan traders and graziers. We woke up to the situation when intelligence reports reached Army Headquarters in March 1961 that the Chinese intended to occupy Barahoti and Longju. The nearest Chinese troops were at Tolingmath, 50 miles over an easy track with a divisional headquarter at Gartok further north.

The team was the best one could ever have, with Bull Kumar from HAWS, Tari Cheema, Namdeo Sawant, Sita Ram Jadhav and a selected platoon from the paltan, Ao as doctor and the Everest Signal detachment. Before we set-off from Bareilly on 10 April, an Operational Order was issued. In essence it meant we were to be present but not visible and in the event of confrontation with the Chinese let them have the first say and opportunity to fire and we were to reply and return fire only after grievous or fatal hurt. With such clarity, we decided to forget and forgive and follow our basic military instincts and prudence. Later in 1988, during one of my visits to Lt. Gen. S.D. Verma (Retd.) in Kasauli I narrated this incident, he told me of his own experience. When Chinese intruded into Ladakh in October 1959 and shot up a police patrol, killing and wounding a number of policemen, at that time the defence of Ladakh was the responsibility of CRPF working under the MHA. After the incident Lt. Gen. Verma, the then GOC 15 Corps, received a signal on 31 October 1959, ordering him to take over the defence of Ladakh in addition to other commitments. The written instructions that followed were almost comical. For instance, he was told that if the Chinese intruded into Indian territory, we were to tell them to go back, if they refused to do so, we were to report to Delhi, and take military actions only after getting permission to do so. And presumably, all this had to be done through proper channels, i.e. the patrol commander to his unit, brigade to division, to corps, to command, to Army Headquarters, MOD, and then in reverse. Just imagine the time all this would take, during which, hopefully, the Chinese intruders and Indian defenders would stand still and look at each other. The incident is cited in his memoirs.[2]

On arrival at Joshimath[3] 100 high altitude porters promised by the UP government with a representative were nowhere to be seen. On our protests we were provided with two locals and few selected raw Biharis of the military porter company under raising at Bareilly. They were ill clad and not acclimatized. I decided to use them only up to Ghamsali after driving them hard, a bit inhuman but necessary. We gave them all our blankets, two sets of socks, warm pants and jerseys, snow boots and a set of wind proof jackets and trousers. Beyond Ghamsali we had to hump all loads ourselves and thus we had to move in small parties. We decided to be our own porters, camp establishing teams and assault teams, designation was only to define what one was doing at a given point of time. We arrived at Ghamsali (11,400 ft) on 18 April 1961 and found the village under 8 to 10 ft of snow, we decided to make it our base camp and established the advance camp 7 miles ahead at Kalajabar (14,700 ft) the next day. Kumar, Budh Singh Ale, Achukutty and Bhim Singh (one of the two locals) opened the route from Kalajwar to Chorhoti Pass on 22 April. But due to a blizzard and snowstorm it was only on the third attempt that both reopening of the route and crossing of the pass was attempted simultaneously on 26 April starting at 2 a.m. The crossing was made by me, Kumar, Cheema, with only one section, the Revenue Party from 9 Uttar Pradesh Special Police Force, radio and medical detachment as the rest were employed as porters. We were lucky to reach the eastern shoulder of the pass at 18,800 ft, which though higher, we decided to cross it there itself. Puja was performed at 0700 hours and sacrificial offering made, for which Budh Singh unknown to me had carried a goat. We could not locate the track going down and winds had started building up, therefore we decided to get down immediately. The descent was mostly on our bottoms with ice axes breaking our slide over the ice and rock face which was windswept. At the bottom of the pass, we found traces of track traverses, which could not be seen from top as from the pass to the bottom it was a sheer drop of 3,000 ft in less than 500 m. We negotiated the Bamjar rock face (16,700 ft) under strong winds and adverse weather on 27 April and reached Rimkhim the same day. Standing on top of the Rimkhim ridge, we could see the Indo-Tibet border and spread below us was the Barahoti plain, empty. 'Trishul' had hit its mark. The next morning the Revenue Party was established at Barahoti and a message of success was flashed to all.[4]

We had carried seven days rations and shared these with the Revenue Party, which was established at Barahoti on 28 April. We ran out of rations after a few days, these could not be bought up nor an airdrop could take place due to bad weather. After two days the drop happened due to personal liaison on wireless with Brig. Niranjan Prasad, the Para Brigade Commander, and Lt. Col. Sucha Singh, CO 1 Para. The first aircraft crashed in Girthi Gad of which we had no intimation and we were surprised when asked to trace it. Trace it we did with Kumar and Tari Cheema and saved the pilot, co-pilot and two members of the ejection crew, the aircraft had broken into two on crashing. It was a crash of all crashes but God saves some. This was followed by the first successful drop, which was 2 km away from our location in the adjoining valley and spread over 1 km but gave us some respite. After which things improved and the air force never let us down.

During May and June weather thawed a bit but the snowstorms continued, the longest one was from 1 to 12 May, in which we lost one porter and L/Nk Ajan, who succumbed to its fury due to acute laryngitis. On 12 May a party coming up was caught in a blizzard between the pass and Bamjar rock face. Fearing for their safety, I decided to go and look for them. Budh Singh Ale and Achukutty volunteered to accompany me. We reached the north face of Bamjar after seven hours of struggle through the blizzard and found the party safe but three straggler porters were missing. I decided to search for them across the Bamjar rock face and beyond. While crossing the rock face along the rope fixed for the purpose, when half way the rope gave away and I fell almost 100 ft, Achukutty feeling the tug, dug in with his ice axe. I was dangling for about ten minutes but it seemed like an eternity. Slowly with the help of the other two I pulled myself up. We refixed the rope and went across to search for the porters. We located two of them and brought them to safety, the third one could not be located due to darkness. His dead body was found behind a rock a few days later.

The Chinese had their Border Guards at Sarkia, Regimental Headquarters at Tolingmath and Divisional Headquarters at Gartok 33 km, 58 km and 96 km respectively from our border passes of Tunjun La, Marhi and Shalsh La over an easy track up to Sarkia and fair weather road beyond, while our nearest troops were at Lucknow. Our safety lay in knowing Chinese intentions well in advance and presenting a much larger force level. This was achieved by one rope (4 men) patrols up to the passes and beyond depicting larger strength by footprints and ski marks/trails. These were ably led by Tari Cheema, Sita Ram Jadhao and Namdeo Sawant and NCOs. The purpose was well achieved as the Tibetan revenue representative (known as Sarji) fearful of his safety fetched up only on 29 June and established rapport with our Revenue Party.

Once the Rimkin post was established and administrative base organized in the Rimkin Bowl normal routine of cooking food in the *langar* started for which Namdeo Sawant deserves all credit. One day, Sant Ram, our cook, had made cheese *pakoras*. We found that the troops relished the *besan* and *mirchis* and threw away the cheese stuffing. I was totally stumped and was determined to make them eat cheese. Melting snow for water and cooking were the main problems during patrols. We got over it by carrying two pressure cookers and stoves each in every rope, one for melting snow for water and other for *khichri* which became the staple diet.

As *khichri* was about to boil, one bottle of pickle, one tin of cheese and one tin of butter were added to it and after the second boil, the delicious meal was served. This was followed by a rich brew of bournvita laced with rum. This solved our problem of food for patrols and the men ate cheese. Similarly the Indian habit of early morning ablution caused quite a headache during the initial days but we overcame it by ordering that all such activity shall be permitted only after breakfast when the system like a cold engine gets lubricated after the initial start before slipping into gear. Having achieved the task, we were to be relieved by 8 Dogra by end June when the passes opened but our stay was prolonged up to 13 August due to delay by them.

During my debriefing in Delhi I was asked as to what I felt about the whole mission. I answered that it was an experience of a lifetime but asked why no pre-planning was done and why we had to rush into it; it could have saved a few lives. The answer was a smirk and I was shown the door. Similar was the fate of my report which I had prepared most painstakingly. The new GSO-2 (later VCOAS) told me that some day if I ever qualify and am fortunate enough to be posted to the Military Operations Directorate, I would find it in a leather bound jacket but unread. Hearing this I sent a copy of my report to 14 Rajput who were nominated later to occupy the Rimkhim post next year. My commanding officer received a DO letter of thanks from their commanding officer saying, how 'helpful it was as it saved few lives and a lot of effort'. Looking back a few years later I felt such incidents were a forerunner to 1962, which also largely diluted recognition of my team's efforts.

'Op Trishul'[5] to Barahoti is a tribute to the courage and resilience of 2 Para. Mountaineering expeditions take place in fine weather and assault teams are supported by other mountaineers and porters. Here the process was reversed and everyone along with 1400 loads had to get to Barahoti in winter in severe adverse weather. It is also at Barahoti that Tari Cheema's potential to be the first Indian atop Mt. Everest was discovered. God bless him and all others who made many sacrifices.

The narrative of Barahoti with the fond and everlasting association that we all and me in particular formed with Tari

Cheema will not be complete without remembering the man, soldier and above all a friend.

TARI CHEEMA: FOND REMEMBRANCES

The winter of 1960 was to be our second one in J&K and having survived the first one on the slopes of Gulmarg and freezing sleet of Baramulla and Srinagar, some of us were looking forward to returning to Gulmarg to renew our embrace with its contours. The month of November was passing slowly due to the chilly winds and any event was a break. On 17 November Mathew Thomas returned to the battalion after helping in setting up the Haile Selassie-I Military Academy in Ethiopia. As we were welcoming him, a smiling Second Lt. came forward and introduced himself as Second Lt. Autar Singh Cheema. When I asked him, 'where the hell did you come from', he just said, 'back of the 15 cwt truck'. Realizing that he was the new officer, I told him, 'See you a lot later'.

I had been the officer-in-charge of probation of all the new arrivals for over a year primarily because the commanding officer felt I was fair, though harsh according to some who had been rejected. In one case I had to explain to Ujjal Gupta then 2IC and now CO as the officer ran away from the paltan during probation and had to be brought back from the bus stand in Agra. When Ujjal asked me as to why he ran away, I told him that he was good but a shirker and there was no place for such people in 2 Para. A few years later I met him in Srinagar Transit Camp. He came forward to meet me, we both were Majors. He said, 'Sir, that was a wakeup call, I am doing well'. I thanked him for coming forward and meeting me. Last I heard he had become a brigadier.

Next day onwards I put Autar through the grill and over the month of probation, I found him to be better than excellent in Battle Physical Efficiency Tests and he took the grilling in his stride, never feeling tense or under pressure. I asked him to repeat some of the critical physical and mental tests for the satisfaction of the CO and other officers. When the CO asked him as to what games he played, with a smile and cheer on his face he proudly announced that he was the captain of the college and university Bhangra Team. The CO smiled and when I said what good it will do to Marathas, he said he will teach them and it will add to their versatility of *Malkham* and *Laziem*. I finally wrote just two lines in his probation report. 'A very tough and mentally agile young officer, who can take stress in his stride and has high potential.' In spite of my bidding for him, he was posted to Charlie Company.

It was during our move beyond Ghamsali when we had to hump all loads ourselves and move in small parties, where Tari Cheema's efforts to push the loads forward proved useful. I could depend on him totally and a base camp was established at Kalajabar with all the essential loads of the first party by 24 April, in spite of heavy snow on the previous two days. Cheema accompanied the first party under me to see the route and returned with Kumar to push forward essential medical and other stores. Similarly, Tari Cheema's effort to trace and locate the air crash along with Kumar and later again going to the site of the crash to cremate the dead and bring their ashes was praiseworthy. It showed his maturity, dedication and enthusiasm to perform such difficult tasks at a young age.

We shared the tough patrols and rescue missions between the two of us as Kumar had left after a fortnight for the Neelkanth expedition. Noteworthy are the special patrols to Sangcha Mala and Lapthal led by Cheema in the snowbound virgin mountains. Similarly, his efforts to rescue the 8 Dogra patrol which had got lost in a blizzard and reconnaissance of the Girthi Gad route ordered by 9 Infantry Brigade were commendable. He not only located the lost patrol but also carried out in addition the reconnaissance of Yong area. He was my worthy partner and made me proud of my confidence in him. I have always enjoyed the pleasure of being correct in judgement to pick him for the mission. We were a mixed lot. Ao the doctor could not live without meat and taught us how to trap beavers in the snow for the same. While Tari was happy to eat and drink anything but his thirst for beer increased as time passed, for it was not part of our air drops. All three of us (officers), the signal detachment and our batmen lived in one ten men arctic tent. But we never lost respect and neither did the men feel uncomfortable. We all grew beards and admired it on each other. The best is we remained totally humane and never lost our sense of humour.

We arrived at Ghamsali village, the first habitation, on our return journey on 15 August where people had just returned, after winter in July. We celebrated Independence Day with *chang*, a local brew closest to beer and were presented a handspun *pattu* dyed in vegetable colours, the like of which I had never seen. Our return journey was made all the more memorable due to our visit to the shrines of Badrinath, Govindghat and Hemkund Sahib and the Valley of Flowers. I am glad that we took some time off to do this. Tari's thirst for beer which kept on eluding him as 8 Dogra had no beer, at Roorkee all the beer was flat, as a teetotaller wine member at the Bengal Sappers Mess had kept the old beer as vintage liquor. At Bareilly, they finally met darling beer and by the time I returned after settling the men both the doctor and Cheema had blissfully passed out. Finally the Trishul had stuck and beer flowed. Cheema was awarded the Sena Medal for his work during the special task force along with us. We probably deserved more but the events had over taken due to the Chinese aggression of 1962 and our efforts though recognized had shifted to the margins. On our return, while Cheema, the doctor and the special task force went to join the battalion at Agra, I came to Delhi for debriefing. In Delhi I met Mohan Kohli and Bull Kumar preparing for the Everest expedition. I told them that I had found a person who will climb Everest and put forward to them Cheema's name. I pestered them till they relented. Pre-Everest was his basic/advance course in mountaineering. He scaled Everest, the first Indian ever to do it after Tensing. My faith and confidence in Tari was rewarded.[6] He was honoured with Padma Shri and Arjuna awards by the government for his achievement.

As a sequel to the Everest success, when later he was selected as Principal of HMI everyone felt that he was too young, compared to Brig. Gyan Singh, Tensing Norgay and Bull Kumar. I maintained that if he could climb Everest without much experience, why can't he run HMI? He again proved me right. He saw, learnt and listened and acted as a friendly superior, who was sensitive and humane. People liked to have him around. The Gorkha land agitation was on the boil, it had even permeated to the institution but he made the atmosphere and environment temperate and congenial. Mr. Sareen, the then Defence Secretary, complimented Cheema for it.

I happened to be at the Defence Services Staff College as a Senior Instructor, when Cheema came for the course. I told him, Tari you have climbed Everest, you must tell them what it was like and how you felt. He replied, people know it. I told him they want to hear it from you. I forced him to speak on his climb to the Everest top. It was so well received that he was invited from Coimbatore to Ooty to Bangalore. He became a celebrity and both he and Arjinder were guests of honour everywhere. He reminded me of Maj. John Dias of the Garhwalis, equally shy and full of humility. Maj. John Dias was the leader of the Second Indian Everest Expedition, while giving a lecture on the expedition he covered everything without mentioning that he was the leader of the expedition. A mischievous officer asked him, 'John, who was the leader', he replied 'I was given that honour'.

He went to 7 Para and later was selected to convert and command 1 Para, a special Commando Unit. He was the best person for the job but we felt he had a few odds stacked against him. But he overcame every hurdle and succeeded. 1 Para commando owes a special debt to him for what they are today. He gave them a steady head start and the oldest battalion of the Indian Army 67th Punjabis (1 Para) is grateful to him.

Both me and my wife Sajni kept in touch with Tari and Arjinder, who was the silent strength of Cheema the tough man. She supported him throughout the travails and triumphs of life as she did in his last struggle. I was in Chandi Mandir, when on 25 May 1989 a call came from Arjinder that Tari was not well and he was passing blood. Lt. Gen. F.N. Billimoria, the Corps Commander at Bhatinda was alerted and I requested him to evacuate Cheema in an ambulance along with a doctor to PGI Chandigarh. I spoke to the Director PGI and also kept a team of doctors ready at the Command Hospital. He and Arjinder arrived next day and investigations at the PGI started immediately. Both me and Sajni went to see him and learnt the details from Arjinder. During my second visit he called me in alone and told me that it is 'The Everest', it took John, I feel I have the same. There is a suspicion amongst the mountaineers, particularly about Everest that exposure at that level makes people prone to suffering from leukaemia/blood cancer. John Dias died of it. Tari was referring to his death. I told him it may not be so and even if it is you will prove them wrong. He asked me not to mention it to anyone, least of all to Arjinder. I promised him. What a man, even in his worst hour of trial, he did not want to cause pain to his loved ones. In spite of showing a cheerful and positive disposition to Tari, I became apprehensive and we decided to shift him to Tata Memorial Cancer Institute in Mumbai. He was moved to Delhi and then flown to Mumbai.

This was the first time that my faith in the Indian establishment was shaken. I am narrating it only so that it might help someone else by awakening their conscience. When I spoke to Tata Memorial Institute, they told me that they wanted Rs. 2 lakh before admitting him. I told them that I would be the guarantor. I did not want to pay it from the Command Funds as it would be ethically wrong. So I started working on sources in Delhi. I requested Mrs Margaret Alva, the then Sports Minister in Rajiv Gandhi's cabinet and I also spoke to Harish Sareen, former Defence Secretary and Chairman of the Mountaineering Federation of India. Sareen was most sympathetic and promised to do his best. When I again spoke to Mrs Margaret Alva after two days, she told me that she was still considering it. I told her curtly that Cheema is a national hero and if there is any delay in financial help I will go to the prime minister. Fortunately, with all the cajoling and threatening, help came from all quarters and Tari progressed well. He was discharged and shifted to the Bombay Area Officers' Mess for recovery as it was close to the Tata Memorial Institute.

Our periodic contacts with Arjinder were all positive and indicators of happy tidings. In the meantime I had retired and come to Delhi. Then came the jolt, Tari had to fulfil his prophecy, he developed some infection and in spite of best efforts and prayers of all he did not recover. He breathed his last on 16 November 1989 with a peaceful smile on his face. I accompanied his body from Delhi to Ganganagar with others to pay our last respects to this great human being and soldier. He was as serene in death as in life. He is with us in our cherished memories. We feel his presence when we talk or do things which we did together or have been known to do. Tari you shall ever—ever live and be with us always.

All Everesters believe that they have the possibility of developing blood cancer—Brigadier Mulkraj had told his wife before marriage of this possibility. Roma, his wife, was a doctor. She had replied that the percentage was too low to worry about it.[7]

I was asked by Arjinder to speak at the release of a book of memoirs, *More than Everest* on 20 May 2011 on the extraordinary life of her late husband Autar Singh Cheema. It was a sentimental journey into the past and of our close association with Tari. It was about emotions and pride. In spite of great achievements in various spheres of human endeavour, he remained a good human being throughout life, who brought exuberance, comfort and solace to all who came in contact with him. He responded to the calls of destiny spontaneously and with vigour and rode the tide. He gave up a distinguished military career to respond to his family's need after his brother's accident and knew where his responsibility lay. The enlightened soldier extended his embrace to the farmers of Ganganagar and later to all agriculturists. He made the slogan 'Jai Jawan Jai Kisan' a vibrant successful venture. He answered the final call with the same courage which epitomized his life. God bless his noble soul.

NOTES

1. Maj. R. MacMillan Smith was originally from 4 Raj Rif. which was para trained. On the unit being taken off para status in the reorganization after Partition, he transferred to 2 Para (Maratha) and served with the unit in Lucknow and Agra in the mid-1950s. He commanded 'D' Company and occasionally officiated as the 2IC. An outstanding hockey player he was well-loved by the younger officers and men, with whom he got on famously. His wife Kaye and three young children were very popular with the officers' community. Kaye was a superb cook and a gracious hostess. Major Smith retired from the Army prematurely as a Major's allowances and pay are insufficient to maintain a large family on the lifestyle that he was accustomed to. His efficiency, wit, charm and engaging personality landed him a lucrative job as Secretary of the Bombay Gymkhana Club. He and his family finally migrated to Australia where they are now well settled.
2. Lt. Gen. S.D. Verma, *To Serve with Honour*, published by Lt. Gen. S.D. Verma (Retd), Longwood, Kasauli (HP), 1988, p.115.
3. All villages beyond Joshimath are vacated by the inhabitants during winter, who return only after June/July.
4. The text of the message was:
   From: Special Task Force

To: Indarmy
Eastcom
HQ UP Area
9 Infantry Bde
8 Dogra
OP TRISHUL (.) EST SHIV NAGAR (.) BOL CHHATRAPATI MAHARAJ KI JAI (.) LUCKY STAR CLEAR.

Note: Shiv Nagar and Lucky Star in the telegram referred to Rimkin and Barahoti.

5. (a) *India's Paratroopers* by K.C. Praval (A History of India's Paratroopers), Thomson Press (India), Delhi, 1974, pp. 230-3.
   (b) *Glory and its Price: A History of 2nd Battalion The Parachute Regiment* by Lt. Gen. (Retd.) Mathew Thomas, PVSM, AVSM, VSM, Kartikeya Publications, Meerut, 2002, pp. 427-31.
6. *Glory and its Price*, pp. 479-83.
7. Ibid., p. 483.

CHAPTER 2

War and Peace, A View from Below: A Learning and Unlearning Experience

In the meanwhile 8 Dogra had moved to Joshimath and one of their companies had relieved us at Barahoti in August 1961. On return from Barahoti, we visited the holy shrines at Badrinath, Govind Ghat and Hemkund Sahib in the area, which was a most exhilarating and enjoyable experience. In Joshimath men were put up in the tented 8 Dogra lines and the officers—me, Cheema and Dr. Ao in the Nissan hut near their officer's mess. I told my batman Guruputer Padwal that from now on we would eat in the officer's mess. Next morning Guruputer brought a tea tray and put it on the bedside table and with a confused look on his face asked me as to what is wrong with the officer's mess that they cannot even make tea properly? Looking at the three pots on the tray I understood his predicament. I told him to first pour the brown coloured water from the big pot, then pour some milk, add a spoon of sugar to it and then stir it. On stirring when it became tea as he knew from the *langar*, he was thrilled as a child and clapped with joy. After I had finished my cup of tea, Guruputer asked us to have another cup as he wanted to practice the magic, lest he forgot the trick. He was from a shepherd clan in Aurangabad district of Maharashtra and had seen and tasted tea only after he joined the Army.

During our stay at Barahoti while living, food and shelter-wise we were comfortable and had all our requirements but we missed the small pleasures of civilization, one of these was to get off our feet and move on something other than our feet. A desire fulfilled as we were entering Joshimath, Tari Cheema saw a man riding a bicycle and when his pleading to loan him the cycle for a while did not succeed, he threw him off and took it. He rode it in a wobbly fashion for some distance till he became steady, all the while with a satisfied smile on his face. We all took turns riding the cycle to the amusement of bystanders who had collected in quite a large numbers. We paid the owner Rs. 30 in spite of his protests, it was our first money spent in more than six months. At Bareilly we learnt that the battalion had moved from J&K to Agra to be part of the Para Brigade and we rejoined the battalion at Agra.

OPERATION VIJAY: LIBERATION OF GOA

The battalion was busy with the routine of returning to peace station from field, of survey boards, changing to peace system of accounting and functioning, opening up of stores and property of various regimental institutions and establishing them. Over 25 per cent of the JCOs and men were sent on leave and the bulk of the officers including all the married ones were on leave. CO Ujjal Gupta, a bachelor and other young and not so young bachelors were holding the fort. I was the Adjutant and also looking after the Bravo Company. It was a Sunday and we along with the CO were in the officers mess opening and checking the silver, when a call from the Brigade Headquarters summoned the CO. He returned after an hour and told us to repack again and ordered me to call all the officers and JCOs present in the station for a meeting after an hour. We left one officer to pack up the mess and the rest left for the battalion lines. In the conference, the CO told us that we were moving to Goa to liberate it from the Portuguese but not to tell the troops as yet. He ordered me to open the war box, take out the mobilization orders and start taking action. In case of any doubts I was to ask Havildar Benedict, the President Regimental Institutions clerk, who had been with the battalion during the Second World War and J&K operations. I sat with Benedict and started taking action. While preparing the recall notices to the personnel on leave, I was a bit confused as to whether they will reach Agra before we left. I asked the CO, he told me to ask all leave personnel to report to the MLI centre at Belgaum.

After attending the Brigade Commander's operational conference, the CO during his briefing told us that we were to be in airborne role and the launching air field will be either Secunderabad or Bangalore. The land tail consisting of heavy stores and equipment would move to Belgaum by a special train that night. He also told the companies that the personal weapons, combat equipment and clothing of the leave personnel will be carried with the land tail to Belgaum. The battalion was to be on hard scale and self-contained for 72 hours. We all felt very light with personal loads of 30 to 50 kg, which were all packed along with door and heavy loads. The land tail was loaded in the special rake and left the next day. Next morning we were given the operational briefing and learnt that our objective was the Dabolim airfield in Goa. After the operational briefing, the battalion was quarantined and we spent the waiting time on numerous rehearsals on a sand model prepared from outdated maps and old sketchy air photo mosaic. We could get familiar with the terrain as was humanly possible. We were next waiting for the call to emplane for Secunderabad en route to Goa.

Forty-eight hours had passed and still there was no news of the aircraft. Having packed all our belongings and except for the normal physical training and rehearsals, we were getting bored of lying idle in our bare rooms. Having been in the same uniform for more than two days, we did a quick washing with the help of our batmen and the company *dhobi* did the ironing on the study table. To break the boredom we rang up the duty officer frequently. It was probably on the third day that the disappointing news came that there would be no airborne operation and we were to be part of the ground operations. We were to leave by train on white hot priority from Agra Fort station. Our land tail having left, our officers mess and the company *langars* had to buy/borrow new set of utensils and other cooking equipment for the train journey. We boarded the train in less than half an hour as there was nothing to load except the ammunition, rations and cook houses. To preserve our uniform for the actual battle after we detrained, the CO agreed that we could be in reasonable state of minimum dress or undress. After boarding the train we asked the CO as to why there was no air borne operation. With a smirk on his face he said that the Portuguese have super sabre fighter (SAT 7) aircraft in underground hangers and a very high level of air defence around Dabolim airfield. As we were to learn later, such intelligence reports were based on rumours floated by the interested parties and came in handy for unwilling people. This is when a large number of officers and men from the services belonged to Goa and nearby areas and they had been going there on leave and some of them were there even as we concentrated for the operations. We never made use of them, so much for planning. Probably professionals were not consulted and decisions were taken by the politicians and their advisors including those from the intelligence agencies. This malady continues till date with its various ups and downs.

We really moved on white hot priority and the train hardly stopped for the first 24 hours except for change of engine and the train staff. It certainly gave us the feeling that action was in the offing. It was alright for the first 24 hours but on the second day the CO told the guard that the train must stop for at least an hour for each meal as the food could not be cooked in a closed C wagon, moreover it could not be distributed to men as there was no corridor connecting the compartments. The guard pleaded his inability to do so due to orders from above. He was told that the NCO manning the telephone in his compartment had orders to shoot him in the case OC's orders for halting the train were not obeyed. After this we had regular halts for meals and some connectivity between the compartments was provided, though not fully, at Pune. During our halt at Poona (Pune), we found a lot of our men in *mufti* waiting for the train to join the battalion at Belgaum. We took them on board, the process continued at all halts and by the time we reached Belgaum we had picked up all except 65 of our men on leave. By the time we reached our concentration area everyone had joined barring one sweeper who was court martialled, which some of us thought a bit unfair as the poor man belonged to a remote village in Bihar and may not have got the recall telegram. A few days later when we mentioned it to the CO, he told us that if everyone else could join why could not he, he was punished on principle. This part of the narration will not be complete without paying a tribute to the railways, which has always risen to the occasion whenever there is any emergency, they have never failed the nation and the Army. This has been our constant experience during all wars and emergencies.

We reached Belgaum early next morning and were received by Brig. Bhatia, the Brig. i/c Adm. of Headquarters Southern Command, with one 3-ton and one 15-cwt vehicle from the MLI Centre. He informed us that we were to move to our concentration area short of Sawantwadi. The CO asked him as to when would our land tail train reach, to which he replied that it would take another three to four days as priority has been given to troop movement. CO told him that the troops can march but how could heavy weapons, equipment and reserve ammunition be moved? The Brig. Adm. replied that these can be left at Belgaum to be fetched later. The CO curtly thanked him for the suggestion but he would not leave the weapons, ammo or warlike equipment and how could he trust Command Headquarters after such a reception. He asked me to pass the orders to the companies to unpack the heavy weapons and equipment and be ready to move out in tactical groups (F, A and B echelons) in four hours. While we got busy with the unpacking and breaking the loads into the F, A and B echelons, the CO and the Sub. Maj. got into a huddle with the officers and JCOs of the MLI Centre. After about ten minutes the Sub. Maj. asked for five men from each company belonging to the nearby areas and along with the men of the MLI Centre sent them on some errand. This was followed by the Sub. Maj. producing a local bullock cart and the CO asked me to work out along with the Nb. Sub. Adjutant Vithal Kadam as to how many of these will be required for each echelon for all the companies, the specialist platoons and the Battalion Headquarters. We worked out that each company will require 4 for F, 6 for A and 4 for a truncated B echelon.

Similarly, the requirement for the specialist platoons and the battalion headquarters was worked out, the total requirement for the entire battalion worked out to nearly 100 bullock carts (local bullock carts are smaller). After a couple of hours bullock carts started arriving and as soon as these were allotted to the companies they moved off with men marching on the sides and the bullock carts in the middle. By midday we had left Belgaum and marching throughout the night we reached the concentration area before the first light of dawn. Brig. Bhatia, a gunner, was amazed at 2 Para's innovation and improvisation. While marching along the

Sub. Maj. told me that the Battalion when at Casino in Italy had a troop of mules, a platoon of T-16 carriers and a full authorization of mechanical transport and could rig combinations for different situations. One can never fathom the infantry's flexibility and ability to innovate.

The details of the liberation of Goa are recorded in the official records of Operation Vijay and the Battalion's history. It was more or less a walkover for the Para Brigade advancing cross country on three axes. The main force of the 17 Infantry Division along the main axes Londa-Ponda entered Goa after it had been captured by the Para Brigade. The credit for this bold action goes to Brig. (later Lt. Gen.) Sagat Singh, the commander who after a few hours advance seeing the enemy resistance crumbling ordered advance on a broad front with three battalions on three widely dispersed axes, to capture maximum territory in the minimum of time. Sagat was to prove his mettle as a bold commander during the operations in Bangladesh in 1971 for its liberation. During the operations in Goa, the myth of Portuguese having Super Sabres and mechanized forces in strength was proved wrong. We always get surprised by the lack of enemy intelligence and open information even when we have men and resources sitting in our backyard. The only exceptions have been at the local unit level. 2 Para fully exploited it by using smugglers of Sawantwadi to help in infiltrating C Company under Capt. N.S. Uthaya for the capture of Sanquelim Bridge, which unfortunately had already been blown up. The Portuguese came to know about the Indian troops crossing the border from the All India Radio broadcast. The liberation of Goa is replete with instances of initiatives at the unit level and even below and the Infantry's innovative and improvisation skills. 2 Para crossed the Usgao backwaters on improvised rafts made of coconut trees and locally procured drums with 1 Para doing a similar exercise under even more difficult circumstances at Banastarim. When 1 Para reached Banastarim crossing they found the bridge to be blown up. So they crossed over by swimming and using improvised aids. It was then that they heard the news that the governor might escape. Moreover by then Para Bde had been ordered to move into Panjim. So Lt. Col. Sucha Singh CO 1 Para decided to get hold of any transport as they crossed and the chase started with their clothes drying on the vehicles. The sight of Lt. Col. (later Brigadier) Sucha Singh, VrC and MC, CO 1 Para chasing the Portuguese Governor in a tipper dressed in a *kucchha* (an Indian underwear) with a rifle just out of Banastarim, water dripping and capturing him before he could fly out, is part of the history of paratroopers and shows their aggressive spirit for which they are known and take pride in.

During operations in Goa, the image of one of our paratroopers Jai Ram Mahabidi chasing an enemy armoured car with a loaded 3.5 rocket launcher is still ingrained in my memory. He was trying to keep the armoured car within 150 yards which was the effective range of the rocket launcher. Every time it misfired, he carried out the misfire drill and continued his pursuit of the armoured car, till we physically caught hold of him from the scruff of his neck and brought him to safety. I gave him the firing of his life for his stupidity. Later when I narrated the incident to Ujjal Gupta, the CO and Shankar Bodhe the Sub. Maj., the CO's response was 'Stupid but brave'. Bodhe sahib told me later not to ever forget the incident as although Jairam made a stupid mistake but a positive and a brave one. Years later when I was the CO of the unit in J&K, Jairam's name came up for promotion as a Havildar. He had barely passed the promotion cadre in his third and last chance and his company commander was not in the favour of his promotion. I had to take the decision, and remembering the incident in Goa I promoted him. He did well for us during the Bangladesh war in 1971. Army can afford to have simple and bold person but not a clever coward.

ROMANCE INTERRUPTED

I have an uncanny knack of getting into situations not of my making. I had just met the girl who was to become my wife and the courtship was blossoming. I had reserved all weekends in pursuance of it, fully utilizing the nights for travelling to Delhi from Agra and back, with a day in her company. We had just finished long night of training on a Saturday morning and I had got the CO Lt. Col. Dhillon's permission for leave of absence over the weekend. He had asked me to finalize the programme of field firing for the next week before leaving. I was working on it when at about 7 a.m. Brig. Sagat Singh, the Brigade Commander, rang up and asked for the CO. I told him that he has just left after night training and I could send him a message. He told me to do so and to stay in the office as I was also required. The CO came after half an hour followed by the Brigade Commander. After a few minutes of discussion with the CO, I was called and told that I should be ready to load up my company group with full complement of weapons, equipment, air-borne special equipment and parachutes in a special train for an operational role in the eastern theatre. I was told that our destination was the Borjor airfield and we will get further orders on arrival there. After some discussion we decided to carry in addition a section of 81 mm mortars with us. My plans for the weekend went for a toss and communications being what they were then I could not even inform Sajni (my girl) that I will not be with her for the weekend and for quite a few days later on. The fog of 1962 had started to descend.

TO THE EAST: 1962 AND AFTER

We boarded the metre gauge train at Agra Fort railway station and headed for Gauhati (Guwahati) on 16 September 1962. After four days we reached the northern bank of the Brahmaputra River and were told to unload quickly. I learnt that we have to cross the river by a ferry at Pandu to go to the Gauhati airfield known as Borjor. When I reached the ferry site I found utter confusion prevailing there and each unit pressing its claim to cross first and a harassed Movement Control Officer, a Captain, at the receiving end. Nobody seemed to know the reason for the hurry. Talking to some senior unit commanders I learnt that the moves had been ordered by none less than the CGS Lt. Gen. Kaul commonly known as Biji Kaul. Having had the recent experience of him during the Barahoti episode I decided to invoke his name. I told the Movement Control Captain that we are the special operations Para Company which has been moved on personal orders of the CGS and we have to reach Borjor airfield immediately. The Movement Control Officer felt concerned and put us on the next ferry. On reaching across I used the same trick to commandeer transport for our move to the airfield. We reached the Borjor airfield late in the evening of 22 September and pitched our camp next to the runway near a water tank. I tried to find out if there was any headquarters nearby or anyone in-charge to report our arrival and to find out as to what our task was but failed. Next morning I contacted the supply depot to arrange for the rations, I was told that we could not be issued rations without an order from the Headquarters 33 Corps or the Area Headquarters at Shillong. I managed to locate the only other army unit near the airfield, an air dispatch unit, and with great persuasion succeeded in attaching ourselves with them for rations on a LRC (Last Ration Certificate), least realizing that providence had willed it. A few days later a Lt. Col. from the 33 Corps arrived who as we learnt later was the AQMG. When I asked him as to what our task was and who will give us orders, he had no knowledge but he promised to find out and made a note of my request. We also learnt that a new Corps Headquarters was going to take over soon. With nothing to do and having established good liaison with the Air Force, me and my JCOs took the opportunity to go on supply dropping sorties to the forward areas, this made us familiar with the area and the terrain. The Air Force took us willingly on these sorties as paratroopers were always treated as special friends. After a few sorties we were familiar with the area and most of the DZ's (Drop Zones). It was on one of these sorties on 19 October that while dropping at the Tsangdhar DZ that we saw smoke on the DZ and smoke puffs around the aircraft. It took us some time to realize that the DZ was being shelled and the smoke puffs around the aircraft was anti-aircraft fire. The war or the conflict had started but no details were available. What was worse was that all the communications had broken down; was it failure or sabotage, everyone was blank. I told the men that the war seems to have started and we are likely to get some task soon but I could not say what it would be.

Next day as we were waiting at the airfield with nothing else to do, an aircraft landed and as we watched the people coming out of it I saw Lt. Col. Surinder Singh (later Lt. Gen., Director General Artillery) from the MO Directorate who had been my instructor in the Junior Command Course. He was surprised to see me and when I told him that we had been there for two weeks waiting for a task and that we had come fully prepared with full equipment, weapons, ammunition and parachutes, he said thank God nobody asked you to jump as any drop at those altitudes would have been disastrous. I told him that with 28 ft parachutes I had decided that if we were asked to jump at high altitude it will be with personal weapons and on weapon ammunition and rest as door loads. Looking back even this would have been a disaster and we would have had very heavy casualties. Without saying anything much he told us that things have moved fast and for the worst and he cannot say as to what we would be asked to do. We felt, rather than knew, the gravity of the situation when the new 4 Corps Commander, the feared Biji Kaul, was evacuated on 21 October and Lt. Gen. Harbaksh Singh took over. With new formations being inducted the demands of air maintenance escalated beyond the capacity of the air maintenance platoon and being paratroopers and available we ended up in helping them in ejection duties. The task became so enormous that one more company from the battalion and one from 4 Para joined us for the task. During the later sorties dropping to stragglers after each disastrous withdrawal we were awestruck by their plight and the aftermath of the debacle in spite of our later successes is a grim reminder of those dark days. It has been covered by various authors but truth still eludes. It is high time that the Gen. Henderson Brooks inquiry report is made public. In the absence of truth, we will continue to have a sense of guilt even after we have got over it militarily. After return to the Battalion we continued with the aftermath of the Chinese invasion in the shape of long marches with heavy loads, privation and hardships generally termed as 'toughening up' as if we lost due to our inadequate soldierly and physical capability; what a cover up for political and military higher command failure! This was destined to stay for a long time and has still not left us entirely.

50 (Independent) Para Brigade trained hard during the 1963-4 collective training period (winter months mainly). 2 Para (Maratha) with the other battalions of the Brigade carried out company and battalion level training in the various operations of war (e.g. advance, attack, defence and withdrawal). Affiliated supporting arms and services were attached to battalions for unit level exercises. Training was carried out mainly in Dholpur and Sir Mutra (near Gwalior) areas and occasionally at Jagnair and Dauki. Troops with their commanders speed marched from Agra to these training areas.

Training camps were set up under the sparse cover that existed there and we bivouacked under hard field conditions. The CO and the 2IC were housed in 112 lbs tents with 40 lbs tents as their toilet, while the Company Commanders and lesser mortals were in 40 lbs (dug in for maximum coolness) and communal toilets. The men were under bivouacs. The officers reverted to bivouacs on exercises. No Officers Mess functioned while out on training. The CO was privileged to have a mess detachment with a cook and of course a wine waiter—and occasionally shared a 'burra peg' with the Company Commanders. The latter formed an ad hoc association called the 'CCA' (Company Commanders Association) and after a particularly welcome 'Shabash' from the CO, Ajit Dhillon, the CCA invited him over to their bivouac area for a glass of beer 'loaned' from his mess detachment, with the connivance of Kardar Khan, the indefatigable wine waiter, who had served many previous COs and could take such liberties. Before conferences a 'grapevine' would indicate to the CCA what Battalion Headquarters wanted, for example, a Mess Havildar, an Regimental Police Havildar, an Intelligence NCO, a Stick Orderly, etc., from Rifles Companies for the next change over, with certain inherent qualifications/qualities. The CCA decided amongst themselves 'who would offer what at the conference'. Invariably Samir Sinha, the 2IC, would be 'sounded' on our choice(s) and adjustments made where necessary. At the conference there was no 'heat and dust' over such issues and on such occasions 'business' was transacted in record time, with the CCA being invited by the 'Tiger'[1] for a glass of beer, this time chilled by ice from the MI Room (meant for heat-stroke cases, of which there were none).

My preparation for the Defence Services Staff College were resumed after the unseen war against the Chinese under the personal supervision of Samir Sinha (later Major General), our old 21C and then raising and commanding 6 Para. This is also the time that I married the person I loved and missed during the Chinese interlude. Samir's dedication to our professional improvement and army's cause can be gauged from the fact that my one month old wife thought that it will be a disaster if I did not put in the prescribed number of hours studying. The odd visit to the mess was termed as improving our drinking handicap. So much so that one day when I took my younger sister visiting us, to a restaurant for dinner and Samir and Mukul, his wife, entered the restaurant, my wife thinking that Samir would be annoyed jumped to my rescue and told him that she had brought me here. I went to the Staff College in 1963 and like most others who benefited from Samir's dedication, I owe a debt of gratitude to him. In my humble way I tried to repay it by helping others in later life and my wife was always an encouraging party to it. Today's army could do with some people like Samir. During the course I plodded on with neighbours like Tirpat Singh (later Lt. Gen.) of EME, who probably was the most serious and industrious student. I had no option but to work hard. He proved in later life that hard work pays and held the posts of the DG Financial Planning and later MGO. A month before the course finished Maj. Gen. Amrik Singh, the MS, who had been the Para Brigade Commander arrived with our postings. During the interview he told me that I had done well and was now posted as a GSO-2 in the MO Directorate, possibly the best staff job for a major. I was most happy till I realized that it was meant to be in Delhi. With our pay those days and with both mine and my wife's families there we just could not afford it. So next day I went back to Maj. Gen. Amrik Singh and requested for a change in posting to a field area, preferably in the high altitude. He promised to consider my request and asked me to see him the next day. Next day he told me that I have been posted to Ladakh as BM of a brigade. This suited me fine as my wife could stay with her parents during summer as they had a house in Srinagar.

LADAKH: SRI VALLEY AND 1965 INDO-PAK WAR

My Brigade Commander in Ladakh was Brig. Narinder Singh of 20 Lancers who was originally from 8 Cavalry. He was physically very fit, relaxed and down to earth and practical in operational matters. I learnt operational staff work from him, he preached and practised that major staff duties cannot be sacrificed for the sake of minor staff duties. In other words, sound operational thinking and plans should not be sacrificed for the sake of military writing's form and layout; substance cannot and should not be sacrificed for style. He always asked for a draft of all important letters to be put up to him but never criticized them or asked me to re-do them. If he did not like a draft, he would cross the entire letter and himself re-write it and return it with a polite note to issue it. During one of the reconnaissances he asked me to arrange a horse for one of the COs accompanying us while both of us were on foot. I found it a bit strange and even told him as to how could we have such an unfit CO. He replied, this is what we have and we have to make the best of it. He qualified it by adding that you cannot slight a person and then expect the best out of him, particularly a CO. If anything you should build people up and not break them. These words came back to me during the operations in the Kashmir Valley in 1965, as the same CO performed better than the so-called fit ones.

Being a reserve brigade we were quite used to alerts, whenever forward brigades sited some Chinese or intrusions even if a suspected one and all of those were not real, but the 1962 experience did not permit these to be ignored. In August 1965 I went on a few days' holiday to Srinagar to spend some time with my family during which we also visited the holy shrine of Amarnath. The next day after my return the GSO-1 of the division rang up to say that this was both a warning as well an executive order for the brigade to move to the Kashmir Valley next morning. When I told him that I had just returned from Srinagar and everything was normal, he told me that large-scale Pak infiltrations have just been detected and the Valley is threatened. We had only two battalions with the brigade, 1 MLI and 6 Rajput, the third battalion 1 Guards had moved to Kargil for operations earlier. The new Brigade Commander and CO of MLI were on leave and after the CO of 6 Rajput and Suresh Sharma the DQ left for Srinagar to be briefed at the Corps Tactical Headquarters and to arrange for logistics, I was the seniormost officer left in the Brigade. I prepared the orders for the move and briefed the 2ICs of both the battalions. 6 Rajput was to lead followed by the Brigade Headquarters and 1 MLI bringing up the rear after the administrative units. I positioned myself behind the company after the CO's party under Maj. Hardev Singh of 6 Rajput, who had just about four years' service. Our move went off smoothly till the bridge short of Kargil, approaching which we heard some firing and saw some smoke on the bridge. I told Maj. Hardev, the officiating CO, to rush the bridge with his leading company. The bridge was under attack by a small party of infiltrators, the quick and aggressive action by the Rajputs saved the bridge and after securing it we moved to Kargil. We again got stuck at Kargil as the Harka Bahadur bridge just beyond it was blown up by the infiltrators. As our convoy was spread over a few kilometres, I closed the convoy and ordered one company each from both the battalions to secure the hills overlooking the convoy. In the meantime Brig. V.K. Ghai, a paratrooper gunner, and the Commander at Kargil, came and told me that we were under his command. I found it strange as our orders were to move to Srinagar. I told him that I was in command and we have nothing to do with him and as soon as the bridge is ready we would move to Srinagar. A short while later we received a very silly message from the AQMG of 15 Corps that he was sending 100 vehicles from Baltal for us to transship. I told him as politely as I could that it was a very impractical idea as by the time the vehicles reaches us and the load of the last vehicle is transshipped across the river, ten bridges could be constructed by the engineers, moreover turning around hundred vehicles will be a bugger's muddle. Better sense prevailed, the bridge was ready in ten hours and we moved to Baltal. At Kargil, Mr. Kotru, a correspondent from the *Statesman*, who had been stuck there joined us up to Srinagar and subsequently wrote about happenings in which our enforced halt at Kargil and journey to Srinagar were prominently mentioned.

We arrived at Baltal in early hours of next morning after two hard days going. Enroute we had received a message not to proceed beyond Baltal as our arrival in the Valley would constitute a ceasefire violation due to induction of additional troops. So on arrival I told the units to have a break, cook a hot meal, check and refuel vehicles, relax and wait for the next orders. I felt that this would also give a chance to the stragglers to catch up. Just as the units had settled down I received a message from the Corps Tactical Headquarters in Srinagar to move immediately with all speed as the town was threatened by the infiltrators who were closing in. I let the troops have their tea and something to eat and then started for Srinagar. We had crossed Gund and were nearing Ganderbal when we met the Officiating Commander Lt. Col. Mutasad Ahmed Khan along with Lt. Gen. K.S. Katoch, MC, GOC 15 Corps. They issued orders as troops arrived. Generally speaking 6 Rajput were assigned the Badgam sector and 1 MLI the airfield sector. The Brigade Headquarters was located in two barracks short of the airfield. On arriving at the Brigade Headquarters I met the DQ Maj. Suresh Sharma and Capt. Gautam Narain the GSO-3. They briefed me on the situation and told me that we were on a counter-infiltration role and responsible for the area from Banihal Pass, inclusive of Gulmarg. In addition to our two battalions we had been given 8 J&K Militia, two Punjab Armed Police (PAP) battalions and other units located in the area. I asked them if we knew the location of all units under us and their area of responsibility. They told me that except for 8 J&K Militia, whose headquarters was in Srinagar, locations of the other units and their area of responsibility were not known. I told them to find out and continue functioning as per orders given to them and in the meanwhile I would take a stock of the convoy and arrange for the recovery of troops and vehicles stranded en route. Within a few hours I was able to account for all the vehicles and personnel and I felt the situation was under control. Just as I was returning to the Operations Room, I heard a siren and saw a flag car convoy entering the Brigade Headquarters area—it was the Corps Commander. On getting down from the staff car he asked for the BM, I stepped forward. He wanted to know as to what was the situation, I requested him to step into the Operations Room and asked the DQ and the GSO-3 to brief him. He turned towards me and said what sort of a BM I was to let the DQ handle operations. I politely told him that I had arrived with the convoy and just finished accounting for the vehicles and arranging for the recovery of the stranded personnel and vehicles, the DQ and GSO-3 have been here for over two days and were in a better position to brief him. The Corps Commander lost his temper and told me that was no excuse. I was equally angry and tired and replied that this was the best I could do. Hearing this he was about to lose his temper again but somehow controlled himself and told me to shut up and proceed with the briefing. After the briefing when he was getting into the car, he called me and told me that I probably had a point and to get into the picture soon. I thanked him and told him that by next morning I would be fully 'in the picture'. The Brigade Commander and CO 1 MLI Lt. Col. Minnie Mohite joined us a few days later and we were placed under 19 Infantry Division and later under Headquarters Victor (V) Sector on its raising. During the period under 19 Infantry Division their main interest in us was to take away our signal communication equipment and weapons as these were better. We not only prevented it but also made sure that they did not interfere with our functioning. We were to learn later that we were moved into the Valley for offensive operations against Pakistan but got involved in counter-infiltration role due to the chaos and panic prevailing and our role got interchanged with 68 Infantry Brigade. The panic and confusion was to be with us most of the time and mostly not due to us but a creation of others.

Most of the time we were as much fighting with the V Sector as against the infiltrators which was to a large measure due to the subservient disposition of the Brigade Commander towards the bully GOC and what made matters worse was the Brigade Commander was equally charmed by the local political hierarchy from D.P. Dhar, the then Home Minister, to Mir Lasjan, a low level political functionary. This was to result in a situation where the COs and the staff were left to fend for themselves and fight on two fronts. After the initial experience of the first few days we in the brigade headquarters decided to function as per our best professional judgement and give no quarter to extraneous pressures as we felt that we had no alternative. This resulted in my removal from my job as BM twice and being reinstated as I was proved right. The events and complete happenings are recorded in the War Diary of 163 Infantry Brigade. I shall confine myself to a few events to give an insight into the environment prevailing at that time.

A column of 1 MLI was ambushed by a strong party of infiltrators on a track 20 km north of the airfield and they had suffered some casualties. The news reached us at 4 p.m. The CO Minnie Mohite and me decided on a plan of action based on the information given by the Column Commander. Just as Minnie was leaving for the operation, the Brigade Commander accompanied by D.P. Dhar, the IG Police Mr. Kaul and Mir Lasjan walked in. We briefed the Commander about the situation and the action being taken, during the course of this conversation Kaul told Minnie, '*phir unko grenade phenk phenk ke marna*', that we should kill them with grenades. I could not contain myself and retorted that the CO has

18 years service and me 14 years, we are professionals and did not require advice from novices. The Brigade Commander and Dhar flared up and the Commander asked me to leave. The reason for my outburst was that this sort of interference had become frequent and in spite of our requests the Commander had continued to bring them to the Operations Room and the visit was a pretext to entertain them. I went to my tent and ordered a drink from the mess. Next morning I did not go to the office and remained in my tent. At about just before mid-morning news came that 1 MLI operation was successful and they had killed over 20 infiltrators. A few hours later Gautam the GSO-3 came and told me that the Commander wanted to see me in the Operations Room. I went there and saluted the Commander. He told me that the operations planned by Minnie and me was a success and asked me to resume duty.

Those were the days when senior commanders dictated most things including operations at unit level rather than giving the task and leaving the implementation to them. In case it did not work out or for that matter any failure resulted in sacking of the CO irrespective of circumstances or lack of justification. It was similar to the story of the monkey who got hold of a mirror and a razor and he cut-off his own ear to spite his image. Similar was the case of 8 J&K militia in our formation, who were asked to move in a hurry and piecemeal with whatever troops they could muster to stop a big column of infiltrators moving into Yusmarg area. The CO was denied time to brief his troops and issue them enough ammunition and rations. The leading elements of a company moved at night by road to Yusmarg and while moving along a track in the early hours of the morning were ambushed. They were totally outnumbered, unprepared and had casualties. The CO who was following got hold of the situation and they gave a good account of themselves in the ensuing encounter and subsequent operations. The Army Commander when briefed of the incident during his visit to Srinagar after a few days ordered the CO to be removed for his failure. Both the GOC and the Brigade Commander who were responsible for rushing the unit just said, 'yes sir . . .'. The CO incidentally belonged to the same Gorkha regiment as the Brigade Commander. When we learnt of it we felt most upset as we knew as to how the CO was hustled into sending troops in a hurry and was unprepared. When I raised the issue with the Commander he told me that it was none of our business and we were not to give any help to the CO. After a few days the CO asked me if I could confirm the orders given to him as also the fact that his request for time to organize and brief his troops was denied to him. I told him that it was all recorded in the Operations Room log book, he can see it and that I will also give him a certified copy of the same. I did this and informed the Commander, he was most annoyed and told me that I will be in trouble for it. I later learnt that it helped the CO as he was only posted out and not demoted. The irony of the situation and the fate of 8 J&K Militia were both distressing and comical. The new CO of the battalion was from 4 Sikh who had been moved by the same Army commander to give command to another officer, probably a favourite. 4 Sikh as we all know went for a task behind Pakistan (PAK) lines in Punjab under the new CO and were surrounded and surrendered.

GOC of V Sector, Maj. Gen. Umrao Singh, an Armoured Corps officer, was a highly strung, excitable and impatient person. Immediately after he took over, the very next day he rang up to say that a large column of infiltrators was heading from the direction of Yusmarg and we should send someone to intercept it. I took the call as the Commander was away, I told him that we would send a column soon. We always had a column ready for such contingencies—in this case it was a company of 1 MLI under a young Maj. Biswas. When I rang up the CO to tell him about the task I learnt that he was visiting a company away from the battalion headquarters, so I asked the Adjutant to send Biswas to me for briefing as we were next door while the Company was getting ready. I also told the Adjutant to group a section each of 81 mm mortars and machine guns as the infiltrators were reported to be 200 strong. Just as I had finished briefing Biswas, the GOC rang up and asked if the Company had left I told him that the Company Commander has been briefed and after he has briefed his men and the mortars and machine guns deployed in another part of the air-field had married up with them they would leave. After another ten minutes he again rang up to say why the delay and they could leave even without mortars and machine guns. I explained to him that it was a weak company and the enemy is strong, therefore sending it unprepared may result in failure and casualties. He shouted at me and told me that if this column gets through he would hang me. The total time since his first call was just over an hour, the company left after fifteen minutes. When they reached short of Gogji Patheri after two hours they saw villagers running towards them. When they asked them the reason they told them that infiltrators have taken some of them as guides and porters and taken their food grain and livestock. The Company Commander deployed the Company on the hill astride the road and waited for them. When the infiltrators were within range he opened up with mortars and machine guns. The infiltrators suffered heavy casualties and were not only decimated but the column also disintegrated. On getting the news I took great pleasure in ringing up the GOC that the infiltrating column does not exist and it is all due to the gallant action of the company ably assisted by the mortars and machine guns. He told me I was lucky that our troops reached in time. I did not argue but I was quite clear in my mind that if Biswas's company was not equipped with mortars and machine guns they would not have given such a good account of themselves.

It was the same general who rushed to our headquarters when Srinagar airfield was bombed and after the first raid in which a UN and an airforce aircraft were destroyed and a 2,000 lb bomb landed near our headquarters. As luck would have it the GOC reached when warning for the second raid had been given and we had re-entered our trenches. Seeing his convoy approaching I came out of the trench and saluted him. His opening sentence was there is no air raid, you people are yellow and still in trenches, I explained to him that there was actually an air raid and a bomb had exploded next to our headquarters and we had just re-entered the trenches as there was a warning for a second raid. While he was still contemplating his next remark, the DQ Suresh Sharma walked up to him with a poker face carrying a shrapnel about 5 ft long and 9 inches thick and told the GOC 'believe me, sir this is one of the smaller pieces'. His reaction was a mixture of reluctance and suspicion but we were spared the wrath. We often used to receive baulking from him as the PAP and the Madhya Pradesh Special Armed Force were not using the appointment code on radio and talking clearly. Shivmohan Singh, commandant of one of the battalions often used to pull my leg that after working with the Army, from human beings they are being asked to become animals as the appointment code was based on animal names. The GOC failed to accept that police forces are different and had a system suited to their requirements and ethos; even today we have senior officers with similar disposition. At times it was frustrating but it also had its lighter moments.

The COAS Gen. J.N. Chaudhuri visited Srinagar some time in the third week of August 1965. Brigadier Narinder Singh, who was our previous Brigade Commander and now DMO, accompanied him. We had provided security to their convoy from Srinagar airfield to the town and back as it fell in our area of responsibility. The COAS convoy returned from the town after four hours to the airfield but we did not hear any aircraft taking off, so when the road protection party under Maj. Bajwa of Central India Horse asked if they could stand down I told them not till the COAS aircraft had taken off. After about twenty minutes the COAS's party drove into our headquarters. Brigadier Narinder Singh told me that there was some problem with the aircraft so instead of waiting at the airfield and knowing that we were nearby he asked the Chief if he could visit his old formation headquarters to meet us all. The COAS said he would also come. We took them to the Operations Room as it was the most decent place there and served them tea. The Chief asked me to brief him. I briefed them on the latest situation, our area of responsibility and location and the tasks of the various units. The Chief and DMO exchanged glances and the Chief asked me as to what was the situation on the periphery of the town and the outlying areas. I told them that town is not our responsibility but all movement between Srinagar-Tangmang, Srinagar-Badgam, Srinagar-Airfield, Srinagar-Yusmarg and Srinagar-Banihal is controlled and administrative convoys protected. In addition, based on the latest intelligence and the Sub-Sector Commander's judgement, road opening is done. The COAS said that he had not seen anything on the way from the airfield to the town and during his return. I told the COAS that two companies and two troops of Central India Horse were deployed so that nobody could take a pot shot at his convoy. I made Brig.

Narinder Singh talk to Maj. Bajwa of Central India Horse, who was in-charge. The second question he asked me was if we were short of troops. I told him no. The COAS said, if so then where is the problem. I told the COAS that everyone except us, which included the tactical Corps Headquarters and V Sector Headquarters, were deploying and tasking the troops and after this was done we were told about it and they are placed under our command. After that I explained to him that our proposed deployment and tasking plan was based on Armed Police and Para Military units to be located near selected population centres for surveillance, intelligence and protective duties and army tasked to seek and destroy infiltrators. He just said 'looks good and workable so implement it'. A short while later news came that the aircraft was ready and they left. A few minutes later Brig. Narinder Singh rang up from the airfield and told me that they were given a very different picture at V Sector Headquarters and the State Control Room. He told me to do the right thing and not to succumb to pressure and that he trusted me. He also told me that he has told the COAS the same thing. In the evening the Brigade Commander came back to the headquarters. I informed him of the COAS's visit and the gist of my briefing. He got very upset. I learnt later that in Srinagar during briefing both by GOCs of V Sector and 19 Infantry Division and by the state government, a very rosy picture showing complete control of the situation had been painted. A few days later, we started enjoying a greater freedom of action to deal with the situation in our sector but interference still continued.

The story of that period will not be complete without narrating the episode of the three companies of PAP which were sent into the hills to deal with infiltrators by Headquarters V Sector. We learnt of their existence when two of these companies were reported missing and we were asked to locate them. We sent patrols from 1 MLI and 6 Rajput as the reported area of their operation was on their boundary. They found no trace of them anywhere in the area, till a 6 Rajput patrol located them in the villages far from the hills by the trail of dead chicken left behind by them. The lesson is very clear that troops must be used for roles for which they are suited and trained and not what we want them to do.

After the ceasefire, the brigade could not go back to Ladakh as the Zojila Pass was closed. While biding our time in the comparative peace but frozen winter of Srinagar I received my posting to 50 Independent Parachute Brigade as BM. It was a total surprise as I had already done my staff tenure. I joined 50 Independent Parachute Brigade in Ferozepur under Brig. I.S. Gill, MC who had taken it over after the ceasefire. On arrival I learnt that he had asked for me and the MS being one of our earlier Brigade Commander had agreed. How this was to influence me and my future, I had not realized. It was to be a very different and entirely a professional experience.

BACK TO THE PARA BRIGADE

I had seen Inder Gill as CO 1 Para and heard of him as he belonged to my battalion but had left before I joined. Like most others I had also watched his drinking bouts, however, which never let him ignore his soldierly and human duties. When 1 Para was in Gaza I had requested him for a Grundig radiogram for my sister as a wedding present, which he brought along. He had refused the same for my CO as he was late in asking and the quota of what 1 Para could bring was full. Such was his sense of fairness. I looked forward to serving with him after the somewhat disappointing experience of the last assignment. I was confident as I had done my job well without any fear or reservation. The very first night exposed me to what was in store. In the evening at dinner time, Inder as he was known kept on drinking and I joined him as a courtesy but I could make out that some of the other officers were getting a bit cheesed off as they had gone through the ordeal for a long period. I spoke to some of them during the day and they were frank in expressing their feelings. As President of the Mess Committee I decided to deal with the problem immediately. I ordered the Mess Havildar that from next evening onwards, he should report to me that dinner is ready at 9 p.m. sharp. The next evening things went as usual till at 9 p.m. the Mess Havildar reported to me that dinner was ready. Inder Gill asked me what is this, I am not ready. I politely told him that some of the other officers who want to have dinner should go ahead. A few officers excused themselves and went for dinner. I waited for Inder. After another drink he told me, let us go and have dinner and we could have a drink later. In spite of his not liking it, his considerate self made him realize the suffering of others.

A few days later, we were scheduled for our first flag meeting with the Pakistani commander opposite us. A detailed set of instructions for the same had been received from Army Headquarters. After reading and 'side lining' some salient points, I sent it to the Commander. It was received back duly initialled by him. Next morning I was ready in my field dress, without the regimental insignia and formation sign and the tactical and formation signs of vehicles had been obliterated with mud as per instructions. Inder Gill came out of his room wearing maroon beret, medal ribbons, paratroopers insignia and formation sign. Looking at me, he smiled and asked me if I was going for field training. I replied that I was dressed as per instructions. He told me, 'My dear Tubby, go and change into full dress, everything you have and earned, medal ribbons, para insignia, formation sign, name tag and of course the maroon beret. Let us show our Pakistani friends with whom they have been fighting and what to expect.'

Having been brought up in the same British military tradition, Pakistani Army instructions must have been similar. They had obeyed the order and they were in field dress, with smudged vehicle identifications. After shaking hands with his Pakistani counterpart, Brigadier Abbas Rizvi, Inder gave him the next shock. 'I am Inder Gill, I was not on the receiving end of your guns, I have just taken over. I have 2 Para, 3 Para, 6 Para, 17 Para Field Regiment, 411 Para Field Company and some machine guns and armour'. Then introducing me he said, 'this is Tubby Nayar, he was dealing with you people in Kashmir and like me he has just joined'. Brigadier Rizvi and his BM Maj. Baluch were stunned and just as they were about to recover, Inder dealt the final blow. He handed over some captured document, 'Abbas, please hand over these personal notes prepared most diligently by one of your gunner officers with our compliments. He appears to be a real professional and these are of no intelligence value.' We had won a moral victory and after this as long we were incharge of the border in the Ferozepur-Fazilka sector there were no problems with Pakistanis and all problems were solved at my level. I would ring up Baluch and tell him what has happened and to tell his people not to create trouble.' His response was equally informal 'Tubby, don't worry, I will sort it out'.

With the impending exchange of prisoners of war, we received another set of instructions, the covering letter said that the Deputy Director Personnel will be attending as Army Headquarters representative. I put up the letter to Inder Gill. He asked me to explain to him the procedure in brief. I told him the procedure agreed between the two countries as given in the letter was that prisoners from both sides will be brought to the border and the officer-in-charge from one side would read out a name and the prisoner would cross over to his country, then the other side would do the same till the list was finished. I told him that the DC with some prominent citizens also wants to be present and welcome our prisoners. After listening to me, he offered me a cigarette and lit one himself and asked me as to who from our side should be the officer-in-charge. I told him, I was thinking of asking one of the 2IC of the battalions to undertake this responsibility. He said, 'Good, ask Maj. Mansoor Yar Khan 2IC 3 Para to be the officer-in-charge from our side, it would convey the right message'. He followed it with the orders; first, there would be nobody except the officer-in-charge, no prisoner's escort or provost representative present for the exchange, no Army Headquarters representative, no DC or reception party or *band baaja*. Don't they realize that the POW is a humiliated and a disturbed man, he wants to go back home quietly. After briefing me, he ordered me to be present short of the check point and ensure nobody except people actually concerned with the exchange go near the site. I called up 3 Para and asked them to send Mansoor for briefing to the headquarters. When Mansoor reached the headquarters, Inder Gill briefed us. The gist of his briefing was: Mansoor, a POW, is a humiliated person, let him leave us with as good a feeling as possible. When the special train arrives they would be taken to the Ferozepur Fort, given a cup of tea, a hot bath, a new set of clothes and served a hot breakfast and driven to the Hussainiwala border at the appointed time. Then he asked me as to how wide was the road at the border and how many people can stand abreast comfortably in columns on it. I told him six. He asked Mansoor to form them into columns of six and check them as per the list. When the gates open, give the list to the Pakistani officer and give the command, '*Pakistan ke bahadur sipahiyon, aap apne watan jaayen*' (brave soldiers of Pakistan, go back to your country). When the gate was opened the lists were exchanged, the Pakistani POW crossed over in a few minutes, ours took a lot of time as each crossed individually as his name was called out. Once again we had won the mental war with Pakistan.

The border had been mined heavily by both sides, which had to be cleared after the ceasefire. The responsibility of the Ferozepur-Fazilka sector was given to 50 Independent Parachute Brigade although these minefields were not laid by us as we were not in this sector. Our engineers, 411 Parachute Field Company had managed to obtained the minefield records from the engineers who had laid the minefields. After a few days our sappers had familiarized with the layout and located it on the ground. When they started the de-mining operation, Inder Gill was present. Looking at one of the charts, he enquired from the JCO incharge, if it was one of the lanes to be cleared. As soon he heard, 'Yes Sir', he took off his cap, grabbed a prodder and started locating and marking mines. The entire clearance party went silent but then got onto the job with greater enthusiasm. After a successful bit of mine clearing, he told the troops, I am not stupid, I am an old sapper and I was just putting my training to use. Inder was a trained sapper officer in the British Army, who was decorated with a Military Cross for demolition tasks behind enemy lines in Greece in 1942. He was probably doing it after a lapse of a couple of decades. The entire minefield clearance was carried out successfully in good time and without any mishap.

During the 1965 War, the Para Brigade had taken heavy casualties during the capture of road and rail bridges over the Ichhogil canal at Jallo. 2 Para and 3 Para the attacking battalions had taken heavy casualties. Both units and for that matter the entire brigade was unhappy that their gallantry and sacrifices were not recognized due to differences of opinion between the previous Brigade Commander Brig. A.H.M. Nambiar with the divisional and the Corps Commanders. Due to the fact that brigades were already destroyed and therefore after the capture of the near bank, the Brigade Commander decided to reorganize short of the bank to avoid exposure to enemy direct and indirect fire. Although the division as well the corps did not know that the bridges were blown when the attack was ordered. Inder Gill had taken over the brigade after the ceasefire but he took up the cases of awards to people who had shown bravery with both the division as well as the Corps. He was blunt with both the divisional and the Corps Commander, 'You may not like the Commander or COs for one reason or the other but the fact is that the troops did a wonderful job and suffered heavy casualties and deserve recognition.' The operation was marked with confusion and misunderstanding between the Division Commander and the Para Brigade Commander. To clear our minds and to convey to junior leaders that in spite of the fog of war a professional approach to problems and frank opinion of commanders to higher authorities is essential. To achieve this aim an exercise named 'Tracy' was conducted to run through the events. After the exercise, we concluded that the available intelligence and information from a number of sources was not fully collated, analysed and passed by higher headquarters. Similarly, there was ambiguity in orders leading to confusion. It was neither a criticism nor a justification but a learning experience and revival of the spirit of the people who had fought bravely but remained unrecognized. What struck all of us most was that here was a commander who would not launch us unprepared when and if we ever were go to war under him. The above experience was reinforced during exercise 'Betwa', when he refused to do anything but as actually in war. He redefined the glossary of military terms and operations of war in terms of reality and actuality.

A month after our return to Agra, Inder Gill asked me as to when the 50 Independent Parachute Brigade was raised. I told him 1941. He said it as much to himself as to me, as we do not know the exact date, it was raised on 3 November 1941, a good day for celebration of its Silver Jubilee and it would be good weather too. We discussed the programme for the celebrations and Inder asked me to finalize it. He asked me to pick up another officer to help me. I picked Maj. B.S. Ramdas, OC of 2 Para Independent Workshop. Inder told me it was a paratrooper's celebration and only for the paratroopers and no one else was to be invited. Once programme was finalized and responsibility allotted, everyone worked on their own. To save effort and avoid duplication, the celebrations were combined with one of the major annual sports event—the brigade athletic finals. It was a full and hectic programme spread over two days organized at minimum cost. All guests stayed either in the messes or with married officers of the brigade, cost of everything was minimal. We produced a memento for the event for less than Rs. 10 with the help of the command workshop. The decoration were done by the wives of officers, who made over 5,000 silver roses. Similarly, the JCOs, men and their families and even children contributed some way or the other. The chief guest was the seniormost paratrooper Gen. P.P. Kumaramanglam, DSO, the then COAS. As per the army protocol the Army Commander Lt. Gen. J.S. Dhillon had to receive the COAS as he was visiting his command. Inder Gill insisted that the Army Commander will only be present to receive the COAS and during the ceremonial parade but would not stay for any other function because he was not a paratrooper. This posed a big problem and a lot of embarrassment but the message was conveyed to the Army Commander and Inder had his way. The two-day function went off very well as did the para dinner on the second day till late into early morning as the grand finale. We all went home and slept well past dawn. It was an administrative day next day. Just as I had got into the bed the telephone rang. I ignored it for quite some time hoping it will stop but when it did not, I picked it up. It was a few minutes before 6 a.m. It was Inder Gill. Who asked me the initials of Col. Malik, OC of the 509 Command Workshop. When I asked him as to why he wanted to know it now, he told me that he was writing demi-official letters of thanks to all who had helped us in organizing the silver jubilee celebration. This was Inder Gill at his deadliest best.

One learnt from him that socially all officers were equal and he displayed this in dealing with the officers, their wives and children. During an X-mas party once, we were all enjoying ourselves. Inder had dressed up as Santa Claus and he was amusing the children and giving them gifts. He asked my son who was five years old as to what present he would like. My son somehow did not like Inder the clown's face, and told him, 'You nit wit', words he must have picked up from some young officer uncle recently. Inder laughed it off. Some officer told me about the incident and I went to Inder and apologized to him saying, my son was as ill-mannered as his father. Inder's response was, 'Tubby don't feel sorry, he is probably a better judge of human beings than either you or me'.

Inder was fond of his liquor and I as President of the Mess Committee of the brigade officers mess closed the bar on a number of occasions. He shouted and even cursed me but came to my office to apologize next morning. He made us conscious of the fact that all human beings have weaknesses and we should judge them and know their best and worst. He could be obstinate to the point of being obnoxious and could be kind to a fault and people took advantage of it. At times it resulted in poor judgement and embarrassment. But above all he had the capacity to be fair even when he differed or hated you. I was to have more experience of it when he took over as the colonel of the regiment and I was to take over my battalion.

NOTE

1. *Glory and the Price: A History of 2nd Battalion, the Parachute Regiment (Maratha)* by Lt. Gen. (Retd) Mathew Thomas, Kartikeya Publications, Meerut, 2002, pp. 421-2.

CHAPTER 3

Command: Challenges and Successes

I had done over a year as BM of the Para Brigade and was enjoying being with my family after four years. We had taken Exercise Betwa in our stride and celebrated the brigade's silver jubilee. We had hardly recovered from the celebrations, when a shock awaited me. I learnt that in the promotion board held for our year of commission I had been deferred as I did not have the required number of Company Commander's reports in the last five years before the board. I had commanded a company for over seven years, was it my fault that I was posted from one staff job to another. I wanted to return to the battalion but did not think it proper to tell it to Inder Gill. I was really disappointed and waiting for my posting to the battalion in the normal course. Looking back, I would not have missed the experience of serving with Inder for any thing in the world. An opportunity came my way, when Lt. Col. Mathew Thomas (later Lt. Gen.) from my battalion who had taken over 5 Para, a new battalion, wrote to me if I would like to command the Maratha Company which had joined the battalion from my battalion 2 Para. 5 Para had just moved to Mizoram after a tenure in Nagaland when in March 1966 Mizo insurgency erupted. I readily accepted Mathew's offer, for me it was a God sent opportunity. I received my posting to 5 Para and joined them in Mizoram in May 1967.

MIZORAM

5 Para had just finished a tenure in Nagaland, when while waiting for their train at Silchar for de-induction, they were moved to Agartala (Tripura) for Internal Security duties. They had lost their CO Balbir Jaijee in a drowning accident and Mathew took over. When, in March 1966, Mizoram blew up, the battalion was moved

there. On induction into Mizoram in March 1966 they were landed by choppers on the southernmost part of Mizoram near Dimagiri. They worked their way up along the central ridges clearing them of MNF insurgents and securing the main communication artery till they arrived at Aizwal. The battalion had done well and was earmarked as reserve and for special operations. The battalion held a post at Durtlang, short of Aizwal on the Silchar-Aizwal Road and was also responsible for road clearance and protection with PMF deployed under its command. In addition it was required to provide company columns for operations anywhere in Mizoram, of which one company was to be ready at four hours' notice. As soon as one company had moved, the next one was put on notice. As I was to find out after joining, we were only notionally in Aizwal, otherwise all over Mizoram. Mathew had instituted a system whereby each company took its turn irrespective of the nature or area of operations. Each column was accompanied by two officers and was of two platoons' strength. The Support Company was also organized as a column and all officers of Battalion Headquarters and Support and Administrative Company accompanied the columns. The system was fair and gave equal opportunity to all. I commanded Alpha Company at Durtlang but spent most of the time on columns.

Mizoram was different from Nagaland. The Mizo as an adversary was also different in more than one respect. The environment was a strange mixture of what the British experienced in Malaya and that of Nagaland underlined by the Indian Army's thinking that these were our own people. We did grouping of villages as in Malaya as a temporary measure and it was resented then. Today after years of being their own masters it has not been reversed by the Mizos as it has turned out to be a boon to the people due to easier provision of civic facilities particularly water, communications, education and social cohesion. I shall deal with the entire spectrum of insurgency later and end by saying that the feelings I had as a sub-unit commander in 1967-8 will never leave me. I am richer by that experience and benefited a lot. I shall only confine myself to some major recollections.

5 Para had an abundance of successes. Operationally we were effective under all circumstances and innovative, fair and just in

our dealings and sensitive to the feelings of locals. Punitive action was the order of the day but in spite of grave provocations we never lost our balance and remained humane. In an ambush on my sub-column in 1968, which was the only setback the battalion had amongst the tremendous successes, we lost thirteen men and six were wounded but we fought and stood our ground. We returned to the village (Kelkong) we had just left with our dead and wounded and put them in a house on a dominating hillock. The villagers had vacated and moved to the jungle in anticipation of it being burnt. I was about to give the order when I saw a young pregnant girl with a child holding her hand. The look of anguish and hatred in her eyes was unbearable. I ordered them to go back to their houses as I was not burning them. It took time to sink in. During the night the column was attacked twice as MNF knew I had only a handful of men left. We withstood the attacks and next morning the rest of my column built up. After cremation of the dead and evacuating the wounded, we followed the gang, had encounters and inflicted casualties on it and were on top again. After a few days while negotiating cross country at night through a *jhoom*, I had a fall and hurt my back and my old para jump injury became very painful. After having tried to continue for a few days, I had to give up. Maj. Farook Mistry of Bravo Company relieved me and finished the task most successfully. When we returned, we learnt that the elders of the village had walked from near Champai to Aizwal to tell the commander what a humane lot 5 Para was. I learnt of human rights then and never deviated from it since.

5 Para is still remembered in Mizoram for its operational achievements and humane approach. The battalion captured Sai Kaka, the then home minister of MNF, in a very daring operation by a sub-column of D Company under young Capt. Bisht (later Brigadier). While screening a village for suspected MNF hostiles he sensed that something was amiss but nothing came out of the screening. Sensing the tenseness of the village council president, Bisht quietly interrogated him, away from the eyes of the villagers. With very scanty information provided by the village council president he decided to search the likely hideouts away from the village. It was raining heavily and while searching an old *jhoom* they stumbled on a sentry, after overpowering him they located a

track leading to the river but it had a sharp bank. Further search revealed a twine rope hanging from the bank. Leaving the two men on top Bisht climbed down the rope and found a cave on the sharp bank of the river. While still hanging from the rope he shouted that the place has been surrounded and all inside should surrender. A lone man came out and Bisht told him to climb up on the rope ahead of him. The captured hostile was brought to the village and while the sub-column's radio operator was trying to contact the main column, a message was received that the rumour in Aizwal was that Sai Kaka has been captured by 5 Para. Bisht confirmed that there is a person who calls himself by that name. The column was asked to be careful as hostiles will try and attack the column. Half way a helicopter was sent to pick him up. When produced before the Brigade Commander as a prisoner with his hands tied, Sai Kaka looked around, chose a chair from the side of the room and sat down, saying he was the home minister of MNF and should be treated as such. Sai Kaka is a friend of 5 Para and when I visited Mizoram in 1997 I met him. He remembered the old days with special affection for the battalion which captured him. Bisht's operation is a fine example of initiative and courage at the junior level.

Similarly, when their Director of Intelligence Lova was captured and during interrogation in Delhi he was asked as to how was it that 5 Para produced over 50 per cent of the results as a single unit in Mizoram, he replied, 'they are brave, innovative and never do the same thing again'. It was named as the 'Bhoot Paltan'. Lt. Gen. Sam Manekshaw, the then Eastern Army Commander was so fond of the unit due to its effectiveness that he resorted to his 'Hello Sweetie' ways to first get around Mathew the CO, followed by the Sub. Maj. and the company commanders to agree to stay on for three extensions and finally letting it go only after clearing the ridges from Aizwal to Silchar on their way out. In recognition of the unit's achievements Mathew Thomas was selected to establish the Jungle Warfare and Counter-Insurgency School at Vairangte and awarded a VSM, a number of other officers, JCOs and men were decorated for outstanding performance during operations in Mizoram. We saw different commanders from Sam Manekshaw as the Army Commander, Brigade Commanders Kabraji and Jaswant

Singh and Mathew as CO to create the environment in their own ways to success by building up people and units and tolerating setbacks, a lesson I was to carry with me.

TO BE OR NOT TO BE

After I had earned my full reports and we had returned to Agra I was approved for my next rank as Lieutenant Colonel. I was told that I could take over the next battalion falling vacant. I informed the Colonel of the Regiment that I will wait for 2 Para and the only other battalion I would have considered was 5 Para, which was not available as a new CO Lt. Col. J.A. Khan (Ahmed) had just taken over and I was his 21 C. In the meantime I was detailed on the Senior Command course as a Major. I must have done well as I went there as an instructor later. There was temptation to go as an instructor on promotion to Staff College before command but I decided to wait. But I was to undergo a couple of shocks and near misses before I finally got command of 2 Para. In the meanwhile Inder Gill had taken over as Colonel of the Regiment. In a development unknown to me, Inder promised 2 Para to Lt. Col. N.S. Uthaya who also belonged to 2 Para and was senior to me but was already commanding 10 Para (Cdo). Lt. Col. Uthaya had to be moved out to make place for Maj. M.K. Bhawani Singh, the Maharaja of Jaipur, a good friend of mine, as he did not have the professional background to command a parachute or an infantry battalion. The Cdo operations are mostly at the lower level of a team (company) or lower and team commander is the person who plans and executes the tasks. CO's role is essentially to analyse the task and supervise the execution.

It was an ordinary and normal day and I was sitting with Lt. Col. Ranjit Singh Dayal MVC, CO 1 Para and writing an exercise for the Brigade, a task given to us by the Brigade Commander. He received a telephone call and ended the conversation by saying he is here, I will tell him. He told me that it was Inder Gill, who was on leave in the station telling him that he has been posted to the Army Air Transport School and I was to take over 1 Para from him. I was a bit taken aback. I had a feeling that this was the outcome of the manoeuvring of 1 Para lobby which was very strong in the regiment at that time and to resolve the situation created by the early move of Uthaya. Ranjit told me 1 Para was the oldest battalion of the Indian Army and conqueror of Hajipir and I was the right person to command it. I was more livid than upset and told Ranjit, it is not my battalion and I will not be a convenience. I rang up Inder Gill and told him that I wanted to see him not as Tubby Nayar, his old BM, but as Major Nayar and he as Colonel of the Regiment. I went and saw him but he was adamant and told me that it was his decision for me to command 1 Para and Uthaya 2 Para. Finding him unreceptive before leaving I told him that I had been promised 2 Para and I had waited for it for over a year. Moreover, I have given something to 2 Para which no other officer of my vintage has, under my command, the Special Task Force earned 12 decorations including three Sena Medals, one Ati Vishisht Seva Medal and eight commendation cards during Operation Trishul in 1961, that too after our action got diluted due to the debacle in 1962. Finally, I told him that I will not command 1 Para even if I have to go out and command a battalion in any other regiment. Just before leaving I told him I will represent to the MS to get justice. The irony of it was that Uthaya, a friend of mine, was staying with us along with his wife. He did feel bad but told me he was equally struck. I told him, we should not let this sour our friendship, come what may. I went over Inder's head to the MS Branch and registered my claim, I always felt having chased my dreams for so long that I could not lose. Fate finally smiled and a toss in my favour done by Uthaya made him relent in my favour. I received my posting to command 2 Para.

The orders for me to take over 2 Para (Maratha) arrived in October 1968 and I was asked to move immediately. As 2IC of 5 Para, I could not leave Farook's, an officer of the battalion, and Maherengez's marriage midway. I moved after two days, making up the delay courtesy the IAF who gave me a lift up to Pathankot. I reached Jindrah, 2 Para's location, to be told that the battalion was still in the Valley, to act as exercise enemy to 'V' Sector in a forthcoming exercise. I decided to leave immediately that night for Khrew, but the Brigade Commander advised me not to do so, as the Battalion's 2IC was already acting in the capacity of CO for the exercise and there was no need for me to go. I told the

Brigade Commander that in a battalion there is only one CO and it is me. He did not like my abrupt reply. During this meeting he also laid out his policy parameters about honesty, frankness and straightforwardness in dealing with units. I did not want to miss the opportunity to respond and told him that nothing could be better for the unit. I also told him that whatever he wanted to know about 2 Para, he should ask me and he will be told the truth. I did not realize that the occasion was to come soon. I left for Khrew early next morning. 2/Lieut. Verma met me at Banihal and informed me that unless I reach the Battalion before 5 p.m., Panditji says the 'muhurat' will be over and I would have to spend the night at the transit camp in Srinagar and take over next morning. It was nearing 3 p.m. I drove like a mad man to reach the battalion before 5 p.m. They had given up hope that I would be arriving in time, till they saw dust kicking up on the track leading into the battalion area. There were shouts of '*aa gya, aa gya*' and as I got down from the jeep a hearty welcome was sounded on the Sinh[1] and I was rushed into the mandir EPIP tent. After the puja, Naib/ Subedar Religious Teacher (RT) Patil, the Panditji, who had joined the battalion from the Kolhapur Shastri Academy when I was the Adjutant, addressed me as follows:

Aap jab is EPIP tamboo se bahar niklenge to aap hamara commanding hoinge lekin us se pahle mai Nb. Sub. Patil, Paltan ka Pandit, apko kuch baten batata hun. Pahli, hum ko malum hai ki aapko gussa ata hai aur aap peet te bhi ho, badli mat hona, iski sakhat zarurat hai. Dusri baat—command dar kar nahin hota—Aap kabhi nahin daren, abhi aap commanding afsar hai, badli nahin hona. Tesri baat—Commanding afsar aur palton ki kismet ek hoti hai—woh ek dusre ko par le ja sakte hain—agar ek ki kismat achchhi hai to dusra bhi kamyab hota hai—Badhai ho 'Ram Ram'. (As you step out of the EPIP tent you will be our CO, however before that I Nb. Sub. Patil, the battalion's Pandit want to tell you a few things. One, we know that you are short tempered and you even beat up people, don't change as it is required. Second, you were never scared, now that you are CO don't change. Third, the fate of the battalion and CO are interlinked and they carry each other—congratulations, Ram Ram). *Bol Chhatrapati Shivaji Maharaj Ki Jai.*

As we were walking out of the tent, Panditji reminded me that since after 1957, when Col. Sucha Singh, VrC, left you are only the second CO after Ujjal Gupta from the battalion, this has affected the battalion, there are great hopes and responsibility on you.

I walked out of the tent rejuvenated, looked at the sprawling battalion camp and silently vowed never to compromise on the battalion's interest. Major Ram Nath Sethi, the 2nd-in-Command, briefed me regarding the exercise. The task of the battalion was to simulate infiltration over the Pir Panjal Gallis into the Valley to destroy value targets and to test 'V' Sector's counter infiltration plans. I felt the plans needed a change. Ram Nath Sethi informed me that the plans had been approved by GOC 'V' Sector, Maj. Gen. Umrao Singh. I sought a meeting with the GOC and established my credentials by informing him that I had intimate knowledge of the area and Pak's infiltration tactics, as I had been the BM of the Infantry Brigade during the Indo-Pak War of 1965. It was essential not only to establish my credentials but also to remind him of 1965 war days when I was the BM of 163 Infantry Brigade and he was appointed as the first GOC V sector. This was essential to convey to him that I was not hiding an old association of 1965. I added that despite the onset of winter, to simulate authentic crossings, columns and sub-columns of the battalion should traverse the Pir Panjal Gallis in the manner that infiltrators would do in good weather. He approved the revised plans and the exercise was a great success. We achieved all our tasks and 'V' Sector defences were modified based on our actions. On the very first night of infiltration, my party (CO's) with 'A' Company was moving rather slowly. When I went forward I found that my tactical HQ was carrying a tent for me, I got livid, and my temper got the better of me and I lashed out with my stick, the first blows fell on the Adjutant Tootli (Capt. V.K. Bhandre) and Nb. Sub. Vithal Kadam. I told them to drop the tent and that I would use my sleeping bag when required, like everyone else. The first night's stick wielding, including one on the Exercise Umpire did wonders and we were moving better than the Bakarwals. When we got back Panditji presented me with a new stick, since the old one had been broken. Wherever I went I received smiles and stolen looks at the stick.

To get a feel of the state of the battalion, I took it out for a month's training to Ram Nagar on the Udhampur-Dhar Road. On the third day, the Sub. Maj. Dubal arrived in the training area from the rear and reported that an NCO from the C Company's rear, Krishna Bhosle, had deserted taking a 9 mm pistol with him. I had known this NCO from the day he joined the battalion and told the Sub. Maj. that this NCO could not have acted in this fashion, without some provocation and that something was amiss. I went to the battalion rear and after checking details, I sent a letter to his home address asking him to return with the pistol. I further told him that he would be punished for the offence, but if he had a genuine reason for doing what he did I would look into the matter. We also sent a JCO from his area to trace him. Simultaneously I informed the Brigade Commander that if the OR did not return within 15 days, I would report the matter officially. The Brigade Commander's reaction was that he would not acknowledge that I told him about it. I knew then that all his talk of honesty, frankness and being straight forward was just talk and a pretense to impress. Meanwhile the JCO returned empty handed, but on the twelfth day I received a letter from Krishna Bhosle stating that he had absented himself taking a pistol with him as the Senior JCO had refused him leave despite compelling circumstances at home. There was also an element of caste superiority, the JCO was a Maratha and Krishna a Mahar. He also wrote that he was returning the pistol via parcel post and promised to return after attending to his domestic problems. The pistol arrived by parcel on the 17th day of absence and Krishna Bhosle rejoined duty after a further period of ten days. I court-martialed Krishna Bhosle, awarding him one year's rigorous imprisonment and dismissal from service. When I told the Brigade Commander, his reaction simply floored me, he said, 'you are a funny person, he has done you a favour and you have sent him to jail'. I told him politely that I do not believe in compromises and I have to command the battalion on my terms and not on favours done. Within the battalion everyone accepted as they expected it from me and appreciated it. I promised Krishna Bhosle that after he comes out of jail I would get him a job in the 'civvy street'. With the help of Major R. MacMillan Smith who was then the Secretary of the Bombay Gymkhana Club, Krishna Bhosle got a permanent job with BEST (Mumbai Transport). Some years later while I was on tour as a part of the National Defence Course, he (Krishna Bhosle) drove me around Pune in a State car.

2 Para (Maratha) earned a name for itself and respect not only in the Bakarwal Brigade[2] but in the entire Valley, as well as in Jammu, as a unit on the move. Besides operational responsibility in which we excelled, Battalion teams won the Khad Race, General J.N. Chaudhuri Trophy and were tested and retested as a part of the Corps Reserve in projected operations in the Valley and Jammu. Apart from our other achievements, during our tenure in J&K, two events warrant mentioning as these have a bearing on the history and traditions of the battalion.

I was returning from a spot of leave, when on reaching Pathankot I was met by my driver Kuriakose and he informed me that we will have to walk a bit as he has parked the jeep in a hidden location. When I asked him why, he told me no jeeps were permitted by a Corps order. I was surprised as it was authorized to me as a CO for legitimate duties. We got in the jeep and I told him to drive to the Sub Area Headquarters. I did not see any Army jeep en route. At the Sub Area Headquarters I asked the AQMG as to what the orders were, he told me that these were Army Commander's orders and my jeep was confiscated. I told him that it is my unit property and he should mind his business. En route to Jindrah, every traffic check post of the Army warned me and took my particulars. After reaching the brigade location, I asked as to what exactly were the orders and what instigated the issuing of such an order. I was told that during the Army Commander's recent visit to Srinagar in a party at the Amar Singh Club, where Governor Vishnu Sahay was also present, he mentioned to the Army Commander casually that Amar Singh Club was overflowing with Army vehicles. The Army Commander instead of telling him that these officers had come to attend the party in his honour and as such were on duty, moreover in J&K they have no other transport to use, instead he passed an order for all vehicles to leave. There was some unpleasantness as some drivers refused to leave without their officers and without their orders. As expected the Military Police report on my journey from Pathankot to the unit arrived saying that I had used the jeep against orders and as such was liable for disciplinary action. Military Police reports are addressed to the OC unit (in this case me) with copies to intermediate headquarters. I replied that I was in a field area and was using the jeep for legitimate duty and that it is authorized on the establishment of the unit.

Some time later, we had to give a presentation at the Corps Headquarters in Udhampur on China. The Brigade Commander offered to take me in his staff car but I along with my 21C drove in my jeep to the Corps Headquarters and parked in the car park. The BGS, Brig. R.D. Hira, MVC (later Lt. Gen.) whom I had the privilege to serve in the same capacity, seeing me in the jeep told me that I was asking for trouble. Even he had come in a one ton. I told him, he is a staff officer whereas I am a commander even though only a Lt. Col. The presentation went off well and the Corps Commander invited me and my officers for a drink to his house, Tara Mount. During the evening his Brig i/c Adm told the Corps Commander that I was one of the two COs who were not obeying the order on the use of jeeps. The Corps Commander ignored it but when the Brig i/c Adm persisted, he asked me if I was disobeying the order and if so why. I had anticipated such an eventuality and was prepared for it. I requested the Corps Commander that it was a social occasion and I was his guest, I would prefer not to answer it now. He smilingly told me not to worry and say frankly whatever I have to say. My reply stumped everyone, as I did not apologize, instead I told him, 'it is an illegal order, the jeep is authorized on my establishment for the CO and I am using it for a legitimate duty only'. I further went on to say, what is being exploited is not our sense of discipline or loyalty but our need for our job. Moreover, we are told that the COs were the backbone of the Army and you want everyone to look up to the CO. What impression would be created on a JCO or on his men when he visits them in a hospital coming in a one or three ton vehicle. They are bound to feel that he can do very little for them when he cannot even find a decent vehicle for himself. Nothing was said after that and the party finished soon afterwards. Next morning I was asked to see the Corps Commander. He fired me for my ill discipline but orders were issued a few days later permitting COs to use jeeps. In the adjoining 11 Corps Lt. Gen. P.S. Bhagat, VC, the Corps Commander refused to carry out these orders and people continued to use jeeps for authorized duties. The incident left a lasting impression on me and I always upheld the position of the Commanding Officer. You cannot take the shelter of disciple in to pass incorrect and illegitimate orders. If people misuse transport, the defaulters should be punished. Almost more than 50 per cent of the transport plying in J&K is government transport including Army and para military forces and comparatively much junior level officers, even below inspectors and others use jeeps in the police forces. Senior officers need to look after the interest of junior officers rather than indulging in slighting them.

MLI RAISES 3 MLI

In 1969, I received a letter from the Colonel of the Regiment, Maj. Gen. I.S. Gill, MC stating that the Maratha Light Infantry during their last reunion had decided to re-raise the 3 MLI.[3] It would be a befitting gesture for the battalion to present a centrepiece to the new unit. I was both non-plussed as well as livid at such a suggestion. The MLI had no right to re-raise 3 MLI, when 2 Para (erstwhile 3/5th MLI) was in existence and thriving. After some quick thinking I called the officers and JCOs and after giving them the news, I told them that I shall represent against it to the Supreme Commander, the President of India. Due to the shortage of time and exercising my moral right as the Commanding Officer, I submitted a petition to the President of India, for undoing the wrong that had been done, with copies to the COAS, AG, Headquarters XV Corps and my Brigade Headquarters. I also wrote to the Colonel of the Regiment enclosing a copy of the petition. As luck would have it the Colonel of the MLI, Maj. Gen. E. D'Souza, took over as the GOC of the division in Baramulla. I met him at a sports event where he told me that the re-raising of 3 MLI decision had been approved by the Chief and that nothing would come of my petition. I told him that I respected him in his capacity as Colonel of the MLI, but that I would oppose tooth and nail the re-raising of 3 MLI. To say the least it was a difficult time as I got support from no one in the higher echelons. Nevertheless I continued to wage a lone battle, till one day a letter was issued that the new 3 MLI will have no claim on past history, battle honours or traditions—it was only a partial victory. The credit for this goes to Gen. (later FM) Sam Manekshaw, MC, who as COAS saw an

Infantry Battalion Commander's anguish over such a historically absurd decision. Even though I relinquished command in January 1971, the battle continued.

In 1975 I was commanding an Independent Infantry Brigade Group in Trivandrum, when the newly raised 3 MLI became a part of the formation. I told Lt. Col. Keshav Puntambekar, their CO, to remove the photograph of Nk. Yeshwant Ghadge, VC, from their Quarter Guard, the Officers Mess and that I did not want to see anything of the original 3 MLI's past in the battalion. My struggle was continuing. The final success came in 1976 when 3 MLI was re-designated 8 MLI. The damage had been undone and honour fully restored. I celebrated the occasion with 8 MLI and wished them well in their new and genuine designation.

The second event concerns the return of 2 Para (Maratha) to 50 (Indep) Para Brigade. Our relief programme showed 2 Para (Maratha) moving to an Infantry Brigade in Dehradun. We had been out of the Para Brigade for over five years and I felt it strange that we were to do another peace tenure outside the Para Brigade, followed by the inevitable field tenure before we could hope to be on airborne status once more after a total gap of 12 years. In the meantime a new generation had come up who knew very little about the battle drills and procedures of airborne operations and had little opportunity to imbibe the ethos, camaraderie and *esprit-de-corps* of the paratroopers. Formal pleadings met with no success. I decided once more to take this on as a personal battle. In the Quarterly Security Intelligence Report, I clearly spelt out that if we could not at this stage form part of the Para Brigade, I and All Ranks of the battalion were seriously considering becoming non-para volunteers and return to the MLI. We were serious about this, every man jack in the battalion. The orders were changed and we moved to the Para Brigade, replacing 1 Para (Punjab) who had been with the Brigade for five years and now moved to form part of the Infantry Brigade in Dehradun.

BACK TO THE PARA BRIGADE

We joined the Para Brigade in January 1970. The Brigade Commander, Brig. Tirath Singh Oberoi, VrC, a fine soldier, put the Battalion through a test exercise in defence and withdrawal while in contact. The battalion did well and the Brigade Commander was happy. Taking advantage of this euphoria I told him that since we had operated in the mountains of J&K recently, instead of training in mountain warfare which was scheduled next, we should be given a chance to catch up on our airborne training. I also requested that instead of 5 Para which had been earmarked for the forthcoming airborne exercise, 2 Para (Maratha) should be given this chance, particularly since the Battalion would remain with the formation the longest. The Brigade Commander accepted my request. This was to give us the chance of our lives.

After the battalion had completed its parachute refresher training, at my request, we participated in skeleton in the airborne role in a Corps exercise. Although it was a success, it brought home to me, how much we needed to improve our airborne operating techniques. The two major weaknesses that I observed were night rendezvous (RV) after the drop and night navigation in the plains environment. Since the basic ingredients for success in an airborne operation were to drop at night, RV and move to the objective in the least time, I decided to move the battalion out of the barracks, to Kheria (near the Agra airfield) and concentrate on both the airborne and ground aspects of airborne operations. There was some murmuring amongst the officers and men, since the battalion had just returned from field service and they wanted leave to go home, to bring their families to Agra and generally enjoy the benefits of peace tenure. At a Sainik Sammelan, I explained to the officers and men that the period of training would only be a month, following which they would have an uninterrupted stay in Agra except for the period of brigade training next year. I found the men enthusiastic to prove their mettle and so we moved to Kheria.

I then decided that we would only jump at night, three times a week in rifle company lots, followed by RV drill. On other nights we would practice night navigation, move and attack. After a week I got the affiliated Para Field Battery, Platoon Para Field Company and Section Para Field Ambulance of the battalion group together and integrated them into the training schedule. During daylight hours, after a debrief of the previous night's RV drill, movement, navigation and night attack practice, practice of loads both individual and heavy drop, 'hang-up' drills and whatever else company commanders wanted to practise their companies in, was programmed.

After about ten days, I was satisfied with the progress made, except the timings for RV which could not be brought down below 45 minutes. The Brigade Commander, Brig. Oberoi, VrC, who jumped with us regularly, was pleased with the timing, but I felt that unless we were able to RV, collect our loads, move off with our field artillery and mortars ready to fire in less than half an hour, we would lose the element of surprise. I knew the officers and men had done their best and that we could only hope to improve on the timings marginally and in case of a dispersed drop, it could be worse. The problem was with the current procedure itself, which we had acquired from the British. This procedure required that after jumping, each individual after collecting his load (heavy loads by detachments), moved to a prominent landmark on one flank of the Drop Zone to the designated company RV marked by light (coloured) on which the men were required to rally. This involved movement over a distance of anywhere between a 1,000 yards and up to 1.5 mile. This may have been tactically sound but was time consuming and delayed resumption of command by sub-unit commanders. I lived with this problem, as did my Company Commanders, and finally came to the conclusion that RV should be on the Drop Zone itself, by each sub-unit and the Company Commander himself would put up the company coloured recognition light wherever he landed. To facilitate this procedure further we did away with tactical loading of the aircraft sub-unit wise, instead paratroopers were loaded in each aircraft of each wave in the order in which I wanted them on the ground. If I wanted 'A' Company on the approach edge of the Drop Zone, followed by 'C' Company followed by Battalion Headquarters in a wave, men of 'A' Company were loaded 1 to 7 on both port and starboard side of the aircraft, followed by 'C' Company followed by Battalion Headquarters. I tried this out in one aircraft and then in a wave of aircraft and found that this procedure worked. After the third practise, we demonstrated the technique to the Brigade Commander who was very pleased to see that we had cut down on RV timing by about 15 to 20 minutes. Similarly guns of Para

Field Battery[4] were dropped with the crews jumping immediately after the guns.

For the final exercise (Ex) 'Circus' we were given photographs of an airfield. Our task was to capture the airfield and thereafter prepare the airfield for air landing of 5 Para. The tactical plan was worked out. I selected a practice Drop Zone 3.5 km from the airfield and practised our tasks. There was a technical hitch in marking the airfield after capture as the Kerosene Bread[5] used for it would remain lit for 10 to 15 minutes at the most which was not enough. We overcame this by improvising our indigenous markers made of cotton waste prepared into 'balls' and dipped in a mixture of used engine oil and kerosene which remained lit for a minimum of two hours and even three by increasing its size. I always shared professional problems with men. In a *durbar* during our stay at Kheria, I told the officers, JCOs and men the problem of marking the airfield with Kerosene Breads and asked all to think for possible solutions. A few days later Paratrooper Jagannath Singh of Bravo Company while sweeping the area near Mechanical Transport Platoon observed that the cotton waste thrown by the drivers after cleaning the vehicles had caught fire and kept on burning steadily. He rushed out reported to the Havildar Major. It came up to me and we found the solution for marking the airfield.

Just prior to the commencement of the exercise the weather got bad and the IAF suggested we cancel or postpone the drop. But the Brigade Commander backed my resolve to continue the exercise as planned. During the approach to the Drop Zone, the weather was turbulent and some of the men affected by the buffeting in the aircraft started throwing up. But just ten minutes flying time away from the Drop Zone the weather cleared and winds abated. It was a dark, moonless night, but the jump was smoothly executed five minutes after the designated 'P' (Parachute Drop Time) Hour. The battalion moved off from the RV, with full loads, guns and mortars ready to fire in 28 minutes and secured the airfield by 'P' plus 135 minutes. The airfield was ready to receive 5 Para landings immediately thereafter. In retrospect this training was of great help to 2 Para (Maratha) in the Tangail drop on 11 December 1971.

Two incidents during the preparatory period of Ex 'Circus' are worth mentioning. During one of our practice night jumps we had a 'hang-up', a gunner from the Para Field Battery. He was released after ten minutes and we located him within half an hour. During his release the sling of his sten carbine snapped and the weapon plummeted to earth somewhere on the 10 miles circuit of the aircraft. We were happy to have the gunner safe. After I narrated the incident to the Brigade Commander in the presence of the IAF Station Commander, Air Commodore Zaheer, the former ordered me to search for and find the weapon. This order not only startled me but Air Commodore Zaheer as well. But orders are orders and I organized the battalion for the search, it was like looking for a needle in a haystack. But luck favours the brave. We found the weapon embedded in a field, none the worse for wear.

The second incident concerns the IAF. Their Officer Commanding of the Parachute Training School traditionally leads the airborne train, but we found in practise drops, that he always dropped the 'stick' short or beyond the Drop Zone. Once we almost had two of our men drowned in Sikandra Rao Canal during a practice jump. During the coordinating conference for Ex 'Circus' in Western Air Command, I stated that I would prefer either Squadron Leader Ambagaonkar 21C of PTS or Wing Commander Naidu OC of another squadron to lead the airborne train. It was but natural that the IAF was upset. But I had my way and the final drop led by Wing Commander Naidu was a great success as mentioned earlier.

Life now settled down to peace time routine at Agra. We won the Brigade Boxing Championship against the best boxers of 7 Para, trained by Lt. Col. S.R. Das Gupta, their CO, a veteran boxer himself. We won the brigade wrestling finals entering in only five weights as Marathas could not produce the heavier weights. During the finals we won the first four fights and we had to win the fifth to get the championship. In this fight an elderly Shamu Bhosle was pitted against a 6 ft tall experienced Khalsa wrestler of 8 Para. The odds were against us. Before the fight, I walked up to Shamu and told him in a loud whisper, '*Beta Shamu agar tu aaj har gaya to tera CO sar aur muche mundwakar jayega*' (Son, if you lose, your CO will leave the place without his moustaches and a shaven head). God alone knows what Shamu did. We found that within the first 10 seconds, the hefty 8 Para wrestler was down under Shamu's vice-like grip; the referee counted him out and we won. I hugged Shamu Bhosle and lifted him up. His opponent told him he would see him next year. Shamu replied that he was going on pension and therefore would not have the pleasure of defeating him a second time. Shamu won a Vir Chakra in the Indo-Pak War 1971 (at Tangail) and after serving the Battalion with distinction went home on pension as a Naik. Of such stuff are the paratroopers of 2 Para (Maratha) made.

Major Kulwant Singh Pannu, had left the battalion before I took over under unpleasant circumstances and was not approved for command. He wrote to me saying that he wanted to return to the battalion as no other CO will have him. I asked for his return to the battalion so that he could eventually take over. He now became my 2IC, but after he was approved for command, he was getting restless. I told him to wait for command of 2 Para (Maratha) as he would not last long in any other battalion. I had just completed one and a half years in command when I was selected for a Military Assistant assignment abroad. I refused and requested that I be posted after I complete my tenure. This was not accepted so I refused the offer and stayed on. This was not agreeable to Pannu who could not bear the delay and with the help of his friends in the MS Branch had me posted as OC Commando Wing, the Infantry School, in March 1970. Having just refused a Military Assistant assignment, this was too much and I told Pannu that I would leave when I had completed my tenure. I sought an interview with the MS and my posting was cancelled. I stayed with the battalion till January 1971 when I was posted as an instructor to the Senior Command Wing of the College of Combat, Mhow.

My innings with 2 Para (Maratha) was indeed the best period of my service. I left the battalion, with a sense of great fulfilment and satisfaction that I had done my best and from Ganpat (a Maratha sepoy) upwards all had acknowledged that I was tough and harsh with them for their own good. 2 Para was in fine fettle and that was proved within a year after I left in the 1971 war of liberation of Bangladesh. They returned as victors and with the honour of being in the first airborne operation of free India. I met the battalion at the Republic Day Camp, when they were specially asked to participate in the parade. I asked Kulwant, the

CO, and Sub. Maj. Sita Ram Jadhoo as to what were their biggest achievements. They said battalion receiving one MVC, six VrC and four SM and being the first troops to enter Dacca. The greatest honour of all was when the battalion was awarded, 'Poongli Bridge 1971', as a battle honour. After listening to them I told them that these will be part of the national and Army history and the unit can be truly proud of these achievements. In addition I told them never to forget that each man in the battalion performed and contributed and is well trained. This is well proved by three incidents during the war. First, that 2/Lt. L.J.S. Gill and one OR made their first jump in operations at Tangail, both in years to come will be recognized as born leaders. The second incident of paratrooper Mahadeo Gurav, when hung up did every thing right and his actions brought credit to him, the battalion and every soldier. His story as recorded in, *India's Paratrooper* by K.C. Praval is attached as Appendix 'A' in this Chapter. It shows the courage, ingenuity and spirit of an average paratrooper of 2 Para. The third incident relates to Subedar Victor Sequera's initiative and leadership at the junior level and operational judgement. His aircraft of a mixed load of a gun detachment of artillery and elements of Support Company were dropped far from the battalion dropping zone. He collected this mixed lot and retrieved the gun from the pond where it had landed and proceeded to join the battalion. Enroute he met Mukti Bahani and fought a few actions and rejoined the unit. He was awarded a well deserved Sena Medal. I told the unit that these events are part of the same history and never to forget it. I requested late Maj. Gen. D.K. Palit to write about it, which was widely covered in most papers. Paratrooper Mahadeo Gurav's hang up incident was also published in *Times Weekly* of 27 February 1972. Apart from the nation and the Army at large, it was a historic occasion for the battalion in more than one way. The link up with 2 Para was effected by 1 MLI, the Jangi Paltan, which further strengthened our ties with the parent regiment MLI. For both units the occasion was of historical importance as it strengthened the ties with the Marathas, these regimental ties are the backbone of the Infantry and the Army. Tangail was shaken by the resounding battle cries of '*Bol Chhatrapati Shivaji Maharaj Ki Jai*' by 2 Para and the Jangi Paltan.

Tangail was important for the unit and the paratrooper fraternity and everyone took advantage of the success as nothing succeeds like success. Under the circumstances it achieved success but it failed to meet the much higher operational parameters for which the battalion had been trained. I was personally disappointed and I shudder to think of the consequences of a drop spread over 50 minutes during daytime in a hostile country as even a mild enemy reaction would have resulted in a massacre. Its planning lacked total professional judgement. It was an ideal opportunity for us and particularly the Air Force to try out a night drop. Moreover, we must not forget that it was the outcome of a series of coincidences which made it happen, first 50 Indep Para Brigade happened to be in Calcutta in Eastern Command, GOC-in-C Eastern Command Lt. Gen. J.S. Aurora was a paratrooper and finally Maj. Gen. I.S. Gill, the Col. of the Para Regiment was the DMO and was the moving force behind it. While the decision to employ this potent strategic force was correct, implementation was shoddy primarily due to IAF's inability and unwillingness to undertake such operations at night which was a serious constraint. 2 Para was fully trained for it.

2 Para's biggest asset has been its young leadership and its nurturing by the dedicated senior fraternity. The battalion has traditionally been very harsh in selection and probation of its officers and only accepted the best. Most of them like K.S. Pannu, J.B. Bhada, V.K. Sarda, J.S. Mahalwar, V.K. Bhandre (Tootli), J.S. Sethi, M.L. Tiwari (Tues), V.D. Varma, K.R. Nair, K.R. Rao (Gundu), T.C. Bhardwaj (Chotu), K.N. Mehra (Krish), S.M. Kunzroo were mine and later the battalion assets, who proved themselves in the Bangladesh War and in difficult years of the battalion in J&K and the North-East. Similarly, different generations of JCOs and men have shown their mettle in operations and all other fields of employment in true traditions of the paltan.

NOTES

1. The traditional Maratha trumpet that is sounded on auspicious occasions, spelt 'Sinh'.
2. The formation was known as the Bakarwal Brigade as it moved, lived and survived like the hardy Bakarwals. We never moved in transport, always on foot using hill tracks and were self-contained. Even our

moves from Jindrah in Udhampur to Khrew in the Valley during summers were on foot on hilly tracks and gallies on Pirpanjal and self-contained.

3. The 3/5th Maratha LI (Para) had on the creation of the Parachute Regiment in 1952, been redesignated 2 Para (Maratha). The battalion disaffiliated from the Maratha LI in 1952 when it became part of the Parachute Regiment.
4. The Bty belonged to 9 Para Fd Regt, which had rotated for parachute duties with 17 Para Fd Regt.
5. Kerosene bread is made of kerosene extract (paraffin oil) and thus is combustible. These are used to mark the DZ by path finders and to mark a captured airfield for subsequent air landings.

APPENDIX A

PARATROOPER MAHADEO GURAV'S 'HANG UP'*

This was the first time that India used paratroopers in a military operation after Independence. Subhash Kripekar talks to Paratrooper Mahadeo Gurav who survived in spite of a 'hang-up' and despite landing in enemy territory.

Little did paratrooper Mahadeo Gurav know that he would be creating history when he got into the Fairchild Packet C119 aircraft, which was to drop him and his colleagues outside Tangail, north-west of Dacca, on 11 December 1971.

He was the 19th man in a 'stick' of 20 paratroopers on the starboard side of the aircraft. There was another stick of 20 paratroopers on the port side.

Flying at twilight—the sun sets around 4 p.m. over Bangladesh—the pilot gave the 'Green on, Go' signal and pressed the buzzer when he saw the dropping zone (DZ) below. The DZ was marked earlier by a group of 80 'path finders' who landed well ahead of the rest of the 2nd Battalion Parachute Regiment, in two Packet aircrafts.

Mahadeo Gurav saw his colleagues leap out of the aircraft. The drill was: count thousand-one, thousand-two, thousand-three, thousand-four. If the parachute did not open in these four seconds, then it meant that the chute would not open and the paratrooper would plummet down to earth if he did not open the reserve chute strapped to his belly.

Mahadeo also jumped when his turn came. But he was rudely jerked into realizing that his parachute strap linked to a wire running down the length of the aircraft had not snapped off when he leaped out. He was hanging 15 ft below the aircraft, upside down. From mid-air, he saw his colleagues floating down, their parachutes ballooning open. Soon, the aircraft and he were well past the DZ. Only the ponds, bamboo groves and mustard fields swirled below him hazily.

The IAF crew inside the aircraft, had realized that a paratrooper was hanging in mid-air. The Packet aircraft was flying at 1,200 ft when it was engaged in dropping 2 Para (Maratha) Group.

Mahadeo Gurav knew that he was now what was called a 'hang-up' case. He also knew that hang-up rarely survives for more than five minutes.

*Based on an account of Mahadeo Gurav's 'hang-up' published in *Times Weekly*, New Delhi, 27 February 1972.

The wind pressure at that height, the exhaust fumes from the aircraft and the constant buffeting against the belly of the aircraft were factors that beat the life out of even the toughest of men.

To make matters worse, Mahadeo's helmet had fallen down when he was jerked up by the 15 ft long strap that failed to disconnect. As the aircraft gained and lost height in an effort to somehow free him he was repeatedly smashed against the belly of the plane. His face was swollen and his eyes were streaming with tears because of the strong wind.

Time stood still for Mahadeo while he held on for dear life. He braced himself up, and although the parachute straps running over his thighs were cutting into his flesh and causing indescribable pain, he was determined to remain alive.

A little later, when he found himself free from the aircraft, his joy knew no bounds. He had been 'hung-up' for exactly 22 minutes, which is probably a world record for a hang-up in an air-borne operation.

The Para Jumping Instructor (PJI) ejection crew inside the aircraft had provided him with another parachute and cut-off the first strap that had almost taken his life. But Mahadeo's troubles were not over. In 22 minutes, the aircraft had taken a circuitous route over East Pakistan territory and when he was finally dropped, he was over Nator which was then held by Pakistani troops. More than 80 km of enemy-held territory separated him from his battalion.

Paratrooper Mahadeo landed in waist-deep water, a sten gun slung on one shoulder and a 2-inch mortar on the other. Within minutes, curious villagers gathered around the pond wondering who this creature was.

'I had to prove that I was an Indian soldier. The disc tied around my wrist inscribed with my name, number and religion helped me establish my identity. I also showed them photographs of my wife and two children kept in my purse and Indian currency too. Once they were convinced, they were helpful. They gave me some rice to eat and attended to my bruises and cuts', 24 years old Mahadeo Gurav told me.

After a few hours of rest, Mahadeo found himself leading a band of Bangladesh guerrillas in a night attack on a Razakar stronghold. Since there was no ammunition for his 2-inch mortar, it was useless. But he equipped himself with a Chinese light-machine-gun, a weapon he had never used before, and went into action. In a second attack on another Razakar stronghold, Mahadeo was able to retrieve his parachute which had drifted away when he unstrapped himself, after landing in the pond.

Mahadeo now realized that he had landed some 25 km from Nator. In collaboration with Bangladesh guerrillas he fought the enemy for nine days. When the mass surrender by the Pakistani forces was announced, he went to Nator and presented himself to the Brigade Headquarters at the Dighapatia Palace, which was the East Pakistan Governor's residence.

CHAPTER 4

Mhow, Wellington, Kerala and Desert

On joining the newly-formed College of Combat, I was told that instead of joining the Senior Command Faculty I was to join the Faculty of Studies and assigned a special task. My designation in the Faculty of Studies was Head of Department of Military Doctrines and Studies. College of Combat was formed after detaching the Senior Command and Junior Command wings from the Infantry School and adding a Higher Command Wing. Faculty of Studies was the new institution's think-tank and thereby the Army's, number of such organizations were to follow in true tradition of escalation in government organizational structure. The college was inaugurated with traditional fanfare by the then Chief General S.H.F.J. Manekshaw MC. A few days after the inauguration I was called for a briefing by Maj. Gen. Onkar Singh Kalkat, the Commandant of the College, an Officer better known for his operational and field command capabilities than as a military thinker. He told me that a new Higher Command Course on the lines of the Russian Army and some other armies was to be introduced and the College has been established with the primary aim of putting Higher, Senior and Junior Command training together. I was given the charge of the conceptualization, formulation and programming of the Higher Command Course and was to work directly under the Commandant and could meet and seek his guidance any time. He also told me that he has selected me on the recommendations of the Director Military Training Maj. Gen. I.S. Gill, my Colonel of the Regiment. I asked him if any concept paper or any material on such courses was available. He told me that it will be with the Director Military Training and I could go to Delhi to get it.

Inder Gill told me that the idea germinated during Gen. P.P. Kumaramangalam, the previous Chief's visit to Russia, and he briefed me on the level, orientation and broad content of the course in the USSR. I told him that I felt totally inadequate as I have only commanded a battalion. He thought I could do it with guidance from the Commandant. I went through the material available and selected the relevant ones and the COAS tour notes covering it. After discussion and deliberations at Delhi I was clear on two aspects. One, Higher Command cannot be of only a level higher than Senior Command but much above it. Second it has to incorporate doctrine, formation level operational, tactical and logistical planning, inter-service dimension of higher planning and execution, command and staff functioning at higher levels and higher direction of war. The senior officers' fortnights held for brigadiers and major generals at Infantry School and other arms and services schools could give useful inputs. Having cleared my mind I made a brief presentation to the Commandant and made suggestions as to how we should proceed. I told him that I wanted to visit all arms and services prime training institutions as well as joint warfare institutions of the IAF and Navy as seeing and knowing what their level of training is would help us to plan better. Moreover, we could not be doing what they were doing, it had to be higher and oriented to our requirement. His first reaction was that I wanted to have a Bharat Darshan and have a good time. It took some time to convince him and he agreed. I also asked for a grade two officer to assist me during these tours to collect relevant material as per the list prepared by me as it will be difficult for me to hold discussions with the faculty as well as collect material. He agreed and gave me his Staff Officer, Maj. Rustam Nanavati, who turned out to be an ideal choice. Rustam retired as Northern Army Commander.

As war clouds built-up most of us who could be employed elsewhere, moved out. I went to the Headquarters Western Command in Jalandhar as GSO1-Ops but stayed unemployed as no one wants to share power and position. On the day war was declared, I was asked by Col. (Int) Col. Pasricha, later DMI to write a press release for the Army Commander to make the announcement. It must have met the requirement and I was taken in and took part in the proceedings of the operational branch then onwards. A few days later I was picked up and ordered to visit the hot spots as the Command Headquarter's/Army Commander's observer to report back to the Army Commander. It probably came about as I had commanded the battalion when Lt. Gen. Candeth was the Corps Commander and I was known to him. It turned out to be the most educative, thrilling and rewarding experience and of these visits ones to the battles of Basantar River, Sejra bulge, Fazilka bund and Nagi sand dune were the most satisfying.

We rejoined the college after the war and we had a new Commandant Maj. Gen. E.A. Vaz (later Lt. Gen. and Eastern Army Commander). During my first meeting with him on the Higher Command Course, he told me that I should see him only in the afternoons, when he is free from other commitments. It meant longer working hours but was totally fruitful. He clearly defined the professional structure of teaching in the college in his very first address. He said, in Junior Command you practice tactics and battle drills, at Senior Command you understand tactics and doctrines and in Higher Command you question doctrines. One afternoon I put up a draft DO letter to the Cammandant inviting an eminent person (still not decided) to give a talk to the Higher Command Course on 'Higher Direction of War'. He approved the draft after some changes and when I asked him as to who we should invite without any hesitation he said nobody better than Lt. Gen. P.S. Bhagat, PVSM, VC. We sent the DO letter to him inviting him for the lecture. We received a reply from him accepting our invitation and suggesting that a more appropriate subject at their level would be, Operational Art of War and Irregular Warfare, rather than higher direction of war as suggested by us. General Vaz asked me as to what I thought of it. I told him that I have been thinking about it and I feel he wants to base his lecture on his earlier writings in *The Shield and the Sword* and *Forging the Shield*, but it was not our requirement. General Vaz questioned me a lot on the difference and he put across the difference most distinctly and we wrote to Gen. Bhagat saying it was not possible to change the subject of the lecture. General Bhagat accepted and asked for three months' time for preparing it. It was one of the best lectures ever to be given in the Higher Command Course. General Vaz believed in doing the best and the most challenging. I could not do the Higher Command Course as I was closely involved with its preparations.

Two months before the commencement of the course, four brigadier instructors joined the Higher Command faculty. Their commander was Brig. S.C. Sinha from my regiment. He requested Gen. Vaz if I could be posted to the faculty. General Vaz asked me and I refused saying I have done my bit, I don't want to be a convenience and the brigadiers should do their job. He appreciated my frankness and I was posted back to the Senior Command Wing as an instructor.

The tenure in the Senior Command was the most satisfying professionally and amongst the faculty and students one met a large number of officers, who were to be my contemporaries, colleagues and juniors in the years to come. We were sharpening the cutting edge of the Army—the battalion/regimental commanders—and used our experience to teach and to learn from them. The faculty was a small well-knit body of one brigadier, two colonels and eight lieutenant colonels, who respected each other but were socially individualistic. However, individual social trends were blended with collectiveness, the hallmark of which was the monthly get-together at each member's house by turn. With our meagre pay those days we had to resort to very stringent measures for a couple of months after one's turn to recoupe. One of these get-to-gethers in Arvind Inamdar's house, a colleague from the Sikh Regiment is worth mentioning. Both Arvind and Nalini were an amiable and lovely couple and very good friends of ours. On arrival at their house we found a big table laid with arrangements for eleven people. Each arrangement consisted of a bottle of Black Night whisky, one dozen sodas, four Coca Colas and two sets of excellent cold cuts with each couple's name written on it. There was a placard saying, 'You are welcome and can have your food and drinks as much as you wish but you cannot leave till you finish it all'. Half way through the party we realized that they were serious about it. It became a challenge for people like me whose better halves did not help by sharing the booze. We decided to reduce the physical quantity by doing away with the soda and water, it worked but with a much greater blurring effect. My wife and me were the last lot to leave on my Vespa scooter. I felt great with an impromptu halo around my head. As I was negotiating a curve on the road leading to the college main gate from the Bombay Hotel side, when my wife shouted 'cow, watch out', I saw it too but it was too late. I shouted for her to jump as I hit the cow. The scooter hit the mass of flesh and in the split second that it stayed still my wife jumped off but I got entangled between the scooter and the cow. My head hit some thing solid but I got up and straightened the scooter and asked my wife if she was alright. She said 'yes' and then she saw something dark on my face, touching it she cried out 'oh my god, its blood!' I took out my handkerchief and wiped my face and found that my left cheek and eye were bleeding. The cow just got up and walked away unconcerned. She forced me to go to the hospital which was closeby. I got two stitches on my left eyebrow and three on my left cheek. The doctor on duty gave me a pain killer and asked me to stay in the hospital for a few hours. I could not do so as I had to take an outdoor class in the morning. I left my scooter in the hospital and an ambulance dropped us home. Next morning (a few hours later) when I was getting ready, I saw the swollen left side of my face covered with yellow marks of the medicine. I considered the alternative of covering it with a sticking plaster as I could not rub it off but gave up the idea. I asked Gurdev Kler to pick me up and when I reached the class everyone asked me what happened. I sheepishly explained the episode. It was quite customary for the Commandant to visit the Senior Command course and partake in its instructional deliberations. Luckily, he did not come to my class that day. However, during the tea break on seeing me he asked as to what had happened. Before I could say anything Arvind blurted out, 'Tubby ran into a drunken cow'. Laughter and mirth followed the remark. General Vaz very seriously asked if I was wearing a helmet. On the spur of the moment I said 'yes'. He was most pleased as it was one of his favourite points during the opening talk to all courses. Leave alone wearing one I did not even possess one. To continue the facade, I always borrowed a helmet for going to evening show movies on weekends in the college and made it a point to display it while passing the Commandant's sofa. He often quoted me as an example. I had to keep up the joke.

General Vaz had a very innovative mind and enjoyed throwing up new ideas. Having tossed them he loved to seek and watch people's reaction and considered these before taking a decision. While working with him on the Higher Command course, he asked me as to what would be my reaction if he started coming to the College on a bicycle. I thought for a while and then told him not to do so. He asked me why. I told him that when I gave the answer, I was thinking not so much about him but me and other officers. Our problems would be manifold—one, we might not notice him. Secondly if we saw and recognized him then after saluting him there would be certain amount of hesitancy in our minds whether to overtake him or carry on. I asked him if he had noticed that when his flag car passes the shopping complex all the shopkeepers who stand outside their outlets salute, they don't even look to see if the Commandant is inside the car, they just salute the flag. If he was on a bicycle more often than not they will ignore him, which in turn would have an adverse effect on us junior officers. I saw the famous glint in his eyes and could not help adding that the Agarwal tailors' greetings/salutes to Junior Command course student officers is always more enthusiastic than to us. When I asked Mr. Agarwal as to why he was so enthusiastic in greeting a Junior Command course student just ahead of me and a listless good morning to me. He explained that Junior Command students get new suits stitched, whereas we only get old ones altered. General Vaz laughed and told me, 'you win, I will not cycle to the college'. In one of his addresses to the Higher Command course he narrated the incident and told them that symbols of authority are as important as the authority they represent.

In the early part of the third year of my stay at Mhow, I received news of my approval for a colonel and later to the rank of a brigadier. The second letter informing me of approval for brigadier was signed by Brig. Bhardwaj, Deputy MS, a paratrooper. Below the typed portion, he had put down in his own hand that I had been earmarked to take over 50 Independent Para Brigade. Both me and my wife were delighted. A fortnight later came my posting as Deputy Commander of Para Brigade to report by 15 April 1973. On 7 April a crisp signal cancelling my posting as Deputy Commander was received as the vacancy was tenable only during the Emergency, which had expired on 31 March 1973. I was quite happy to be where we were and did not mind moving directly to take over the brigade a year or so later. However, destiny had willed otherwise. A fresh posting was received posting me as a Senior Instructor at the Defence Services Staff College. I did not want to move just for a year or so and then again move to 50 Para Brigade. I requested General Vaz the Commandant if it could be cancelled and I could stay on, even in my present rank. He saw merit in my request and spoke to the Military Secretary. Next day he informed me that the posting cannot be cancelled as my name was on the list selected by the Commandant of Staff College. We decided to move with minimum luggage and sent the rest to the Para Brigade. Two days later I was invited by the Senior Command faculty to an informal dinner at the Golf Hut. The new Commander of the Wing, Brig. Farhat Bhatti had started this trend instead of the formal function in the mess.

We were all enjoying the party and had wined and dined well. Both me and my wife were getting ready to take leave, when Shiv Sharma from my regiment who had recently joined the faculty told the Commander that no paratrooper's dining out is complete without a para jump and roll. When everyone insisted I could not control my wild urge and looked around for a suitable aid to climb on top of the Golf Hut. I found a pipe going up and I started climbing up and was almost on top when the power went off. I tried to adjust my vision to the darkness, then jumped down and did a roll. When I tried to get up I found my feet aching all over. It was because I had landed on the hard cement floor wearing only Peshawari chappals. The power came on and when I asked why it had gone earlier, Shiv told me that he had switched it off intentionally as I was climbing a pipe carrying electric wires in it.

We travelled to Wellington with my sore feet and walking on tip toes. To top it all, I got the scolding of my life from my wife for my irresponsible behaviour. My children nine and eight years old sympathized with me and could not fathom my wife's stern behaviour when I was suffering. Later when they grew up and understood, they often pulled my leg that I could not do a para roll properly. I proved my credentials as a paratrooper years later in 2004 to my granddaughter's delight, when I jumped at Bangalore on the regiment's golden jubilee. I was 72 years old then and continued to jump for a couple of years afterwards too.

My one-year stay at the Staff College was good, enjoyable and professionally satisfying. At the end of it I earned my dagger. Staff College's traditions centred around protocol and I created a bit of an upheaval when I refused to follow the protocol based on seniority of your date of joining the college and insisted that Army seniority should be observed. Both the Commandant Maj. Gen. S.P. Malhotra (later Northern Army Commander) and Brig. H.K. Kulkarni, the Chief Instructor, were most intrigued when they learnt I was the juniormost senior instructor while other seniors had accepted it.

The posting of one of my colleagues Baba Giri was received, to take over a brigade on promotion and I was waiting for mine to Para Brigade. A few days later Col. (later Brig.) V.K. Saxena, Military Assistant to the Chief, who had done the Staff Course with me rang up to congratulate me on taking over the Independent Brigade Group in Trivandrum. I told him that I was earmarked for Para Brigade, he told me he did not know anything about it. I later learnt that Gen. Bewoor, the then COAS, felt that Southern Command always got a raw deal as this was his experience as its Army Commander and he wanted to correct it. When this Independent Brigade Group fell vacant, he asked for a list of approved brigadiers. The list along with the dossiers was put up and he ticked my name. When the MS told him that he himself had earmarked me for the Para Brigade, he said, 'I am the Chief and I can change my mind. I will send the best according to me to Southern Command'. The journey from Wellington to Trivandrum was short and we had to wait for our heavy luggage for six months from Agra. Though located in Trivandrum I was more out of it than in and my children shifted from learning Tamil to Malayalam.

As instructors at the Staff College, most of us were competent in the art of public speaking as there were ample opportunities for the same when we took central classes. But some of the instructors practised it to its extreme regardless of the occasion. When two of my colleagues and me were invited for dinner in the officers mess on our posting out on promotion. I was the juniormost. After the Commandant had spoken and complimented us on our contribution to the faculty and the college at large, the first speaker amongst us in reply spoke for over 20 minutes covering his and his wife's activities during their stay. It tried the patience of the officers and the ladies present. The second officer was a bit more considerate and took only five minutes. When my turn came everyone looked at me longingly for mercy. I told them that they have heard a long speech and a short one and I would give both. I saw murderous glances being exchanged. I said first the long one, 'thank you very much, and now the short one, thank you'. There was loud applause and one lady even came up to me and almost kissed me. The art of public speaking lies in realizing the occasion and understanding the state of mind of the audience.

DESTINED CHANGE FOR GOOD: COMMAND OF AN INDEPENDENT INFANTRY BRIGADE GROUP

From Wellington to Trivandrum was a short journey deeper into the south, a real blessing for an infantry officer. Professionally it was most rewarding because of the new desert environment where the operational area was and seniors that I served with. Lt. Gen. Sartaj Singh, GM, the Army Commander was my direct boss who was known for his tough and no nonsense approach and at times could be obnoxious but what was good was that he was only interested in the profession with no extraneous demands. Maj. Gens. K. Sundarjee and Prithiviraj and Brig. V.N. Sharma (Titch) were other formation commanders. My predecessor Brig. Bakshi Joginder Singh, MVC, who commanded the Brigade Group in Bangladesh and captured Bogra had already left so there was no handing over. My BM, Maj. Gurdeep Singh from the Dogras told me that there were two major events soon, a war game at Command Headquarters after a fortnight and a brigade exercise to be set by the Command after a month, for which the brigade should move while I was still in Poona. The move of the Brigade Group had already been planned. I discussed it with the Quarter Master General staff and went over it with Lt. Col. Mianwala, CO J & K LI who was the seniormost commanding officer. The Gorkha Battalion who were due to move out of the brigade were left in Trivandrum to prepare for their next field tenure. My children's admission to schools and setting the house was left to my wife and she did a marvellous job of it.

Desert was a new environment and my only exposure to it was the comparative study done of the wars in the desert in 1965 and 1971 for the Higher Command course and the exercises during the recent tenure at the Staff College. After the operational briefing and having studied the plans, I was convinced that familiarization with the terrain and latest enemy intelligence was important both for the presentation and the war game. After study of the maps and air photos I decided on my reconnaissance plan. I spent the better part of the fortnight available in the area familiarizing with the terrain and our operational role. I was greatly helped during my reconnaissance by Lt. Col. A.D. Singh, the CO of the motorized battalion, who was from my Company at the Indian Military Academy, I fully exploited their expertise both as camel mounted and motorized troops. The defensive plans were sound and I only had a small variation to offer. However, there were serious reservations and apprehensions regarding the offensive task. The brigade on return from Bangladesh had occupied the area (as captured territory) till they returned in 1972. They had detailed maps and sketches of the area. On planting the intelligence inputs since 1972 on these sketches and air photos, the objective appeared more formidable and a well coordinated battalion position instead of an advance and a weak battalion position in the rear. We double checked it and later an independent check by a CO confirmed that our plans were based on the 1972 position.

As is customary in the Army the briefing at the commencement of the war game followed the seniority, first the two divisional commanders, Sundarjee followed by Prithiviraj. Both were excellent presentations with a lot of charts and other aids. I only had an enlargement and a map and my notebook. I made a few changes in my briefing notes as I listened to their briefings. My turn came after lunch. I started with terrain and went into the minutest details. After 10 minutes Gen. Sartaj interrupted and said he knew the terrain and I should proceed further. I had heard about Gen. Sartaj's abrupt and rude ways but it came as a total surprise, probably a part of his impatience was boredom and post-lunch ennui. However, in my mind I was convinced that unless I presented everything as planned, it will be difficult for me to justify the difference in opinion I had on the current plans, so I carried on as planned. He interrupted me twice more but when he did it for the third time, I told him, Sir, you know it but it is important that you should know that I also know it and it is important for me to project certain issues. After this, though a bit unhappy he did not interrupt. After presenting the defensive plans, I projected no changes except location of the reserves, which in the plan were located within the brigade defended sector. I placed them 30 km behind the sector. General Sartaj felt it was most unconventional and was reluctant to accept the change. Some amongst the formation commanders also had the same opinion. I argued that desert terrain and our location permits investment of the sector from more than one direction and the sector could be cut-off, the reserves may get involved in the initial battle making their movement and application for the main tasks difficult. These are mobile elements with good radio communications and therefore could be applied from any direction once the enemy design was clear. It was decided to war game it. During the war game it turned out to be a better option and was adopted.

In the second part, when I presented the enemy layout for the offensive task assigned to me projected that it was a formidable battalion plus position and not an advance company position with a weak battalion defensive position in-depth. The first to interject was Brig. Suri, the BGS, followed by Maj. Gen. Sundarjee under whom I was to carry out the offensive task. I also said that I could not do it unless I have additional resources. General Sartaj's first reaction was, if you cannot do this task, I will sack you. I kept quiet but said in my mind 'better now than after one fails'. I took the marked air photographs to him and explained to him the positions marked based on intelligence reports from his headquarters, whereas the planning was based on the 1972 positions. He ordered a break and took all the formation commanders to his office and asked me to once again authenticate what I had said. I was prepared for it. I took out a set of air photos with 1972 positions and then built it up based on later intelligence reports. He asked the BGS to do an independent check. I knew he will probably get after his intelligence staff, so I told him that if I were not new, I would also probably do the same. He asked me what additional resources I required. I asked for one more infantry battalion, one field regiment, one medium battery and an additional squadron of Armour. He approved it after discussion and much to the annoyance of Sundarjee, who was asked to provide these additional resources. After the war game, he asked me about the exercise and said it could be postponed as I was new. I told him I have inherited a very fine formation, which did well during the war, I was what I was and won't improve in a month. Sartaj thought I was being cocky, as I learnt later he told Sundarjee who was to conduct the exercise to throw the book at me. The Chief of Staff Lt. Gen. Kundan Singh who was my instructor at the Staff College, called me and told me '*shagird* (pupil) well done, keep it up'. Sartaj appreciated frankness and even bluntness, as he was quite frank and blunt himself.

DESERT AND ENCOUNTERS OF THE DIFFERENT TYPE

I just had about three weeks in desert and to know my units and officers. General Sundarjee was to exercise my brigade on behalf of the Army Commander and the entire control and umpire staff was from his division. The initial scenario of the exercise was along the expected lines depicting the mobilization and move of the formation to its area of responsibility and occupation of defensive positions. Recce (R) and Order (O) groups had moved to the area and the Fighting (F) group consisting of the rest of the Brigade Group were moving as per the plan. This is where the similarity ended. While waiting for the F group at the designated RV, I was painted a picture that in a surprise move enemy has ingressed in strength into the area and put a road block on the main axis between us and the F group. I asked Gen. Sundarjee as to how it could happen as there were no intelligence reports of a build-up, his crisp reply was that was the situation. I decided not to fight the whites. My first order was for the 2ICs to take over and the seniormost to act as the commander. Based on map appreciation I ordered the leading battalion to firm in 2 km short off the road block and rest of the brigade to go into a harbour behind it. I ordered the firm base battalion to locate the enemy extent and told the BM to coordinate the patrol programme. It had taken me the better part of two hours to assess the situation and issue orders. After listening to my orders, Gen. Sundarjee told me he was happy to see my reaction and that I would be flown into the brigade location for further action and execution of the task. I was flown into the brigade sector and we removed the road block after 36 hours and moved into defences after clearing the area. This was the defensive and first part of the exercise. During this phase we reacted to situations based on the level of our preparation and met most contingencies painted to us successfully. My contention of placing the reserves where I had proposed during the war game was tested and its viability was fully established.

After a day's break, we changed posture and shifted to the offensive part of our role. It was a day of catastrophe and jubilation. Catastrophe as the J&K LI battalion which was to lead the advance lined up in the harbour as they would have done in the convoy park in Badami Bagh in Srinagar, with consequent disastrous results when enemy aircraft picked them up. This battalion had for the first time crossed Banihal and the first train they saw was when they boarded it at Pathankot. Depend on the Army to overdo things and send them to the southernmost tip to Trivandrum and for a role in the desert. The irony was as we heard the news of the nuclear blast of 1974 on the radio, we were so close but knew nothing about it. The jubilation overshadowed the minor disaster, all to good effect. The battalion adjusted well and did well under Mianwala.

On the lighter side there were some interesting episodes on the sidelines. General Sartaj at times took upon himself to tell me as to why I was not doing this or that. I listened to it for a couple of days without following any of it. On the third day I told him as politely as possible to let me command the brigade and at the end of the exercise tell me all my mistakes as in actual war neither he nor Sundarjee would be there with me. That kept them quiet for the rest of the ten days of the exercise. Secondly, everyone is thirsty in the desert and there was no distinction between the umpire or the ones being exercised. Between me, Suresh Rege, CO of the field regiment of my brigade group, another paratrooper and our Chief Umpire and Director of the exercise Sundarjee, we drank over 350 bottles of beer while working at full speed. This also established a bonding between us for the rest of our professional lives, while we did not agree with each other on a lot of things but we listened to each other and were tolerant of differences.

While we were away in the desert, a sad and fatal accident took place in the Gorkha Battalion left behind in Trivandrum to prepare for their next field tenure. With few days left of their sojourn in Trivandrum, the unit had organized outings and visits for their men, JCOs, officers and their families to religious and scenic spots around the city. In one such picnic outing by the officers and their families at the Kovalam beach resort at night, one of their young officers while easing himself in a secluded corner slipped and hit his head on a rock. He was immediately rushed to the Medical College Hospital without first being taken and referred to the Army Hospital as the Medical College had the best facilities. But in spite of the best efforts of the doctors, he could not be saved. Next morning the CO reported the accident on the rear radio link giving me the details. I told the CO that I agreed with his actions and he did the right thing. As per the orders then, the officer's family was not entitled to pension as he did not die while on duty. I discussed the case with my staff and after checking all the orders they told me that the officer's accidental death was not covered by the rules. After thinking for a while I ordered that the officer could be shown on duty on a pre-course training for a rock climbing course at the HMI and he would also be shown having been referred to the Medical College hospital by the Army Hospital Trivandrum. I told the officer conducting the inquiry that all these details will be tied up in the court of inquiry proceedings and that I would give my opinion that the officer died while on duty in a training accident. I did this with a clear conscience that the wrong was justified in the interest of the officer's family. In spite of the fact that some of my staff felt that we should take the Higher Command Headquarters in confidence, I did not agree and took full responsibility. We helped the officer's wife to get her pension, a job in her home town and an allotment of AWHO house. We even had to fight and set aside the officer's father's claim on the family pension. While I was doing the National Defence course in Delhi, the CO who had been posted as a staff officer to the AG who was also the Colonel of the same Gorkha Regiment, rang me up to say that the AG wanted to see me. When I went to see him, the CO told me that he had told the AG about the officer's accidental death and how we managed to get family pension for his widow. I went in to meet the AG. While he thanked me for helping an officer from his regiment he said I could get into trouble for doing it. I told him that I was happy that I did what I did and given similar circumstances would do it again.

Initially for the first six months I was chased and tested by Sartaj but later I became well established and became a part of his command team. This gave me the opportunity to work on command exercises and be associated with their conduct, thus providing me a great opportunity to learn and improve myself. Sartaj was a rough and overbearing superior, gruff in his manners and language but once you stood up to him he listened. According to Lt. Gen. Kundan Singh who was Chief of Staff, I could do no wrong as far as Sartaj was concerned. He had a human side too which I discovered when he was retiring. He decided to write a report on me, even though I had not done the requisite minimum time required and which was therefore set aside. I was very intrigued by the role allotted to my formation. It was defending one of the forward-most areas in the desert, right in the shop window, while we took the longest to reach it. It would have been ideal to earmark us as the reserve due to our late arrival and composition of the formation. I decided to ask Sartaj about it after a few months. He looked at me sternly and replied that he would tell me before retiring. True to his promise he told it to me during his farewell. He said, in India we panic in times of crisis, to some extent even in the Army, and throw well-planned actions overboard. He continued to say that he knew that we would not reach our operational area in time, so he had planned to fly out my reconnaissance and order groups and earmarked troops from Gen. Sundarjee's division, who were the nearest and that I would command this force till my brigade arrived. Once I was committed my brigade group was deemed to be committed too. If I am in reserve and uncommitted, where was the guarantee that he will not lose my formation if there is a crisis in the adjoining command. Since I was the only reserve he had, he could not afford to lose me and that could only be ensured if I was committed. I understood the logic. When the new Army Commander Lt. Gen. O.P. Malhotra raised the same issue, that due to our late arrival in the op location it will be best for me to be command reserve. I told him that even I had the same view but after the previous Army Commander explained to me the reason for it I was convinced. He decided to change my role and we became the command reserve. He did not lose me but lost other valuable assets of armour and artillery due to a perceived likely threat in the neighbouring command. Here were two army commanders both professionally right but guided by different experiences.

After taking over, Lt. Gen. Malhotra after some time planned to visit me. Both me and my wife got ready and reached the airport to receive them. There was no news of the aircraft till after one hour beyond its scheduled arrival time. When I rang up the Air Traffic Control, I was told that the aircraft crashed just after take off but all were safe. Lt. Gen. Malhotra had sustained some bruises, Mrs Malhotra had also sustained some injuries and was in the hospital but out of danger. I spoke to him and told him that we were relieved to know that they were safe. I could not help telling him they were safe because they were in the good old Dak (Dakota aircraft), whose air aerodynamics were so good that in any other aircraft, this kind of crash could have resulted in a disaster. He told me, that he was most upset when the IAF gave a Dakota but felt relieved after hearing this.

One of Gen. Sundarjee's brigade's located at Bangalore was earmarked as the command reserve. The Army Commander Lt. Gen. Sartaj during one of his visits asked Sundarjee to exercise it in its role. Sundarjee asked me to join him in the writing and conduct of the exercise. He told me that it had the Army Commander's approval. On arrival at Bangalore I asked him as to how I can help him. He told me that by writing the exercise I could do so. The general area of the exercise was around Kolegal ranges beyond Bangalore. I told him that I had no idea of the deployment of reserves at the command level. He told me, neither did he, except for the broad roles allotted to this brigade. Between us we analysed each task and contrived two divisional sectors widely separated, where these tasks had to be performed. We decided to develop the rest of the exercise and situations to be created as we went along. We located the brigade where it would be possible for it to move cross-country in the desert with a desert track for its maintenance to execute the tasks. For ease of control and to do the maximum in the least possible time, we condensed time and distance. After the exercise, we were quite clear about the approach to execute such tasks and the core issue of planning deployment of reserves at the command level in desert terrain. The broad conclusions were that in the reserve brigade one battalion was to be designated as the lead battalion for each sector for counter-attack and counter-perpetration tasks, the third battalion was to act as reserve and be prepared to occupy a covering or a containment position in case of a breakthrough. The remainder of the brigade was to build-up on the leading battalion in each contingency. Each battalion was grouped with armour, affiliated artillery and engineers to ensure fire support and obstacle clearing capability. Detailed movement plan and air support was planned for each contingency and outline orders prepared in a diagrammatic form (on a sketch) on a single page. Detailed preparations and rehearsals are the key to success for such tasks. It was a great learning experience and came in very handy when later I became the command reserve. General Sundarjee always picked on other people's brains on problems and used them as sounding boards. He was a great thinker and one could learn a lot from him. At the same time he did not have commensurate experience of combat or experience of live situations. He was obsessed with mechanized warfare and lacked ground level exposure, which could result in failure. He would ignore deployment of major components of infantry brigades, and chase and get involved in a small mechanized column, whereas the success or failure of a brigade attack could decide the outcome of a battle. He at times overlooked the Indian reality while taking decisions, this deficiency was visible even later when he became the Chief.

Talking of Kolegal ranges reminds me of an incident which took place during my field regiment's course shooting there. During a break in the shooting while we were having tea, I asked the Sub. Maj. of the regiment to call the police inspector-in-charge of the range clearance and offer him a cup of tea. The inspector came and after saluting us he sat down with the Sub. Maj. for tea. He took off his white plastic hat (which is the head dress of the Karnataka police) and kept it on a chair. Suddenly a gust of wind came and blew off the hat and children who were standing closeby started playing football with it. The inspector ran after the children shouted at them in Kannada and retrieved his hat. He was very upset and agitated. We cooled him down and told him that children don't understand that playing with the hat was bad. He said it is not the children's fault, it is the fault of the hat. He said he avoided wearing it unless it became absolutely essential. He continued and said that when their headdress was the Mysore turban (*safa*), the moment it was seen anywhere people respected it and seeing it felt the authority was there. The inspector talked a lot of sense, the symbols of authority have to be sober and impressive to convey the authority they represent. I have never forgotten the incident.

The Expert Committee under Lt. Gen. Krishna Rao along with its other members Maj. Gen. Sundarjee and Maj. Gen. M.L. Chibber visited my brigade group and apart from the questionnaire which they had sent they had a detailed discussion with me. Their real purpose of the visit was to see Indian Space Research Organisation, visiting my brigade was only a side event. During the discussion there were two issues on which I distinctly disagreed with them, one was dealing with the officer management and other on pruning the manpower in combat arms. General Krishna Rao asked me if in the promotion boards an officer should be only given one look as compared to three as currently. I told him one look would be fine if the system was fair and just, both in terms of opportunity and assessment. I told him that I was speaking from experience. I explained to him that in our year of commission, 1951, when the board for promotion from Major to Lt. Col. took place, three officers including me were deferred because they did not have the requisite number of reports as company commander before the board. This was in spite of the fact that I had commanded a company for over seven years. I did not have five reports before the board as I was posted from one staff job to another. It was not my fault. I had to earn my reports again to be cleared more than a year later than others of 1951 batch. It is also a fact that some people come to know and manage to serve under the 'right' persons, whereas others did not even know if MS planning went against their interest. The system should stay as it is, and thank God it does. Secondly, in our enthusiasm to save manpower, we should not reduce any manpower in armoured regiments, artillery regiments, infantry battalions and engineer regiments as full strength is never available at the time of mobilization. The strength of the combat units or armoured regiments, infantry battalions and artillery regiments have remained unchanged. But during the limited warning period the tasks have multiplied. Which include preparation of main, secondary and alternative positions, dumping and stocking of ammunition in all these positions, rehearsals for various tasks and contingencies. We would be lucky if 75 per cent of authorized strength is available on mobilization, normally it is closer to 60 to 65 per cent. We could not meet these tasks even with full strength and any reduction would be telling on their capability. I think they probably paid heed and I am sure that others would have also projected similar views as the proposals were shelved. The Expert Committee report was the talk of the Army. I was only able to glance though it. I really went through it when I was the Western Army Commander. My findings were that barring some, most recommendations were not implemented even by its authors as ground realities and actual operational environment are different from the perceived ones. The lesson I learnt was that one should change things after due consideration and only after seeing their implementation with people concerned at the operational level.

My tenure with this wonderful formation will not be complete without talking about Trivandrum and Kerala, not in the geographical, historical or even cultural context but of contemporary events. The state was governed by a mixed coalition of left parties, Congress and a number of smaller parties, a full house of nineteen. Shri Achuta Menon of the Communist Party of India was the chief minister and N. Karunakaran of Congress was the home minister, two people I dealt with and came to know. The coalition was held together and functioned efficiently due to the stature and personality of Achuta Menon, whom I respected and found easy to deal with. Karunakaran on the other hand was a shifty character, a manipulator and not fully trustworthy. Forty years later he confirmed his image of those days. Achuta Menon was a true communist in every sense of the word, truthful and morally upright. I was told that once he called the owner of the Poonalur Paper Factory, a Marwari, and told him that he had received complaints from the union that he was hiring people from outside while qualified people were available in Kerala. The owner told him that it was not true. Why should he hire a person on higher wages, give him home leave and travel expenses, when he could get someone to do the same job at lesser cost and with minimum perks. He ended by telling the chief minister that he was a businessman and worked for profit, the union leader from your party is a trouble maker and instead of doing his duty and putting forward genuine grievances, he only incites people. The chief minister thanked him and by the time the industrialist reached back to Poonalur, a distance of 40 km, the union leader had been sacked and the new union leader welcomed the owner.

Similarly, when the junior engineers of the Electricity Board went on strike on some frivolous issue, he asked for Army help to keep the Trivandrum lights burning. The brigade's engineer company had not been raised. We asked for help of technicians from the Madras Engineer Group at Bangalore. We were not certain of their capability and the chief minister was told that while we will keep the Trivandrum lights burning we were uncertain of the damage that may occur to the generators. He said he was quite happy. We managed to do just that and after 24 hours some non-striking civilian engineers took over. He dismissed a large number of striking junior engineers with one stroke of the pen, which had a salutary effect.

There was also the incident of serious indiscipline almost amounting to mutiny, when the Kerala Armed Police units went on strike. The cause was an altercation between them and the CID branch. He took firm action with the help of the Army. In spite of his being a cadre man and a strong supporter of trade unions he never tolerated indiscipline and took firm action. Everyone respected him and as chief minister where people's interest was concerned he was above politics and his own party. He was never bothered about his post and was ever prepared to quit but would not do anything morally, ethically and legally wrong. There was a proper platform outside the State Secretariat up to which agitators were permitted. Processions were permitted on approved routes and after every 500 m there had to be a gap to permit public movement. Processionists could inconvenience public to record their protest but could not cause disruption of life or harassment to the public. It was a new experience for me.

The story of Trivandrum will not be complete without recording our entire family's feeling that it was a most rewarding and enjoyable experience. Initially we were taken to be Malayalis but even after it was discovered that we were from the north, the warmth and friendship we received did not decrease. My children 11 and 10 years old, picked up things fast and learnt Malayalam in no time and my son even took part in a Malayalam drama on AIR. Amongst our very close friends were Mr. and Mrs. Hari Das, brother-in-law and sister of Tiger (Brig. E.A. Thayagraj) from my battalion. Both were much older than us, Mr. Hari Das's son-in-law too was older than me. They took to our children most warmly. Hari Das was a retired chief engineer of the state and after retirement was in-charge of the Kovalam Tourist Development Project. He had been a chief engineer in Libya. He was a good sportsman and had represented Kerala in cricket.

Trivandrum was also the place where I was forcibly introduced to golf, something which I have never regretted. Membership of the Royal Trivandrum Golf Course under the patronage of the erstwhile Maharaja was beyond the reach of the average officer due to its very high entrance fee. I was able to convince the Maharaja that service officers on short tenures could not afford the huge entrance fee, however, the monthly subscriptions were a reasonable and legitimate charge. I was inducted as the vice-patron and managed to get the entrance fee waived for all services officers with transferable jobs. But I had to invest in a golf set and also learn to play.

We saw the length and breadth of the erstwhile Travancore State from Kanyakumari to its border with Coorg. This also gave us the opportunity to see Mysore and Tamil Nadu. We loved the backwaters of Kerala and the Allepey boat races were our favourite. My children loved Kerala so much that my daughter and her husband spent their honeymoon at Kovalam. My son after doing his staff college at Wellington travelled with their twin son and daughter the whole of south and Goa by road of which they spent the maximum time in Kerala visiting his childhood haunts and showing these to his children. We made a lot of friends and are still in touch with a few of them. Mr. and Mrs. Hari Das shifted to Bangalore and we often visited them there. Unfortunately we lost them for ever, first Jumma in 1981 and next year Hari Das who could perhaps not bear her separation.

My tenure with the Brigade Group was most satisfying. During one of his later visits Gen. Malhotra told me that he had asked the Military Secretary to post me as his BGS and that I should be moving to Pune soon. I duly received my posting after I had done a two years' stint but before I could move, it was cancelled as I was selected for the next National Defence Course (NDC). Ultimately I moved after I had done two years and nine months. When Gen. Sundarjee heard about my selection for the course, he told me that I was a good candidate for the Royal College of Defence Studies in UK. I told him I would give him two bottles of scotch if I go and if not he would have to give me the same. I took a similar bet with my old Brigade Commander on his bidding. I understand I was a contender but I did not go and a colleague of mine did. The four bottles of whisky came in quite handy during my stay in Delhi. NDC was a very good experience. I thoroughly enjoyed it. One found that with our service background, training and rational approach, we could find very workable solutions to problems in the economic, social, political, diplomatic and administrative fields. This amazed the officers from IAS, IFS, police and other central services. It was an experience which gave me tremendous know how and confidence in fields beyond my profession.

Right at the beginning of the course in the second week I lost my father. I wanted to stay with my family for at least a year but without knowing that there was a vacancy in Delhi I did not want to make the request. By the time I found out, my posting had already been announced. Here also I learnt later that it was changed as out of the two officers posted no body wanted to go to Central Command under the then Army Commander Lt. Gen. J.S. Nakai and had managed to get out of it. Lt. Gen. Kundan Singh who was the MS and earlier Chief of Staff in Southern Command and knew me, told the Chief that I was just the person as I could serve with anyone, so I was to be the sacrificial lamb. When I learnt this, I went and met Lt. Gen. Kundan Singh, but my protest did not help and he warded me off by saying I will do well. The reality, as I was to learn later, was grimmer than anyone knew. It seems that my predecessor in Lucknow was due for promotion in a few months and should have moved later on promotion direct but he did not want to stay on. What was more surprising and even shocking was that he was nominated for the NDC course, which he left to go on promotion after a few months. He was two years my senior and his counterparts had done the course two years earlier. The MS knew it fully well as the officer was one of his brigade commanders. It was a waste of a vacancy at the NDC to help this officer.

As BGS with the same Army Commander I did what was professionally correct and never succumbed to pressure. I had my differences and earned his displeasure at times. It was never on professional issues but only on extraneous ones. One of the major issue was his dislike for some officers working under me, he thought I was protecting them, whereas I was only countering his prejudices. Ultimately we established a very workable and later even a pleasant relationship, when he discovered that while I gave him respect but would not be subservient and did not seek favours. I served with him for the better part of two years and later with two other Army commanders. I must have done well as I was promoted and moved to Command the Mountain Division in Manipur and Nagaland. It was an experience, which confirmed my conviction, do your job and be forthright, so that nobody takes you for granted. I believe it was also appreciated by the same Army commander and hinted as such when he retired.

CHAPTER 5

Tryst with Manipur and Nagaland: Insurgency, Upheavals and Success

On approval for the next rank to Major General in mid-1980, like anyone else my natural instinct was to work out the division I was likely to command when my turn came. One was falling vacant in Central Command itself and would be there for the asking. Orders for raising of one more division had also been issued about the same time. Soon afterwards I accompanied Lt. Gen. R.D. Hira, PVSM, MVC, the Army Commander, for the biannual Army Commander's Conference to Delhi. During the Conference Gen. O.P. Malhotra, PVSM, the COAS, congratulated me on my approval for promotion and asked as to where I was likely to go. Having served under him in Southern Command and knowing his good nature one could take liberty. With a smile I replied, 'It is one hell of a question for the Chief to ask, you should be telling me'. Finding him receptive I added that now that he had asked, I only want to request as to where I did not want to go. I did not want to go to a new raising and spend my command tenure in collecting personnel, equipment, arms and getting the formation together. His response was encouraging, with a smile he said, 'Don't worry, Tubby, we would send you to the right place'. A day later, I ran into Col. Joginder Singh, Col. G.S. (Operations) Headquarters Eastern Command who had accompanied his Army Commander Gen. E.A. Vaz, PVSM. He introduced himself and told me, 'Sir, you take it from me that you would go to the Mountain Division in Manipur and Nagaland, whenever it falls vacant'. I was a bit intrigued and asked him as to how could he say it with such confidence. He just said, he would let me know when I came on posting to join the division. Over six months passed, there was no news. Two officers junior to me were promoted and one of them, to my great relief, went to the new raising. Lt. Gen. G.S. Rawat, the then MS spoke to me on a number of occasions on some MS matters as I was the officiating COS. In March 1981, during the course of one such conversation, I asked him if there was any news about me. All that he said was, soon.

The posting came in the beginning of April to the mountain division in Manipur and Nagaland. On my way to join the division, while passing through Kolkata, I met Brig. V.K. Sood, the then BGS and a friend of mine, and Col. Joginder Singh. They told me that Gen. Vaz, the Army Commander, had asked for me to command the division, thus solving the mystery. The situation was volatile in Manipur due to Meitei insurgency and the Naga insurgency was gaining renewed vigour. During the meeting with the Army Commander, the major issue discussed was whether the present arrangement of Manipur and Nagaland being handled by two separate divisions should continue or the command of troops both in Manipur and Nagaland should revert as originally to my division. I was aware of the fact that an additional division had been inducted into Manipur to deal with the Meitei insurgency, which had created problems locally. My opinion was that the problem could not be divided and it certainly is not the best way of handling it. As dual perceptions result in dilution of effort and fragmentation of responses, the responsibility should rest with one commander. The Army Commander told me that he had already decided it and was happy to see my response. As a matter of fact, orders for the move out of the headquarters of the additional division in Manipur had already been issued, leaving behind troops till the situation stabilized and command of all troops given to me. The Army Commander asked me if I required anything else. I told him I will come back to him if required. My immediate requirement was an equal number of additional flying hours of helicopter for Manipur, as for Nagaland, to facilitate better operational control and supervision. He immediately agreed and promised to get the air effort allotted from Headquarters Eastern Air Command. He wished me luck.

CHANGING MINDSET TO MEET NEW CHALLENGES

Based on the briefing at Headquarters Eastern Command and by my predecessor Maj. Gen. Venugopal, MVC, I worked out a schedule of my familiarization visits to the formations and units. A word about my predecessor would be most appropriate and valid. More than his briefing, it was our one to one discussion which was most beneficial. I asked him a number of questions, some justified but also a few irksome ones. I found him to be most forthright and honest, he was particular in emphasizing some of his mistakes and particularly his aversion towards the political and administrative establishments in the two states. He advised me to have an open mind in dealing with them. This helped me a lot and his advice is still etched in my memory. We were not destined to serve together but I shall always remain grateful for his advice.

The well-planned scheme of visits for familiarization and work went for a six by the incident at Fakmile on the Nagaland-Myammar border on 12 May 1981, three days after I had taken over. I was in Manipur, which was of higher priority, when I received the news. One of our standing patrols protecting the Khemugan Nagas displaced from Myanmar had been attacked, one JCO and 6 OR were killed and badly burnt.[1] I landed at the incident site and was horrified to see the badly burnt patrol base. When I talked to the refugees and the surviving personnel of the patrol, inadequacy of our operational stance was clear. The incident clearly brought out the marked shift and focus and nature of hostile operations. The Naga hostile sanctuaries had shifted from the west in East Pakistan to our eastern borders with Myammar opposite northern Nagaland and Somra Tract opposite Ukhrul in Manipur. The insurgents could strike across the border and return before we could react, the critical area was up to a depth of 15 to 20 km. Unless we could detect them during infiltration and close to the border it was difficult to deal with them in the interior areas in the absence of real time intelligence. The changed scenario required quick reaction capability near the borders, ability to execute cross-border operations to strike at their bases and well executed deliberate operations in the interior based on good intelligence. We were still deployed as in the late 1960s and early 1970s. I ordered strengthening of the border posts, redeployment of reserves located as far back as Dimapur and in other depth areas and emphasized the need for air mobility. There was opposition to these changes from amongst my commanders and in the higher echelons. The new COAS Gen. Krishna Rao and Army Commander Lt. Gen. A.S. Vaidya were both old Nagaland hands and advised caution. I had to politely remind them that we are not fighting the Naga hostiles of 1950s and 1960s, who were operating in large groups within Nagaland equipped with Second World War leftover weaponry. The Naga insurgent today is modern, wears jeans, listens to pop music, and is more sophisticated and has the latest weapons given by the Chinese or bought in arms bazaars of the Far East. I requested for a free hand and promised to produce results. They agreed but told me that if I do not succeed my neck was on the block.

Realizing that time was of essence, I ordered the readjustments and move of troops for implementing our new operational stance. Brigadier Vishwanathan from the Kumaon Regiment, Deputy Inspector General Assam Rifles (DIG AR) at Tuensang, told me that his troops in permanent locations cannot be moved without the sanction of the MHA. I told him that he will move troops as ordered and if assets of accommodation for troops and families require shifting, my engineers will do it but move he must as ordered. I finally told the officer that I would be landing at the Tuensang helipad next morning and if by then his troops were not on the move, it will be my personal pleasure to remove him from command of the sector. I had known the officer when he was commanding a brigade in Lucknow. At night I got a call from Director General Assam Rifles (DG AR), Lt. Gen. Sushil Kumar, whom also I had known but I refused to relent. All Assam Rifles (AR) and Para Military Forces (PMF) were under my operational command and I had no ambiguity about it in my mind. After this readjustments took place without any hitch and smoothly. The brigade from Dimapur moved to Ukhrul and all AR, Border Security Force (BSF) and Central Reserve Police Force (CRPF) units ordered to occupy new positions did so smoothly and in time.

Redemption came a month later. Naga insurgents in strength came to attack Phomching, the northernmost post in the division on the Tirap-Nagaland boundary. They were in for a big surprise, both by the resistance and the reaction due to our strengthened dispositions and the changed operational stance. They were isolated and hunted within our borders and chased and killed across the border in their forward bases. We killed a total of 35 to 45 insurgents within and across the border and lost two soldiers.[2] This set the trend for future operations in Nagaland and hill districts of Manipur against Naga hostiles. These two incidents bring out the vital need of updating perceptions as operational environment changes, for neither time nor situations remain static. During the operations at Phomching, I asked for MI-8 helicopters to lift troops from Mokokchung to the area of operations. The Air Force Liaison Officer Gp. Capt. Pardesi, posted in my headquarters told me that the Eastern Air Command wants it to be routed through the Eastern Command. I told him that he had been posted with me to meet my requirements and not only for coordinating my helicopter flights. I asked my Col. G.S. Ravi Bhalla to send a personal signal from me to Eastern Air Command that if I did not get MI-8 choppers in the next two hours, the Indian Air Force did not exist for me. There was a big uproar and calls for me were flying from Eastern Army and Eastern Air Command but I was in the area of operation at Phomching. My staff came under pressure but they conveyed my messages as bluntly as I had directed using my name. In spite of all the hot air, I got my choppers and the results more than justified my demand.

As a follow-up of the above operations and numerous visits to Konyak areas of the Mon district I realized it was the most backward and neglected area both by the administration and the Army. The area was dormant during earlier hostilities but most active then as Konyaks formed a major constituent of the newly-formed NSCN and Kholay Konyak, a Hemi Naga, was its Commander-in-Chief. Apart from intensifying operations, we decided to carry out sustained civic action and build it up as a major thrust of our policy. Both me and Ramesh Kulkarni, the Brigade Commander, visited most of the villages to find out their requirements and to convey our sincere desire that we meant well but their response was that of suspicion. I firmly believe trust begets trust and there was no better time to test it. We started small by leaving a medical team under a doctor and an engineer detachment with a dozer under an officer in the centrally located village Shinga-Chignu to attend to the sick and to construct a playing field and level the ground for a school building. They were all unarmed and we told the villagers that they were there to work for them and it was up to them to ensure their security and look after them. In spite of grave apprehension, it worked and gave us the breakthrough to consolidate our gains. The battle for the hearts and minds had been won. I never forgot it and it paid handsome dividends later in the Punjab. Another area of major NSCN activities was Ukhrul district in Manipur, to which their Secretary General Muivah, a Thangkhul Naga belonged. Thangkhul Nagas have dominated the NSCN and continue to do so. Even after the split in 1983, they dominate the major break-away faction NSCN(IM). We inducted a brigade from Dimapur and while the area was brought under control it remained a hot bed of NSCN activities.

During one of my frequent visits to the posts, at one of the highest and most important post of Mollen under 5/1 Gorkha Rifles, I met a young newly-commissioned officer 2/Lt Das Gupta. As was my habit I asked him a number of questions about his area of responsibility, terrain, villages in the area and across Myanmar (then Burma), population, insurgent activities in his area and across the border in Somra Tract. Being new I realized that he needed to learn a lot more about his duties as an officiating post commander as the company commander was away. I encouraged him and briefed him and before leaving I told him that he should know everything about the area, even the number of pregnant women in each village, as in the time of crisis they would come to him for help which would require his asking the CO to send a doctor before their due time. He cannot afford to fail them if he wants to earn their trust. I visited him again after a month, he told me all that I wanted to know and even more. I was rather intrigued by his detailed description of the area across the border in Somra Tract. When I asked him as to how he knew all this, he told me he has been to all the areas in Somra Tract on a patrol with two of his Johnnies (Gorkha Sepoys). After explaining the danger of doing such a thing without the knowledge of his superiors I patted and complimented him. Later he did well in various operations and was awarded the Shaurya Chakra. People learn fast if they know what is required of them.

I was in the second year of my command and I had accompanied Gen. K.V. Krishna Rao to Italy. It was a most welcome change and the outcome of a decision taken by him that field commanders in operational areas should be given due recognition for the operational achievements and good work and in appreciation given the opportunity to accompany the Chief on his foreign tours. Unlike other Chiefs, who preferred to take their own staff or officers close to them. I was the first beneficiary. After a very enjoyable and fine trip, bad news awaited me on return. Elements of a newly-arrived Sikh battalion moving into Ukhrul were ambushed by the NSCN and one officer, two JCOs and 13 OR were killed.[3] More than the incident what upset me more was the lack of adequate aggressive follow-up action, which had been amply demonstrated and drummed into all commanders during the Phomching and subsequent operations. I took the defaulting commanders to task and told the battalion to establish in the area and retrieve its lost honour, which they did very successfully later during the rest of their stay under a new CO. The defaulting CO had been removed by me earlier. In an insurgency environment while you reward success and tolerate omissions you don't condone lapses resulting from command failure as human lives are involved.

The success of the Sikh Battalion generated its own dynamics. The state administration under a Thangkhul Chief Minister Rishang Keishing and the Thangkhul population of the area, instigated by the Thangkhul hostiles, demanded that the battalion be moved out of the area. They built-up political and public pressure right up to Delhi and the prime minister and I was sounded on this by the MO Directorate. I told the Army Commander Lt. Gen. Vaidya to convey to Delhi that it will not happen as long as I am in command and nobody except I decide as to which troops will operate in what area. I won ultimately and told the chief minister that he has to deal with me and cannot go over my head on issues concerning security. The authority of a Commander should not wilt under pressure, for then he loses his credibility both with his subordinates and with the other people he deals with.

The above period of turmoil in Ukhrul district coincided with one of political instability and uncertainty in Manipur due to inter- and intra-party feuds. This naturally drew attention and visits from the central political hierarchy and media whose main concern was political and administrative failures. When one of the many high-powered media party started probing and asking searching questions to the chief minister, he found it expedient to divert them to the issue of the high-handed behaviour of the Sikh battalion in Ukhrul after the ambush on them. Not only that, he even sent them to the ambush site and to visit some of the villages closeby. The party was accompanied by Thangkhul political workers close to the chief minister. On return they were agitated and wanted to meet the army authorities, to which we readily agreed. The party arrived at the Manipur (M) Sector Headquarters and was led by senior journalists Shamim from the *Times of India*, Guru Dutt from the *Statesman* and Shekhar Gupta from *India Today* and ten to twelve other journalists. Brigadier Jhingon, the Commander in Imphal, tried to brief them but they wanted it from the horse's mouth. I was a bit late in arriving. When I spoke to them, I said that I will tell them the truth and the whole truth including the murkiest of it and that I trust them as the national press. I gave them the details of the incident, our actions in the area to date and what we are trying to achieve. I also explained to them that the well-being of the people is as much our concern and people were the focus of our endeavour to secure the environment but we would not be pressurized into inaction. I ended up by telling them that we were the national Army and they were the national media. They appreciated my frankness and were correct and fair in their reporting, much to the chief minister's discomfiture and disappointment. It also resulted in a very congenial relationship with the media. I have always maintained that truth always triumphs. After that episode, Guru Dutt and Shekhar Gupta and I developed a lasting friendship based on mutual regard and trust. Unfortunately Guru Dutt died after our last meeting in Shillong in 1997. My friendship with Shekhar Gupta continues till date, irrespective of our infrequent contact.

The spate of allegations against the Sikhs continued. We investigated all and found them to be false. However, in one instance after an operation one teacher and a clergyman were reported missing. On investigation we found a few people responsible for it. I took action against the JCO in-charge of the detachment and men responsible. They were dismissed and awarded rigorous imprisonment in a civil jail. The officiating commanding officer, who was approved for command, was removed for lack of adequate command supervision and debarred from further promotion. This established our credibility. However, the instigators in connivance with local politicians and self-appointed human rights defenders filed a case against the security forces in the Supreme Court. We defended the case successfully with due concurrence and permission of the then Prime Minister Mrs. Indira Gandhi and no strictures were passed against the Army as the punishment awarded by us was more stringent and justice prompt. The entire case was fought by the Attorney General based on briefs prepared by me, the main thrust of our argument was that in the insurgency environment some aberrations were bound to happen but lapses should be dealt with firmly. During my meeting with the prime minister I had emphasized the need to defend the case so that army's effectiveness is not dented. I reminded her of the government succumbing under pressure in the earlier case of Dr. Haralu, a prominent doctor of Kohima who was killed in the early hours of 2 July 1956 in an unfortunate incident. Although the Army took strict measures to prevent reoccurrence of such an incident, they did not make public the actions taken. Hostiles made much of the incident and used it for propaganda against the Army. Due to adverse publicity Pt. Nehru the then PM took personal interest and became the guardian of Dr. Haralu's daughter who later joined the Indian Foreign Service. Mrs. Gandhi saw my reasoning and the fact that we had acted firmly and punished the defaulters. Throughout this period Gen. Krishna Rao's support and encouragement was most helpful. The Supreme Court absolved the Army of any blame due to our stringent and timely action against defaulters but recommended compensation to the bereaved families on humanitarian ground. The instigators led by Nandita Haksar and her Naga husband, having lost the case propagated that the Army should pay compensation. The issue came up again at the political level and in a meeting held in Mrs. Gandhi's office in the Parliament House, which was attended by the home, defence and law ministers. I attended the meeting on behalf of the Army and clearly and categorically stated that neither the Army nor the MOD should ever be involved in compensating any aggrieved party in such circumstances. The reasoning put forward was that the Army and for that matter the security forces act in support of civil administration when called out under special provisions and circumstances beyond them, as such they should not be involved in compensating people as a consequence of their legitimate actions under the law. The decision was that compensation would be paid on behalf of the MHA by the state government. This was a befitting reply to the instigators. The lesson is very clear, commanders have to be correct, just and humane in their approach and keep a tight grip on events. At the same time, we cannot be the whipping boys for the authorities. Sincerity and credibility finally won the battle.

MEITEI EXTREMISTS, NEW PLAYERS, NEW ENVIRONMENT: NEED FOR A DIFFERENT APPROACH

Manipur received my major attention and I spent the maximum time there. The situation was volatile, confused and complex and our responses were equally disoriented. Most of the troops were deployed on protective duties and fear psychosis had gripped the authorities. Troops of all shades including Army were guarding anything and everything from petrol pumps, post offices, treasuries, government offices and buildings and even police stations, a protective syndrome was all-prevailing. After discussing the situation with both the brigade commanders Dalip Sidhu and Som Jhingon, I appraised the state government of my assessment of the situation and that a change in approach was imperative but there was no reaction. I issued orders that the Army will hand over all protective duties to the civil administration and PMF under it after 30 days and we must go on the offensive to locate and destroy Meitei Extremists (ME). L.P. Singh, the then governor who was in control as President's Rule had been imposed, was against it and it became a big issue between us. In spite of our repeated requests there was no reaction and no orders were issued by the administration to relieve the troops. Two days before the expiry of the 30 days period still finding no reaction I issued executive orders withdrawing troops (including PMF) under Army's operational control even if they are not relieved. This drew immediate but unexpected reaction. Next day Giani Zail Singh, the home minister, and the Cabinet Secretary Rao Sahib Krishna Swamy arrived in Imphal as the governor had contacted them. I was asked to meet the home minister, which I politely declined, as no orders were received through Army channels. I was later rung up by the Army authorities and asked to meet the Home Minister. When I met him, he told me that there were a lot of complaints from the state government that I was not cooperating with them. In the most diplomatic language that I could muster, I told him that as a professional I am doing my job to the best of my ability and I am not in a popularity contest. I ended up by telling him that I was answerable to my chain of command and no one else, part of the conversation requiring major emphasis was in Punjabi. I got full backing of the then Chief Gen. Krishna Rao and the Army Commander Lt. Gen. Vaidya. Ultimately the state government had to face the *fait accompli* and all protective duties were taken over by the PMF and police under their control. This freed us to pursue and execute our offensive strategy. Having succeeding in having my way, I was fully conscious of the predicament of the civil administration. The situation was so bad that in some areas SHOs had hung their uniforms in the police stations and disappeared, ME had the run of the Valley. Police required help and support. Looking back, one feels greatly satisfied that we did not let our professional judgement be influenced by external pressures, it paid us rich dividends.

The ME were operating in small groups in towns and urban centres and in larger numbers in rural areas. Policing, particularly in urban environment could best be done by police using police methods and with the support of the armed police and PMF. I was fully convinced that police and PMF need to be activated at the earliest to take over policing and responsibility of towns and population centres. The hub of these activities had to be the police stations, with police gradually assuming full responsibility for protective duties and developing capability to deal with the ME and their supporters with help from PMF in their area of responsibility. This required building up of intelligence by activation of the special branch, which was to prove the cutting edge particularly in the urban areas. However, we reserved the right to operate in the towns, the main area of ME activities. The town was divided in sectors and units allocated responsibility for each sector. By experience, we found units should be located on the periphery of the town and not in the towns. Locating units within the town compromises their security and operational secrecy, it is easier to move into the town for operations than within it. This required a different orientation than followed so far, the basic ingredients of which were dealing with small groups in towns, policing of urban centres and supervision and control of activities within. This demanded both surveillance and intelligence and quick reaction by small mobile teams. It also required the ability to build-up on chance encounters with surveillance and other elements. Army and PMF so far had been operating in sub-units with security as the main concern. It required total reorientation. We organized quick reaction teams based on light vehicles, both Army and civil commandeered. Simultaneously, foot and cycle patrols moving in civvies for surveillance and to act against ME if encountered were undertaken. This was a sea change from the way Army and PMF had been operating. Success came our way gradually as troops understood the requirement, got familiar with the changed operational environment and gained confidence. This encouraged both police and PMF and they became active. We had successes everywhere.

On 6 July 1981, within two months we had our first major success, when in a well executed operation at Tekcham in the semi-urban hilly area in the marsh land of Loktak Lake we captured N.Bisheshwar Singh, the Lhasa trained Chairman of PLA, along with one more hardcore PLA member and killed four Lhasa trained ojhas (leaders) and two hardcore PLA members. Colonel R.P. Singh, the CO of the 14 J&K Rifles, during my visit the previous day had briefed me on some intelligence available of the area and that he was trying to confirm it. In spite of lack of hard intelligence I had a gut feeling that there was something wrong in the area. I ordered RP to mount the operation that night without waiting for confirmation. He wanted more time as he had no troops, but my feelings were getting stronger as we did a map appraisal and discussed the terrain with the available intelligence. Before leaving I ordered him to send a small column out of the personnel of battalion headquarters under his Intelligence Officer (10), 2/Lt. Cyrus Pithawala cross country on foot at night and reinforce it later if required. That night while at dinner with the chief minister of Nagaland I got the news of Cyrus hitting something. We built up on it at night. In the morning when I landed on a cart track in the marsh near the site, the encounter was still on, 2/Lt Pithawala was wounded and he was evacuated in my helicopter. Pithawala was awarded an immediate Ashoka Chakra, one after seventeen years in Nagaland and Manipur and Col. R.P. Singh, the CO, a Kirti Chakra.[4] The capture of Bisheshwar was first announced by the Prime Minister Indira Gandhi in the Parliament as it was in session, followed by the announcement in the State Assembly and then to the press and public by me. L.P. Singh was so thrilled that he flew from Shillong to Imphal to congratulate me. This marked the beginning of a very warm and lasting friendship between us. We received a message of congratulations from the prime minister through the COAS, from the COAS and the Army Commander. With our success public morale picked up and the civil administration and police become active and effective and many a good actions were carried out by them. We encouraged active and brave police officers and built them up. We ensured that their contribution was recognized, they were decorated and absorbed in the IPS cadre. Those deserving special mention are Karnamai Singh, SSP Imphal, and Roman Kumar, SP City, Imphal. In a daring action, Smt. Lalit Kumar Singh, wife of the president of the Manipur Congress (I), fought single handedly and unarmed with two armed ME and saved her husband's life. This represented a change in the people's psyche, I flew to Imphal and presented her the formation's memento as a token of our appreciation and regard. I recommended her for a Shaurya Chakra. It was thrilling and most satisfying to see her being presented it by the president along with us during the same investiture ceremony. She was honoured by the state government at a public reception. The peoples' morale ran high.

The capture of Bisheshwar presented both an opportunity and a challenge, the enthusiasm it generated set into motion dynamics in fields beyond security and even in the political arena. L.P. Singh was keen to make use of him, I was of the opinion that we should do so only after we know of his attitude and response, rather than pushing him into a situation beyond his and our control. Moreover his health was a consideration, he had not been treated properly for his kidney problem by the Chinese in Lhasa, all this required time. During my discussion with L.P. Singh I told him that we should learn from our past experience. Phizo was not what he actually was but what we made him, same was the case with Laldenga and Bhindranwale later. We put him on a pedestal and when it did not suit us we discarded Phizo. We were also constrained by our respective positions, he because he was the constitutional head and I because I was an officer in uniform. We were clear in our minds that he could not be left to the local politicians as then his options will get limited to either joining them or be eliminated possibly physically but most definitely politically. We required time to be clear of our options and this required complete control of Bisheshwar. I decided to keep Bisheshwar in Army custody and not to hand him over to the police as mandated under the law. This had the tacit and silent connivance of the governor. He was kept in Army custody till I handed over the division. He was handled only by two officers under my guidance both R.P. Singhs, the CO, whose battalion had captured him and the Deputy Brigade Commander of the brigade in Imphal. Even during his imprisonment in Naini Jail, Allahabad under the National Security Act, one of these officers regularly visited him. On his return to Manipur, we took custody of him and kept him with us at Liemakong Cantonment. I refused to hand him over in spite of the continued insistence and agitation by the state government. I asked the state government to declare the building he was being held in as a sub-jail, to meet the requirement of law.

Finally, a few months after his return from Naini Jail we succeeded in gaining his confidence and established intimate rapport with him. In spite of his long absence, he continued to enjoy command over and respect of not only PLA and other Meitei insurgent groups but of the entire Meitei population and thereby had a sway over the whole of Manipur Valley. He was totally sincere, honest and devoted. He had the potential to lead the Meiteis. We were also able to confirm that he still had control over Temba, who along with some of the other PLA cadres had ex-filtrated to Myanmar, and he was in contact with them and they would follow his decision. With this background we got him to agree that he would bring all the Meitei insurgents over ground and persuade them to surrender with weapons. On our part we would help him to meet his aspiration to enter public life and provide him full opportunity and support in achieving it. I got this agreement, attached as Appendix A in this chapter, in writing from him and took it up at the highest level with the help of Gen. Krishna Rao. Mrs. Gandhi agreed to give him her blessings.[5] I was very hopeful and looking forward to taking Bisheshwar to Delhi to meet her. However, I was in for a disappointment. The General Secretary of the Congress (I) in-charge of the North-East Moopanar rang me up and told me that Bisheshwar should be sent to Delhi along with the local party leaders. I would have agreed to it if it was confined to Tompok Singh, the Meitei deputy chief minister, who was totally a nationalist and trustworthy but I did not trust the rest. I found out that the local leaders had got the wind of what was up and had worked through the party channels to get Bisheshwar under their hold. They feared that if he was able to establish himself, their position would be compromised and hold weakened. It amounted to throwing him to the wolves. Failing to get a firm assurance on our part of the deal and it being executed as I had visualized, I retracted. I told Bisheshwar that the deal was off and he was free and on his own to plan the future. I am still convinced to this day that the deal if executed as proposed by me, the Meitei insurgency would have finished and we would have had a charismatic Meitei leader to guide Manipur's destiny. Between Tompok Singh and Bisheshwar Singh, Manipur would have never sunk into the black hole in which it is today. However, it was not to be and my worst fears were proved right when I returned to Manipur in 1993. After I left, the civil administration had their way and they took Bisheshwar over from the Army. He fell on the mercy of the local politicians, who manipulated him and he became a victim of their dubious designs.

Our successes in Manipur continued and in another well-executed operation the second PLA headquarters under Kunj Behari was destroyed in April 1982.[6] It was a complete success, the back of Meitei insurgency had been broken but there was no political and administrative follow-up action to consolidate the situation. With the departure of L.P. Singh the administration now under full political control became complacent, inefficient and politics became the mainstay and the only concern. I was also to discover later, like their Naga counterparts, the Meitei politicians had also developed close links with ME groups to foster their common goal of power, patronage and corruption. It is my firm opinion that in the prevailing political environment in the North-East, the people will remain deprived and poor and the Security Forces will continue to be the convenient whipping boy to divert attention. The politicians and insurgents both exploit public annoyance and anger against the most visible symbol and only effective instrument of government the Security Forces—to divert public attention from their misdeeds. Manipur is a prime example of it though not the only one. However, in spite of all the noises all of them make, they still want the Security Forces for protection from each other.

Public sympathy and some cases of support to the insurgents in the insurgency environment is a well-known phenomenon and a fact due to ethnic ties and 'our boys *versus* them' Security Forces syndrome. It was no different in the Imphal Valley, if any it was more intense, one of its major manifestation was when woman agitators hampered our operations and thereby supporting ME activities. On a number of occasions in Imphal town and other urban centres they surrounded the troops during operations while on hot pursuit of ME. The highlight of it was when Brig. Som Jhingon commanding the brigade in Imphal town while proceeding to supervise an ongoing operation was surrounded by 200 volunteers of the Nupi Samaj, a women's organization. He contacted me on radio and asked me as to what was to be done. I told him to sit on the bonnet of his jonga, whistle and smoke cigarettes and do nothing else but to offer cigarettes to their leaders as most women in Manipur smoke. Our patience, perseverance and determined efforts not to antagonize the public paid us handsome dividends in the long run. At the Manipur Sector Headquarters, popularly known as M Sector, which was established on the main road next to Raj Bhavan, it was an open house where everyone and anyone could walk in, lodge his complaint, have a cup of tea and get a reply to his/her query or complaint. President of the Nupi Samaj (women's torchbearer) and its other members were regular visitors. Though initially belligerent, but over a period of time we won their confidence and support which established our credibility and contributed to our success.

The other major constraint and irritant which caused frustration and harassment was the legal battles we had to fight against the self-proclaimed defenders of human rights. Although the Armed Forces Special Powers Act and the Disturbed Areas Act had been promulgated to give Security Forces powers of arrest, search, detention and to protect life and property by adopting the extreme step of shoot to kill if circumstances warranted but motivated interests always questioned our actions. We took deliberate and sustained action/measures to educate our junior leaders and troops and kept records so that evidence could be produced when required. A cell was formed in the M Sector Headquarters for this purpose and after each action an FIR was filed with the police and record of events, captured weapons and material and witnesses kept. This and our stance of openness helped a lot as did our experience of working with the Nupi Samaj. Even later when I returned to Manipur in 1993 this proved of immense help.

In the insurgency environment knowledge is the most potent weapon, of this intimate and deep understanding of the place and its people in all aspects is vital. The geography, history, culture and language provide the basis, which need to be tempered with the contemporary developments in all fields. In addition a continuous updating of the knowledge of peoples' perceptions is essential as nothing is static—human beings, attitudes and behaviours change. Perceptions are equally important as facts. I was made alive to this reality when the placid environment at Fakmile was disturbed, forcing a reorientation and reassessment. Hierarchy in the Army disapproved of my assessment, they were old hands seeing new environment entirely through old experience. They were unaware of the changed environment of insurgency and changes in peoples perceptions and attitudes. Phomching a month later justified our new approach.

CHALLENGES BEYOND OPERATIONAL AND MILITARY

Toward the end of 1981, the Congress which was in opposition in Nagaland, tried the toppling game. I felt that such a political move will not only be counter-productive as it will not only create political instability but will also disturb the settled security environment adversely. J.B. Jasokie, the Naga National Democratic Party chief minister, was a credible person, a nationalist and respected by all. Any change at that juncture was most uncalled for. I conveyed my views through the chief to the prime minister. These must have been accepted as the government lasted its full term. This was followed by the elections in 1982, which was to test our neutrality and credibility both in people's perception to whom we were a just and fair instrument represented by the institution of the GOC as its head. While political parties have to play politics and do everything to win elections, which include strong arm tactics and use of insurgent power and influence. The Army should be completely out of it and be the watchdog and prevent use of strong arm tactics by the political activists and sympathizers which should be dealt with by the civil administration and police. In the environment of Nagaland expecting both the police and civil administration to be completely neutral at the lower functional level would not be pragmatic, however, if the top echelons remained neutral then it has a salutary effect. I always felt this was achievable. Over a period of time I had developed a good rapport and mutual confidence with Z. Obed the chief secretary and the IGP Tripathi and we had formed a club of three, confidentially known amongst us as 'Ke Kolay Club' (KKC), of which I was the convener. But anyone could ask for its meeting, we met to discuss all sensitive issues and situations in all spheres of public life, administration and security to find an honest solution to these problems. We met when required and without any aides. Two months before the elections I raised the question of free and fair elections. After discussion we decided that any problem or any issue connected with the elections, we should all three handle it together and the person most involved should deal with it and issue orders with others present and agreeing. In most cases they told me to be the front man. We travelled together, mostly in my helicopter. Two incidents require special mention in this regard. S.C. Jamir, the Congress (I) leader, and later the chief minister was bullying and using strong arms tactics with the help of the DC in Mokokchung, both were from the Ao tribe of the area. All three of us visited Mokokchung and after listening to all parties, we admonished the DC and told him to pack up and orders will be issued by that evening. As we were leaving, the Congress (I) representative told us that Jamir was on his way to see us. We told him, we could not wait and left. In the second incident, DC of Phek, a sympathizer of NNDP and close to the Finance Minister Vamazo decided that the Prime Minister Mrs. Gandhi cannot land at the district headquarters as the helipad was not safe due to a building on one side which acted as a reception area. Following our well-practised routine we visited the ground, my view was that the prime minister cannot be denied a visit if she desires. After seeing the area, we found that the building was an obstruction but the DC was partisan in his attitude. We ordered the building to be demolished and to be rebuilt after the visit. The prime minister visited as planned.

We had a similar incident at Dimapur, which was developing as a major town on the entry to Nagaland in the foothills. Mrs. Gandhi during one of her visits to Assam wanted to hold a public meeting in Dimapur. The state government and even the IB was against it due to it being a stronghold of NSCN with formidable presence in the nearby Itinki forest. The problem was dumped on my lap. I was quite clear that the army could not be involved in any activity which may even remotely be connected with a political function. After a week I informed Delhi that she can come on any of the two days suggested by me and if required her Assam programme should be modified to meet this requirement. She came and addressed a public meeting attended by of over 5,000 people, which in those days was unheard of. The state government provided normal security by its police but took no responsibility for it. Later I was asked as to how I had ensured her security without getting involved. I refused to give any details and just said in an unconventional way that I followed the dictum of to catch a thief, you set a thief to do it. I used my trusted friend and ex-commander-in-chief of the Naga Federal Army, Zehato Swu and his ex-underground men to sanitize the area, a secret which remained between us till now. I trusted him fully and he returned my total trust and confidence. This kind of trust takes time and an honest and open understanding. Trust and understanding are required both at the individual and organizational level. Its foundations are laid at the highest individual level and it permeates down to the lowest levels. We did this both in Nagaland and Manipur between me (GOC), the Chief Minister, Chief Secretary and the IGP. The same is true of various segments of the security forces.

The story of politics and elections in Nagaland will not be complete without mentioning an interesting sidelight. Before the elections I was asked as to what my assessment was of the outcome of the elections. I took a week and conveyed that with a slight edge, National Nagaland Democratic Party may get 25 seats, Congress 23 and there will be 10 to 12 independents in a house of 60. The local Congress leadership had painted a rosy picture of a total walkover. When results were declared both were 24 each. I was wrong by two. My assessment must have been accepted as the Congress High Command acted fast and formed the government after buying independent MLAs. It was rumoured that Rs. 5 crore was brought of which only a portion was given to the independent MLAs, the rest was taken back and shared amongst Delhiwalas. A small portion that was given to independent MLAs was enough to satisfy them then. Some of them had not even seen Rs. 5,000, leave alone ten, fifteen, twenty or fifty thousand rupees. This was also probably the first time that big money was inducted into the body politics of Nagaland, which further spread to other areas of the North-East.

After taking over as GOC, I found a tendency amongst some of my staff to complain against the PMF and vice versa. I have always believed in dealing directly with all commanders in the insurgency area. We had six BSF battalions and five CRPF battalions under me the immediate problem was with the BSF. I spoke to the DIG of BSF Beant Singh and asked as to what the problem was. He told me that there was always a problem with the Army on the strength of the people on the posts and they do not understand as to how BSF functions. I asked him frankly as to what were his requirements. He told me that he was obliged to provide one platoon for the IG headquarters at Shillong and in addition one platoon for duties at his own headquarters and one platoon for escorting rations, stores and ammunition to the forward battalions. Also, each battalion had to have a training company. I agreed for him to take out one company worth of troops for the administrative duties in turn, one platoon each from three of his battalions. These platoons will be from the training companies of these battalions and training companies in these battalions will have only two platoons. I also agreed for the training company to be located with the battalion headquarters, it will perform battalion's local administrative duties also and in addition if required provide two platoons for operations for short duration, which will require DIG's clearance. Having discussed and agreed on this arrangements, I told Beant Singh that rest of the six battalions be fully deployed and be operational. I followed similar agreed parameters with the CRPF. Having established this trust and understanding with them I got the best out of them and they produced good results.

People operating in an insurgency environment should not look for a quick fix or instant solutions as such attempts normally result in ugly and disastrous consequences. Towards the end of my tenure my Col. G.S. (Ops) moved out on promotion. I requested the MS branch to post my Col. Adm. Col. Vinay Shankar (later D.G. Arty., Lt. Gen.) in his place as he had been there over a year and had officiated as Col. G.S. (Ops) to my satisfaction. But the MS branch decided to post a new Col. G.S. (Ops) belonging to the regiment of the additional MS Maj. Gen. R.K. Sood. This officer appeared to be intelligent but a bit disoriented and not suited for the job. He wanted to dominate the other members of the staff and unduly concern himself with other peoples' sphere of activities. He would be more interested in the visit of senior officers, arrangements for it and the mess functions in their honour. I told him a number of times that the deputy GOC and the President Mess Committee were there to look after these things. He also had a habit of interfering in the operational activities in the brigade sectors and I had received a number of complaints about it for which I had to admonish him. His habit of seeking prominence and glory caused us a huge embarrassment and almost resulted in a disaster.

We had been working in the central Nagaland area under Brig. P.L. Kukreti to capture the mastermind and destroy the complete network for money collection and recruitment by the NSCN in Nagaland. To achieve our aim we had patiently built-up intelligence for over four months. One of our sources code named doctor, who was working with me and also knew Brig. Kukreti, was to confirm as to when the NSCN finance minister (Kilenosar) was to come from Somra Tract to the area. During this period I went for the investiture ceremony at the Rashtrapati Bhawan to receive my PVSM from the president. Before leaving I told the Deputy GOC and the Col. G.S. that if an individual calling himself 'doctor' comes, he was to be sent to Brig. Kukreti. A few days later when the source (doctor) came to the divisional HQ, the Col. G.S. instead of sending him to Brig. Kukreti started interrogating him. After that without informing anyone he mustered troops from the divisional Defence and Employment Company and the Flag Staff house guard and launched an operation on his own. Not being familiar with the area, they raided the wrong place and opened fire killing two and injuring a few innocent villagers. Before leaving they set the houses on fire. The villagers lodged a complaint with the Brigade HQ and ultimately the news reached Deputy GOC. When I was informed by the Deputy GOC in Delhi, I was livid. On returning to Nagaland it took me a number of days and a lot of effort to repair the damage and retrieve the situation. I admonished the Col. G.S. and wrote in his report, 'this officer's professional judgement is impaired by his desire to seek prominence and glory and he needs strict supervision'.

When I was in the MO Directorate the officer encouraged by my successor decided to represent against my report for which he was fully entitled. When the MS Branch sent his petition to me for comments, I had to give details of the incidents, including the above-quoted major one, to clarify the basis of my remarks in his confidential report. After finishing my comments I added a few lines which are quoted below: 'This officer represents a new breed of officers who progress professionally not due to competence but due to extraneous reasons. The number of such officers was on the increase and we need to take a note of it.'

The COAS Gen. Vaidya while reviewing the officer's petition, told the MS that my above remarks were uncalled for and I should be asked to delete it. When the MS asked me to do so I refused. The officer was given some relief. A few years later I learnt that the officer had been promoted and posted as BGS. He was removed by the Corps Commander and put on adverse report. The above incident illustrates vividly that in the live environments of a war and insurgency and terrorism, commanders and staff in key appointments should not be appointed on considerations other than professional competence. There is no place for self-centred glory seekers.

REMINISCENCES

Credibility, Key to Success

The issue of realistic and correct perceptions is linked to credibility of perceptions as unless these are true and honest they do not convert to reality, resulting in loss of credibility. I learnt as GOC in Nagaland and Manipur that as head of the security forces my credibility with the troops, the administration, with the people and even with the insurgents was sacrosanct. You cannot profess one thing and do another or act as high and mighty with subordinates and succumb to pressure of superiors. The handling of the situation both in Nagaland and Manipur initially against established norms, support given to Jasokie, neutrality in 1982 elections and stand against the move out of 21 Sikh after the ambush and pressure from interested parties went to establish my credibility and of the Army of which I was the head. Manipur was a tough call but ultimately our credibility prevailed; it was cemented by our professional stance, honest handling of the Bisheshwar issue and the following incident.

In 1982, late Rajiv Gandhi who was then an MP and General Secretary of the Congress (I) and a member of the Defence Consultative Committee visited Manipur. I received a message both through the Army and the state administration that the prime minister had desired that I brief him on the situation in Manipur. I saw the merit of the intention behind it as everyone thought I would give an unbiased opinion. A message was also received from Governor Burney to meet him at Raj Bhavan. It posed a problem as in keeping with my policy of maintaining an independent stance I never went to see anyone who was not in the chain of command, at the same time irrespective of who the person was, whether a politician of any affiliation, an official or a civilian, a common man and even the underground or their sympathizer I always received and met them. I informed the army hierarchy and the governor that in keeping with my policy it will not be possible for me to meet Rajiv Gandhi in Raj Bhavan but I will be very happy to receive him in my headquarters at M Sector. I was very happy when I received a message that he would call on me at my headquarters. I appreciated his magnanimity and graciousness and thanked him. He just smiled and told me he has not forgotten what Rajesh Pilot told him after the Nagaland visit. When he arrived, he was accompanied by Saighal, a DIG level police officer who was incharge of his security, whom I told to stay out of the briefing. We had a very free and frank discussion and after the briefing I offered a few suggestions and recommendations. I was very happy that prompt action was taken on some of my recommendations, as one of the ministers was removed. The incident with Rajesh Pilot in Nagaland related to their visit to Nagaland during the elections. Rajiv Gandhi accompanied by Rajesh Pilot visited Nagaland during the elections. While Rajiv Gandhi was at a meeting the pilot of their private helicopter landed at our Chakabama helibase and told the ASC JCO in-charge of aviation fuel to refuel the helicopter. He told him that he cannot do it without orders and when the captain incharge was called he said the same thing. The pilot, a retired Air Force officer, was rude to the officer and told him as to whom he was flying. When I was informed of the incident, I told the officer to order the pilot to fly off from the helipad and put him under arrest if he refuses. The pilot took off and after some time Rajesh Pilot rang me up and asked for help. I told him of the misbehaviour of the pilot and that we cannot refuel a private helicopter without the sanction of the Ministry of Defence. By late evening the sanction came and the helicopter was refuelled. Later I had the opportunity in Delhi and Chandimandir to brief Rajiv Gandhi on some very sensitive issues as Additional DGMO and Army Commander respectively.

Credibility won me the respect, confidence and trust of the people of Nagaland and Manipur apart from respect and love of my own officers and troops. This was demonstrated in a very touching manner. When the Chief Minister Jasokie and the leader of the opposition S.C. Jamir jointly invited me to the Nagaland Assembly to address the house, a singular honour given to me. It had never happened before or later. Similarly, during each of the visits to Manipur after I left I was given honour and respect beyond my status and rank, which was always a moving experience.

Building up a Sense of Involvement

In an insurgency and during protracted operations troops and particularly commanders must develop a sense of involvement, then only can they understand the complexity of the situation and respond quickly to situations keeping in mind the fallout of their actions and the long-term objectives. This also generates responses in the command, creates mutual confidence and all work towards the attainment of the goal. During discussion with some formation commanders I came across a view that in an insurgency environment troops get tired and become careless and there is a need to cut down tenures. This is not entirely correct and mostly prevails amongst people who have no experience at the ground level and have not served in such an environment at unit or sub-unit level. This view is also influenced by our exposure to Western and particularly American practice in recent years. The reality is that people who do not have a sense of involvement with the task remain detached, get bored and tired, whereas a person with high level of mental involvement with what he is doing does not get tired or bored. Physical tiredness can be overcome by periodic rest and recuperation but it is involvement which provides the stimulant to overcome fatigue. To the involved every new situation is a challenge and stimulant to perform. This is also true of all activities even in peace, troops get tired of training if done in a routine fashion and there is no challenge and involvement. I have not heard of any successful and fully involved unit or its junior leaders complaining, whereas some who only think of passing time get bored and lethargic. At the same time commanders must guard the tendency to flog the willing, a balance needs to be maintained and all must be motivated to do their best and their effort recognized. Junior officers and troops have come under stress in recent years because while unit tenures are regularized, personnel both officers and men, return to field tenures with short peace gaps and some even without the minimum gap due to our system of providing manpower for the Rashtriya Rifles. It is a serious problem requiring attention.

Motivation and Capacity Building

Units and troops resent unproductive effort as it amounts to flogging. This is the result of aimless tasking and employment. Troops employed on well thought out productive tasks and employed in a productive fashion produce good results, have a sense of achievement and remain motivated. In cases of harsh and inhuman behaviour of troops, it was found that these troops were not motivated and their failures outnumbered their successes. Underlying this is the truism that it is the unsuccessful troops who have such an attitude and behaviour and indulge in human rights violation. We must create the right environment and operational conditions for troops to perform well. One of the finest and motivating forces is leading by personal example. It was a point of honour with me and my commanders to be present where the action was and share the danger and hardship with the troops. I and my brigade commanders were present at Phomching, Tekcham and Operation Kunj Behari and all other major and minor operations. Even as an Army Commander and Colonel of the Parachute Regiment, I visited units of my regiment and other troops in Sri Lanka, although this area was not my operational responsibility. Units and sub-units were deployed all over Sri Lanka, I visited them all and even landed in the Vavunia jungles to meet sub-units on operations in different parts of the jungle, whom I could not have met otherwise. A helicopter parked besides mine was blown up by the LTTE minutes after we took off from the helipad at the Brigade headquarters just outside the outskirts of the jungle. Later on our way to a mountain division headquarters, we lost our way in the fog and landed in the dark by following the railway line. It was a lucky escape. You do not command by issuing orders, driving troops and issuing of messages of appreciation, you have to be with them physically and seen by the troops during operations.

Linked with the performance of troops is the key issue of building up their capacity, which requires orientation and preparation before their induction into operations. Even in an emergency when troops are moved for operations, this capacity should be built up as operations progress. We did this in Manipur during active operations against ME by reorienting and training them in operations in urban environment by quick reaction teams and small groups. Sri Lanka was an example in the opposite, where there was a marked tendency to blame troops for failure, whereas actual failure was at a higher command level as troops were not given any opportunity to adjust and prepare for the new environment. Instead command cohesiveness was broken and formations and units split and launched. The art of command lies in planning based on capability and enhancing it as we go along. Failure is a challenge and situations are redeemed by building and enhancing the capability of our command continuously.

Support, Reward and Recognition

Commanders in insurgency and any operational environment need support, encouragement and backing so that they do not get pressurized and go ahead with the task in hand unhindered. In this regard we were lucky to have Lt. Generals Eric Vaz and A.S. Vaidya as the Army Commanders and Gen. Krishna Rao as the Chief, they all had served in the division and Gen. Krishna Rao had also been its GOC. They knew the environment and backed us. Gen. Krishna Rao along with backing, firmly held us responsible for lapses, along with support there was a fair amount of chasing. We worked flat out knowing failures will not be accepted and successes will be rewarded. I personally looked forward to his visit as these were totally professional. It will not be possible to recount every bit of his incisive questioning and advice, but its essence can be summed up quoting one ingrained in my memory, 'Well Tubby, don't let up on operations and pressure both on hostiles and troops and do what is right in national interest. I will not let any b… touch you chaps.' The experience was most refreshing and I passed it on to my commanders.

Reward and recognition along with accountability are essential to get the best out of people. The tendency to play favourites must be curbed. I am mentioning it deliberately as it has been the subject of discussion in recent years. I had laid down certain norms and stuck to them. Sustained good performance of the units was rewarded by distinguished service award to the CO and key personnel of the unit after due verification at all levels and ranks, majority going to the men. Gallantry in operation was rewarded based on acts of valour. The only grey area I found was how to reward the unit as a whole without disturbing military traditions and ethos. The question of honouring units as in the US Army or for that matter the present system of unit citations was examined and rejected as there will be discrimination and may cause resentment. In consultation with Lt. Gen. A.S. Vaidya, the Army Commander, and Gen. Krishna Rao, the Chief, it was decided that the three best units performance wise in the insurgency area, should be awarded with a shorter tenure of two years and given a peace station of their choice. I am proud to say that the first three units, 14 Bihar, 28 Madras and 17 Rajputana Rifles (Sawai Man Guards), were from my division. While in the MO Directorate immediately after commanding the division, I ensured that the best unit from the insurgency area, 5 Garhwal Rifles from Mizoram was moved to Delhi and given the honour to be the battalion for duties at the Rashtrapati Bhawan. My division won more awards in two years of my command tenure than any other formation ever in an insurgency area. It is a tribute to the men, JCOs and officers whom I had the honour and privilege to command.

Building up Trust

Army in Nagaland and Manipur has had a very close association with people there and strong feeling of trust and oneness developed over a period of time. However, there are fluctuations in the level of mutual trust and responses. A study would reveal that this has very little to do with the level of operations. On the contrary, whenever the intensity of operations has been high as during my period of over two years, we have had greater trust and respect for each other and responses of the people and administration has been good. I attribute it to two factors, one the sincerity of purpose and second credibility. Similarly, if in our civic action endeavours there is lack of sincerity and it is in the realm of lip service, then it fails to create an impact. If our civic action efforts are directed to help people in areas of their real well-being then these have a permanent effect. The motivation for these actions should not be image building but genuine desire to help. It must have a sense of involvement and generate participation of people. This was continuously emphasized to the commanders and we did a lot of useful work in the fields of education, health and hygiene, social well-being and sports. We never promised anything which was not warranted or we could not deliver.

People talk a lot about psychological operations in such an environment. Theoretical models of intellectuals may be useful but unrelated to ground realities they do not succeed. At formation level, what succeeds is genuine responses to people's feelings and truth. Our themes should be based on these, should be simple so that our troops can understand and implement. Our main asset is our personal contacts with the people and it is also the best means to implement these.

Rewarding Return

I went back to Manipur in 1985 to visit 6 Para, then serving in the division as Colonel of the Regiment. I told the CO that during my visit I would like to meet a number of people whom I had known and some friends. I was totally unprepared for what I experienced when I landed at Tulihal airfield in Imphal. There was the deputy chief minister, Tompok Singh, the Chief Secretary Barua, IG Police Almeda, Karna Mai SSP, Lalit Kumar Singh Congress (I) president and Bisheshwar Singh (now an MLA), to receive me. I was only an ex-GOC purely on a regimental visit, I was touched by their affection. In the evening over 100 people came to see me uninvited. Thank God for the Army *langar's* capability, nobody returned hungry. When I reached Kohima the next day, the Chief Minister Jamir, with officiating Chief Secretary Lotha and the IG met me at the helipad. In the evening at dinner I met old friends from Nagaland, like Jasokie and Obed who had driven from Dimapur to meet me. The meeting with Gen. Krishna Rao, now governor was also like old times.

On my daughter's marriage in Delhi in November 1984, I invited friends from Nagaland and Manipur. I asked my old PRO to distribute the invitations. To my pleasant surprise a number of them did turn up. Rishang Keishing, the chief minister, Barua, the chief secretary, along with two MLAs from Manipur and one MP and few Gaon Burahs from Nagaland. Also present was Burney, the governor. We were thrilled and felt rewarded. Our heart goes out to the wonderful people of Manipur and Nagaland.

NOTES

1. The details of the incident are recorded in 8 Mountain Division History, *Forever in Operations*, in the chapter titled 'Quick and Aggressive Response', by Col. R.D. Palsokar, pp. 176-7.
2. Ibid., pp. 178-81.
3. Ibid., p. 185.
4. Ibid., 8 Mountain Division History, pp. 182-4.
5. *Threat From Within*, by Lt. Gen. V.K. Nayar, PVSM, SM (Retd.), Lancer Publishers, New Delhi, 1992, pp. 228, 241-3.
6. Op. Kunj Behari, n. 4, pp. 185-8.

APPENDIX A

From, N. Bisheswar. Singh

To,

Major General V.K Nayar

GOC M. Sector,

Imphal

Dear sir,

Please refer to our conversation at number of occasions since my return from Naini Central Jail Allahabad. I have deliberated over the various aspects of our discussions and I have come to certain conclusions which I would like to put accross to you for consideration and subsequent action. I feel, if the revelations made by me in this letter are given dispassionate consideration, it would resolve the problems of my beloved motherland Manipur.

I had raised the PLA because the conditions in the state at that time were so bad that no patriotic individual(s) fired by the love of the motherland, could have ~~been~~ accepted the prevelent corruption, nepotism and maladministration. It is generally alleged that the PLA has a seccessionist designs but I would like to clarify that this allegation has been coined by certain vested interests to defame the organisation. To

From, N. Bisheswar Singh

To,

Major General V.K. Nayar

GOC M. Sector

Imphal

Dear sir,

Please refer to our conversation at number of occasions since my return from Naini Central Jail Allahabad. I have deliberated over the varous aspects of our discussions and I have come to certain conclusions which I would like to put across to you for consideration and subsequent action. I feel, if the revelations made by me in this letter are given dispassionate consideration, it would resolve the problems of my beloved motherland Manipur.

I had raised the PLA because the conditions in the state at that time were so bad that no patriotic individual(s) fired by the love of the motherland, could have accepted the prevalent corruption, nepotism and maladministration. It is generally alleged that the PLA has a secessionist designs but I would like to clarify that this allegation has been coined by certain vested interests to defame the organisation. To support my argument I would request you to go through the articles given by me in the party magazine, "Dawn". Also over a period of things have changed considerably and I feel as a patriot, wishing always best for Manipur, I should now adopt such methods which may speed up the progress and prosperity of this land of jewels. Therefore I have decided that my party should join the mainstream of the country and work hand in hand with other well-wishers of the state to achieve the common goal.

I have at times been thinking to have a seperate political party to serve the people of Manipur. But after weighing all the pros and cons I have dropped this idea because I feel it may again not be the right solution to achieve the desired development and prosperity of Manipur and its peace loving people. I have strong conviction that too many small, small parties hinder the progress rather than speeding it up.

I, therefore, request you to use your good offices and innitiate the case on my behalf for the merger of the PLA with Congress (I). I am making this proposal with all the sincerity and confidence that I have the backing of all members of PLA whether overground or underground. I am making the support my argument I would request you to go through the articles given by me in the party magazine, "Dawn". Also over a period things have changed considerably and I feel as a patriot, wishing always best for Manipur, I should now adopt such methods which may speed up the progress and prosperity of this land of jewels. Therefore I have decided that my party should join the mainstream of the country and work hand in hand with other well-wishers of the state to achieve the common goal.

I have at times been thinking to have a separate political party to serve the people of Manipur. But after weighing all the pros and cons I have dropped this idea because I feel it may again not be the right solution to achieve the desired development and prosperity of Manipur and its peace loving people. I have strong conviction that too many small, small parties hinder the progress rather that speeding it up.

I, therefore, request you to use your good offices and initiate the case on my behalf for the merger of the PLA with Congress (I). I am making this proposal with all the sincerity and confidence that I have the backing of all members of PLA whether over ground or underground. I am making the

above suggestion after deliberating over this
matter for almost over six months. I am
convinced that this merger will be an
ideal solution for the speedy progress of the
state and elimination of the malady of corruption.
Furthermore, this merger with the Congress (I) will
not only involve PLA but all Meitei extremist
organisations which include Prepak and KCP etc.
This is for your information that all other Meitei
extremist organisations owe allegiance to me
and to my party and will abide by the
instructions given by me. However I would not
accept any sort of surrender or general amnesty
as is being propagated by the state Government.
The merger of the party has to be in a respect-
able way giving due consideration to the
sentiments of all members of PLA and other
parties. I do not consider it necessary to
elaborate this aspect at this juncture. However,
I have full faith in you and request you to
work it out yourself with assurance from my
side to abide by the reasonable decisions taken
by you. I would, however, re-emphasise that I
would like to resolve all problems including
discussions with the government, working out
of the modalities of merger and merger itself
through you as I repose more confidence in
you than any one else. Further I would like
to suggest to you that this matter may please
be discussed at the highest level and not

above suggestion after deliberating over this matter for almost over six months. I am convinced that this merger will be an ideal solution for the speedy progress of the state and elimination of the malady of corruption. Furthermore, this merger with the Congress (I) will not only involve PLA but all Meitei extremist organisations which include Prepak and KCP, etc. This is for your information that all other Meitei extremist organisations owe allegiance to me and to my party and will abide by the instructions given by me. However I would not accept any sort of surrender or general amnesty as is being propagated by the state Government. The merger of the party has to be in a respectable way giving due consideration to the sentiments of all members of PLA and other parties. I do not consider it necessary to elaborate this aspect at this juncture. However, I have full faith in you and request you to work it out yourself with assurance from my side to abide by the reasonable decisions taken by you. I would, however, re-emphasise that I would like to resolve all problems including discussions with the government, working out of the modalities of merger and merger itself through you as I repose more confidence in you than any one else. Further I would like to suggest to you that this matter may please be discussed at the highest level and not disclosed to the local leaders till this idea mooted by me gets the approval of the Congress(I) leaders at the helm of the affairs. I am making this point because I am aware of the fact that many local leaders will try their utmost to sabotage this plan.

If the above proposal made by me is accepted by the Congress (I) High Command, then I propose that the merger be carried out stage by stage which could be as under :→

Stage 1 : I would stay with Army as a free citizen and not under police custody and through you get all the undergrounds to a place as mutually agreed between both of us, and arrange disarming of the undergrounds.

Stage 2: Working out of the modalities of merger of the two parties. During this stage we may include mutually agreeable Congress (I) workers to resolve differences, if any.

Stage 3: Merger of the two parties. However from the start till the merger takes place I would like you to be the negotiator. All aspects must be handled by you. I am repeatedly re-emphasising this point as I do not want that my party should be deceived/let down at any stage. For this purpose, to my way of thinking, you are the only person I can trust and depend on.

disclosed to the local leaders till this idea mooted by me gets the approval of the Congress (I) leaders at the helm of the affairs. I am making this point because I am aware of the fact that many local leaders will try their utmost to sabotage this plan.

If the above proposal made by me is accepted by the Congress (I) High Command, then I propose that the merger be carried out stage by stage which could be as under:

Stage 1: I would stay with Army as a free citizen and not under police custody and through you get all the undergrounds to a place as mutually agreed between both of us, and arrange dearming (disarming) of the undergrounds.

Stage 2: Working out of the modalities of merger of the two parties. During this stage we may include mutually agreeable Congress (I) workers to resolve difference, if any.

Stage 3: Merger of the two parties. However from the start till the merger takes place I would like you to be the negotiator. All aspects must be handled by you. I am repeatedly re-emphasising this point as I do not want that my party should be deceived/let down at any stage. For this purpose, to my way of thinking, you are the only person I can trust and depend on.

Before implementing this plan I would request you for the assurance from the highest level that myself and my party members after merger will be given the full opportunity to develope their political talent. There would be no discremination shown against us and we will be as good members of the party as others.

In the end, I would not like to make any tall claims but I can assure you and the country that I have such good hold over the people of Manipur Valley that any appeal made by me would not only get the favourable response but will be taken as total truth by all young and old. Therefore with the merger of my organisation with Congress (I) the latter will get tremendous boost in the valley. At the same time members of my organisation will have the satisfaction of serving and improving the plight of Manipuris who we feel have been left behind in the race of progress as compared to others.

With the above I have handed over the destiny of my organisation in your hands and I have no doubt that you will up-hold the confidence I have reposed in you. I am sure hereafter, myself and my organisation

Before implementing this plan I would request you for the assurance from the highest level that myself and my party members after merger will be given the full opportunity to develop their political talent. There would be no discrimination shown against us and we will be as good members of the party as others.

In the end, I would not like to make any tall claims but I can assure you and the country that I have such good hold over the people of Manipur Valley that any appeal made by me would not only get the favourable response but will be taken as total truth by all young and old. Therefore with the merger of my organisation with Congress (I) the latter will get tremendous boost in the Valley. At the same time members of my organisation will have the satisfaction of serving and improving the plight of Manipuris who we feel have been left behind in the race of progress as compared to others.

With the above I have handled over the destiny of my organisation in your hands and I have no doubts that you will up-hold the confidence I have reposed in you. I am sure hereafter, myself and my organisation will not be held responsible for the alleged antinational activities and onus of failure of talks would be on the ruling party.

N. Bisheswar Singh
(N. BISHESWAR SINGH)

13 Dec.'82

will not be held responsible for the alleged antinational activities and onus of failure of talks would be on the ruling party.

N. Bisheswar Singh

(N. BISHESWAR SINGH)

13 Dec. '82

CHAPTER 6

Military Operations Directorate: Myth and Reality

My posting out of Manipur and Nagaland had as much of a drama as my posting to the division. It was towards the end of February 1983 that Gen. Krishna Rao, the COAS, during his visit to the division got stuck with us due to one of the worst weather spells in Nagaland. Lt. Gen. Vaidya, the Army Commander, was also present. They were staying with me in the guest rooms in the GOC's hut, as they liked the place for its beauty and due to sentiment of the past association. Even a day after the scheduled end of the visit, the weather did not let up, torrential rains accompanied by landslides closed even our option of taking them by road to Dimapur and then flying out in a fixed wing aircraft. I left them on their own except at meal times when I joined them. It was on the fourth day when I was taking their leave after breakfast that I was asked to join them in the lounge. The conversation was of a general nature and centred around Manipur and Nagaland and the personalities known to us. After a while, Lt. Gen. Vaidya told the Chief, 'Sir, if you have made up your mind then you better tell him'. General Krishna Rao with a smile said he also thought so. He looked at me and said, 'Tubby you have done well in the command of the division and your tenure is also ending, I want you to come to the MO Directorate as ADGMO-A dealing with all operations in a few months.' I was surprised and to be honest a bit taken aback. After a while I replied that I was most thrilled and grateful for the appreciation of my work and confidence in me. On second thoughts, I said while I am most thankful but if permitted can I make a request. Chief said, yes. I continued, 'Sir if you think I have done well for you, then why cannot I get a cushy job and save a bit of money for my Army Welfare Housing Organisation flat'. Lt. Gen. Vaidya asked me what was that job. I told him, head of the Army Training Team in Iraq. Chief interdicted, 'Good idea but you won't get that job as it is not for people like you. Moreover, you don't know how the army works, it is simple—reward for hard work is more hard work'. With this he smiled and said, see you in Delhi in a few months. This put an end to any speculation and I received my posting in May 1983.

Even before I joined the MO Directorate, I was asked to join Gen. Krishna Rao during his visit to one of the Corps in the North-East. We toured the forward division's new defences and saw the progress in what was termed as Forward Posture, with which I became familiar after joining. The visit was most useful and saved me a lot of legwork. It was also during this visit that I learnt about my new boss, the Chief, as to how dedicated, sincere and professional he was. Each day started at sunrise and normally ended late evening, resulting in our landing up for dinner unwashed and unchanged. Coming from Nagaland and Manipur, I was quite at home but I found some of our hosts were perturbed.

The day I joined the MO Directorate, I found it to be in a bit of functional confusion. I was to find out later, it was due to two reasons, one there had been no ADGMO-A for a few months as the previous incumbent Maj. Gen. Baljeet Mehta of Dogras whom I was replacing had retired. Baljeet was an excellent officer, who was approved for the next rank but retired due to lack of a vacancy. The second reason for the flux was that Lt. Gen. K.K. Hazari, DGMO, was going on posting and his relief Lt. Gen. Sommana had arrived a day before and they were in the process of handing and taking over charge. My counterpart ADGMO-B dealing with operational infrastructure was senior to me in service. The absence of ADGMO-A for a few months resulted in the two brigadier Deputy Directors for the East and West and the section heads of other operational sections (MO1, 2, 3, and 10) dealing directly with the DGMO. I reported to Lt. Gen. Hazari and also met Lt. Gen. Sommana but did not disturb them, as they were very busy. I spent the day in familiarizing myself and meeting various section heads and finding out who was doing what and what was where. One of the things on my mind was as to how to get to the Directorate without losing oneself in the South Block labyrinth. In this the civilian peon, one of the few in the Directorate, was of great help to show me the correct gate and lift. While talking to ADGMO-B I asked him as to where my office was. He told me that he had occupied it and I could either take his office on the second floor or find another one. I left him after telling that my job required that I be next to the operations room and the DGMO. By the end of the day I had a good idea of the layout and functioning of the Directorate. That evening sitting in the Battle Honours mess bar, I decided to confront the confusion frontally as this was what I was doing in Manipur and Nagaland and was adept at it.

Next morning on reaching office, I went to the operations room, called the deputy directors and told them that from now onwards they will send all operational files to me and come for all decisions to me. If the DGMO calls them, go to him and on return let me know as to what transpired. I told them that I will be functioning from operations room till my office is set up. I also worked out a schedule of briefings by the section heads starting the same afternoon. At about midday I walked into ADGMO-B's office and told him that I wanted my office back as it is essential for my functioning. I requested if it could be done the next day. He asked me to speak to the DGMO, I told him there was no need for it as it should be resolved between us.

Next day, I arrived early and went to my designated office. It still had ADGMO-B's nameplate, I asked a *chaprasi* to remove it and take it along with his other belongings to his office upstairs. We started the day by briefing by section heads as per practice. I never heard about the office either from the ADGMO-B or from the DGMO but I could guess by their demeanour that my blunt and abrupt manner was not appreciated. I carried on and slowly things fell into place. Initially I also got a feeling that in the elite MO Directorate, like all other elitist organizations and set-ups, a sense of pedigree superiority prevailed. You have to have an MO stamp before you can have a top MO job. My mind went back to my posting to MO Directorate after Staff College. Later at an opportune moment I told them that after Staff College I was posted to the MO Directorate but I got it changed to avoid coming to Delhi. I also made it clear to all that I was posted on the Chief's bidding and intended to do the job to the best of my ability.

There is more interaction between the MO Directorate

and the MOD as compared to other directorates or between directorates within the Army headquarters and most of it is on sensitive operational matters. The white hall system of functioning prevalent in the GOI is neither conducive nor efficient to meet the requirements. My first taste of it was when on a very sensitive issue I drafted a note and addressed it to the JS(G), a couple of days later we received a reply signed by a desk officer. I told Col. G.S. (Ops) of MO-2 to send it back saying it is not acceptable till it was signed by an appropriate level officer, which is the JS(G). A few hours later I got a call from the JS(G) K.A.A. Nambiar to telling me that it was the system. I told him the system is faulty not because I am standing on protocol seniority of my rank but because I want to be sure that the recommendations which we have formulated after great deliberation and care have been seen and considered at the appropriate level. After a discussion between me and Nambiar the issue was resolved and the response from the MOD was as I had requested. A part of the problem was due to the upgradation of appointments and lack of knowledge of each other's functioning. People who man the system cannot be its slaves.

Lt. Gen. Sommana, a typical Guardsman, had a lot of style, thunder and bluster with him but at heart was a very kind and considerate person. The proof of it was, as some in the directorate said, he tolerated my frank and at times blunt ways. In spite of the fact that initially we were very formal and aloof with each other but over a period of time we understood each other and forged a very close relationship. After a couple of months he complained to me that I was taking decisions beyond my jurisdiction and level and at times he felt left out of the picture. I told him that I was sorry that he got that impression as after the morning briefings I always informed him and where required briefed him of decisions taken and sent important files for his information. I also asked him if any of the decisions taken by me had rebounded or been wrong. He smiled and told me to forget about it and carry on working as I was doing but to always keep him informed. Lt. Gen. Sommana was a sound professional but very deliberate and slow in decision-making, which could be a bit of a constraint during an emergency and on occasions requiring quick operational responses. Later, as Deputy Chief of Army Staff, he did extremely well.

The system thrived on file pushing and meetings, which delayed and diluted responses. If you didn't want to take a decision, you marked the file with a very innocuous remark, 'May we have your comments', and sent it to a number of appointments. It disappeared for weeks and months. This became a bone of contention between me and a few others. One case which is a striking and glaring illustration of this and is still fresh in my mind would be an appropriate example. The Army had decided to equip the infantry battalions with heavy machine guns after due deliberations and trials. The file with the trial reports and operational and organizational aspects was sent to me by my counterpart ADGMO-B asking my comments from the operational point of view. I was aware of the decision that operational clearance was given years back. However, to be sure I glanced through the minutes and after that I wrote the following comment, 'The decision that infantry battalions will have heavy machine guns was given operational clearance years back. That being so, what heavy machine guns, how many and organization of the platoon is the job of the Infantry and Staff Duties directorates, I therefore have no comments.' This upset the ADGMO-B and he sent the file to the DGMO but I did not budge. When Lt. Gen. Sommana called me I told him that I do my job but am not prepared to do other people's work. Similarly, too many meetings were a major waste of time, and led to unproductive activity and in most cases side stepping the decision-making responsibility. If the DGMO attended all the meetings, he was expected to attend in addition to briefings and discussions within the directorate, he will be working almost 18 hours a day with no time for thinking on serious issues. In over two years' command of the division I never held a brigade commanders meeting, I met them personally when required. To dilute the impact of meetings, over a period of time, we devised a system whereby the burden was shared between the DGMO, me, the new ADGMO-B and even the deputy directors at times. The system worked well except at times it caused some protocol problems, which we got over by our personal rapport with officers in the MOD and other ministries by clarifying that the person had the necessary authority not only for expressing views/opinions but also to take decision. At times, we even left meetings to attend to urgent operational calls and requirements. A mention of two meetings will be relevant to illustrate the above. To decide the requirement of defence bricks for the Army, a meeting was to be held by the Additional Defence Secretary Agnihotri. The people concerned were the section dealing with the engineering equipment under ADGMO-B and the E-in-C Branch. As normal in all letters for such meetings it was addressed to DGMO and E-in-C. I was the officiating DGMO. The right person to attend the meeting would have been the ADGMO-B who was to be accompanied by the Col. G.S. of the section concerned. Since ADGMO (B) was away on duty, I told the Col. G.S. to attend the meeting along with the Brig. Engineer Staff from E-in-C's Branch. Agnihotri refused to hold the meeting till the DGMO and E-in-C attended. The meeting was postponed twice for the same reason. I told the Col. G.S. to tell him the responsibility for defence preparedness does not rest alone on the Army, it is equally that of the ministry, if he does not want to hold the meeting it is upto him but as long as the present officiating DGMO is in chair, he will not attend it. The matter was reported to the VCOAS but I still refused. He was quite upset as I told him the same what Col. G.S. had conveyed to Agnihotri. When the new DGMO Lt. Gen. Prem Hoon took over, the VCOAS told him to attend the meeting. Lt Gen. Hoon asked me what he should do. I told him it is up to him. He attended the meeting.

The second incident concerns an incident on the India-Bangladesh border, which was manned by the BSF on our side, who had some casualties during an incident. The DG BSF told the MHA that the Army should take over. A meeting was called by Narasimha Rao, the then minister of external affairs, and the MOD, minister of external affairs and MO representatives attended it. MEA was represented also by Secretary East, Romesh Bhandari. Birbal Nath, the DG BSF, gave details of the incident including use of mortar fire by the BDR saying that the situation was beyond BSF and the Army should take over. Discussions went on for some time and when the minister asked my opinion, I told him that BDR is a paramilitary force equivalent to our BSF which is better equipped. If they cannot tackle BDR, then they might as well be disbanded. The Army's 'response' has to be only in a situation when Bangladesh has to be taught a lesson, the present situation is only a border incident. Birbal Nath started arguing with me. I cut him short by telling him I was discussing it with the minister. The message went home and BSF was asked to handle the situation. I had become a bit allergic to PMF and state administrations throwing in the towel, passing the buck and getting the army involved.

Apart from dealing with skirmishes and incidents on the LOC in J&K and keeping in touch with the operational and internal security situation in the country, a fair amount of time was spent on review of operational plans, of which Forward Posture against the Chinese in the east and west received special attention. It was a well-conceived plan and move by Gen. Krishna Rao to improve our military posture and infrastructure. When I joined it was well under implementation and making good progress in the east. In Ladakh in the north it was in an advance stage of finalization and Gen. Krishna Rao was keen to start it during the current season in 1983 and everyone was seized of it. During our discussions one felt a simmering of reservations but no forthright dissent. When I raised the issue with Lt. Gen. Sommana, the DGMO, and the ADGMO (B), my counterpart, they told me that the Chief is very keen on it and wants it to start before he retires. A few days later having time at my disposal, I decided to discuss it with the E-in-C Lt. Gen. Parikshit Puri, whom I had known from our younger days in Agra and with the DGOL Maj. Gen. Gurinder Singh. After my discussion with them I was clear that while the operational plan was very sound, the logistic support to implement it had not been given due attention. While movement of additional troops into Ladakh was no problem, maintaining and stocking them for winter would be difficult. The situation will be made worse by the requirement of additional movement of engineer and construction stores and ammunition. The constraint was road capacity during the summer season, with the current capacity it may turn out to be a false start, followed by a hold up soon. We had to upgrade the Srinagar-Ladakh and the Manali-Ladakh (Upshi) roads, particularly the Zojila Pass stretch of the former, which will reduce the road capacity further while work on these is in progress. I gave the details of our findings to the DGMO, who agreed to conduct a review with all concerned.

The review confirmed our findings and we prepared a logistics staff check and presented it to the Chief. General Krishna Rao was most reluctant but agreed when facts were presented to him. He agreed to a postponement and everyone heaved a sigh of relief. Our priorities changed and upgradation of Srinagar-Zojila-Leh and Manali-Upshi-Leh Road was undertaken to be completed by the end of the next season. This was my first experience of dissent at that level and proved that professionalism succeeds.

There was a feeling amongst Army officers including some in the MO Directorate that the BSF and other PMF which were to come under Army's operational control during a war situation were not properly trained for this role, neither did they make an effort to make themselves available to train with the Army even for a very limited period. The feeling was genuine and true. The factual position has not changed till date. The Assam Rifles (AR), Border Security Force (BSF) and Indo-Tibet Border Force (ITBF) deployed in sensitive areas are under Army's operational control and in other areas and borders are under MHA's control. When I joined there was a strong move and the idea was mooted that BSF and other PMF deployed on the border should be placed under the Army and thereby the MOD control. I opposed the idea vehemently, having served with and having had the AR, the BSF, Central Reserve Police Force (CRPF) and other police forces under my command during insurgency and having understood their functioning, ethos and ideology. While it is desirable and definitely required under operational conditions but during peace time the responsibilities of manning the border are different and enlarged to include prevention of smuggling, gun running, human and animal trafficking and other cross-border criminal activities. We were not equipped to supervise these and neither involvement with these additional duties and activities were desirable for the Army. Moreover, accountability and involvement cannot be separated. After heated arguments my view was accepted and the idea shelved.

We as a nation do not have a strategic culture and live in the present, without any long-term planning although we are gradually getting wiser and things are improving. This results in lack of policy. I became more aware of it in the MO Directorate. Lack of policy was most apparent in the Security and the Defence

Fields. The services did this mostly on their own, in the absence of a national perspective on security. The reality became obvious when we realized that the Forward Posture and infrastructure for the same lacked the sanction and recognition of a national policy and thereby came under financial and other implementation strains in spite of their inclusion in the Five Year Defence Plan. After some discussion we asked the MOD for a directive outlining the emerging threats based on the government's strategic vision. There was no response and after a few reminders we were asked to make a draft and send it to them. After a few days it came back duly signed by the defence secretary. We sent it back with a polite note that the directive to the Armed Forces should be signed either by the prime minister or minister for defence on her behalf as it is only the political head who can lay down policy and issue directions and not a bureaucrat. We received a fresh copy duly signed by the defence minister. To the best of my knowledge this probably is the only policy paper initiated by the government during my tenure in the MO Directorate.

SIACHEN: 'OPERATION MEGHDOOT'

The origin of the Siachen dispute lies in the Sino-Pak collusion against India. After the 1962 conflict with India, China felt concerned about India coming closer to the Western powers, as a result of which China negotiated a boundary settlement on the Karakorams with Pakistan, which was finalized in March 1963. This resulted in Pakistan illegally ceding 2,700 sq. miles of Indian territory (in POK) in Shaksgam Valley to China. With the completion of the Karakoram highway in 1978, it provided a direct link between the two countries and opened up Sinkiang in China to Tibet and to Pakistan through the northern areas, which created new security concerns for India. Zulfikar Ali Bhutto even went to the extent of saying that in the event of war with India, Pakistan would not be alone. Alongwith it Pakistan gradually started intruding into the Siachen Glacier area, taking advantage of the fact that the LOC was demarcated only upto NJ9842 and would extend thence north to the glaciers as recorded in the Karachi Agreement of 1948. It started sponsoring expeditions to the area and building up infrastructure towards it. Pakistan's occupation of the glacier would have resulted in physical extension of the line beyond NJ 9842 to the Karakoram Pass. There were clear indications of this in 1983. The clause in Pak-China agreement of 1963 on the boundary, that after Kashmir dispute is resolved, the side which had sovereignty over the area can once again negotiate the boundary with China, would have had no value in the face of adverse physical possession of the area. The plan to forestall Pakistan's design of expanding into the glacier was well thought out and the logic of increasing our presence gradually through own and sponsored expeditions had worked well. We were also aware of Pakistan's sensitivity. We decided to occupy the glacier in a surprise move and present Pakistan a *fait accompli*. The then Prime Minister Mrs. Indira Gandhi was briefed in the operations room. The briefing was attended by the Raksha Mantri, the Defence Secretary, the COAS, DGMO and me. She gave her approval. The plan was to occupy the glacier and thereby establish our presence and extend the LOC *de facto* beyond NJ 9842 northwards. Once our presence was recognized, then the process of negotiations to get our claim recognized both by Pakistan and the international community was to follow and once it was done, to withdraw leaving surveillance elements. To achieve our aim, it was imperative that while consolidating our position, Pakistani reaction had to be dealt with minimum possible escalation. This was emphasized and well known to all. It is also recorded in Lt. Gen. M.L. Chibber's, PVSM, AVSM (Retd.) personal account of the operations.[1] Logistics and altitude were major factors. The need for high altitude clothing, equipment and tentage was worked out and sanction obtained. We suggested that a young officer with experience to be sent for procurement of the equipment. But the Corps Commander Lt. Gen. Prem Hoon who had been an instructor at the High Altitude Warfare School decided to do it himself. In spite of our opposition this took place. While shopping in Europe for clothing and other equipment Lt. Gen. Hoon almost encountered a Pakistani officer on a similar errand and a game of hide and seek ensued. Fearing this might result in loss of surprise, the operation had to be rescheduled and brought forward and Operation Meghdoot was launched on 13 April 1984, the auspicious Baisakhi day. Reaction from Pakistani 'Burzil Force' specially earmarked and trained for tasks in the area materialized only on 24 April. After a time we in Delhi got the impression that the Corps and possibly the Command as well had got swayed by the developing situation, resulting in avoidable escalation of the situation and accretion in personnel and weapons. When we noticed it in the MO, we had specific instructions as a 'Personal For' message from the COAS to the Northern Army Commander issued, 'there will be no escalation repeat no escalation'. We were horrified when Chief Gen. Vaidya after his visit told us that the Northern Army Commander has planned an increase in force level and induction of some more heavy weapons. When we told Gen. Vaidya that this is against his own instructions of no further escalation, he just kept quiet. Later during Mrs. Gandhi's visit to Northern Command, the Northern Army Commander Lt. Gen. M.L. Chibber not only highlighted the strategic importance of the area for future operations into POK but also recommended further offensive actions to thwart Sino-Pak collusive designs in the area. Our protestations to Gen. Vaidya were of no avail. We realized that he just did not have it in him to confront his Army Commanders. I felt that somewhere down the line we seemed to have lost our aim and situation escalated as much due to our over-reaction as to Pakistan's actions, thus mitigating the chances of negotiations and acceptance of our presence. It was possible only in the early stages when Pakistani attempts to dislodge us had failed with heavy cost in casualties and the situation remained within the military's and government's purview on both sides. Once it got publicized the chances of either side backing down reduced. I was to see more of it in Punjab with disastrous results. The situation in Siachen Glacier escalated and resulted in our continued presence with huge personnel, military and financial cost. The stage was set by default and rest is history. After the Kargil war in 1999, the Siachen issue has become all the more a part of the overall Kashmir dispute between India and Pakistan, even though it remains a separate item for discussion/negotiation.

PAK ARMY'S TALK OF PEACE

An avalanche on Pakistan side of the Siachen glacier region at Gyari on 7 April 2012 resulted in 147 casualties to the troops of

6 Northern Light Infantry (6NLI) deployed there. It is the biggest tragedy due to weather on either side since we occupied the glacier in 1984 and which prompted Pakistan to talk peace. During his visit to the area after the avalanche, the Pakistan Army Chief Gen. Ashfaq Parvez Kayani commented that perhaps the time has come to make peace with India and resolve the Siachen glacier issue as a part of the larger Jammu & Kashmir problem. While the offer needs to be examined but it should not be accepted on its face value. The importance of Saltoro ridgeline lies in that along with deployment along the Karakoram axis it thwarts collusive threat from China and Pakistan into the Shyok Valley and to Leh through Khardungla Pass. The increased Chinese activity including permanent structures for troops could be a forerunner of such intentions.

While the Government of India has positively responded to Pakistani civil and military leadership's call for better relations but we cannot ignore our past experience. This coupled with the ground reality that there is no indication of Pakistan winding up its terror infrastructure and its persisting with pushing infiltrators across the line of control (LOC). There is no positive response to our request to bring to book perpetrators of 26/11 Mumbai attack—on the contrary Hafiz Saeed, founder of Lashkar-e-Taiba (LET) has total freedom to continue his tirade against India. Similarly, there is no response to our demand of 50 most wanted fugitives including Dawood Ibrahim and members of his underworld group. Pakistan's continuing efforts to upgrade and stockpile its nuclear arsenal and upgrading its missile capability cannot be ignored. Moreover in keeping with its anti-India policy it continues to oppose India's bid for a permanent seat in the UN Security Council and various other UN forums.

Taking the totality of the situation Gen. Kayani's offer is a tactical gimmick to gain time and respite to deal with its internal turmoil and to ensure a peaceful Eastern border till US and NATO withdrawal from Afghanistan. This is imperative to further its design for its allies, the Taliban, to capture power in Afghanistan. Keeping in mind our long-term interests in Afghanistan, it will be prudent for us not to rush into any agreement to keep Pakistan on the defensive by its involvement on both fronts. Gen. Kayani's move may equally be motivated by his desire to appease the Northern Light Infantry troops who belong to the area and its people who have borne the brunt of Siachen operations, recent catastrophe and the Kargil misadventure of 1999.

Demilitarization of Siachen area should be contingent first of all on recognition of the Actual Ground Position Line (AGPL), marked and authenticated on maps by both sides. Which should then be published and recognized by the international community and recorded in recognized cartographic publications. Then only should we initiate dialogue for demilitarization of the Siachen area, without prejudice to our position on the larger issue of Jammu & Kashmir. The need is to proceed with caution and guided by military security requirement and not by diplomatic goodwill. The talks between the representatives of India and Pakistan, on Pakistan's insistence that these precede the scheduled talks on Sir Creek were agreed to by India. The talks took place in the second week of June 2012 and as expected ended inconclusively.

'OPERATION BLUE STAR': ITS REALITY AND MYTH

During my tenure in the MO Directorate one of the major events which was to have wide ranging impact within India and provided Pakistan an opening to interfere in our internal affairs and finally resulting in Operation Blue Star occurred. A most regrettable and possibly an avoidable incident, the nation continues to pay a price for it in some fashion or the other till today. The killing of DIG Atwal outside the Golden Temple on 25 April 1983 had occurred just before I joined the MO Directorate. Its significance had not been realized by the authorities both in Delhi and Punjab. It was to be the beginning of the end. In spite of increase in violent incidents, kidnappings and killings, life appeared to be carrying on normally, with the state abdicating its authority slowly but surely and militant's writ increasing gradually and surely.

It was only in November 1983 that some of us in the Army informally started taking cognizance of the situation in Punjab. The Army was not privy to any intelligence, we could only take a view based on media reports and information available through open sources. Two conclusions set the alarm bells ringing. One, the manner in which the situation was being handled could only make it worse. Second, the well-founded apprehension based on past experience that when situations get out of control, these are usually dumped on the Army. In this case it was bound to have its ramifications within the Army. As a follow-up of this initial review I visited Amritsar. During the visit I assessed the general environment in the Punjab, particularly around Golden Temple and had discussions with the local formation commander, some journalists and common people which gave a good idea of the worsening situation. I followed it up with informal discussions with my friends in the intelligence set-up including some retired ones who confirmed my worst fears. A key element in the worsening situation was the dismissal of the Darbara Singh Ministry on 6 October and promulgation of president's rule. It signalled the closure of political avenues and brought the centre in direct confrontation with the situation. It was widely believed as did I that if Darbara Singh had been given the support and resources, he was in a position not only to control the law and order situation but politically resolve it too. His dismissal was the outcome of the infighting within the Congress between him and Giani Zail Singh and totally in keeping with Mrs. Gandhi's policy of keeping chief ministers on tenterhooks and not permitting them to be effective. I was fully convinced of the reality of these opinions. In my own opinion it was also the beginning of the marginalization of the established moderate Sikh leadership and further boost to Jarnail Singh Bhindranwala and his extremist followers. The situation had all the makings of a political design with all the ill omens of disaster. Based on the inputs and in consultation with my junior colleagues S.P. Kapoor and Ginger Bal who shared my concern and were a source of strength, we formulated an assessment of the prevailing situation.

I presented the above review in a closed door briefing to the Chief, the only other person present was Lt. Gen. Sommana the DGMO. The briefing was in two parts—my assessment of the situation and major conclusions, the gist of which is covered in the above paragraph. After the briefing, I recommended to the Chief that he should meet the prime minister and convey our apprehensions of the outcome of the worsening situation. He needed to tell her that we were totally apolitical and it is none of our concern to interfere in the running of the government and as to how it handles its affairs in the Punjab. Our major concern is because all the three services have a large number of Sikhs and Hindus belonging to Punjab and any precipitating action may affect the services internally. The aim was to give the prime minister an honest and uninhibited opinion based on ground realities, caution her against hardening of her stance and prevent Army's involvement. As a side effect it was also intended to get involved with the decision-making process and influence it. We were firmly of the opinion that the Army should not get involved with the situation in Punjab. I emphasized with the Chief that Punjab is vital for the Army and we need to be out of it. It was also hoped that it would warn the prime minister and she will not take a sudden decision to get us involved. All the logic and force of my arguments failed to get any response from Gen. Vaidya. He only questioned me on the source of my inputs, which I refused to divulge as I did not want to compromise the confidence of friends, who were so responsive. Even after such a frank and in a manner blunt talking, Gen. Vaidya did not respond. I would have welcomed if he had even told me to shut up and do what I was told. No response was to become a hallmark of his reaction to any crisis. General Sommana told me to continue monitoring the situation and keep him informed. On return to my office, I felt that we had the wrong man to lead the Army at this critical juncture. He had no mind of his own and neither the will nor competence to handle crisis. He would follow the dictates of his political masters and what is worse that he lacked moral courage to restrain his defiant Army Commanders. I reflected back on our admiration for his calm disposition as Eastern Army Commander and came to the conclusion that it was not based on competence or ability to handle crisis but on his attitude of accepting situations and going along with it. He agreed with his superior the COAS Gen. Krishna Rao a strong personality and let us juniors do the job, not for any thing else but to put responsibility on us. There was never any element of guidance or professional discussion, disagreement or correction. He left the ops room with a brief nod and 'You told me' sort of gesture.

A key element in most operational and internal security situations is intelligence. Except for the routine intelligence handouts and the Joint Intelligence Committees briefings, there was nothing worthwhile available. I raised the issue with DGMI Lt. Gen. P.N. Kathpalia, he told me that it was not in the charter of Military Intelligence, and the IB and the RAW, dealing with the internal and external intelligence were sensitive, to our meddling in their affairs. I told him what my view was, which I still hold, that any situation which affects us is our concern and needs intelligence inputs from Military Intelligence, particularly when its resources are deployed in the area. He was most polite but would not budge. I took it up with the Chief and even requested Lt. Gen. Kathpalia to come with me to discuss the issue with the Chief, he did that but no decision was taken. However, it had a good fallout as it resulted in the development of a healthy relationship between the MO and MI and particularly between me and Lt. Gen. Kathpalia, which permeated down to the functional levels. This was most useful and helpful not only in this situation but in our overall functioning. The relationship between the MO and MI soured due to the ego problems between DGMO and DGMI, both belonging to the same course from IMA. I also managed to get some tapes of Bhindranwala's sermons to the congregations at the Golden Temple, which helped me to fathom his impact and analyse his personality. At the government level a committee on the Punjab was formed which initially the Chief and subsequently some of us on his behalf attended, more as observers as nothing of substance was ever discussed.

After the first few meetings, we gradually brought down the level of our participation and I became the permanent representative of the Army as the level could not be brought down any further. P.C. Sethi, the then home minister, and T.N. Chaturvedi the then home secretary rarely attended the meetings. It was either chaired by MOS Home Venkat Subiah or the RRM, K.P. Singh Deo. The other participants were Arun Singh, probably representing Rajiv Gandhi, R.N. Kao, Principal Security Advisor to the PM, Rao Sahib Krishna Swamy the Cabinet Secretary, Director RAW G.C. Saxena, Director IB Rajendra Kapoor and Wali and Prem Kumar from MHA. P.C. Alexander, principal secretary to the PM only occasionally attended. Mostly it was a narration of the day's happenings in the Punjab by the DIB followed by some discussion.

Stictly speaking nothing of consequence was discussed or decided. After a few meetings it was easy to discern that it was a façade and a cover up for some political design. After some time K.C. Pant, who was neither a minister nor a government functionary started presiding over these meetings. I raised the issue with the RRM at a personal level, he told me that I should attend the meetings only when he attends. He also told me that Pant has been directed by the PM and that is why MOS Home and he were attending. Pant dominated the meetings and there was greater expression of hard line views. I kept my counsel and remained on listening watch.

Sometime in February 1984, late one evening VCOAS Lt. Gen. G.S. Rawat, rang me up to say that the Chief has returned from a meeting in the Cabinet Secretariat and as he could not contact the DGMO or me, so he has asked him to pass these orders to one of us. The Army had been asked to take over the border in Punjab to relieve BSF who were to be deployed for internal security duties in the Punjab. We in the MO had no inkling of it nor were we consulted. I thought for a while and tried to contact the Chief as I thought it was not a sound decision and needed a review. In spite of my best efforts I could not contact the Chief, who was attending a reception at the French Embassy, or the DGMO. Both were leaving for the Andaman Islands early next morning. I decided to sleep over it and do nothing till next morning. I felt a bit uneasy on the urgency and the manner of the decision, lest any orders have been passed directly to Headquarters Western Command. I decided to check up and to my surprise I learnt that the GOC of the Corps in Jalandhar had received orders direct from Gen. Vaidya and they were in the process of moving. I rang up the GOC Lt. Gen. Gauri Shankar to stop implementation and freeze all movement till they hear from MO and Western Command. I felt a bit easy after that.

Next morning on reaching the office I learnt that the Defence Secretary Ghosh and the MHA were agitated and perturbed as to why the decision had not been implemented, they had been informed by the BSF. The defence secretary had already rung up twice, when I spoke to him he appeared to be quite agitated, I explained to him that there are good reasons for stopping the implementation of the decision and I will meet him at 10.30 a.m. and explain to him. During the meeting I explained to him that the proposal had serious implications as it required a fairly high degree of mobilization which if implemented suddenly will give Pakistan cause for apprehension even if we informed them of the purpose and they were bound to take some precautionary measures. Army unlike the BSF will have to move forward its command, communication and administrative elements even if we don't move guns and tanks. Moreover, the Army will be in a wrong posture if Pakistan decides to take advantage of the situation and precipitates an incident. Foremost consideration was that Army should not get involved with the situation in any manner at this junction. I also drove home the point that availability of additional 30 to 40 companies will not make a substantial difference to the internal security situation when hundreds of companies of PMF and police were already deployed, it was a question of clear objectives, will and effectiveness. I was totally motivated by the thought to prevent Army's involvement. The defence secretary was convinced of the reasoning for not implementing the decision. He informed the cabinet secretary who was furious and fixed a meeting for that afternoon. I informed the VCOAS and asked him to accompany me for the meeting. We thought three of us were going to discuss the issue with the Cabinet Secretary Rao Sahib Krishnaswamy but when we arrived we found Alexander, Principal Secretary to the PM, Kao the Security Advisor to the PM, Director RAW, Gary Saxena, DIB Kapoor and the Special Secretary Home Prem Kumar present. As the meeting started and the defence secretary started to explain the reasons for not implementing the decision, he was abruptly cut short by the cabinet secretary and asked why government orders have not been implemented. The discussion veered off to this rather than the merit of the issues we were raising. Seeing the trend of the cabinet secretary's argument, everyone else also pitched in and we three felt isolated and left out. They had probably contrived to do so, this is an old trick of the bureaucracy to outnumber and out talk. Both the defence secretary and the VCOAS being gentlemen kept quite for a while, then the VCOAS pitched in to explain why it would be incorrect to implement the decision. He was told that the Chief who was present in the meeting had accepted it. They wanted to know as to why once government had taken a decision for the Army to relieve BSF and accepted by the COAS, it was not implemented. I was by then a bit frustrated and fed up and could not help interjecting. In spite of my agitated state I kept my cool and in the politest language I said that since morning we have heard only why government's decision has not been implemented and nobody has bothered to listen to our reasons for not doing so. We are as much a part of the government and on issues where Army's involvement is sought, there has to be a frank discussion. As regards to COAS's presence in the meeting, we have not had the opportunity to review all aspects of the situation with him. On the spur of the moment I invoked the prime minister's name, saying that unless she is apprised of the implications, we will not implement it. I added that even if she in her wisdom orders us, we will only implement till after the Chief has returned from Andaman Islands and we have discussed it with him. The abruptness of my remarks had its effect as the cabinet secretary was reminded of our encounter in Manipur. The meeting ended in a stalemate and we never deployed the troops. As we were leaving, the defence secretary told me he thought Bengalis were excitable but I was worse. On return from the meeting I sent a note under my signature to the cabinet and defence secretaries reiterating our position. I sent a copy of the note for Chief's information on return. When he saw the note, he called me and admonished me not on my judgement but on reversing the decision when he had given his tacit approval. The writing on the wall was clear that we will be dragged into the situation more by default than by design. There were greater shocks in store of which I had no inkling or idea.

I became more determined to prevent the Army getting involved in Punjab. To do so we needed to know the situation in a holistic and wholesome manner. I thought a good way would be to start a process of dialogue and discussion with the Headquarter's Western Command. I prevailed upon the DGMO and the COAS to ask the Western Army Commander to give us a briefing on the Punjab situation. I rang up Headquarter's Western Command for the same and learnt that Lt. Gen. Sundarjee, the Army Commander, was on leave in Goa, so I asked Lt. Gen. R.S. Dayal, the COS, to do so. He told me that he was quite willing to come but Lt. Gen. Gauri Shankar the Corps Commander in Jalandhar was the officiating Army Commander. After discussing it with the

DGMO, I asked both of them to come, as it will give us a better perspective as the Jalandhar Corps had the bulk of Punjab under its jurisdiction. Both of them briefed the COAS on the situation, me and DGMO were present. We were struck by the disparity of their views. General Vaidya as usual asked no clarifications or questions, both DGMO and me did not consider it pertinent to ask or say anything. Even more than the Chief's presence it was the confusion in our minds that prevented us. Afterwards when I discussed it with the DGMO, who had been the Corps Commander in Jalandhar, he said we cannot have Gauri Shankar handling the situation in Punjab, if ever it comes to it.

Generally speaking there were two views prevailing in the Army at that time. The most convenient and aired view was that we should not concern ourselves with the government's handling of the situation in Punjab, just keep a watch and if we were ever asked, we should carry out the task given. It was a very simplistic and escapist view and displayed an attitude of ambivalence. I could not believe it and was totally against it. I along with some of my colleagues felt that the Army should not at all get involved with the situation in the Punjab. The situation was escalating due to inaction and it appeared to have a political design, which was clear from the perfunctory nature of the negotiations with the Akalis and the treatment meted out to Sikhs during the Asiad, particularly in Haryana. Being by now well informed of the ground realities and aware of Sikh history, I took courage and spoke to Gen. Vaidya face-to-face in his office. I repeated what I had told him in my briefing in November 1983 and again requested him to speak to the prime minister and tell her that the Punjab situation as was being handled will blow up and it will have a very adverse impact within the services, even then I could not imagine how bad it was to be actually. He gave me a patient hearing but gave no indication of his thinking. I went to the extent of saying that there are dozens of secretaries in the Government of India but only one *Chief of Army Staff* and what he can tell the prime minister, no one else can. To the best of my knowledge there were only two meetings held, that too at the staff level and the only issues discussed were the methodology and mechanics of Army involvement and the requirement to maintain a minimum defensive posture. This was not dealing with the problem but side-tracking it. Neither were there any consultations between the Chief and the Army Commander.

By April-May 1984, the law and order situation had completely broken down and extremists had the run of the place. Civil administration was totally neutralized and police was rendered ineffective. There was some semblance of order in areas manned by BSF and CRPF. Akalis were no longer in control of the movement and Bhindranwala's writ ran supreme. The Golden Temple was being fortified and other *gurdwaras* in rural areas were being organized as centres of defiance and resistance. The situation was fast deteriorating. Taking the totality of the situation, me, Ginger Bal and S.P. Kapoor made an outline plan in case the Army was called, hoping that it would not happen. We were clear in our mind that it was a politico-military situation with political element being the dominant one. The diffusion of the situation was the key element and not operational success and there was paramount need for caution. If ever the Army was called, it should move most deliberately with a lot of fanfare and publicity to give heart to the moderates and help public opinion to become as neutral as possible if not against the extremists. The cordon already established around the Golden Temple should be strengthened to tire the extremists and if they sneak out, all to good effect. Our plan was based on the premise that the deliberate and long drawn out actions of the Army will give the established Akali and Sikh leadership heart to regain their position and tell the extremists to relent and make the public opinion favourable if Army action becomes imminent. It will also put the onus of the outcome on the extremists. Military action was the last resort. We were also firmly of the opinion that the Army's involvement in such an eventuality should be confined to the norms laid in aid to civil authority, Army was to be more of a psychological weapon than operational. In many years of involvement in the insurgencies in the North-East, the Army has never damaged or destroyed a single church. Having formulated the plan, I briefed the DGMO and both the Col. G.S. Ginger Bal and Kapoor. I went on leave in the last week of May to bring my family from Lucknow, where they were in a separated family accommodation, while I was in Manipur and Nagaland.

In the middle of my leave, late on the night of 1 June I got a call from Col. Kapoor and in a guarded manner he told me that the Army has been ordered to move and to clear the Golden Temple of extremists. I rejoined the next day and learnt that things had moved fast and in the wrong direction, with no consultation with the MO Directorate. We were mere spectators. On checking up I learnt that Lt. Gen. Sundarjee had been called to Delhi, met the prime minister and was given a carte blanche. He had in his typical blustering fashion ridden the war horse with full fury. I wonder if Gen. Vaidya the COAS had much say in the matter. How he accepted it as the Chief, later events were to prove that he just did not have it in him to stand up or guide the destiny of the Army. The MO Directorate asked for a directive from the government as is the norm in such circumstances. After much haggling the MOD issued a directive. Based on which the MO Directorate issued an operational instruction to Headquarters Western Command outlining the tasks. Which broadly speaking were to seal the border with Pakistan, flush out the terrorist from their strongholds in *gurdwaras*, curb terrorism and restore normalcy in Punjab. The operation to seal the border was given the code name 'Operation Wood Rose' and to clear the *gurdwaras* 'Operation Blue Star'. The detailed planning and execution was left to Headquarter Western Command, based on their assessment of the situation. Army had also asked for the police, PMF and administration dealing with the situation in the Golden Temple to be placed under its control and appoint the officer-in-charge of operations Lt. Gen. R.S. Dayal, MVC as the security advisor.

The operation as we learnt later was ill conceived, hasty and totally military, with complete disregard of its political and social ramifications. The extremists under Bhindranwala, Bhai Amrik Singh and ex-Maj. Gen. Shabeg Singh fought because they were given no option. The operation was launched on 5 June 1984, immediately after Guru Arjun Dev's Martyrdom Day Anniversary (3 June) and Panchmi (3 and 4 June) when a large number of devotees were present in the Golden Temple. The lame excuse that the Akalis had threatened to launch a *morcha* to prevent movement of grain in Punjab does not hold water as the Akali leadership was a captive of Bhindranwala in the Golden Temple. The timing and focus of the entire operation showed a total insensitivity to the religious sentiment and comprehension of the situation. How did it matter if the operation was postponed or delayed by a few days.

I will not go into the details of the actual operations as these have been recorded in the GOI white paper and by various other authors. I will only deal with certain incorrect perceptions prevailing in the minds of the public. First of all there is a general perception that the name 'Operation Blue Star' was chosen after deliberate thought and connected with the blue colour of Akali turbans. This is far-fetched and wrong and is far from the truth. It was some time on 24 or 25 May before I went on leave that late in the evening when I was returning home and Col. Kapoor was dropping me off. I was quite upset and stressed as I had lost my last ditch battle to put some sense in the authorities. Colonel Kapoor asked me as to what name should the operations against extremists in Punjab be given as our involvement looks imminent. As per the norms and practice each aid to civil authority during any internal security situation or in the case of a natural calamity is given a code name, to facilitate reporting and compilation of records. I told him pick up any name, just then I saw a board on the roadside advertising Blue Star Refrigeration. On the spur of the moment I told him to call it 'Blue Star'. This is the truth and this again proves the dictum that truth is stranger than fiction.

The second perception that Lt. Gen. R.S. Dayal, the then COS of Headquarters Western Command, was put in-charge of the operation because he was a Sikh and the same is said about Maj. Gen. K.S. Brar who was in-charge of operations in the Golden Temple. My feeling then and even now is that it was entirely related to personalities. Lt. Gen. Gauri Shankar, the Corps Commander in Jalandhar, as I have said earlier, was probably not considered the right person for the nature and type of task required to be performed. We had the same feeling though for different reasons. As to why the GOC of the division in Amritsar was not given the task which was most logical, my feeling is that he was not favoured by Lt. Gen. Sundarjee. This is further reinforced by the fact that his deputy Brigadier A.K. Dewan participated in the operations as did troops from the division. The upshot of it was that we had people in command of operations who were not in close touch with the situation or had no experience of such situations including Lt. Gen.

Sundarjee. However, the feeling that the government deliberately planned the use of Sikh officers to deal with the Punjab problem did not appear to be true then but the way their loyalty to the government was highlighted later lends some substance to it. Later events were to continue to reinforce this public perception because in J&K we used Muslim officials to contact and negotiate with the Kashmiris. In view of this it will be difficult to deny this mindset. Lt. Gen. Sundarjee was to continue to be influenced by inexperienced officers while dealing with live situations. Sri Lanka was to follow. I have often wondered as to what prevented a pragmatic soldier like Lt. Gen. Dayal to voice his opposition and refuse to be a party to it. It was particularly surprising after his recent experience in Assam just before coming to Western Command. I had known him well enough to say that I was disappointed and was pained to see him suffer in later years for it.

The news of Army operations in the Golden Temple and the rural areas of Punjab spread like wild fire. The government's failure to put out authentic and factual version led to rumours and people turned to other sources, whether Pakistan TV or radio resulting in repeated rumours becoming news. This had a devastating effect and led to disgruntlement and even mutiny amongst Sikh troops in Ranchi in Bihar, Pune and Mumbai in Maharashtra and amongst troops deployed in Poonch in J&K, there were a few more isolated cases. The news had spread even to distant places like Nagaland. The Sub. Maj. of my old divisional Headquarter Defense and Employment Company whose extra regimental employment was from the Sikh regiment rang me up in Delhi and asked me as to what had happened in the Punjab. I conveyed to him the situation in brief and asked him to speak to the men as to what I had told him. I also told him to convey to the men that they should not believe in rumours. I suggested to the Sub. Maj. that he should send a JCO and a few men by the next courier to Delhi. I told him that I shall meet them during their halt at Delhi, after which they should go and see things for themselves and on return convey the truth to others. Our most damaging singular failure was not informing our own commanders and troops. We concentrated on the English national and foreign media and failed to manage and keep the vernacular media informed. On an earlier occasion during a meeting with B.D. Pande, the then governor, I had made the point that vernacular media was of prime importance and should always be given preference during our briefings as that is what reaches and influences locals. However, I must confess that even with my recent experience in Manipur and Nagaland and being totally opposed to the operation, I was surprised by the gravity of the adverse effect that the operation generated. I was so occupied with keeping a tag of events and how to deal with the backlash, that when DGMO asked me to handle press as well, I had to refuse it. My counterpart Maj. Gen. Sharma ADGMO-B was made responsible for it. In spite of some aberrations, he handled the press briefings well. The trend in Army's response to mutiny by some Sikh troops was set by Lt. Gen. Tirath Singh Oberoi, GOC-in-C Southern Command, who set an example in dealing with them personally and was categorical in saying the Army will not accept such acts of indiscipline.

The incoming reports on the operations in the Golden Temple and from other areas were most disturbing. Realizing the gravity of the situation during a meeting in the ops room on 6 June, I ventured to mention to the Chief in the presence of the DGMO that he should visit Amritsar and Golden Temple and see the situation himself. I had a feeling that we were not being given the true picture. The Chief, as was normal for him, declined to respond. On the morning of 7 June we received reports of the completion of the operation in the Golden Temple and that Golden Temple has been cleared of terrorists. Bhindranwala, Bhai Amrik Singh and ex-Maj. Gen. Shabeg Singh had been killed during the operation and everyone heaved a sigh of relief. In the late forenoon, I took some time off and went home to have a bath and change into fresh set of clothes as I was wearing the same for two days. When I returned at lunch time, Col. Niko Bahri met me and told me that he was accompanying the R.R.M. Shri K.P. Singh Deo, who was going to Amritsar and the Golden Temple to review the situation. I realized as to how important it was for the Chief to have gone and seen the situation for himself. Since that had not happened I felt that either the VCOAS or the DGMO should himself go. Col. Niko Bahri was not the officer dealing with Punjab or internal security. Moreover he was not senior enough and may not even get an opportunity to be close enough to the Army Commander and the RRM to know what had transpired. I raised the issue with the DGMO, he thought for a while and then told me to go. He felt it was too late to ask the VCOAS and he was tied up in some meetings. I told Col. Niko Bahri to accompany me as he was all ready. We rushed to the technical area at Palam and just managed to catch the RRM's flight. In the aircraft I was surprised to see Kapoor DIB, Shankaran Nair (Ex-Director RAW and IB) and some representative of MHA. The journey to Amritsar was uneventful and nothing much was discussed. On arrival at Raja Sansi Airport in Amritsar, the RRM was received by Lt. Gen. Sundarjee, who told him that first he will take the RRM for an aerial overview of the Golden Temple before taking him there. Lt. Gen. Sundarjee accompanied the RRM in the first helicopter, I sat in the second and took Kapoor with me. We made a few quick circles of the Golden Temple, we could still see some smoke coming out of some areas of the temple and in its vicinity. After landing, I managed to sit in the front seat of the staff car along with his staff officer in which Lt. Gen. Sundarjee was escorting the RRM.

En route to the Golden Temple, Gen. Sundarjee explained to the RRM that he had ordered the use of a field gun in direct fire role on the Akal Takht due to very heavy resistance. During our journey we could see people peeping at us through their house windows as curfew had been imposed. On reaching the Golden Temple, the scene that we witnessed shocked me totally. Outside the main entrance at the Clock Tower in the open sat a couple of hundred Sikhs, young and old, on their haunches with hands tied behind their back. When I enquired as to who these people were, I was told these were the people captured in the Golden Temple awaiting interrogation and screening. The scene was being witnessed by hundreds and thousands from behind closed doors and windows. When I mentioned that this display will make every Sikh who is watching a terrorist, the response was a smirk. Inside the courtyard the bodies of Bhindranwala, Bhai Amrik Singh and ex-Maj. Gen. Shabeg Singh were laid out along with some weapons on display. As we were going around, we could hear the sound of sporadic firings and there were large parts of the Parikrama still soiled with blood. When we reached the Akal Takht, I could not even in my wildest dreams imagine the sight we saw, the destruction was simply terrifying and we were completely overawed. When I asked Maj. Gen. Brar (Bulbul) as to why the place had not been cleaned up and why there were blood stains everywhere, he told me that the troops were very tired after the operations. I could only respond to this with a curt reply that if troops get tired after a two-day operation then there is something amiss. Also present was Ramesh Inder Singh, the DC of Amritsar, who had just taken over. During my quick interaction with him I asked him as to where will the bodies of Bhindranwala, Amrik Singh and ex-Maj. Gen. Shabeg Singh be cremated. He replied, 'at the Saheed Shamshan Ghat'. I told him 'would it not be the wrong place?' and left it at that. As far as the operation itself was concerned I felt it was planned in a very bull headed manner, with total disregard for casualties, relying on overuse of heavy weapons and force. My overall impression was that Lt. Gen. Sundarjee had totally failed to grasp the essentials of the situation and aspired to quick military success, irrespective the damage and casualties. This resulted in military considerations overruling all other political and socio-religious considerations. At a later stage of the visit, I developed a feeling that the sporadic firings during the visit was probably stage managed for the benefit of the RRM. During our visit to Harmandir Sahib much was made of its head *granthi* Sahib Singh and his help solicited in justifying operation 'Blue Star'. The discussion was essentially between RRM, Lt. Gen. Sundarjee, Lt. Gen. Dayal and Kapoor DIB, rest of us were distant witnesses but within hearing distance.

During the return journey, there was a discussion of what we had witnessed, with Akal Takht as its focal point. Later in the discussion it was discussed as to how to get a statement from the head *granthi* of Harmandir Sahib Giani Sahib Singh to the effect that Army action on the Golden Temple was brought about by the militants under Bhindranwala and the destruction of the Akal Takht was unavoidable. Kapoor and Shankaran Nair were of the opinion that this could be best managed by the Army as they were in control of the Golden Temple. I had kept quiet during the discussion but when mention of the Army was made I politely but firmly told them that it was not the Army's job and can best be done by the intelligence people as they are adept at it. When they insisted, the RRM asked me to make a note of it and do the needful. I bluntly told him we have done the operation and this dirty job should be done by the intelligence agencies, who always have a pack of dirty tricks in their bag. This upset the normally calm, pleasant and well-mannered RRM as he probably felt slighted in the presence of others, he retorted by telling me that he is ordering me to make a note and convey to the Chief. While realizing the reason for his anger, I still did not want to dilute or convey any ambiguity in Army's stance. I replied I don't have to make a note in writing as I can recall it but I want to make it clear that Army will not do it. It is what I had said, it won't be any other way, irrespective of who is talked to. Saying this I left the VIP cabin and came and sat on one of the seats outside.

On return to Delhi, I told the DGMO of what had happened and what a mess we have landed ourselves into, doubting if it will make a difference. There was nothing to add as the issue was never discussed again. During the course of events which followed, it was apparent that both the political and intelligence set-ups got busy with tackling the aftermath of the destruction of the Akal Takht. This was mostly managed by Buta Singh, after a lot of efforts and prolonged discussion with Sikh leaders. Kar Seva was undertaken by Sant Santa Singh. I am not aware of any Army involvement but some senior Sikh officers did visit Amritsar. The government and its handymen seemed to have realized their folly. After Operation Blue Star, the Army's involvement in any case would have further angered the still simmering passions. There was another confrontation between MOD and me representing the MO. The CBI under its Sikh Director, P.S. Bawa asked the MOD to ask the Army to produce individual witnesses to testify that they saw a particular militant with weapon shooting at them at night and that particular *jawan* who confronted him and shot him. The very concept was ridiculous, but not to upset ruffled feathers any more, I explained to the RRM who was chairing the meeting that the operation was at night and the Army did its task of clearing the Golden Temple by eliminating the resistance they met. The ridiculousness of the suggestion was all too clear and I told the RRM that Army cannot meet such demands. I became the mouthpiece of the Army and the MOD on such similar issues as it suited them all to put me in front as people were used to my bluntness. I was in for a pleasant surprise a week later, when I got a call from the RRM. After wishing him I asked him as to what I could do for him. His response surprised me. He said it is more than a week since we both had a fight and he was missing it. I said it was never meant to be like this, we were frank about our views. He said he wanted a favour. I replied, certainly. He asked me to have breakfast with him next morning, I accepted with pleasure. Next day I had breakfast with him, he was an excellent host, very gracious and pleasant. He told me there should be no hard feelings as we both were doing our jobs. In spite of our numerous spats, my judgement of him was correct. Ever since then we have been friends, howsoever, infrequently we meet.

After a month or so the situation seemed to be settling down a bit but the simmerings of the aftermath continued, the hurt Sikh psyche was a serious cause for the nation and to some extent for the government. But except for Kar Seva in the Golden Temple no concrete steps were taken to repair the psychological and moral fissures and smoothen the after blow. Sikh leaders both in the government and outside it fell into their different ways. Sikh leaders in the Congress like Buta Singh and Giani Zail Singh got busy feathering their own nests, they had no following amongst the Jat Sikhs. Majority of them were either with the Akalis or had left the Congress in resentment. What made things worse was that the government and their loyalists in the bureaucracy and even some in the Army like Gen. Vaidya and Lt. Gen. Sundarjee by their action as well as inaction in some respects made the entire Sikh community look like suspects. These feelings were shared by my Sikh colleagues with me as they felt I had their confidence. Attempts by some of us to raise these issues were viewed as anti-establishment and were resented.

Retrospect

I have taken great care of going into most available documents, writings on operation 'Blue Star' by people in authority, independent authors and also talked to people who dealts with the Punjab problem at that time. There is a dichotomy between what people who dealt with the problem said and what has been projected by the government and its functionaries. This also holds true of the events in the aftermath of Mrs. Indira Gandhi's assassination on 31 October 1984. I shall deal with that later.

The very first issue is the growth of Bhindranwala from a *mahant* of Damdami Taksal to a belligerent Sikh leader, who overpowered the established Sikh leadership of Akalis as well as others and denigrated the established Sikh institutions. The common perception that Congress created and encouraged him for partisan or political gains and later failed to control him in spite of his provocative acts is well founded. Even later when he was portrayed as a militant, the government's failure to deal with him firmly puts a question mark on its intentions and sincerity. Simultaneously, the government continued prolonged negotiations with the Akalis which were not in the public domain till much later after the event. With the passage of time the government should have realized that Akalis had lost their control over the situation and the Sikh masses. The time for action against Bhindranwala had come much earlier in the period from DIG Atwal's killing in April 1983 to the declaration of president's rule in October 1983 when the violence and killings escalated. This resulted in Hindu reaction in the neighbouring states of Haryana and Rajasthan, which provided Bhindranwala greater opportunity to defy both the Akali leadership and the government. Bhindranwala's shifting from Guru Nanak Niwas to Akal Takht in defiance of the Akali triumvirate and after a physical confrontation with the Akali leadership was possibly the last straw. It is surprising that an astute politician like Mrs. Gandhi failed to read the writing on the wall or were the intentions different? Timely action could have saved the situation and made negotiations with Akalis meaningful, instead it resulted in Akalis and Bhindranwala competing in defying the government.

The above narrative in essence is similar to the events following Bhindranwala's escape from Chandu Kalan to Mehta Chowk in 1981, which was assisted by Giani Zail Singh, the then HM. Once Bhindranwala had firmly established himself at Mehta Chowk, the Army was asked to capture him. These instructions from Mrs. Indira Gandhi were passed by the then Defence Secretary P.K. Kaul to Lt. Gen. Sethna, the VCOAS. The COAS Gen. Krishna Rao and the DGMO Lt. Gen. K.K. Hazari were on a tour of Nagaland. In spite of the fact that these instructions were passed to Headquarters Western Command (COS Lt. Gen. N. Puri) and troops were earmarked and ready, Lt. Gen. Sommana the then Corps Commander ordered that no action would be taken. This was fully endorsed and supported by the then Army Commander Lt. Gen. S.K. Sinha and later by the COAS Gen. Krishna Rao on return, who also took it up with the prime minister. General Krishna Rao had passed instruction that the Army would not get involved with the situation in the Punjab.

On the ground at Mehta Chowk there were enough Punjab Police and CRPF units ready for action against Bhindranwala, and were waiting for orders of the Punjab government. Therefore asking the Army to get involved with the situation could only be the centre's design and intention as action by Punjab government would negate the political game being played by Giani Zail Singh for and on behalf of the central leadership. Use of Bhindranwala was possibly aimed to denigrate the established Sikh leadership in the Punjab both in the Congress and the Akalis. Was use of Army also aimed to convey to Bhindranwala that he cannot fall out of line with the central leadership and create his own political space?

The second and most critical issue is who was in-charge of the operation and who planned it. Apart from the GOI white paper issued after the operations in the Punjab, the most authentic version of events recorded from the government's point of view is probably by P.C. Alexander in his book, *Through the Corridors of Power*[2] who was the Principal Secretary to Indira Gandhi throughout the period and later. The complete series of discussions and interaction between the prime minister, her advisors and Gen. Vaidya are recorded on pages 294 to 298, attached as Appendix in this chapter. Some of the main points and issues raised and discussed are highlighted in brief to help understanding the subsequent discussions. According to P.C. Alexander, Gen. Vaidya, the COAS, was called by the PM on 25 May 1984 and she asked him to keep the Army on alert as civilian authorities may require their help to deal with the situation in the Punjab. It is also alleged that Gen. Vaidya told her that he had already ordered certain troop movements in anticipation of such a demand and that he will be able to move forces in adequate numbers into major trouble spots in Punjab at short notice. The PM also seemed to have implied that it will involve flushing out terrorists from their hideouts in *gurdwaras*, their arrests and seizure of weapons. General Vaidya was also informed that 40 *gurdwaras* had been taken over by terrorists. General Vaidya also seems to have told the PM his strategy as to how the Army planned to accomplish the mission assigned to it, which he elaborated in the narrative in great detail. The strategy was based on maximum show of force with minimum use. The PM also repeatedly told the COAS that no damage should be done to the temple building, particularly Harmandir Sahib. She also told him that a meeting was scheduled with the Akalis on 26 May but she was not hopeful that he would be informed of the outcome.

Further, Alexander has stated that in a meeting in the cabinet secretariat with Gen. Vaidya on 27 May attended by the Cabinet Secretary, R.N. Kao, Senior Security Advisor, and him, he was informed that talks with the Akalis on 26 May had failed. For his part, Gen. Vaidya told them that troops in sufficient number would be moving in and that they would be establishing themselves properly in all the trouble spots in the next four to five days to be able to start operations on 2 June. Alexander further stated that the military operations which the PM authorized on 25 May and which Gen. Vaidya discussed, were confined to siege and flushing out operations. Till that point there was no reference to any plan except an effective siege, cutting off telephone lines, electricity, water, food and inflow of men and weapons.

Alexander further states that after a quick visit to the Punjab on 27 May for consulting his senior colleagues, the Army Chief sought an urgent meeting with the PM on 29 May to inform her of certain change of plans. He (Gen. Vaidya) met the PM at her South Block office and explained the revised plan and reasons for change. R.N. Kao and Alexander were present and K.P. Singh Deo, minister of state for defence joined the meeting a little later but had to leave (as soon as Gen. Vaidya had explained his new plan) to attend to some other urgent work relating to the Punjab situation. Gen. Vaidya told the PM that he had discussed the plan of siege with Lt. Gen. K. Sundarjee and other senior officers-in-charge of operations and it was their considered view that while the plan for siege could be followed for smaller *gurdwaras*, it would not be practical to follow the plan in the case of Golden Temple. Instead he said there will be a quick seizure of the hideouts of terrorists inside the temple using minimum force. The seizure, he (Gen. Vaidya) said will entail a commando operation inside the Golden Temple, which would be conducted with such swiftness and surprise that it will not result in any damage to the temple buildings.

Alexander's narrative continues to state that the PM was taken aback by this sudden change of plan. She was perturbed by the use of force inside the temple and asked Gen. Vaidya several questions seeking clarifications. She asked what would happen if terrorists put up a stiff resistance. She also wanted to know as to how long will it take to subdue such resistance and particularly what would happen if terrorists took refuge in the inner sanctum where the *Guru Granth Sahib* was placed. She also asked as to why the previous strategy of siege and flushing out was discarded. She also asked about comparative analysis in terms of loss of lives and damage to the temple with respect to the two plans. Another question she raised was whether such action inside the temple would have any adverse effect on loyalty and discipline of Sikh *jawans* in the Army. Gen. Vaidya explained that what he was proposing was the result of very detailed discussion he has had with Gen. Sundarjee who was the person in direct command of the operations and had his (Gen. Vaidya's) full endorsement. Gen. Vaidya explained to the PM that a siege will lead to a mass upsurge and it will be difficult to prevent people from reaching the Golden Temple. Gen. Vaidya also thought that it might lead to Bhindranwala forcing the priests to issue a *hukumnama* asking people to assemble in the Golden Temple. Alexander records that Gen. Vaidya spoke with such confidence and calmness that the new plan that he proposed appeared to be the only option. On the question of adverse reaction among the Sikh *jawans*, Vaidya was quite reassuring. He declared that there need not be any apprehension on this score as Sikh *jawans* constituted a highly disciplined and loyal force and they would always accept the orders of their senior officers.

Here it will be relevant to recapitulate events in the Military Operations Directorate. Consequent to the dismissal of the Darbara Singh ministry on 6 October 1983 and with the situation continuing to worsen during the president's rule primarily due to inaction, Gen. Vaidya was briefed by me on the situation in Punjab in November in the presence of Gen. Sommana, the DGMO. We had also briefed and in a manner warned him on the likely effect the Army involvement may have on the Sikh rank and file in the Army due to sensitivity of the situation. There were clear indications of this due to the deep resentment simmering in the minds of the Sikhs due to the treatment metted out to them in Haryana during the Asiad Games. Although Gen. Vaidya did not respond to it, he was clearly told of the possibility. This was followed by the incident in February 1984, when the MO Directorate refused to relieve BSF on the border in spite of Gen. Vaidya's acceptance in principal. In March after the briefing by Lt. Gen. R.S. Dayal, MVC, Chief of Staff, Western Command and Lt. Gen. K. Gouri Shankar, GOC 11 Corps, we again asked Gen. Vaidya to speak to the prime minister but without success. Our aim was to prevent the Army's involvement and if it became unavoidable then at least become a part of the decision-making process. We in the MO directorate firmly believed that it was essentially a political problem which had developed terrorist overtones due to bad handling and inaction. The motive behind it or reasons for inaction were unknown to us. Taking the totality of the situation it is difficult to believe that Gen. Vaidya had a different perception, idea and a plan in mind and was waiting to be called by the prime minister. Moreover, it is difficult to believe that he had plans ready for the same. To the best of my knowledge Gen. Vaidya was never taken into confidence and the prime minister and few of her confidants dealt directly with Lt. Gen. Sundarjee. I have also learnt from good authority that Lt. Gen. Sundarjee and Dayal were seen coming out of the prime minister's office and Gen. Vaidya was nowhere near the scene. The principal staff office at Headquarter Western Command dealing with operations has further confirmed that Gen. Vaidya did not visit Headquarter Western Command or meet Gen. Sundarjee between 27 and 29 May, as P.C. Alexander purports in his book on page 296. At best he was probably informed that Gen. Sundarjee has been entrusted with the task. Moreover, MO Directorate does not plan operations and there were no plans either. The MO Directorate issues operational instruction tasking commands and formations and it is the commands and formations concerned who make operational plans. That is why when the Army was asked to act, the MO Directorate asked for a government directive which was reluctantly issued by the MOD and based on it Operational Instruction was issued belatedly to Headquarter Western Command. Taking in the totality of the situation it is difficult to believe that the prime minister and her advisors realized the gravity of the situation in the Punjab only on 25 May 1984 and thought of interacting with the army that late unless it was by design.

As I have stated earlier, the date and time selected for the operations showed a total lack of understanding and sensitivity to the situation. We in the MO Directorate were fully conscious of it. Moreover, the pretext that Akalis had given a call for stoppage of grain movement, refused to pay taxes and threatened to converge onto Amritsar were the government's apprehensions, which have been attributed to Gen. Vaidya inappropriately. The very fact that operations against all *gurdwaras* in Punjab were simultaneous would have prevented any large scale move towards Amritsar.

As per Alexander, Gen. Vaidya explained the plans most eloquently and that when Gen. Vaidya was specially asked by the prime minister of the likely adverse effect the operations in the Golden Temple would have on the loyalty and discipline of the Sikh *jawans*, Gen. Vaidya was most reassuring and declared that there should be no apprehension on this score. This appears to be a bit naïve as he had been informed of such a likelihood. It was entirely in keeping with the flamboyant disposition of Lt. Gen. Sundarjee, who had none or very little experience of handling live situations. Compared to him, Gen. Vaidya had ample battle and handling live situations experience in an insurgency environment in Nagaland as a brigade commander and later as the Eastern Army Commander. General Vaidya's only fault probably was that he was not proactive and accepted situations as they arose. In view of the above it will be logical to conclude that Gen. Vaidya was made a fall guy to cover up government and Sundarjee's failures, who was not at all mentioned in Alexander's narrative of events. What further belies the government version is the manner in which the operations were planned. This is amply brought out in Lt. Gen. K.S. Brar's book *Operation Blue Star: The True Story* that tanks, APCs were planned for as well as guns in direct firing role, which belies the government's claim of maximum force but minimum use. The sad part of all this is that in spite of maximum damage we had very heavy casualties (Army personnel killed—4 officers, 4 JCOs, 75 OR (total 83), wounded 13 officers, 16 JCOs and 219 OR (total 248); Terrorists killed 492 (30 women and 5 children), wounded 86 (7 women, 4 children) apprehended 592.

A few questions remain unanswered. Why was the GOC of the Infantry Division in Amritsar who was fully in the picture not tasked for the job? Is it purely personality? Which was always Gen. Sundarjee's weakness? The delay in dealing with the situation remains unexplained, was it due to ulterior motives? What was the political aim? Was destruction of Bhindranwala by design or incidental?

Assassination of Mrs. Indira Gandhi

The superficial calm was shattered by the shooting of Mrs. Indira Gandhi by her Sikh police guards on 31 October 1984. I was in the operations room going through the morning first reports and daily briefing of happenings in the country, when the duty officer told me that R.K. Dhawan from the prime minister's residence was on the line and wanted to speak to a senior officer. I picked up the telephone and gave my name and appointment, he just said, the prime minister has been shot. On my enquiry as to how badly, he said very badly, please inform the Chief, it is only for information. I informed the Chief and asked him if anything needs to be done, he said, he will let me know. I told him that I will check the availability of troops in Delhi, just in case of any requirement. I put the duty officer to monitor the TV and Radio and let me know any news about the prime minister. By midday the news of Mrs. Gandhi's death was announced, followed by news of sporadic firings and riots. It was only towards the evening that the anti-Sikh nature of the riots became apparent. One JCO and a few Sikh other ranks living in civil areas like Paharganj came to me expressing their concern about the safety of their families. I ordered the duty officer to organize an escort from the Delhi Area and evacuate the families to the Army Headquarters Camp. The details of the Delhi anti-Sikh riots and other places are well known and recorded in detail by the lawyers' body and others. I have also recorded my findings in some details in my book, *The Threat From Within*[3] in the chapter on Punjab. Here I only wish to record some of my major observations. These riots were not entirely a result of spontaneous anger after Mrs. Gandhi's assassination, these were to a large extent instigated and had the connivance and support of the pseudo-loyalists in the Congress party. What is worse is that the Delhi state authorities and police became a party to it not only due to inaction alone but by active participation in a large number of cases.

As the only infantry brigade located in Delhi was away in the Punjab for their operational alert rehearsals, I decided to move one brigade from Alwar and one from Meerut to Delhi Cantt and remain available there till further orders. The brigade from Meerut had two Sikh battalions and the GOC Bulbul Brar was reluctant to send them to Delhi. I told him these are our troops and I trust them fully, and the brigade moved to Delhi as ordered. When Maj. Gen. Jamwal, the then GOC of Delhi Area, heard about the move of Sikh troops to Delhi, he expressed his reservations on employing them. I told him the same thing as I had told Maj. Gen. Brar. What was worse was that Gen. Vaidya went to the extent of admonishing me. I told him that I had full faith in them and it was a deliberate decision on my part. I reasoned with him that employment of Sikh troops will have good effect both within the Army and amongst the Sikh community and at the same time it will have a salutary effect on the trouble makers. I told him that restoring faith and trust with the Sikhs was important at this juncture as it was not a spontaneous reaction to Mrs. Gandhi's assassination but a contrived vendetta. Finally, I told him that if GOC Delhi Area is reluctant to employ Sikh troops, make me the GOC and I will employ them and there will be no problems. I believe till today I was right but my plea fell on deaf ears. We missed a very fine opportunity to heal wounds. Unfortunately, the only Sikh unit we used was to look after the refugee camp in Delhi Cantt, which had just the adverse effect. How stupid and insensitive we can be. My conviction proved right and I did the same thing later in my Corps as I had said.

The Delhi riots further deepened the suspicion. Authorities were more fearful and indulged in justifying the happenings. The question that till to day remains unanswered is why the Army was not called out till more than 96 hours after the assassination. While the Delhi state kept on giving the news of riots escalating but no requisition for the Army was given, though we had adequate number of columns ready by the afternoon of 31 October. The GOC even asked us for certain precautionary moves, which we overruled without receiving the requisition. General Vaidya and Lt. Gen. Sundarjee went along with the government's policy of suspicion and keeping the Sikh officers away from Punjab and northern India. Most fresh postings of Sikh officers were to Eastern and Southern Command and mutinied Sikh units were mixed with companies of other group units in spite of opposition of the colonels of the regiments. Both decisions had to be reversed as Sikh officers after completion of their tenures in Eastern and Southern commands returned to the north and similarly the decision of mixing Sikh units had to be reversed as it created serious management and command problems.

No discussion of the Punjab situation can be complete without a mention of the Bhindranwala phenomenon. Most authors and other people have mentioned it primarily in the context of Punjab politics, which to my mind is a very narrow and restricted view compared to its overall impact. It needs to be examined in its totality of its psychological, religious, political and social dimensions. It was fascinating to see how this moderately educated rustic with little or no political exposure could decimate the established Sikh leadership and manipulate public opinion and power structure to his advantage.[4] Even retired senior bureaucrats, army officers and police officers fell prey to his spell as the established polity of all parties refused them public space due to their own insecurity. Our failure to recognize such phenomenon and its exploitation for narrow political gains, resulted in credibility gaps, which was the worst casualty in Punjab.

Sometime towards the end of 1984, we received a proposal for raising of a special task force to deal with situations of insurgency, terrorism and hijacking. The paper was authored by R.T. Nagrani, a police officer in the cabinet secretariat. He had given the paper to Gen. Vaidya, who had passed it on to us. We examined the paper and gave our comments to say that such a force will be duplicating the roles performed by other para-military forces and would be incapable of handling problems of insurgency and terrorism like the one in Punjab on its own. Our recommendations were accepted by the MOD, who sent it to finance ministry before forwarding it to MHA and to the cabinet secretariat. The comments of the finance secretary P.K. Kaul who had been the defence secretary earlier not only agreed with our recommendations but reinforced them further by adding, 'Escalation in the number and type of forces is no panacea for efficiency'. We thought the proposal had died a natural death. Some time later the same person as cabinet secretary, when told by R.T. Nagrani that this will be a force under him, not only revived the proposal but also had it approved by the cabinet. The force later come to be known as NSG and became primarily a VIP protection force. In spite of the fact that its prime cutting edge component is manned entirely by the Army it remains under police control. Their performance during terrorist attacks in Bombay in November 2008 was far from professional and drove home the point that even the best of troops can perform well only under the right leadership. To make matters worse, there is enlargement of the force to cover up lapses in overall policy thinking. Escalation in force levels without due thought and care only helps in spreading inefficiency.

NOTES

1. Lt. Gen. M.L. Chibber, PVSM, AVSM (Retd.), 'Siachen: The Untold Story (A Personal Account)', *Indian Defence Review*, January 1990.
2. P.C. Alexander, *Through the Corridors of Power: An Insider's Story*, Harper Collins, New Delhi, 2004, pp. 294-8.
3. V.K. Nayar, *Threat from Within*, Lancer Publishers, New Delhi, 1992, p. 35.
4. Ibid., p. 23.

APPENDIX A

EXTRACT FROM *THROUGH THE CORRIDORS OF POWER*

P.C. ALEXANDER

On 25 May to be precise, that Indira Gandhi finally made up her mind to summon the Army. She sent for Gen. A.S. Vaidya, the Chief of Army Staff, and asked him to keep the Army on alert as the civilian authorities may require its help to deal with the situation in Punjab. General Vaidya told her that he had already ordered certain troop movements in anticipation of such a demand and that he would be able to move the forces in adequate numbers into the major trouble spots in Punjab at short notice. The prime minister specified to Gen. Vaidya that the top priorities of the Army would be to effectively curb terrorism and violence, provide security to the people and restore normalcy in Punjab. These tasks involved flushing out the terrorists from their hideouts in certain Gurdwaras, their arrest and the seizure of their weapons. Her expectation was that the very presence of the Army and the demonstration of its strength through flag marches would, by themselves, act as deterrents. Consequently, she felt that there would not be any need for use of excess force by the Army.

Nearly forty Gurdwaras in different places in Punjab had been taken over by the extremists. These Gurdwaras were reported to be having adequate stocks of arms and ammunition as well as food and water to enable the militants to offer long-drawn-out resistance if any attempt was made to flush them out. When General Vaidya met the prime minister on 25 May, he explained to her his strategy as to how the Army planned to accomplish the mission assigned to it. He pointed out that he would move a sufficient number of troops into Punjab to deal quickly with the situation in different places simultaneously. The Gurdwaras that had been seized by the extremists would be surrounded by the troops who would prevent movement of water, food, weapons and men into these places and force them to surrender. He said that a similar siege operation would be mounted in the Golden Temple using a larger number of troops. According to this strategy, the troops would fan out to all the trouble spots in the state and thus would be able to prevent movement of troublemakers towards Amritsar, which would be the main scene of the flushing out operations. The prime minister was assured by Vaidya that there would be a maximum *show* of force, but minimum *use* of it. She repeatedly told the general that in any operation *no damage should be done to the temple buildings and particularly to the Harmandir Sahib*. She also told him about the meeting with the Akali leaders, which had been scheduled for 26 May. Although she was not very optimistic about the outcome, she, nevertheless, brought to his notice that if there was a favourable response from the Akalis at the talks, he would be immediately informed about it. Otherwise, she instructed him that he should proceed with all the necessary arrangements to restore order and peace on the lines discussed between them. As stated earlier, the talks with the Akalis ended in total failure.

On 27 May at 10.30 a.m. the cabinet secretary, senior security adviser, R.N. Kao, and I held a meeting with Vaidya at the Cabinet Secretariat to discuss the follow-up of the decisions conveyed to the general and the details of the Army operation. We informed Vaidya that the talks with the Akalis on 26 May had failed. For his part, Vaidya told us that the soldiers would be moving in, in sufficient numbers, and that they would establish themselves properly in all the trouble spots over the next four or five days in order to be able to start operations on 2 June.

We decided, in consultation with Punjab Governor B.D. Pande, the further measures that needed to be taken by his administration.

I would like to state here categorically that the military operations, which the prime minister authorized on 25 May 1984 and which Vaidya discussed with us on 27 May, were confined to the *siege and flushing out operations* in the identified gurdwaras in different places and in the Golden Temple at Amritsar. Till that point of time, there was no reference to any plan except for an effective siege of the buildings involving cutting off telephones, electricity, water, food and inflow of men and weapons. However, there were major and sudden changes in the plan that had been approved by the prime minister on 25 May and discussed with us in considerable detail by Vaidya on 27 May. Vaidya, after a quick visit to Punjab and after consultations with his senior colleagues in the Army, sought an urgent meeting with the prime minister on 29 May to inform her of some important changes in the plan. He met Indira Gandhi at her South Block office on 29 May and explained to her the revised plan and the reasons for the change. R.N. Kao and I were present at this meeting. K.P. Singh Deo, Minister of State for Defence, joined the meeting a little later but had to soon leave (as soon as Vaidya had explained his new plan) to attend to some other urgent work relating to the Punjab situation.

Vaidya told the PM that he had discussed the plan of the siege with Lt. Gen. K. Sundarjee and other senior officers directly in- charge of the operations and it was now their considered view that while the plan of siege could be followed in respect of all smaller gurdwaras then under the control of the extremists, it would not be practical to follow this plan in the case of the Golden Temple. Instead, he said, there would be a quick seizure of the hideouts of the terrorists inside the temple using minimum force. This seizure, he said, would entail a commando operation inside the Golden Temple, which would be conducted with such swiftness and surprise that it would *not result in any damage* to the temple buildings.

Needless to say, the prime minister was taken aback by this sudden change of plan. She was quite perturbed at the suggestion of the use of force *inside* the temple and asked Vaidya several questions seeking clarification. She enquired as to what would happen if the terrorists put up *stiff* resistance? She also wanted to know how long it would take to subdue such resistance and particularly as to what would happen if the terrorists took refuge in the inner sanctum where the *Guru Granth Sahib* was placed. She asked him why the previous strategy of siege and flushing out was being discarded so soon (after all, Vaidya had outlined it only on 25 May). She also sought details about the comparative analyses in terms of loss of life and damage to the temple with respect to the two plans. Another question she raised was whether such an action inside the temple would have any adverse effects on the loyalty and discipline of the Sikh jawans in the Indian Army.

Vaidya explained that what he was now proposing was the result of very detailed discussions he had had with Sundarjee, who was the person in direct command of the operations and had his full endorsement. He pointed out that a siege could lead to a mass upsurge among the Sikhs in the countryside and mobs might start moving towards Amritsar, galvanized by religious frenzy. In such an eventuality, the Army may have to open fire in several places in the state to prevent such mobs from reaching the vicinity of the Golden Temple. Even if the mobs from outside Amritsar could be stopped, he felt serious problems would be faced in preventing the frenzied mobs within Amritsar from entering the temple or attacking the Army from behind. He also thought that Bhindranwale may force the priests in the temple to issue *hukumnama* (diktat) asking the people to assemble in the Golden Temple in large numbers. If that happened, he observed that it would be difficult to distinguish between the troublemakers and ordinary people and the siege may become ineffective. Vaidya affirmed that, after weighing the pros and cons of the two options, he, without any hesitation, would agree with his senior colleagues that no time should be lost by going in for a siege; instead the Army ought to make a quick entry into the temple and take the terrorists by surprise.

On the question of adverse reaction among the Sikh jawans, Vaidya was quite reassuring. He declared that there need not be any apprehension on this score as the Sikh jawans constituted a highly disciplined and loyal force and they would always accept the orders of their senior officers.

He also clarified that the extremists holed up inside the Golden Temple would be given adequate time to consider the option of surrender without resistance and there was every possibility of their accepting that option when they realized the odds against them.

Vaidya spoke with such confidence and calmness that the new plan he was proposing appeared to be virtually the only option open to the Army. He said that the other option was fraught with dangerous consequences and hundreds of innocent people may fall victim to firing along the roads leading to Amritsar and in the vicinity of the Golden Temple. He noted that Army casualties could also be heavy as the siege may last several days in view of the reaction to be expected from the frenzied mobs. On the other hand, he emphasized that the new plan would be executed so quickly that everything would be over by the time the people came to realize what was happening. On the question of damage to the temple, Vaidya asserted that *strict instructions* would be given to the Army to ensure that no damage was caused to the temple buildings under any circumstances.

The convincing manner in which Vaidya explained the pros and cons of the two plans left the prime minister with no other option but to ask him to go ahead with the plan proposed by him. On 29 May, when Vaidya was explaining to the prime minister so eloquently and with so much confidence about the soundness of his new plan of operation, he himself could never have anticipated that events would take the turn they eventually did.

After Vaidya left the room, the prime minister told Kao and me that she was accepting the general's advice since he was, after all, the person responsible for delivering the goods. She added that during the Bangladesh war in 1971, she never interfered with the decisions of those in command of the field operations. She used to discuss with the senior generals the broad objectives and apprise them of the important political considerations to be kept in view, but would leave the decision on the specifics of the operation entirely to them. In other words, she respected the professional judgement of the generals.

Events now started moving very swiftly. All paramilitary and armed police forces stationed in Punjab and the union territory of Chandigarh were placed under the command of the Army. Chandigarh itself was placed under the charge of the governor of Punjab.

On 1 June 1984, some extremists fired upon a BSF contingent from inside the Golden Temple; the contingent promptly returned the fire. The firing continued intermittently during the afternoon and resulted in seven persons inside the temple and three outside losing their lives and sixteen persons inside and nine outside being severely injured. This 'test firing' looked like a probing on the part of the extremists to ascertain the reaction of the armed forces stationed outside the temple.

Indira Gandhi addressed the people over national television and radio on the night of 2 June, just a few hours before the new agitation called by the Akalis was to start. In her address, she recapitulated the various concessions offered by the government to accommodate the Akalis' demands. Even at that last minute, she offered to sit around a table to find a solution through discussions. Addressing her 'Sikh brother and sisters', she reminded them how Sikhism was born as a faith to bring together people of different religions and how the great Gurus taught love and tolerance. 'Let not a minuscule minority among Sikhs', she declared, 'be allowed to trample underfoot civilized norms for which Sikhism is well known and to tarnish the image of a brave and patriotic community.' She concluded by making an impassioned appeal: 'Even at this late hour, I appeal to the Akali Dal leaders to call off their threatened agitation and accept the framework of the peaceful settlement we have offered. Let us join together to heal wounds. The best memorial to those who have lost their lives is to restore normalcy and harmony in the Punjab which they loved and served. To all sections of Punjabis I appeal: *'Don't shed blood, shed hatred*.'

As anticipated, there was no response either from the Akali leaders or the militants to this appeal. The government announced on the night of 2 June that the Army had been called in to support the civil authorities. Lt. Gen. Ranjit Singh Dayal, a Sikh himself, was appointed as adviser (security) to the governor of Punjab and Maj. Gen. Kuldeep Singh Brar, another Sikh officer, was placed in direct control of the operations inside the Golden Temple.

Some of the Akali supporters close to Dayal's family tried to persuade him to turn down the assignment. He was one of the seniormost among the Sikh officers in the Army hierarchy at that time and some of his friends thought that if he refused the assignment and resigned on religious grounds, this move would be viewed as a great victory for the Sikh cause and might encourage some other Sikh officers also to follow suit, thereby causing considerable embarrassment to the government not to mention the resulting problems. But Dayal was a good soldier and a patriot. He informed his friends that he would not be true to his profession, his country and his religion if he shirked his duty. As subsequent events showed, Dayal and scores of other brave and patriotic Sikh officers and jawans proved their commitment to their country and their profession by performing the duties assigned to them with exemplary courage and loyalty.

CHAPTER 7

Vajra to Chandimandir

I received my posting on promotion to the Corps in Jalandhar and was ordered to report by 25 July 1985. The posting like all my earlier command postings helped me to maintain my record of not serving under a known superior. I always found it to be challenging but rewarding as you could never take anything for granted and were judged on merit and performance. Before leaving the MO Directorate, I was told by the COAS Gen. Vaidya that I was going to the Corps in Jalandhar because I opposed Operation Blue Star, as such placed best to deal with its aftermath. Secondly the other two officers due for posting to a Corps were already lieutenant generals and had requested they not be placed under Lt. Gen. H.K. Kaul the then Army Commander. My opposition to Operation Blue Star according to my friends was a sound professional and moral stand but was looked upon by the Army hierarchy as being obstinate and anti-government. It is a long story and does not merit elaboration here. Suffice to say that the issue will come up whenever the internal security situation in Punjab is discussed. The Rajiv-Longowal accord had just been signed on 24 July, a day before I took over.

On taking over the Corps I was clear that my main task was to train the Corps and brings it up to a state of best operational readiness. As far as the internal security situation was concerned, the main task was to ensure Army's non-involvement and bring about a change in its orientation to it. A natural corollary to it was to re-establish our credibility and close relationship with the public in Punjab, which had always been our greatest moral strength and support in wars against Pakistan. It was also important as a large segment of the Army belonged to Punjab. Events were to prove it was easier said than done. During my reconnaissance and visits to the border areas, I sensed a definite break in our relationship with the people and felt the vital necessity of cementing it. While I was clear of the requirement and was confident of achieving it, the problem was where to start. The opportunity came in a very sad and painful manner and to the great suffering of the people of Punjab. There were flash floods just a week or ten days after I took over the Corps. The entire area of Gurdaspur, Amritsar, Ferozepur and Kapurthala districts was badly affected. Realizing the great havoc caused and the resultant suffering of the people, I suggested and got permission from the then Army Commander Lt. Gen. H. Kaul, to help and share the sufferings of the people even before being asked to help formally by the state administration. He was totally in the spirit of it and gave us all the help. I asked my formation commanders to go all out in their areas of responsibility and utilize all their resources, and whatever more was required would be provided, but the task was to be done with sincerity and without any ulterior motive. We put in over 30 medical teams with large stocks of medicines, a vast number of rescue teams and reached everywhere with food and shelter and constructed alternative routes over bridges and swamped areas. After three days when the civil administration could reach them with our help, we quietly withdrew except for medical help and efforts to re-establish the communications. We lost two brave sappers by drowning during these rescue operations. Commanders and men were without food for two days along with the villagers and whatever came was first given to the suffering public. I visited most of the areas and was touched by the feeling of oneness between our men and the people. The ice had been broken and we had made a good start to re-establish mutual trust.

During the flash floods due to flooding of the Kali (Black) and Safed (White) Bein (rivulets), the entire Corps Headquarters complex and parts of the cantonment got totally flooded. Seeing the rising water I visited the Corps Headquarters and ordered its evacuation to the Corps Central School and we functioned from there for over a month. During my visit to the flooded areas of the Jalandhar Cantonment apart from evacuating people, equipment and stores, it helped us to redraw the drainage plans of the cantonment. The COS of Western Command visited us and I demanded extra allocation for the repair and maintenance of affected areas and for relaying the drainage system. I got the QMG late Lt. Gen. Rajinder Singh to visit us and a substantial additional allocation from him.

ASSASSINATION OF SANT LONGOWAL AND ITS AFTERMATH

Sant Longowal's assassination on 20 August 1985 was a major setback to the accord and the ongoing process for resolution of the Punjab problem. There was panic reaction by the centre and it affected the state administration adversely. There was fear and apprehension that it would result in the breakdown of law and order, encourage extremists and instigate communal violence. It was a testing time for Punjab and its people. I knew that it would be a test for the Army as well and would we display the resilience and forethought to protect what the accord had achieved and continue to retrieve lost ground and consolidate our gains. I was convinced that our best hope lay in the accord and political process as a result of it. From the Army's point of view a total non-involvement in Punjab was important, as we were a symbol of the past happenings. Any involvement of the Army would affect our credibility, ethos and most importantly put us once again on a confrontation course with the public. I was determined not to give in on what I believed in and staked everything on it. The authorities had not understood the real implications of the shooting of Sant Longowal. It was an extremist act to vitiate the emerging environment of peace, re-establish their position and invite harsh reaction by eliminating the symbol of sanity and more important what he represented. People who have not been exposed to similar live situations do not understand it and fall prey to the extremist design. It requires mental resilience and clear vision not to lose sight of the aim and accept such reverses and continue to work towards the goal. I knew, we could not undo what had been done. I kept my counsel and fingers crossed.

The bombshell came just a few hours later. I was leaving for a visit to Ferozepur, when I was shown a log message from Army Headquarters by the BGS asking all formations in Punjab to deploy and indulge in activities similar to Operation Blue Star. I was struck by both the order for deployment and its nuance. I knew the extent of panic prevailing at various echelons of the government, including the Army. I cancelled my visit to Ferozepur and spoke to the Army Commander and asked him if he had seen the log message. He had not seen it. I quickly briefed him of its contents and told him that I was not deploying, as it was a thoughtless order. I also told him that I was sending a detailed log message giving my views, I was categorical and firm in expressing my views. After the receipt of my log, the Army Commander asked me to come to Chandimandir to discuss the issue. In the meantime, in a few areas in Punjab, not under my Corps, the Army had started deploying. During the meeting, the other formation commanders gave what they thought was the situation and that the Army deployment was wise, and they also wanted the provisions of various special powers/acts to be invoked. The Army Commander asked me for my views and as I had already told him I was totally opposed to it. I gave him my assessment of the implication of Sant Longowal's shooting, the nature of terrorist activities and finally and most important of all that any undue steps would negate the accord and process of normalization. The Army Commander then gave his decision that we should not precipitate the situation and issued instructions that there would be no deployment till he has had a word with Delhi. This timely decision by the Army Commander Lt. Gen. Kaul saved the situation and troops in the other Corps who were in the process of deployment were quietly withdrawn. Later in a separate discussion with me in his office, the Army Commander informed me that he has had a talk with the Governor, Arjun Singh, and the state government had also received similar orders. The Army Commander told me that he was meeting the governor that evening and suggested that I should also meet and discuss the situation with the governor during his visit to Amritsar the next day. He promised to go by my views as I was the most affected Corps Commander.

The governor was holding a meeting with the administrative and police officers of districts north of the Sutlej River along with his advisors at Amritsar. I met him the next day at Amritsar, I took the GOC in Amritsar Maj. Gen. A.K. Dewan (Cheeky) with me. The governor's meeting with the officials took place at the airport lounge and we got involved with it by default as when we arrived it was still on. There was panic visible all around, each and everyone of them wanted a large number of additional paramilitary companies and wanted the Army to be deployed. At the end the governor asked for my views. I told him that I had not come to attend the meeting but would discuss the situation with him separately in private. In the discussion between the two of us, I told him that I had been authorized by the Army Commander to take a decision. I gave him my assessment and told him that the accord had achieved a lot and that he had a big part in bringing it about. It would be wrong to undo it and all of us would be blamed for it. The situation was tense but considering the greater national interest, it should be tackled by the police and paramilitary forces. The Army was a symbol of all that went wrong in Operation Blue Star and we should avoid displaying it again so soon. He was most concerned on two counts, one that Delhi had ordered it and secondly everyone in the state was advising him that the Army should be deployed before things got out of hand. I assured him that as the person most concerned, he had my word of honour that before things got out of hand we would be there to help but based on our assessment and not on that of that state administration. As far as Delhi was concerned we should tell them to leave the decision to him and the Army Commander who knew the situation in Punjab the best. He agreed to my proposals and to reassure him, I met him again in Ferozepur along with my GOC Maj. Gen. D.S.R. Sahni (Dewan Sahni) there.

I informed the Army Commander of the discussion with the governor and he assured me that he would take it up with Delhi and put his foot down. I still kept my fingers crossed and kept in touch with the state administration to give them heart and kept the Command Headquarters informed. I also ordered that no troops be moved or deployed in aid to civil authorities without my personal permission. I flew to Amritsar, Gurdaspur, Ludhiana, Ferozepur and other sensitive areas and met the local authorities. As a precautionary measure, we positioned a few troops in suitable camping grounds near sensitive areas, on the pretext of training. They were to be visible but remain uninvolved. Each of the company commanders deployed for the task was briefed by the formation commander in person. We thus stalled our involvement much to the annoyance of Army Headquarters and the central government. I was rung up by a number of people in higher echelons in Delhi both from within the Army and people who had taken the decision. I was also threatened that if things went wrong I would be held responsible and pay for it. However, I told them that the Army could only be deployed in Punjab after removing me.

We thought that we had got over the problem and had started to concentrate on other things, when I got a call from the Army Commander summoning me to the Command Headquarters at Chandimandir. On reaching there, he told me that he had met the governor the previous evening and the government had given a requisition for the Army to clear the Mand Area, as there had been a number of killings in that area by the terrorists over the last few days. He also told me that the governor had taken us on our word that we would come to their aid before the situation gets out of hand. During the discussion I told him that this was a gimmick to get the Army involved but to maintain our credibility we would handle it. I was also convinced that some people in the state were putting pressure on the governor by painting a grim picture. The Army Commander approved the plan I gave him. I also told him we should insist on two conditions for accepting the request, one that there would be no formal requisition for Army aid and secondly, the police would impose curfew, establish surveillance on villages astride the river and deal with the public and terrorists there. He agreed to it but the police showed reluctance and said that they did not have the 18 odd companies required for it. We informed the governor that unless this was done the deal was off, the same was also conveyed through the police channels. It had the desired effect. I briefed Dewan and Sahni, the two GOCs involved and the plans were put into action after 72 hours. We inducted 10,000 troops with BAUTS (army boats) and three Engineer Regiments were deployed. Troops entered the Mand after last light in their designated areas and cleared it by first light. We found only some *bhattis* (distilling plants), and people indulging in illicit distillation. The police caught some extremists in the villages around Mand. The state administration wanted us to stay on, but we refused point blank. We had achieved our task, established our credibility with the state and did not get involved. The papers gave good coverage to this operation supposedly carried out by police and PMF and a number of police officers were decorated. There was no mention of the Army. When Delhi came to know of it, they were upset that we did not get recognition and credit for the work done. They missed the point that we wanted to give confidence to the state administration to handle the situation and not get involved.

ELECTIONS AND AKALI FAILURE

This was followed by elections in Punjab in 1985. We firmly told everyone that we would not get involved. There were a lot of pressures and although we never got involved, we kept the environment secure by our invisible presence. During elections, the prime minister visited Punjab, and both the central and state governments wanted, for security reasons, that his public meetings should be held in the Cantonments. I flatly refused and said the Army is apolitical and in the disturbed environment of Punjab, we derive our strength from our credibility. There was complete understanding between the Command Headquarters and me and I was given a free hand to take on people concerned on these issues. All meetings were held in civil areas. We evolved plans for quick reaction and knew minute to minute as to what was happening at these meetings but were nowhere near them. Even the Army Commander was surprised as to how I was giving more or less a running commentary of where and what the prime minister was doing during his tour of Punjab. He was very inquisitive to know as to how I managed it. I told him that I would explain to him when we meet next. I explained to him when we met after a week or so, it was a simple methodology based on experience. I would not divulge more as I wanted to protect the identity of some officers who worked with me and some may be putting it to use even now.

The Akalis were helped to coin a victory and in spite of pretences Congress made sure that they (Akalis) won as a measure of political appeasement not only to them but to the Sikhs at large. The Akalis won 73 of the 117 seats and formed the government under Surjit Singh Barnala. I met Barnala for the first time during a function at the PAP Headquarters in Jalandhar soon after he took over. I was sitting with him when the then DIG of the range

Bhullar came and informed him that a fight had ensued between *Jathedars* Santa Singh and Pritam Singh for control of a certain Dera. Bhullar also told the chief minister that Pritam Singh is our man (Akalis) and Santa theirs (Congress), thereby implying action against Santa Singh. Barnala continued to stroke his beard but said nothing. I thought the right course would have been to arrest both and after a while I told the chief minister the same. I qualified it by saying that if you arrest both then it will send the right message that you mean business as the vision of *jathedars* is limited to control of *gurdwaras* and *deras*. I later learnt that Santa Singh alone was arrested. I even then felt an inkling that in spite of a clear mandate, he lacked the courage and will to govern and was likely to succumb to petty pressures of Akalis, *jathedars* and *granthis*. The later events proved me correct.

Barnala became a victim of Akali infighting and failed. The extremists found the environment conducive to revive militancy. The Mathew and Venkataramiah commissions failed to effect transfer of Chandigarh to Punjab and Abohar and Fazilka to Haryana. Consequent to the formation of the Panthic committee and declaration of Khalistan from the Golden Temple complex in April 1986, police entered the Golden Temple complex to clear the precincts, 300 extremists were arrested. The year was also marked by killing of 15 passengers in a bus near Muktsar, killing of Gen. A.S. Vaidya and an attempt on the life of new DGP Julio Francis Ribeiro. After an ineffective rule of 20 months, the Barnala government was dismissed and president's rule was re-imposed on 11 May 1987.

RE-ESTABLISHING TRUST

During 1986 and 1987, we were deployed on the border and the BSF was placed under us. To function effectively, some of the commanders wanted Acts giving special power to the Army to be invoked. I categorically told them that it would not happen and we should act within the existing laws and do nothing to antagonize the people in the border areas. We were to use our presence to stop trans-border movement with minimum disruption to public life. The aim of our presence was to further activate the BSF, police and local administration, reassure them with our presence and not get involved. The *modus operandi* for it was worked out which gave fruitful results and it had a healthy fallout. The Army's presence even in normal times is irksome and we were so conscious of it that we did not let the people feel it and never caused any hardship to them. It had a very good effect and we brought the Army back into the hearts of the people. For this, credit goes to our men, commanders under me and superiors in Punjab at that time. When one of the officers of the Higher Command Course in 1986 during their visit to the corps asked me as to what would be the response of the people in Punjab, particularly the Sikhs, if we were to go to war with Pakistan. I told him that in my area, I was confident that the response would be better than in 1971 and I planned on the same. All of us in Punjab felt this way, it was only the people outside, even in the Army, who still didn't understand it. If this trust gets eroded, it would be primarily due to lack of faith and we should not let that happen. There is a distinct tendency amongst people to feel insecure because they have never been involved in live situations.

On taking over the Corps in Jalandhar, I discreetly inquired whether we had a guard from a Sikh unit at the Corps Commander's residence during Operation Blue Star or afterwards. I learnt it was not so. I ordered the very next guard from a Sikh battalion which had mutinied in J&K during Operation Blue Star. There was opposition to it but I insisted. I fully trusted them and we were able to resolve their problems without causing any aberrations. I always had a Sikh guard in their unit's turn when due as Corps Commander and Army Commander. I never moved with escort in Punjab and encouraged people to do the same. We are obsessed with security, which is entirely different from legitimate precautions only when a particular situation demands. I firmly maintained that trust begets trust, and my experience in Mizoram, Nagaland, Manipur and Punjab fully justified this conviction.

TRUTH IS BITTER BUT IT PREVAILS

My friends tell me that I have an unerring instinct for things and to feel the underlying truth. They essentially mention this in respect of my time in the division in Manipur and Nagaland and during some of the episodes during my tenure with the MO Directorate. I never felt that such a situation would arise during my stay at Jalandhar. Before I left the MO Directorate, Headquarters Eastern Command had ordered an in-depth study of insurgency in the north-east. By that time a Corps had come into existence and they were ordered to conduct it. I was a special invitee as Headquarters Eastern Command and the COAS felt that I had an in-depth knowledge and could contribute to it. The event scheduled was to take place after I had moved to the Corps. Some wise person got the idea as to why not discuss Punjab also and the scope of the meeting at Calcutta was enlarged to include it. Headquarters Western Command naturally asked my Corps to prepare the paper. I asked my BGS Virender Oberoi to prepare the paper as they had been involved in the situation during Operation Blue Star. After a few days the paper was put up to me. When I read it I found it was nothing but a justification of what had happened and not a critical analysis. I told the BGS that I will write it myself. I wrote the paper with an analysis of what the situation was and how the situation should have been handled. The main thrust was that a badly handled political situation was converted into a law and order one and its aftermath was handed over to the Army. The problem had political, religious, fundamentalist and human content and the challenge was to create a secure environment by the activation of the civil administration, police forces and giving support and heart to moderate political leadership and isolating the fundamentalists under Bhindranwala were the key issues. The problem required a politico-social approach with police and other law enforcing agencies playing a key role. The involvement of the Army was strictly to be confined to the norms of aid to civil power and police and paramilitary forces had the major role. It was at the most a politico-military operation, with political part being dominant. The aim was to diffuse the situation and bring the moderates to the forefront. Time was not a factor, it should have been a slow and deliberate effort with minimum Army presence and the entire Punjab should have been the area and not only the militants in the Golden Temple or elsewhere. The Army Commander agreed with my approach, the aim was to learn for the future in case we got involved in such a situation again.

I did the presentation at Calcutta and while it was widely appreciated, the COAS Gen. Vaidya, VCOAS, Lt. Gen. Sundarjee and some others who thought it was a criticism of their actions were very unhappy. I became a *persona non grata* with them. Some went to the extent of saying that my future was sealed and efforts were made by some loyalists to get a copy of my presentation to tell the government of my disloyalty. This did not deter me from my approach, which I have outlined in the above narrative on Punjab, the results were for everyone to see.

OPERATIONAL PREPAREDNESS

Operationally I found that for no fault of the commanders and troops, there was total disorientation due to preoccupation with Operation Blue Star and by and large people were still in an internal security frame of mind. This struck me during my visit to the first operational alert in one of the formations. People just moved around in their areas, carried out routine drills of occupation of defences and stand to, no movement of tanks, guns and reserves was practised and neither contingencies were discussed or rehearsed. I thought it was a total waste of time. Similarly, I found that the operation instruction was outdated and did not meet the present or future operational requirements and I decided to start with the commanders *ab initio*.

We started with an intelligence assessment of the enemy to include its intention, capability and likely battle scenarios. I held this discussion for three days with all the commanders. This was followed by ground reconnaissance down to battalion commanders to familiarize and examine our deployments; this was done over a couple of weeks, which was followed by a war game at the corps level. Based on these discussions, the current deployments were examined and modified. This was followed by the review of different contingencies and tasking of reserves at divisional and corps levels. Once this basic framework was evolved then movement and administrative plans including dumping to support these were formulated. This framework was ready at all levels before the next operational alert and it was rehearsed during it. I have always maintained that operational alerts have value only if everything is actual and environment is created which is as close to war as possible and level of activity even higher than actual war to put maximum pressure on commanders and troops. To that end before each operational alert, I held a discussion at the corps level, when after presentation of plans, likely battle scenarios were discussed and contingency planning done. Similar, discussions were held at the divisional and brigade levels, after which the battalion commanders discussed and briefed their troops and immediately after this troops moved for the operational alert. Operational alerts were for 15 days, of this five days or one week was allotted to the battalions and the remainder for practice of contingencies at brigade, divisional and corps levels. A minimum of two contingencies at the divisional and one at the corps level were practised during each operational alert. Time utilization was modified depending on the requirement. Everything was practised with full compliments and full movement of troops, equipment and ammunition. Due to security reasons operational alerts was staggered formation-wise. During the first operational alert on the very first day I found that tanks could not be inducted into one of the enclaves, this was practised every night till both the armour and engineers became proficient and confident. After two operational alerts and accompanying discussions I was in a position to re-write the Operation Instruction, which I did over a period of time and it was issued.

During operational alerts and discussions, it became clear to me that we were hazy about both what constituted an adverse situation and how to restore it. So I decided to hold a sand model exercise on it. When I mooted the idea to the Army Commander, he liked it and asked me to hold it as a command event and enlarge the scope to also include restoration of an adverse situation at the command level. This was held as a command event and was attended by all formation commanders down to brigade commanders in the command and staff of Command Headquarters. It was most useful and successful. We practised some of the contingencies during the next operational alert.

ADMINISTRATION

I have always maintained that it is only a happy and satisfied soldier who fights well. Since troops come to Western and Central Commands for peace tenures they look forward to good living conditions, reasonable family accommodation, adequate time with families and full quota of their leave entitlement. I found that married accommodation was not adequate for corps troops and the two brigades in Jalandhar, for the independent armed brigade and the newly-raised corps reserve brigade. The division in Ferozepur was comfortable, the division at Amritsar and Tibri was reasonably housed and the division in Meerut had adequate married and Other Than Married (OTM) accommodation. After going around Jalandhar Cantonment I found that a number of big bungalows with large areas were occupied by civilians. I ordered their resumption and followed it uptill a number of them were resumed. In the area along the Mall Road a number of officer's quarters came up and JCOs and ORs accommodation in the adjoining areas. A number of NCE one-room accommodation was also converted with modification by joining two quarters for one OR. I also found that a large number of barracks had been recommended for demolition and auction. I ordered a board of officers to select the best few with good residual life and which could be restored. We bought these from the corps funds and restored them. These were allotted to men on compensation in lieu of quarters (CILQ), who were living outside in the town under most adverse conditions. Men paid the CILQ money less some amount to the Vajra Fund, the money left with the men was to be used by them for replenishment of bulbs and for other small maintenance as MES could not do so as these were no longer on their charge. By the time I left in October 1987, there was at least 25 per cent improvement in family accommodation. The divisions did the same and the level of satisfaction was heartening.

During my visit to the Vajra School I found that the headmaster spent a lot of time on minor administrative details rather than looking after the education. The reason for it was that he had to run for every little thing to the Brig. i/c Adm. Similarly, I found that the Vajra Canteen could not cope with the number of people dependent on it due to its anarchic method of functioning. I told the Brig. ASC who was in-charge to change over to the self-service system and to adopt cost accounting audit rather than survey boards. This was done after a suitable large shed was found for the canteen. Not only were people satisfied but our profits also went up substantially. I do not believe in changing any system, unless I have understood it and there are reasons for change. I found that almost everyday there were a large number of sanction books coming to me and found that the COS had even more. These included doing up of new vehicles, Vajra School requirements and those of other corps institutions. After detailed discussion with the staff and officers responsible for various Corps institutions, I decided to change over to the budget system. Each institution was to be allotted a yearly budget after examining their requirements and discussion. The officer-in-charge of the institution could spend up to his budgeted allocation for the purpose for which it was allotted. He was to maintain proper accounts which were to be audited. At the beginning of each year in April a budgeting meeting presided over by me, with COS, Brig. i/c Adm. and officer-in-charge of institutions was held, demands scrutinized and funds allotted. We found that it not only saved a lot of unproductive effort, it also resulted in saving as everyone functioned with responsibility. People perform best when given responsibility and trust.

The corps Army Wives Welfare Association (AWWA) did their bit for the welfare of troops and families in a thoughtful and productive fashion. In keeping with my thinking that corps headquaters should not impose on lower formations, my wife left them to function on their own. One of the major thrust in the welfare field was to reach to the people of Punjab. With this aim in view a part of the welfare was to reach the ex-servicemen and civilians in their areas. Two ex-servicemen rallies were held, where emphasis was to give them information and health care. An area of special concern was provision of dentures to ex-servicemen, for which I gave generous allocation to the Corps Dental Centres for equipment and material and they did an excellent job. The height of AWWA's effort to reach the people of Punjab was the light and sound show 'Glimpses of India' in which over 450 officers, JCOs, OR and their families and children took part. It was inaugurated by the Army Commander and it coincided with the command event mentioned earlier. It ran for over four days and was open to the general public. The theme covered our cultural diversity from J&K in the north to Kanyakumari in the south and Manipur in the east to Gujarat in the west. It was an excellent show and was appreciated by the public and had a good effect. A video cassette of some of them was made and kept in the corps headquarters.

When I left on 31 October 1987 to take over Western Command, I was a very satisfied man personally and professionally. I was able to achieve it with the wonderful team of formation commanders like Bulbul Brar, Cheeky Dewan, Dewan Sahni and my staff under Tirlok Singh my COS, Virender Oberoi my BGS and Sudarshan my Brig. i/c Adm. and all others; the associations formed last till today.

When my turn came for promotion and a vacancy (VCOAS) existed, after a few months the rumor mill started working again and the ghost of Kolkata emerged once again. Whenever people asked me as to what was happening, I told them I am probably out of the race. Then one day Gen. Sundarjee rang up and told me that there is a delay in announcing my promotion as he wants me to take over Western Command and both the existing vacancy of VCOAS and Western Command will be filled together without affecting my seniority. I kept it to myself till the formal announcement. It goes to the credit of Gen. Sundarjee and possibly the authorities in Delhi that in spite of my open criticism of Operation Blue Star, I got my due. My belief both in professional life and everywhere else that truth prevails was further reinforced.

BRASS TACKS: WAR OR NO WAR

Most people and public at large are aware of the famous exercise 'Brass Tacks' in 1987, which almost led to a war with Pakistan. It generated a lot of controversy and received attention of domestic and international media, particularly after the press briefing by Gen. Sunderjee and Arun Singh followed by the Prime Minister Rajiv Gandhi in January 1987. This was followed by intense diplomatic exchanges and activity to defuse the situation. These events were more than adequately covered in *India Today's* cover story 'Indo-Pak

Border, Game of Brinkmanship', 15 February 1987. Ravi Rikhye's book, *The War That Never Was* which came out in 1988 while I was still in service added to the controversy. I have also studied the ACDIS Research Report, *Brass Tacks and Beyond: Perception and Management of Crisis in South Asia* first published by Program in Arms Control, Disarmament and International Security, University of Illinois at Urbana in January 1995. I think time is appropriate to revisit the events and the issues. I wish to confine myself to facts known to me or later confirmed.

As a prelude to the actual exercise, Brass Tacks, there was probably the biggest war game held by the Army in Delhi in which I participated as a corps commander. This was the brain child of Gen. Sundarjee the COAS. It tested our operational plans and commander's capabilities. I was probably one of the most tested corps commanders during it. During the war game, Arun Singh the then RRM, was present throughout and was a quiet but keen listener to all discussions and watchful during its conduct. During the war game Gen. Sundarjee took special care to explain to him the reasons and implications of all major discussions and actions by commanders. It was very apparent during the defensive and offensive stage in my sector and the way my plans and actions were analysed and questioned.

After the war game, Gen. Sundarjee asked me to write and conduct the war game at the command level. During my discussion with Gen. Sundarjee on the parameters of the command war game he told me that the enemy build-up was to be similar as in the war game in Delhi and mainly opposite Punjab, whereby a counter-offensive in the desert would be the best alternative. The war game virtually incorporated all corps in the western theatre and the Army reserves, with emphasis on offensive by the strike corps of Western Command. The logic of exercising the syndicates from both strike corps and also one of the holding corps in an offensive role made good sense to draw maximum benefit from views of all commanders. I tailored the exercise to meet the above broad requirements. COS of 1 Corps Maj. Gen. G.S. Grewal approved to be a corps commander acted as a semi-controlled enemy. The air force participated in full strength in the exercise including Air Marshall M.M. Singh AOC-in-C Western Air Command and his operational staff. During the war game, Gen. Sundarjee wanted to play one particular corps commander against another. I objected to it as both were my junior colleagues. The Army Commander Lt. Gen. Hoon was upset and wanted me to conduct the discussion as the Chief wanted, I refused to be a party to this murky game. The episode ended as the Chief agreed to run the exercise as I wanted. I picked up the best from each of the syndicate's solution and dovetailed it into a plan which was then war gamed with each syndicate giving their reaction to situations and actions at each stage of the war game. The air participation was discussed at length and it was generally agreed that the air force would be using considerable effort for counter air operations to neutralize enemy airfields from which their aircraft will be operating in support of their army. This would ensure that our strike formations would be free from enemy air attacks to a large extent. Air effort for counter air and close air support would be closely monitored by Western Air Command on daily basis and allotments made based on operational requirement. In this context both the role and effectiveness of air defence groups were examined in detail. The war game at the command level was successful and lessons learnt were to be incorporated in the exercise with troops named exercise 'Brass Tacks'. One of the aspects glossed over was the logistic support for the entire operation. Although the syndicates had prepared detailed plans for resupply, track construction and maintenance during the offensive. Similarly, they had also prepared detailed requirement of transport, movement plan and dumping schedule for ammunition, fuel oil and lubricants and track material for the concentration and beyond into enemy territory. It, however, remained a worry in my mind and I made up my mind to do a detailed check of it during the actual exercise with troops, for which I had catered for additional staff in the control headquarters. I took it up again with Gen. Sundarjee when I took over the Western Command. The details will be of little interest to the reader.

Exercise 'Brass Tacks' was formulated incorporating lessons of both the war games held before it. After the troops had concentrated for the exercise, the control headquarters was established and I started functioning from it. We went through the entire routine of listening to the holding corps' plan for the defence of their vital objectives in-depth and the plan of the RAPID Division to oppose the enemy advance from the border in the open desert terrain and as to how they had planned to discern the main offensive and its objective. Based on this intelligence from various sources was tailored and fed to the strike corps to the extent that it would be available in a war situation. After the strike corps had done its planning, these plans were examined with particular reference to its advance in the open terrain, plans to deal with the intermediate objectives and up to contact and investment of the final objectives. Along with this we discussed air cover planned for the advancing elements, logistic and maintenance plan and the track plan. The last bit did not engage Gen. Sundarjee's real attention. A staff check by my staff found the plans sound and workable. Gen. Sundarjee asked me to match the plans and tell him if there was any requirement to modify the enemy's defensive plan. I told him that we should leave the plans as it were and exercise control by picture painting in terms of reaction and additional unreported positions and action of flanking formations through intelligence and situation reports. Having done all this we were gearing up for the start and conduct of the exercise.

At this stage my headquarters informed me that some Pakistani build-up had been reported opposite our sector as per intelligence reports from Army headquarters. At the ground level neither BSF nor local sources deployed by Intelligence and Field Security Groups reported anything till much later. There were indications of concentration opposite southern Punjab and opposite Gurdaspur and north of it. Later the exact areas opposite Fazilka-Ferozepur in the south and north of Gurdaspur and DBN area in the north were confirmed. I sent back my BGS who was in the control headquarters assisting me to my corps headquarters to monitor the situation. I raised the issue with the Army Commander but got no satisfactory answer, he just said keep a watch. I returned to my headquarters and after reviewing the situation, I estimated that elements of Pak Army Reserve South (ARS) had moved to opposite the Fazilka area and Army Reserve North (ARN) opposite Gurdaspur and DBN and both my flanks were threatened. I briefed the division commanders and told them to deploy surveillance elements and take precautionary measures based on their judgement without waiting for any orders. When I returned to the control headquarters still no warning had been issued. We discussed the situation informally amongst the formation commanders.

Reflecting back on the past events, I discovered a marked similarity between the enemy buildups in the war game in Chandimandir, the enemy build up to be fed to the strike corp for exercise 'Brass Tacks' and the actual Pakistani reaction to our movement and concentration for the exercise. These also had a striking similarity to Gen. Sundarjee's briefing to me before I wrote the 'Brass Tacks' exercise. Was he reading the Pakistani mind or was Pakistan feeding the design anticipating our motives and plans. Another person who was most concerned was my colleague in the adjoining holding corps, who was to act as the exercise enemy and was deployed a bit away from his area. He had just finished exercising his recently reorganized RAPID Division. I was surprised a bit more when I asked Air Marshall M.M. Singh, who was later to be my counterpart. Although a bit concerned but he had no inkling of it from Air Headquarters. Ultimately he decided to go to Delhi next day and discuss with his Chief, Air Chief Marshall Dennis Lafontaine. His concern which I learnt later on was due to the fact that he was privy to an informal discussion on Operation Trident plans between Gen. Sundarjee, Arun Singh and Gen. Hoon. During his meeting with the CAS and VCAS he conveyed the Army's Operation Trident plans as he had learnt. He was surprised to learn that the Air Force had not been told anything about it by Army Headquarters. During the meeting Air Marshal M.M. Singh also conveyed to them the inadequate WWR (War Wastage Rates) holding for the Jaguar fleet. Next evening, on his return, Air Marshall M.M. Singh told me as to what had transpired at the Air Headquarters but he was not aware of the follow-up action by the CAS. At about the same time or may be a day later or earlier Arun Singh and Gen. Sundarjee left for Delhi. It is much later that we learnt of the press conference by Arun Singh and Gen. Sundarjee and other developments.

At this stage two events need to be mentioned of which I had no knowledge till much later. The first was the visit of Lt. Gen. G.S. Grewal COS Western Command to Delhi to present the plans (probably offensive) of Western Command to the COAS

Gen. Sundarjee. Secondly, that telephonic orders had been issued to GOCs of both the corps being exercised to redeploy in new concentration areas. So when GOC 2 Corps Lt. Gen. Hanut Singh, MVC asked me as to why he has been asked to shift to a new concentration area, I could only tell him that I did not know but I will check up. When I asked the Army commander, he said Hunty (Hanut) has been given his orders, he should obey it. There was always some kind of antagonism between Hanut and Gen. Sundarjee and nobody wanted to get involved with it. It was obvious during the war game in Chandimandir and during the presentation of plans during the exercise 'Brass Tacks'. So much so that Hanut after he had given his orders refused to be available to Gen. Sundarjee and the Army Commander Gen. Prem Hoon on the pretext of being in meditation as he was well known for his extreme religious disposition. He would only discuss things with me, which became an extra burden for me. I later learnt that Lt. Gen. Prem Hoon was called to Delhi for discussion of his offensive plans. He did not want to get involved with the situation being created for what he felt was an actual war situation. He sent his COS Lt. Gen. Grewal to Delhi which I have mentioned above. I also later learnt that the plan envisaged the holding corps doing enemy in the exercise was required to readjust to do a change in direction by realigning in their exercise concentration area itself to be able to take off for their objectives across the border in Pakistan. Their advance would have also provided flank protection to the strike corps, whereas Hanut's strike corps had to move to new concentration areas, which would have taken 48 to 72 hours and would have given some inkling to Pakistanis. I understood that Hanut thought it was a hoax and that he would be asked to return to his present area for the exercise and thus resulting in quite a wasteful effort. This is why he was reluctant to follow the orders. This was also roughly the time that mobilization orders were given to all in the western sector opposite Pakistan.

On return from Delhi, Gen. Sundarjee announced that he had invited all the Military Attachés (MAs) including from Pakistan, to visit the exercise area and see things for themselves. He asked me to brief them of the salient points of the exercise. A bit later when I had figured out the implications, I asked Sundarjee that the present exercise is based on our actual capability and potential and may compromise our plans. After some discussion we decided to contrive a new setting with different set of objectives for the briefing. I had to work over the next 36 hours to work out the new setting and visualization of the progress of exercise and its broad conduct. Gen. Sundarjee approved it next night, which gave me that night to polish up the briefing. It was realistic but not real. Next day the MAs arrived and were briefed by me. Gen. Sundarjee, Arun Singh RRM and (Maj.) K.P. Singh Deo ex-RRM were present. Maj. K.P. Singh Deo's TA unit 105 Infantry Battalion (TA) Raj Rif had been embodied and was looking after the local Defence of Gen. Sundarjee's advance headquarters. The briefing went off well, there were questions, which were answered by Gen. Sundarjee and me. This was followed by a quick spin around to give the MAs a feel of the area and a visit to a nearby Air Defence unit. This was followed by lunch before they returned to Delhi. One of the most inquisitive MAs was the Pak MA, a brigadier who a few years later was declared a *persona non grata* when he was caught with his Indian agent in the Jama Masjid area. During the lunch, the Pak Air attaché, an Air Commodore, who displayed a very subtle sense of humour told me that we should let the Pakistani Army train in our desert for adequate compensation as most of the open area in their side of the border has been taken over by the senior army officers for cultivation and there is hardly any land left to train. When I asked him about Sind, he just said, let it remain as an actual battleground.

After the exercise, when I was writing the report, I asked Lt. Gen. Hoon, the then Army Commander if we might have actually gone to war. He just said, what has happened is best left alone. Later, after I had taken over as Army Commander during the Army Training Conference in Bhatinda in November 1987, when I asked Gen. Sundarjee, he just smiled and said, your guess is as good as mine, best to forget it. By that time other things had come up and we were fully involved in Sri Lanka.

Ravi Rikhye in his book has covered in detail the political scenario, the intention of the prime minister to create a crisis to meet the demands of political expediency and how later due to his weakened position he backed down. Behind the scene diplomatic efforts to diffuse the situation were taken up which culminated in Gen. Zia-ul-Haq's visit to Jaipur for the India-Pakistan cricket match, I would not like to comment on it as we came to know of these developments second hand from the media later. He has also given his perception of events including build-up on both sides. Neither can I dispute it nor confirm it as it did not concern me. At best it can be viewed as a viable academic exercise of a very fertile mind. All I can confirm is that we had enough troops in Punjab and nearby areas to have launched the offensive into Pakistan. However, I feel the offensive operations envisaged by him under Operation Trident could not have been the main one with Brass Tacks as a strategic deception, both due to the timeframe and the sensitivity of the area after the Siachen operation launched by us in April 1984. Operation Meghdoot in Siachen was launched on the Army's initiative and not on Mrs. Indira Gandhi's suggestion as reported by him. Of course, we had got her approval. This also defaults his theory that we did not launch Operation Brass Tacks because, 'Trident' was not ready. The other issue of professional interest he had raised is that Pakistan had planned and was prepared to trade space for time in the Sind sector. This was well known and both sides were aware of it, and we had catered for it in our planning and worked out various contingencies. This is what war is all about. The moot question is who takes the initiative, achieves surprise and is prepared and not surprised by enemy counter moves. I felt Sundarjee was very much up to it and I never did nor do I after introspection subscribe to the dismal picture of the outcome painted by Ravi Rikhye. It will also not be correct to say that Sundarjee did not spell out the aim of the exercise till late December. I knew it, otherwise how could I have written the exercise. However, such details are not in the public domain.

AN ASSOCIATION OF PRIDE

While at the military operations directorate, I took over as Colonel of the Parachute Regiment, which imposed additional responsibility on me towards all ranks of the regiment. It mandated that I treat all battalions in the regiment equally and on the same footing. Although 2 Para in which I served most of my regimental service and 5 Para which I served in Mizoram held a special place in my heart. In keeping with my new responsibility I decided to have my personal staff in rotation from the entire regiment. I asked 5 Para to ask for a volunteer young officer as my aide-de-camp as I had my earlier aide from 2 Para as GOC 8 Mountain Division. Capt. S. Ravi from 5 Para joined as my aide-de-camp after I took over the corps. He was a graduate NCC direct entry to the Indian Military Academy. I found him to be intelligent, professionally sound, with an inquisitive mind and full of desire to learn. He showed keen interest in professional matters above his rank. I encouraged him by responding to his queries whenever we were together. He was likeable, socially correct and pleasant and gradually became a member of our family. After a couple of years before I moved from Jalandhar, I heard from my children that Ravi wants to leave the Army and achieve something in life. I tried to dissuade him as I thought he had a bright future in the Army. When I was moving to Chandimandir I told Ravi that he will be returning to the unit, as my next aide will be from another battalion. He told me that he was very sincere in his request to leave the Army and do something different and unique. He persisted with his request and seeing his determination and enthusian, I helped him to get released. This was the period of the late 1980s and early 1990s, when new winds of liberalization, globalization and privatization were catching the imagination of young and daring to meet new challenges. In my busy schedule for a time I lost contact with Ravi, till a year after my retirement Ravi told me about the birth of the Pegasus Centre For Excellence and asked me and my wife to see the new baby born out of thoughts during our days together. Seeing what he had achieved thrilled me beyond my dreams. With his innovative mind and after deep study he decided to apply defence forces approach, techniques and management technologies to new challenges facing the industry in the fields of multicultural workforces, management of scales, use of newer and multiple technologies and their integration into the system and above all renewing the thought process of managerial and production staff. An idea we often discussed was that defence is an evolved organization and unless we can continuously integrate new techniques of warfare, weapons and organizations meeting new challenges will be difficult. Today Pegasus has expanded to have

Plate 1: Old adversaries – trusted friends later. N. Bisheshwar Singh and the author.

Plate 2: Mama Satso – Symbol of Courage
A legend in Nagaland, who killed four Naga hostiles with a 'daw' in 1965, who had killed her husband a JCO in Assam Regiment. She died in 1997.

Plate 3: Author with Nripen Chakravarty, Ex CPI(M) Chief Minister of Tripura. An honest person and a firm believer in 'Ideal Politiks'.

Plate 4: Author with Prime Minister Smt. Indira Gandhi.

Plate 5: Author with Yasin Malik.

Plate 6: Author with Gujar Leader Mian Bashir and his son Mian Altaf – a minister in Farooq Abdullah's Ministry.

Plate 7: Author with Shabeer Shah.

Plate 8: Author with COAS, Gen. K.V. Krishna Rao, PVSM.

Plate 9: Author with Gen. K. Sundarjee (then Maj. Gen.) in the Rajasthan Desert during Exercise Parivartan.

Plate 10: Author

Plate 11: Wife – Sajni Nayar

Plate 12: Ritu – daughter with husband Virendar Kapoor and daughters Megha and Ayesha.

Plate 13: Son – Vikrant Nayar with wife Rashmi,
son Adhiraj and daughter Shagun.

Plate 14: Ravi with wife Seema and daughter Yashu.

Plate 15: Signing the oath of office after the swearing in as Governor of Manipur, 1993.

Plate 16: Leading the march past after the veterans jump in 2002 on the occasion of the Parachute Regiments centres Golden Jubilee.

Plate 17: With Inder Gill and Tirath Oberoi after the veterans parachute jump.

Plate 18: With President R. Venkatraman.

five delivery centres in Bangalore, Pondicherry, Pune, Dehradun and Bhubaneswar. It has 650 customers from India and abroad, which include N.R. Narayan Murthy's Infosys, Premji's Wipro and a number of other multinationals in India and abroad. His faculty is drawn from academia, industry, HR, psychologists, behavioural sceintists and defence. He has expanded his sphere of activities to establish a Pegasus Learning Centre, which apart from meeting Pegasus's need in R&D field also caters for new variations and additions to Outward Bound Learning. I am proud to be associated with Pegasus since its inception and see it grow to be the only organization of its type in the world. Well done Ravi. I am proud of you.

ON TO CHANDIMANDIR

My tenure as Army Commander in Chandimandir was in more ways than one a continuation of my tenure in Jalandhar. Operationally, I had been intimately connected with all the planning not only in my corps but also in other corps zones as also in the offensive plans and in the joint planning with the Air Force. The culmination of operational planning at the conceptual level was the series of war games before the exercise, Brass Tacks and the exercise itself tested some of these at the executive level. So much so that the new Army Commander Lt. Gen. P.N. Hoon, who had a short tenure of just one year and his staff considered me a part of the Command Headquarters and frequently consulted me. Therefore arrival and getting settled at Chandimandir was smooth and easy.

Lt. Gen. G.S. Grewal (Guddy), the COS, was known to me since my days in the division in Manipur and Nagaland, he was the BGS Eastern Command then. I was lucky to have him as my COS. He is a very sound professional with a very calm and pleasant disposition. As is customary, Guddy asked me for a message for the command on taking over, which is published as a special order of the day in the command orders. I called him back after half an hour and gave him a draft message as follows, 'My aim is to maintain the highest level of operational readiness of the Western Army and to improve the living conditions in the Command by 20 per cent during my tenure'. Guddy read the message and said that he was sure of the first and operational part but he felt the second part about the living conditions was a tall order. I told him that I am not only aiming for it but together we shall achieve it.

IMPROVING THE LEVEL OF SATISFACTION

The first task in this regard was to identify the really bad stations in the command. I gave this task to Guddy, the Maj. Gen. i/c Adm., Maj. Gen. Raj Bahuguna and the Chief Engineer Maj. Gen. Maharaj Singh. I asked them to work out a statement of accommodation both for troops, vehicles including specialist weapons and vehicles, OTM and married accommodation in each station and highlight the deficiencies and mark out the really bad ones with priorities. The exercise was completed by the end of December 1987. The worst station was Hissar where a newly-raised division was mostly still in hutments and tents even after almost a decade of raising with some temporary family accommodation and very limited scope for CILQ. Some of the other stations considered bad were Bikaner, Lalgarh Jattan, Beas and Kapurthala. The review of the Key Location Plan (KLP) revealed that it also required hastening up for which additional funds for the year starting April 1988 were required. A request for the same was rejected outright by the Army Headquarters. I raised the issue again at the Army Commanders' Conference and minced no words in conveying that inadequate married accommodation, lack of covered accommodation for vehicles (tanks), sophisticated air defence equipment and guns and other technical accommodation was resulting in wastage, discomfort and bad living conditions and would adversely affect morale. While we had pumped in additional troops, sophisticated equipment and arms in the command but development of quality accommodation had not kept pace. Most troops coming to Western Command are on peace tenures and only less than 50 per cent get a chance to bring families.

My constant agitation resulted in the Defence Minister K.C. Pant visiting the command and seeing things for himself. In spite of genuine hardships, wherever he met troops they showed a happy and contented demeanour. I had to coax the COs and subedar majors to put across their genuine grievances of accommodation and children's education, such is the goodness of the Indian soldier but we should not exploit it. Our efforts succeeded and we got additional funds from next year onwards. While the progress of the OTM accommodation improved, the state of married accommodation remained below satisfactory level. After deliberation and further discussion, I came to the conclusion that we need to create temporary married accommodation on a fairly large scale without slowing or disturbing the KLP. We had to construct temporary married accommodation in areas where no construction was likely to come up in the next ten years so that KLP was not affected. Also while constructing temporary married accommodation we should not sacrifice comfort or facilities that are available normally. This requirement could be met by single storey constructions with minimum foundation and temporary roofs with false ceiling, all other facilities being as authorized. The Chief Engineer Maj. Gen. Maharaj Singh worked out a number of designs, we selected three out of these but left the final choice to the formations. We laid the financial limit of Rs. 1 lakh for each unit, thus we could get 100 married quarters for Rs. 1 crore. I decided not to touch the allocations for the KLP as progress in the KLP was equally beneficial in the long run. The money for the temporary married accommodation came out of the additional allotment, that too without any major effect on KLP projects as we touched only 2 to 3 per cent of the allocations. This almost gave us 2,000 additional married quarters in two years, which improved the married accommodation state in the command considerably. Just as we thought we had resolved the problem, we were in for a very unpleasant surprise. The chief engineer reported to me that no contractor is prepared to bid for the temporary accommodation as it is not worth their while. While we were still grappling with this development, Lt. Gen. Roy E-in-C rang me up and told me that he was against the proposal and had told the Chief of the same. I had to be curt with him and told him to mind his own business. I further told him that I am determined to execute the project even if I had to put all the engineer regiments in my command to do so, although I was against such employment of troops. I also told Maj.

Gen. Maharaj Singh that all major KLP construction contracts will only be open to those who agree to execute one task of temporary married accommodation. I had realized that both the MES and contractors are only interested in big projects as this is where the real money and benefits are. The threat worked and we got the projects going. The odd formation commander initially treated this as a fad of senior commanders but when they were told that if they don't select the design for their own areas, it will be decided for them, they got into the spirit of the issue. It was heartening to see the progress of the project and the happiness of the troops who occupied it.

CONSOLIDATING OPERATIONAL PREPAREDNESS

On the operational side the culmination of Brass Tacks series was the operational conference which was to discuss, decide and record the lessons learnt, which in turn became the parameters of our strategy in the desert. This should have been held within a short period after the completion of exercise Brass Tacks but it kept on being postponed by my predecessor. It was finally scheduled in November 1987, just three weeks after I took over. Gen. Sundarjee asked me if I required more time, I told him not to postpone it and we should go ahead as planned as it is already delayed. The conference took place in Bhatinda and we were able to cover all ground and finished it in one and half days instead of the allotted three days. When the Chief asked me as to what we could do for the rest of the period or disperse early, I told him that since all Army commanders were present, we should avail of the opportunity to ask them to update the rest of us on the developments in their commands. The Chief liked the suggestion and agreed, it turned out to be a great boon. We were updated on operations in the Siachen area in the Northern Command and the forward posture and insurgency situation in the Eastern Command. The Chief himself briefed us on Operation Pawan in Sri Lanka. It was most educative but it also brought out as to how far the reality was from what was desired. Of these Sri Lanka and Siachen raised the maximum doubts. I shall cover these later.

The issue which was of immediate concern to me after this operational conference was that while the depth of the offensive planned was both desirable and within the capability of combat troops but our logistic capability, particularly engineer support in terms of track laying and transport could not fully support it. This was generally glossed over by Gen. Sundarjee and other enthusiasts of mechanized warfare. While I was fully with them and all for offensive spirit but I was most unhappy and could not ignore the logistic reality. I took it up with Gen. Sundarjee and told him that I was only planning on the outer limit of our logistic reach while keeping the combat edge sharp. This required an acknowledgement and revision of Army headquarters' operational directive, none of these happened during my entire tenure, in spite of reminders.

There was and probably is still a tendency amongst senior officers and which naturally is followed by juniors to talk big, aggressively, only of offensive oriented operations and conveniently gloss over logistic constraints and enemy capability and likely reactions in their professional posturing during operational discussions and sand models. It is a positive trait and needs to be nurtured but when it results in a closed mind then it requires correction. This was clearly brought out in the first war game in Delhi and later in Chandimandir that the desire to exploit our potential and superiority in armour/mechanized combat power in open desert terrain is well known to the adversary and if he forestalls you as he will try then your offensive options get limited to the plains and obstacle ridden terrain. However, amongst our mechanized commanders there is a tendency to ignore this reality and stick to the convenient terrain and environment. To overcome this I had to declare that the next training year will be devoted to studying of and exercising in the plains and in a obstacle ridden terrain. In the very first war game in our offensive corps we realized it was no sooner than required. Our conceptual grasp and thinking and knowledge of battle procedures in such a terrain were rusty and vague. I drove home the point that along with operational balance there was need for balance in thinking and continuing requirement to update battle procedures and preparations for the same. This is equally true of all other real life situations.

THE TURBULENT SITUATION IN PUNJAB, HOW AND WHY IT FINALLY RESOLVED

The internal security situation in Punjab had improved but remained turbulent and terrorist activity prone. It was marked by a high degree of violence and killings. Instability at the centre resulted in lack of policy guidance, high-handed governance with bureaucratic overtones and police dominance. A large number of militant outfits mushroomed and political, social and civil institutions become non-functional. Punjab came under the dominance of militant dictates and its agenda of social reform, like dress code, no use of Hindi with warnings to the media, Doordarshan and AIR. Militants held courts in the border districts, enforced ban on liquor, tobacco, meat and marriage parties of more than eleven persons. *Bhog* ceremonies of militants not only acted as platform for propaganda but also to raise funds. The killings of both the security personnel and the terrorists increased and there was further deterioration of the environment due to criminalization of the terrorist movement. Ransom demands, kidnappings and extortions by terrorists were matched by fake encounters, illegal arrests and detention and all crimes were covered under the umbrella of terrorism. Even the success of operation Black Thunder II in May 1988 failed to stem the tide. In the prevailing environment Punjab virtually became a police state. The Governor S.S. Ray's experience of harsh measures against Naxalites resulted in people fearing the state as much as the terrorists. In this noise few sane voices of Jiwan Singh Umrangal (politician), Vaishnav, the chief secretary and Chaman Lal and D.S. Mangat of the police got lost but their persistence kept some check on bureaucracy and the police. In such a vitiated environment, I felt it was wise to continue my policy of non-involvement. It was imperative, as by involvement you could neither turn the tide nor influence authorities and at worst become a party to it.

LACK OF VISION AND UNDERSTANDING

After the departure of Arjun Singh and with S.S. Ray taking over as governor, the government's responses were primarily in armed violent actions and essentially by the Punjab Police, which drew equally violent response from the terrorists and the killings and kidnappings increased. The field was left entirely to the police with little accountability. With the sidelining of the Chief Secretary, Vaishnav, a seasoned and mature administrator and the departure of the Home Secretary N.N. Vohra for Delhi, very little sane counsel prevailed. There was no long-term perspective and a total lack of policy. What made things worse was that there was no consultations or review at any level except between the governor and the defunct Punjab Committee under K.C. Pant, the defence minister representing the centre. Ray, a seasoned hardline politician, with his background of successfully tackling the Naxalite problem in Bengal as chief minister tried to apply the same harsh measures, but the dimensions and scope of terrorism were different, requiring long-term perspective in handling the problem. I had been in Punjab for a long time and was clear that we were in for a long sustained haul. Under the circumstances I kept away from state government and ensured that the Army did not get involved, which was the most contentious issue between me and the governor. We only had a limited but pleasant social interaction. The situation remained the same with its ups and downs till I retired in 1989.

During one of his visits to Punjab, K.C. Pant, the defence minister as head of the Punjab Committee, rang up from Raj Bhavan asking for me, my batman informed him that I was away playing golf and was not available. We had taken no notice of his visit as it did not concern us and neither were we formally informed by the Army headquarters. In the evening I spoke to him in Delhi and he asked me to meet him next morning at the Chandigarh airfield, when he would be on his way to Srinagar and would break his journey to consult me on a few issues. Next morning when I met him at the airfield, he was accompanied by Ghulam Nabi Azad. To have privacy we met in the aircraft, while others waited in the lounge. He told me that the prime minister had decided to organize the ex-servicemen in Punjab into a Village Defence Force and the Punjab government has liked the idea very much. He wanted me to help the Punjab government in organizing it. I told him that it was not a very sound proposition and I was not in favour of it. I explained to him that an ex-serviceman was an individual and equally a civilian as others in the village. If you only organize them, they will get marked and he and his family would be targetted and not achieve any results. The scheme should embrace all villagers, then it would be a cohesive force and together they can resist the terrorists without compromising their individual and family security. He told me that the prime minister has decided based on a suggestion from the Punjab government. I informed the defence minister that when the governor had raised the issue with me I had told him the same. I made sure that the scheme was not implemented.

Ray was also fond of speaking in Punjabi, and left no opportunity to portray himself as more of a Sikh than the Sikhs themselves and emphasized his association with Lahore. He was fond of television appearances for self-projection, a trait all politicians have but he looked for such opportunities constantly. A brilliant mind, submerged in political gamesmanship and thus he missed the realities of the Punjab situation. We often clashed in our views but in a civil manner till in one instant he told me that the Army had to come in. I told him not as long as I am here and added for good effect that I am only answerable to my hierarchy. An interesting social occasion highlights the relationship.

Burney had taken over as governor of Haryana. I had known him well when he was Governor of Nagaland and Manipur. He had asked us over for dinner along with Ray and Mrs. Ray, B.K. Nehru, Ribeiro and Mrs. Ribeiro and Mrs. Nayantara Sehgal. B.K. Nehru had come from Kasauli to see Vijayalaxmi Pandit who was admitted for treatment in the PGI, Chandigarh. I had come to know B.K. Nehru well as I used to meet him along with Lt. Gen. and Mrs. S.D. Verma during our visits to Kasauli. During the course of the dinner the conversation naturally turned to the situation in Punjab. Ray and Ribeiro gave a resume of the situation and what they were doing to control the situation. I was not concerned so I kept out of the discussion. Ray after some time said, of course the General does not agree with me. I was provoked but I kept my cool and just said that they are in-charge and as such are the best people to handle it.

After dinner, when we had gone to a side room to smoke, B.K. Nehru asked me as to what was the rub between me and the governor. I told him that Ray is doing what he feels is the right thing but he does not have to justify it on television every time and seek concurrence of everyone around. Moreover, his posturing as a Punjabi and a staunch follower of Sikhism was just having the adverse effect. B.K. Nehru smiled and said, a political animal never changes.

Some time later during the Army Commanders Conference at a dinner where Prime Minister Rajiv Gandhi was present, he asked me what should be done in Punjab. I told him that he should come to the Golden Temple in Amritsar, *matha teko* in Harmandir Sahib and just say, '*Galti ho gai hai, sanu maf kar do*'. I told him Punjabis and Jat Sikhs in particular will lift him on their shoulders as they carry their heart on their sleeve, the problem will be solved. However, he was not permitted to do so by his advisors. He missed a golden opportunity. Manmohan Singh did it in his first tenure as prime minister but it was not the same as a lot more blood had been shed. It was late and he is a Sikh which is not the same as a Gandhi family member and a Hindu.

The Punjab tangle finally resolved somewhat in 1993, four years after I retired. A Congress government came to power with a suspect mandate due to boycott by the Akalis and a low turnout during the elections in 1992. However, it established its legitimacy due to lack of a credible alternative and with a large turnout during Panchayat elections in which Congress won a handsome majority. Both the elections and militancy were handled as an operation of war, with the Army, PMF and police playing their assigned role well. The claim of K.P.S. Gill, the then DGP Punjab, that March 1993 marked the beginning of the end of militancy was largely justified. Both Beant Singh and Gill deserve credit for it. Victory came after a long period of attrition and change of approach under Gen. O.P. Malhotra. At that time in 1992, a clear understanding of the fact that it was neither a Hindu-Sikh problem, nor a religious separatist movement, nor a political movement with Khalistan as the goal and most of all it did not have support of the masses or any religious sanction, finally emerged to the authorities in Delhi. With fragmented militant organizations, local intelligence was vital for success. The militants themselves helped in this by antagonizing the rural Sikh peasantry with their criminal activities of sacrileges of holy places and licentious behaviour of not only their rank and file but also senior leaders like Gurdeep Singh Deepa, Jaspal Singh Bhuri and Sukhdev Singh of KCF, Sukhdev Singh Babbar and Madho Singh of Babbar Khalsa and Harminder Singh Sultanwind and Sohan Singh of Panthic Committee. Land grabbing by terrorists became another course of antagonism with the rural people. Success came from clear understanding, Beant Singh's political will and Gill's shrewdness and understanding of the Jat Sikh mental make-up. There was a clear-cut aim, complete freedom of action and unity of command. However, success also made Beant Singh assume the mentorship and role of sole arbitrator of Punjab's fate resulting in political confrontation with the Akalis, administrative lapses, corruption and police high handedness. The trends continued even after assassination of Beant Singh and the syndrome of political confrontation and administrative failures continue irrespective of the party in power.

SOME IN-HOUSE OBSERVATIONS

Army is a functional organization, which is mandated to deliver and not expected to fail. It has therefore out of necessity to plan for future threats and contingencies. However, in the absence of a strategic culture at the national level and lack of clear policy directives this is mostly done in isolation by the Services on their own, entirely based on their professional judgement, with no or little input from elsewhere. This gets defaulted at times due to extraneous reasons or distorted perceptions of both the individual and the collective. This gets reflected to some extent even in some of its studies. As Army commander I got the opportunity to examine and be exposed to some. One of the first one was a study entitled, 'Expert Committee Report'. I was personally interested in it as I was one of the few brigade commanders who were sent a questionnaire and later discussed it with the Committee during their visit to Trivandrum in 1976. Going through it at Chandimandir, I discovered that to the best of my knowledge some of its major recommendations remained unimplemented and some discarded by the proposers themselves. On closer examination I found that it was so because in its desire for modernization of the Army the Committee ignored the indigenous Indian environment,

Army's long drawn commitments in J&K and the north-east, and the resources the nation could afford to make it available. It was a good study of what Indian Army could be but may not be able to meet the challenges in the environment in which it operates. This was a major lesson and influenced our recommendations during the operational conference after Operation Brass Tacks in November 1987.

There were two more studies ordered by Army Headquarters during my period as Army commander, both of which I rejected after due examination. The first was under a lieutenant general who was a friend of mine from DSSC days. It dealt with savings in manpower in teeth arms and services by reducing strength at the section and platoon levels and by reducing the number of sub-units in the units. I permitted the Study Group an open house and a full discussion with all heads of arms and services and the general staff at my headquarters to examine his proposals in all operations of war and in the terrain in the command zone. In most cases the proposals were found wanting and impracticable. So in a very amicable fashion we rejected the study findings. It naturally upset people in Delhi, who had ordered the study but the reality could not be ignored. The second study was done by another lieutenant general, again a friend of mine. The study aimed to create a separate Tri Service Command for Andaman & Nicobar group of islands and a South Western Army Command. I told him that I will not comment on the need for a separate command for the Andaman & Nicobar group of islands as I have not examined it and neither does it concern me. Today the Tri Service Command under an Army commander (or equivalent) has less troops than an independent brigade group. The Air Force pulled out after the tsunami and most of the naval elements have rejoined Eastern Naval Command. But as far as western and southern theatres are concerned I do not see any requirement for an additional command headquarters as neither there is any accretion in force level nor there is any change in the threat perception. I therefore was not even prepared to consider such a proposal, let alone agree to it. I told him that instead the Army Headquarters should consider and finalize our recommendation after exercise Brass Tacks. The proposal for a South Western Command died a natural death. However, what is sad is that in 2006 the proposal was dug out and we have a South Western Command today. There is no force accretion, the territory of the Western Command and Southern Command in the west has been truncated and its assets divided. This leaves both the commands little flexibility in offensive planning or in scope and reaction capability. Such exercises lead to creation of unproductive costly assets in the shape of headquarters thereby denying assets and resources for enhancing combat capability. Similarly, raising of a new corps headquarters for the area north of Zojila after the Kargil War in 1999 has resulted in more unproductive assets to maintain and mouths to feed across Zojila without improving our operational posture in the sector.

During the review of the KLP projects in the command, I visited the Command Hospital project to review its progress and found that while the main hospital project was making progress, the nurses' mess and quarters and the accommodation for essential specialist staff was lagging behind. The main hospital building also lacked adequate air conditioning for the essential parts like operating theatres, recovery room, ICU and other areas as did most of the wards. The building also had no provision for inter-communication and paging facility. When I told the chief engineer to cater for these, he told me that it will have to be done as a separate project later. To me it sounded quite irrational as it will result in breaking up parts of the building and it will be quite messy. I told them to do it now and put up additional sanctions for my approval. The chief engineer told me that the project may go beyond my tenure and I may not be able to inaugurate it. I told the chief engineer to do it now and complete the entire modifications, it did not matter if my successor inaugurated it. I saw to it being done completely with all facilities and essential married accommodation. It was completed three months after I retired and was inaugurated by my successor Lt. Gen. Rodrigues.

Similar was the case with the Army Hospital which was in temporary Second World War barracks in Delhi Cantt. The KLP for the project was ready but it kept on getting postponed for over a decade for one reason or the other. The latest hold up was due to its location on the ridge, due to some unwritten restrictions on construction on the ridge, whereas a lot of construction was going on it. When I asked for the order to be shown to me, they could not produce any order. I told them to finalize the plan and that construction will start beginning of the new financial year that is April 1988, I also earmarked Rs. 1 crore for laying the foundation. In the next Army Commanders' Conference I informally asked the Prime Minister Rajiv Gandhi and told him that the ban on the construction on the ridge should be invoked only if we overlook the ecological aspect. He told me to go ahead. I asked the Chief Gen. V.N. Sharma to lay the foundation of the Army Hospital (Research and Referral). He told me that the QMG had some reservations and T.N. Sheshan as environment secretary was unlikely to agree to it. I told him that there was no other location suitable and I have got the PM's approval and if he does not come I will lay the foundation. He finally agreed and we started the construction. It has turned out to be a wonderful facility with improved greenery and better ecology. However, the MES construction was not up to the desired standard. Everyone later tried to lay a stone in that building on some portion or the other but I am happy to be nameless.

In keeping with my policy, we left the formations alone to plan and carry out their own scheme of welfare activities to meet the requirement of their men and families. Only one function was organized at the command level during my tenure. My wife organized a Vasant Utsav in 1988, which was a great success and raised a large sum of money for welfare activities in the command. It was in recognition of this effort that Mrs. Sarupi Sharma, president of Central AWWA named an outlet in AWWA Complex in Delhi, 'SAJNI', after my wife's name.

COLONEL OF THE REGIMENT

I became the Colonel of the Parachute Regiment in 1984. It is an honour given to one of the senior officers of the regiment. Normally it is decided during the biannual conference of the battalion commanders which is presided over by the present incumbent. However, in our regiment each and every officer of a major's rank votes for it which is by a secret ballot opened during the Battalion Commanders' Conference. In addition each CO consults all officers and senior JCOs of the battalion and he puts across their views during the conference, it is the most democratic way and everyone has a chance to express his opinion. When I got elected the decision was unanimous as the other two officers withdrew once they knew my name was being proposed. It is an ex-offico appointment and is primarily confined to regimental affairs. He is normally consulted by the military secretary on officer management of the regiment particularly in appointment of COs. However, while rendering such advice to the military secretary he should follow uniform norms and must be just and fair to the officers. I followed a system whereby the seniormost officer of the battalion approved for command was the automatic choice. In case no approved officer from the battalion was available or not likely to be available then the seniormost approved officer of the regiment was the choice, provided there was no chance of his taking over his own battalion. As the father figure he must be approachable by all officers and be fair. Playing favourites is wrong. While selecting COs, special contribution of the officer to the battalion or being in operations should get due weightage. His other functions are keeping an eye on the manpower state of battalions and ensure that there is a balance of field and peace tenures of each battalion in the regiment. He is also to ensure that traditions and customs specific to the regiment are observed as is the case with dress code, these have to be within the Army norms. He should normally keep an eye on the functioning of the regimental centre without interfering in the functional and administrative chain of command. Each CO should be able to freely write and express his opinion on all regimental matters and also be able to seek his help if the unit is not getting redressal of genuine problems through the chain of command. This should only be followed in exceptional cases. Similarly, each officer should be able to approach him freely on his personal problems but this should not be permitted to be used for any advantageous purpose. The colonel of the regiment should visit units regularly, particularly those in field and operational areas.

On taking over as colonel of the regiment, I found that the battalions of the regiment did not have equitable opportunity, this was particularly true of the commando battalions. 1 Para after conversion to Cdo was staying on in peace station, 9 Para Cdo was constantly in field in J&K and frequently called out for operations and 10 Para was constantly in the desert. In addition there was disparity in the pay and allowances between 1 Para and the other two cdo battalions which had a special dispensation compared to the other two battalions. I took up a case for same pay and allowances to be given to 9 and 10 Para Cdos. I also suggested that these battalions should be rotated not only amongst themselves but to different operational areas, so that their expertise is enlarged both operationally and area-wise. I received both formal and informal requests, some even from the Army commanders in whose command these battalions were located against the proposal. I was able to push both these proposals through and men were very happy as their pay and allowances became at par with each other. Moreover, units going to field area benefited not only in getting the field concessions but also additional points of field service for honorary ranks. The system improved the operational capability and professional diversity, which paid us rich dividends in Sri Lanka and later in J&K.

I followed a similar approach to the other six para battalions and floated a case for three of them to stay in the Parachute Brigade for any air-borne role and the other three battalions to go to field in high altitude, an insurgency area and third to another tough field area. This proposal was also accepted and resulted in better employment of this elite force in diverse operational roles and environment. After the first cycle, whenever I visited the units they were happier, brighter and more professionally competent than before. The system let our battalions not only share the burden but greater professional exposure which resulted in each of the battalions performing exceedingly well during operations in Sri Lanka, the north-east and in J&K including in the Siachen glacier.

My tenure as colonel of the regiment was mostly smooth but it had its hiccups. One of my centre commandants indulged in petty corruption and un-officer like conduct. This came to light through some reports and on verification I found them to be correct. I sent a message to his sub-area commander that it should be enquired and strict disciplinary action taken. The officer in the meantime had moved as GOC of a division. Based on the investigation, disciplinary action was taken against him and not only was he demoted but also advised to quit. While the message went home but it left a bad name for the centre and indirectly for the regiment.

The other problem concerned the commando battalions, particularly 1 Para Cdo, who having been equated with the other two for some time adopted an attitude of being distinct. Para Cdo units normally are directly under the command headquarters which gives them access to senior commanders and staff at command headquarters. The situation got further misconstrued when we created a cell in the MO directorate to cater for their special training and equipment, which gave them access to the MO directorate and thus Army Headquarters. They mooted a proposal that as a special unit they should be separated from the regiment and given special status. What added further confusion was that Brig. Rustam Nanavati (later Lt. Gen.) from the MO directorate who had undertaken a course in the USA with the Special Forces, mooted the idea that while the commando units can remain located in different commands but for all operational planning and tasking they should be under MO directorate. This was done without any consultation with the Army Commanders and the colonel of the regiment. When I got to know of it, orders for separation of the commando battalions from the regiment had already been issued. I rang up Gen. Sundarjee, the Chief, to say that both these issues need to be discussed in the Army Commanders' Conference. He very reluctantly agreed as both the VCOAS Lt. Gen. Rodrigues and Lt. Gen. Bipin Joshi, the DGMO, had made it a prestige issue. During the conference when the issue of operational planning and tasking came up, I spoke against it. My reasoning was that all these specialized tasks are to be performed in conformity and support of command plans except may be the odd one of strategic nature and even for this launching and extraction after the task it will be the responsibility of a command because Army Headquarters has no separate resources or capability. In the case of any fiasco who would take responsibility for retrieving the situation. Moreover, even for the odd strategic task of Army Headquarters the commands should be taken in confidence as these cannot be launched in isolation. I ended up by saying we follow other armies blindly without regard to our ground realities. There was a lot of discussion and all the other Army Commanders supported me and the proposal was discarded.

On the second issue of separation of Cdo battalion from the Parachute Regiment, I said that I will speak only as colonel of the regiment and my concern is my men. I was categorical in telling Gen. Sundarjee, Lt. Gen. Rodrigues and Lt. Gen. Joshi that as far as I was concerned they can do what they like with the Indian Army but I am concerned with the men as to who would look after the wounded, maimed and disabled soldiers after a conflict and during counter-insurgency, who will look after the widows and their entitlement. I told him the large number of soldiers wounded and disabled in Sri Lanka, were absorbed in the regiment and those not fit for commando duties are in other battalions. We make up their deficiencies of manpower whenever required and as an example the CO of 1 Para went around the entire Indian Army and got only 17 volunteers. We made up 1 Para when they discarded almost over 50 per cent of their strength. The resilience and strength of the Indian Army is its regimental system and any fiddling with it will be asking for trouble. Finally, I told them that if 1 Para leaves the regiment then let the Army look after them. There was some discussion and resistance from the VCOAS and DGMO but everyone else supported me, the other three Army Commanders from Infantry, who were also colonels of their regiments supported me. The proposal was shelved and the Chief issued a letter cancelling the previous MO directorate letter. People made a prestige issue of it and Gen. Rodrigues and later Gen. Padmanabhan considered reviving it but it met a natural death. Now the entire regiment is being converted to para commandos. Is it a wise decision? We still have to see its usefulness. We tend to follow other armies blindly without regard to our environment and the regimental system adopted from the British, which has been our mainstay.

REMINISCENCES

Beyond professional sphere, my tenure in the MO directorate and later as corps and Army Commander gave me insight into the working of the government and initiated perceptions and ideas which were confirmed in later years. In the GOI an atmosphere of adversary relationship is all-prevailing, between ministries, within ministries themselves and within its departments. In the Ministry of Defence it is a triangular equation, with the politician minister, bureaucrats and service heads. At times Defence Finance is activated to further confuse the equation. While the politician minister always has the feeling that he is the boss, the bureaucrat encourages it without giving substance to this feeling to feather their own nest and create a buffer between the minister and the services. This results in a one-to-one contest between the bureaucracy and the services, which is influenced by personal relationships at various functional levels. It operates on two planes of confrontation or amicability accompanied by compromises from the lowest level up to the PSO level, which is worked out by individuals. In the absence of a formalized system of CDS and integration of the services with MOD, its management at the highest level is of great significance and importance. I saw two chiefs managing it in entirely different manner. General Krishna Rao had a working relationship with the Raksha Mantri Venkataraman, recognized the presence of RRM and totally ignored the bureaucracy. He dealt with the prime minister directly on all important issues, with whom he had developed a good relationship and access. The other chief one heard of having a similar but more dynamic and direct approach with the prime minister was Gen. (later Field Marshal) Manekshaw. While FM Manekshaw was more direct and open, Gen. Krishna Rao was equally effective but more sophisticated. The second chief I served with was Gen. Vaidya. He was most inconsequential and in the very early period of his tenure he had compromised his position with the government as well as within the Army. I felt that management of this relationship is important by the service chiefs in order to get the services their due. A direct relationship with the politicians, both the prime minister and the Raksha Mantri is important, if possible without confrontation or even with confrontation with the bureaucracy. Such direct relationship has tremendous value and is crucial in times of crisis. I recollect that it was Gen. Krishna Rao's direct access to Mrs. Gandhi which prevented our involvement in Mauritius, not due to lack of Army capability but because we did not have airlift for the same as our aircraft lacked a turnround capability without refuelling in a third country. Similarly, sensing trouble brewing up in Sri Lanka, after discussing it with Mrs. Gandhi, Gen. Krishna Rao asked me and Brig. Narsiman to update our information and keep up with the smallest developments in that country. It was to be kept under tight wraps, till required, even the highest of bureaucrats had no inkling of it. Under Gen. Vaidya it degenerated into a purposeless open exercise without any well-defined aim. Lt. Gen. Sundarjee initiated it *ab initio* without regard to past studies and knowledge, which resulted in a bit of a fiasco. The value of this relationship was proved beyond doubt during 1971 war of liberation of Bangladesh. But the nation refuses to learn. Most chiefs spend more time in managing the Army, which could be entirely left to the army commanders with suitable policy guidelines.

An open and healthy relationship between the politician and the army hierarchy is not only in the best interest of both but of the nation. It became vividly clear to me as the Western Army Commander later. I am quoting the incident here as it illustrates the point well. During the Army Commanders' Conference in September/October 1988, the Defence Minister K.C. Pant, hosted a dinner for all the commanders of the three services. We arrived at the appointed time and were received by officers of the MOD, but K.C. Pant had not arrived, which I thought was inappropriate as he was the host. A bit later Pant arrived and positioned himself in the centre of the hall. A few minutes later a junior bureaucrat came and told us to go and meet him. I felt it was odd and as a host he should go around and meet his guests and not other way round. Our politicians (so-called public men) are more feudal than the British, in this they are ably assisted by the bureaucrats. We ignored the bureaucrat as we thought he knew no better. After a while the RM came round to our group and Air Marshall Sinha, AOC-in-C Eastern Air Command, introduced himself and the RM shook his hand and asked him how is Calcutta. Air Marshal Sinha told him, he was in Shillong and it is Army's Eastern Command which is in Calcutta. When my turn came, I just wished him. He shook my hand and asked me how I was. I told him 'good'. After the RM had left a senior bureaucrat in our group asked me, General Sahib, all of us introduced ourselves, you did not. Why, I think there is something behind it. I told him I have met the RM a number of times, I wonder whether he even remembers my name. I continued that it does not matter if he knows Tubby Nayar or not, but it is important for him to know the Western Army Commander not only as a person but more importantly his capability, for the outcome of any conflict with Pakistan will be determined by what the Western Command does or fails to do. That is why it is important for him to know us. I have a feeling that the bureaucrat conveyed the message to the RM as all army commanders were asked to meet him individually the next day. But the system is still wanting and both the nation and the services continue to lose by default.

From the above narrative it should be evident that our structure for security management and response to defence requirements is inadequate and the functional relationship between different organs and institutions is distorted and unresponsive. We need to rectify it, for which more than adequate studies and deliberations have taken place and are available. I shall confine myself to highlight some of the major aspects.

Flawed Structure

The present structure for security and defence planning is flawed and there is no institutionalized professional interaction. The Cabinet Committee of Security (CCS)—(earlier Cabinet Committee on Political Affairs)—is the highest policy making body on security and defence matters. Next is the Committee for Defence Planning, which acts as a chain between the CCS and Chief of Staff Committee (COSC), which is the highest policy making body within the purview of the Defence Forces. The three committees represent the political, bureaucratic and the defence services. Interaction and intercommunication between them is minimal and virtually non-existent and essentially restricted to during crisis. They work in an isolated fashion. Defence and civil services are compartmentalized to such an extent that these are considered antagonist to each other. The situation had been made worse by the interjection of a Strategic Policy Group and a Crisis Management Coordination Committee under the cabinet secretary and a National Executive Committee under the home secretary. The Armed Forces have also fallen a prey to the ethos of committee system by forming the 'Defence Services Crisis Management' Group under the integrated Defence Staff. A sneak review of the system confirms that for long-term policy planning for defence and security, the system is flawed and lethargic and for emergency and crisis it has added to confusion and delays. Committees without proper professional representation and inputs can never take sound policy decisions and neither can they be accountable. Institutions respond to situations and not committees. A prime example of the failure of the system is the response to the 2008 floods in Bihar. Having constituted the Disaster Management Authority, its basic recommendation of positioning relief bricks got lost in the maze of committees. Who can be blamed? If anything, it has added to the turf war and disjointed actions.

The need for integration of the Defence Services with the Ministry of Defence and establishment of the Chief of Defence Staff system as recommended by the Arun Singh Committee can no longer be delayed. A natural corollary to this would be the institution of the theatre commands. In conflict situations as in Jammu & Kashmir and the north-east, the system has resulted in ad hocism and total lack of policy for conflict resolution and management. The concept of unified headquarters and civil-military liaison committees adopted in conflict areas is only a contraption to soothe the turf war between the administration, Para Military Forces (PMF) and the Army. The need is for unity of command. This existed in the troubled areas of Nagaland, Mizoram and Manipur till the late 1980s. It worked well and there was never any problem either with the civil administration, the PMF and the Army. The problem has its roots at the centre, where each head of PMF wants to control (really interfere) in field operations more to establish its turf but without accountability.

In a globalized environment, need for strategic culture and thinking is greatly enhanced, which requires a strategically responding military providing advice to a similarly competent civil authority. In such an environment, effect of action and inaction will be magnified and the threshold of crisis for the decision maker will be lowered and response time for decision reduced. Also the need for immediate attention and action is enhanced and requirement for coordination and cooperation of all organs is clearly mandated.

The need for being strategic is best illustrated by the global threat of terrorism, the MHA needs to fight terrorism at the strategic level and leave the fight against terrorists to the police and the intelligence agencies.

In Western democracies, the military over a period of time has learnt to respect the capability of their political leaders. It cannot be said of our system. The concept of civilian control in our democratic system is accepted and honoured by the armed forces. Unlike Pakistan, the legitimacy of the political authority has a traditional acceptance in India, irrespective of its shade and complexion. But what is worrisome is the misplaced concept of civilian control as to who the controller is? It is the political master and not the bureaucracy, which is just another executive instrument. Without going into the why and how, of it the current state of affairs is dismal. The ignorance of national security by our political elite has resulted in lack of political direction and ineffective mechanism for formulation and execution of national security policy. Governments' response to frequent acts of terrorism is a prime example. The void can only be filled by professional advice to and understanding of it by the political leadership. The preparation and execution of a war is even a more complex issue requiring intimate and continuous professional advice. The success of the 1971 War for the liberation of Bangladesh was essentially due to the sound professional advice by the service chiefs to delay the operations till the winter, which was accepted by Mrs. Indira Gandhi in spite of pressing international and domestic compulsions. The requirement is for an objective civilian control, wherein the power is distributed between civilian and military with maximizing of military professionalism. Instead what we have in the country today is a type of subjective control, which is undermining the military security of India.

Broad aims of national security continue to be to protect the nation and its institutions against external and internal threats. Since both the civil and military instruments are involved in its planning and execution, therefore civil-military relations became a function of security policy and essential for its implementation.

Before I get down to the actual functioning and implementation of the civil-military relations at the operational level, a word on aid to civil authority is essential. Instructions on Aid to Civil Authority

1970, lay down that aid to civil authority is a constitutional obligation, albeit the instrument of last resort. What needs to be clearly understood is that it is the instrument of last resort and therefore does not bear procedural compliance as is the impression of some junior administrative officers. There have been a number of occasions when request for Army requisition has been made without utilization of police and PMF resources available with the administration. To prevent this the central government has laid down the following additional guidelines:

(a) Employment of troops for normal law and order situations other than having communal overtones may be responded at the Command Headquarters at the discretion of GOC-in-C. Army Headquarters will be kept informed.
(b) In the case of communal disturbances it will be referred to Army Headquarters and cleared by the COAS and MOD.
(c) All election related deployment of troops will be projected by the MHA and cleared by Army Headquarters and MOD.
(d) Employment of troops for more than ten days will require sanction of the central government.

Civil-Military Relations

The foundations of civil-military relations in a conflict situation should be laid on sincerity of purpose, mutual trust, tact, perseverance and above all professionalism. Of these sincerity of purpose is most important as we should be quite clear of our long-term aim and work towards it in spite of all pressures, and should not compromise these for the sake of good relationship and short-term gains. There is a tendency amongst politicians and some bureaucrats to succumb to pressures and wash their hands off unpleasant situations. This results in erosion of government's image and loss of credibility, which must be avoided. The need is to be frank and even blunt at times but there should never be a break in the relationship.

The sphere of our civil-military relations are primarily confined to conferences at state level and down to districts and updating on Internal Security Schemes. These are all in the formal domain and deal with only some of the major problems of mutual interest, even these linger on from year to year. There is no continuous and progressive relationship developed between civilian and military officers, there may be odd exceptions. During the British period, John the DM, Jim the SP and Joe the local Garrison Commander met regularly socially and otherwise, which projected the government's functioning in a united and cohesive fashion. Today there is greater need for it as areas of civil-military cooperation have expanded beyond routine land acquisition, cantonments, excise, pensioners and ex-servicemen welfare. The disturbed social, political and economic environment have made handling of law and order more complex, to say nothing of terrorism adding more complexities to our internal security situation.

I intend to suggest some guidelines for actual working of civil-military relations at different levels by narrating actual incidents in my experience. During my visits to the outlying areas in Manipur and Nagaland as GOC, I always made it a point to meet the local officials and functionaries irrespective of their status. My new *aide-de-camp*, a young officer, initially thought that I was observing some kind of a traditional ritual but found that the conversations and interaction was related to the area and their functioning. One day he could not contain his anxiety and asked me as to the purpose of my doing it. I told him to figure it out. However, after a month or so I told him that irrespective of how low a status we might think they have, in their own environment and domain they are important, whether an ADC, Circle Officer, BDO, Gao Burha, Dobashi or a panchayat representative. By giving them respect and importance we help in enhancing their status and build them up among their people and it reinforces their authority and helps in drawing their willing responses. Everyone irrespective of his comparative low status is important in his own environment.

During the Assam agitation in late 1970s, a newly-posted DC gave a requisition for dispersal of an agitated crowd to a Major in-charge of a column, which had been pre-positioned in anticipation of such an eventuality. Having received the requisition, the Major deployed his men but took no action against the agitators who were over a couple of thousand strong. The DC asked the Major as to why he was not dispersing the crowd which was shouting slogans, beating drums and utensils and blowing conch-shells. The Major told the DC, the demonstration is peaceful, they have done no harm to anyone and not damaged anything, they are just agitating. The young DC told the Major that once he has given the requisition, it must be obeyed and the crowd dispersed. The Major told the DC, you have done your duty, I will do mine based on my judgement. The DC complained against the Major to the Commissioner when he visited the area. The Commissioner was a seasoned veteran and explained to him that the Major's action was right and if he had taken action as the DC had thought, it would have precipitated the situation. Without discouraging the DC, the commissioner told him that the Major has 13 to 14 years service and he should respect his age and experience and not let ego come in the way of doing the job. I had similar experience in Manipur while implementing the Armed Forces Special Powers Act. No law is bad, it is bad implementation which causes problems.

I took over the Division in Manipur and Nagaland at the height of the Meitei insurgency in Manipur and renewed phase of the rejuvenated Naga insurgency in the districts of Nagaland and Manipur bordering Myanmar in May 1981. The situation in the Imphal Valley was so bad that the elected government had washed their hands off and president's rule had been imposed. Both the government and the security forces were on the backfoot. Administration and police were nowhere to be seen and SHOs had hung up their uniforms and disappeared. Anything and everything was being guarded, from petrol pumps to all government offices, institutions and officials and all civil installations of any consequence. L.P. Singh, a towering personality and one of our most distinguished and able civil servants, was the governor of all the seven north-eastern states. A few days later he arrived from Shillong and I went to call on him. During the meeting he outlined the situation as a true professional covering all the core issues, then he asked me as to what my initial assessment was and as to what should be done. After a brief resume of the situation I told him what we were doing was wrong and that we should get out of the protective mindset and go on the offensive. I told him that to do so I intend withdrawing all Army, AR and other PMF under Army's control from protective duties and after reorientating them to go on the offensive to seek and destroy ME. I informed him that I intend doing this after 30 days to give the civil administration time to readjust and take over all essential protective duties and throughout this phase I shall help the civil administration and also be available for dealing with any untoward situation. He was visibly upset and told me that he cannot permit this as civil administration was not up to it and there was bound to be a backlash. I issued orders that all Army, AR and PMF under army's operational control employed on protective duties should hand over to the PMF and police under the civil administration control. I gave a copy of the order to the chief secretary. Nothing happened for 25 days and when I reminded the adviser, he told me that he will ask the governor. Two days later L.P. Singh arrived in Imphal followed by the Home Minister Giani Zail Singh and the Cabinet Secretary Rao Sahib Krishna Swamy. I received a message from the Raj Bhavan to meet the home minister. I sent back a message regretting my inability unless I received orders through Army channels. A couple of hours later I received instructions to meet the home minister and convey my point of view. I met him and conveyed my professional assessment and the line of action. Gradually the troops were relieved and we got on the offensive, while simultaneously helping the civil administration, police and PMF under it to be active. Results started coming in slowly with successes in small encounters followed by bigger ones. In July just two months later, we captured Bisheshwar Singh, the chairman of PLA and one of the main ojhas (leaders) of the seven who had returned from Lhasa. Hearing of it L.P. Singh flew to Imphal and after congratulating me, told me that my professional judgement was correct and he is happy that I stuck to my guns. While there was sincerity of purpose on both sides, commonality of perception and trust took time. L.P. Singh was one of my biggest supporters and we developed the highest degree of mutual trust and respect. Due to our professional stance the credibility of both the Security Forces (SF) and administration was established.

CONCLUSION

The present structure is not conducive for efficient functioning. There is urgent need for reforms and these have to be top downwards. The CCS should be more representative and include service chiefs as professional heads for security and defence planning. The Arun Singh Committee report on integration of service headquarters with the MOD should be implemented. The CDS system should be instituted as without it integrated approach will remain elusive irrespective of the integrated defence staff's existence.

The scope of internal security has enlarged. It includes the expanding dimensions of terrorism. There is an urgent need for a long-term strategic response and improvement in dealing with it effectively at the tactical level requires immediate attention.

The number of committees should be reduced as you do not govern by committees. They have no accountability and are a hindrance against decision-making and implementation. When you constitute committees for specific purposes then its recommendations should be examined and implemented.

Today we depend on the Army and other services to bail us out of dirty situations resulting due to failures of others. What is worse, we take it for granted and refuse to give them their due.

NEED FOR STRATEGIC CULTURE

The absence of a strategic culture or a long-term vision is all too evident in most spheres of national life. There are manifestos by all political parties but once in power these are never translated into vision documents or white papers on policy issues. We have five-year plans but these do not reflect any long-term goals and therefore there are no progressive achievements in any field.

The same is the case in the security and defence fields, which in spite of the institution of a National Security Advisor (NSA) does not reflect any defined policy and vision. Based on the Kargil Committee report, we followed it up by setting up committees on Defence, Intelligence, Internal Security and Border management. I was member of the Committee on Internal Security and generally aware of the work of the other committees as there was fair amount of interaction on common issues and areas. These committees did commendable jobs but their recommendations though accepted by the group of ministers were left either unimplemented or implemented partially in an adhoc fashion. We continue to function in the same lackadaisical fashion and the field is left to bureaucratic committee of secretaries with limited vision, knowledge and experience.

Lack of strategic culture has resulted in piecemeal responses to events. It is so evident in our dealings with China, Pakistan and even our other neighbours. Internally it is reflected in our handling of the situations in the north-east, J&K and lately while dealing with Naxalites and terrorism.

Closer at home, the service chiefs need to concentrate more on strategy rather than conduct of operations in commands or day-to-day happenings in the service. Based on their experience, they should display a long-term vision of the global strategic scenario and developments in India's areas of interest and neighbourhood. This should not remain isolated but extend to interaction with the political set-up particularly with the CCS. Even with the institution of the NSA and its secretariat, the chiefs need to act independently with CCS on issues of national security and they should not hesitate in conveying their views even if these are in conflict with the NSA or even with members of the CCS. Till the CDS system is fully instituted, the service chiefs need to put up a joint front on issues of national security and defence. However, the position of the COAS is unique due to our external security dynamics on the borders and internal security environment and he should render direct advice to the CCS. It is also imperative that he renders advice on internal security situations even if we are not involved as its mishandling like in the Punjab can be detrimental to national interest and security. This is totally in the realm of professional advice and cannot be construed to be interfering or acting independently. This should also help the other organs of the government to inculcate culture of cooperation and consultation, which will generate greater consideration of the problem at the strategic level.

It is also imperative that the chiefs pick up a few critical issues or items whether these be in the operational, logistic, technology, equipment and doctrinal fields and achieve these during their tenures or make a start, which then fructifies in due course. The chief's main battles are in Delhi and not in commands or in the service, if he can win a few during his service then he has contributed to it. Two clear examples that come to my mind are resolving the Bangladesh crisis in 1971 by FM Manekshaw and the forward posture against the Chinese by Gen. Krishna Rao.

DEMYSTIFYING APPROACH TO STRATEGY

To develop strategic thinking, it is imperative that we understand the nuances of strategy and define our approach to it. Without going into the academics of it, opportunity for which is available to professionals during their careers but is rarely practiced due to the constraints of our environment, where immediate takes precedence over real and long terms issues. I wish to suggest a simple approach based on my learning and experience during service and later. The process and steps in formulation of strategy are discussed below. The first step is a clear vision.

A Clear Vision

An individual's physical vision can be defined as limits of his sight. However, it is the mental vision which is our concern, which is the horizon of one's imagination depending on his faculties and varies in each individual. But it is the focused perspective related to the issues which draws its parameters and defines its critical areas. Such a clear vision provides the basis for strategic thinking and formulation. This when put in writing can be termed as a vision document, which must be clear, discerning and focused. If more than one issue or aspect is included, then it is essential that not only each issue is clearly defined, in addition in the concluding portion their correlation, inter say priority/importance or relevance is indicated to make it cohesive and wholesome.

Strategy

In military terms strategy is defined as the art of generalship - science and art of war employing political, economic, psychological and military forces of a nation to achieve national goals. Beyond military and general civilian sphere applicable to all situations it implies employment of all means, resources, instruments and relevant infrastructure to achieve evolved goals. Broadly speaking it lays down a set of goals/aims, which are derived considering all known or influencing factors, which can be generated over a time, fallout of our actions (reaction) and imponderables. The last will ensure flexibility of responses. While strategy is to win wars, tactics is to win battles or engagements. Strategy must indicate clear parameters leading or focused towards find or ultimate goal. Militarily, out of strategy should flow operational parameters for each goal, terminating on the final one. In non-military arena it should result in policy.

Policy

It can be defined as a plan of action with managerial wisdom. It is the instrument to implement the strategy within identified parameters. It must therefore fulfil all requirements for execution of strategy, which implies that it must have an overall plan of action for achievement of goals and managerial guidelines for doing so.

Security: An Obsession

As a nation we are prone to traits as anyone else, these normally reflect the national character. However, two traits of recent origin reflect on us adversely and are not entirely in keeping with our history or culture. The first one is of dealing with real and important issues in a superficial manner, while non-issues take most of our energy and attention. This is obvious in the way our democracy has been functioning in recent years and lack of response by the instruments of governance for common man's concerns. I have illustrated this in Chapter 10 under 'A Nation in Disconnect'. This is a result of our current political culture, which is only oriented to electoral politics and power wielding.

The second one is our obsession with security which is more founded on perceptions rather than reality. The government and the media are equally to be blamed in engineering and reinforcing it. Security is a state of mind and a sense of insecurity in the public is generated not so much by incidents of terrorist violence but due to state failure to secure the environment for the public. What makes insecurity more pronounced is when state appears to be insecure itself and employs SF mostly for its own protection. This results in the state and its instruments getting obsessed with security, thus adding to the feeling of insecurity. Once this syndrome manifests security managers lose their orientation. After Operation Blue Star in Punjab in 1984, security has become an obsession with our politicians and higher the status more a sense of insecurity and demand for higher security. Ultimately it gets linked with status and in turn becomes its symbol. The intelligence agencies and police forces find it a convenient ploy to keep the leaders isolated, thus losing contact with the public. Greater display of security causes public irritation and resentment. Which also diverts effort and resources from securing the environment, which can only provide real security. Because of disorientation of the agencies responsible, they are found wanting at the time of crisis. Prime examples of this are the attack on the parliament and the 26/11 Bombay terrorist attack. The normal excuse given for failure is inadequacy of forces, which results in further reinforcing of an ineffective security apparatus. I have discussed these issues in the chapter on conflicts.

Real security can only be achieved by securing the environment. This requires improvement and rejuvenation of the basic infrastructure at the ground level of district police and Special Branch. Creating diverse intelligence agencies and more PMF and armed police will not enhance security without an efficient basic ground level set up. It is not a question of resources but correct orientation and realistic appraisal of threats and long-term approach to counter these. This can only happen if our obsession with security is overcome, which will also ensure that security agencies do not indulge in empire building without accountability to deliver real security. I have been in disturbed areas in the length and breadth of our country and exposed to dangers long enough to understand what security is and how it can be achieved. I have brought it out repeatedly in the context of different disturbed environments and repetition of it has become only irksome for me.

NOTE

1. Ravi Rikhye, *The War That Never Was*, Chanakya Publications, Delhi, 1988.

CHAPTER 8

Back to Manipur and Nagaland: An Insight into Our Democracy and Governance

My tenure as governor of Manipur with additional charge of Nagaland was one of the shortest, of just 16 months and of my own making. In spite of it being brief, it was most eventful and satisfying. I left with a tremendous sense of achievement and with equal disappointment as I could not finish the good work we had started. In a way it was probably as disappointing for the common people of Manipur and Nagaland, although the same cannot be said of most of the polity, the elite and some of the bureaucracy, as for them an irksome thorn in their side, had removed itself. It had similar though limited reaction in Delhi. Amongst the politicians both Narasimha Rao, the then prime minister, and Rajesh Pilot, MOS (Home), were genuine in their disappointment that I had resigned. They were sincere in their feeling that I was doing good and had achieved quite a lot in the limited time, to others it did not matter one way or the other. To the then HM S.B. Chavan it was good riddance of a defiant governor. Amongst the bureaucracy to the then Home Secretary K. Padmanabhaiah it did not matter but I had a feeling that Ahuja, special secretary, was sorry that I left. N.N. Vohra, in whose tenure as home secretary I went and was probably responsible for my appointment was genuinely sorry. The reaction amongst my friends was uniform, 'it was just like Tubby to do it'. The reaction amongst my near and dear ones was mixed, while some felt it was silly to have left, I should have done my full tenure of five years and let things carry on, but others took pride in my bold and upright stand. I never felt the need to justify anything I did, although the issue was raked up in the media for some time after my resignation and for a longer duration in Manipur.

Before I left Delhi to take over the appointment, I was briefed in detail by the then Home Secretary N.N. Vohra. The situation in Manipur was really bad, there were large-scale ethnic clashes between Nagas and Kukis, there had been communal clashes between Meiteis and Pangals and in addition there was high level of armed violence perpetrated by the Meitei and Naga insurgents. Similar views were expressed by the Prime Minister Narasimha Rao and Rajesh Pilot during my discussions with them and they felt I was the right person to handle it. When I asked them as to what they expected from me and if there were any instructions, they both told me to do what you have to do to bring the situation under control. I was also told that I would be given additional charge of Nagaland once I had settled down, they went to the extent of telling me that they were prepared to impose president's rule as soon as I take over. I told them that I will take some time to assess the situation and send them my recommendations. It is under these circumstances that I took over as governor of Manipur.

I arrived in Imphal on 31 August 1993 and was received by the CM R.K. Dorendra Singh and Deputy CM Rishang Keishing, other cabinet ministers, the Chief Secretary H.V. Goswami and the DGP R.K. Sharma with the customary guard of honour. I was given another guard of honour at Raj Bhawan before the swearing in ceremony by the Chief Justice of the Guwahati High Court on the same afternoon. During tea, after the ceremony, I met a lot of people I had known earlier. Dispensing with all formalities I asked the CM to brief me, followed by a briefing by the Chief Secretary Goswami and the DGP Sharma. All in all it was a grave situation. The coalition government was a conglomeration of Congress (I), Manipur Peoples Party (MPP) and seven other segments of defectors and unattached elements. Apart from the political fragmentation, there was no cohesiveness even amongst the communities—Meiteis, Nagas and Kukis. The Meitei CM, the Naga Deputy CM and Doungal, the Kuki FM, as I discovered later were encouraging factional, ethnic and communal fights by aiding and abetting ethnic and communal militant groups, thus providing impetus to ethnic and insurgent violence. The NSCN(IM) had increased their area of influence beyond Senapati and Ukhrul districts to Tamenglong and Chandel districts in the hills with the connivance and support of Naga politicians and their over ground adjuncts. The administration and police were both partisan and ineffective.

Due to government's failure to check it, it drew reaction from Kuki organizations and militant groups. The ME indulged in extortions and kidnappings and most people in the valley were captive of their design and tolerant of their activities. The Pangal-Meitei riots in May 1993 had disturbed the communal harmony in the valley. Rising insurgency, Naga-Kuki ethnic clashes and communal tensions provided spurt to anti-social and criminal activities. The situation in Nagaland always influences the situation in the hill districts of Manipur, which had also started escalating. The factional clashes between NSCN(IM) and (K) to increase their area of influence had added to violence and it spread to other areas. The partisan attitude of the state government and unfortunately to some extent that of the security forces had further precipitated the situation. The areas of conflict and violence both in Manipur and Nagaland had enlarged territorially and engulfed most tribes and ethnic communities. The insurgency had developed ethnic and political dimensions. In Manipur itself killings by NSCN(IM) had increased to over 150 up to August 1993 compared to 20 in 1991 and 30 in 1992 and over 300 Kuki men, women and children had been killed and over 80 Kuki villages had been burnt. The situation had been deteriorating since the previous year (1992) and after the May riots it worsened in the valley as well. The state government had bumbled along in their own sweet lackadaisical way. There was no governor after Panigrahi left in March 1993. It was looked after by Raghunath Reddy, the governor of Tripura. Centre was not fully apprised of the situation. I spent the next 24 hours in briefings and discussions with the intelligence agencies and the security forces and another day to make up my mind on the actions required to control the situation.

Under the circumstances, I was quite clear in my mind that I could not be a spectator to happenings. I had to influence these and ultimately take command of the situation, if influencing the popular government failed. I decided to be proactive and was later to be referred to by all as an activist governor. In my opinion it not only succeeded but also generated positive public opinion and responses. I therefore decided to confront the situation headlong. I called all the three senior political leaders—the CM Dorendra Singh, Dy. CM Rishang Keishing and the FM Doungal and told them bluntly that they were not Meitei, Naga or Kuki leaders but senior Manipur leaders and they should behave as such. I asked them to act jointly and visit areas most affected by violence and deal firmly with the situation and arrange and distribute relief in a non-partisan and fair manner. I told them that I will watch the situation for a few days and will interfere if required. After this I called the Chief Secretary Goswami and the DGP Sharma to act and take administrative measures and decisions on security based on their judgement without waiting for orders or nod of political approval for their actions. I told them I will not accept any inaction. I heard some muttering from the DGP and I told him to cut it out and then told both of them that I have given directions to the CM, Dy CM and Doungal, if they have any doubts they can ask them as they know me better. I called the other heads of the security forces and told them to curb violence in their own areas of responsibility. During our discussion I discovered that some of them including the Army thought that dealing with ethnic violence was not part of their charter. I told them that in the disturbed areas of Manipur any violence or any activity leading to violence and which disturbs peace and endangers lives is part of their mandate and there should be no ambiguity about it. I followed it up with a meeting with the community and church leaders and conveyed my feelings of distress to them and asked them to soothen the feelings within their own communities. I ended up by telling them that I will be watching their actions, some of them who knew me smiled and said, 'GOC is back'.

It was on the third day after my arrival that the first major incident of ethnic killing of Kukis by Nagas took place in the far-flung Tamai area in Tamenglong district. The reports I got were most disturbing, it was a complete failure of the security forces and what was worse, relief again was provided in a partisan fashion. While Doungal went with relief to Kukis in Tamei, Reshang went to a small pocket of Nagas in Senapati who were attacked by the Kukis. When I spoke to the CM he pleaded total ignorance and helplessness. In spite of my resolution of not to interfere for a few days, I could not restrain myself. I flew to the area next morning along with the DIG AR, the only security forces officer readily available. I saw dead bodies mostly of women and children as the men had run away and only returned when I landed. I went around the village and after finding out the details of the incident, I walked to the next Naga village and spoke to the villagers. I was certain that this was not the end of killings in this area. After discussion with the DIG AR I identified two Kuki villages which could be the next target. I told the DIG AR to inform the GOC that it is a point of honour for the SF that these two villages are fully protected. After a gap of ten years my gut feeling and ability to seek and sense trouble were live and kicking. Alas my warning did not result in the prompt action required. One of the village was attacked after 48 hours and the GOC had to pay the price for it. I had him removed and a new GOC Maj. Gen. S.P. Chopra was posted in his place. My visiting the area and taking action against defaulters had the desired result and things started moving.

I decided to tour all the districts and visit all violence prone areas where ethnic clashes had taken place. I told my staff to organize the tour as per the priorities given by me. They were against it but I overruled them, I had to overrule them even on the means of transportation. I insisted on travelling by road throughout. My ADC Th Brojan Singh a Manipur police officer, spoke to my wife to dissuade me but having known me for years she told him, 'Brojan, he does what he wants'. We had planned to spend three to four days in each district and I told my staff to be self-contained for the tour so as not to pose any burden on the district authorities. The tour commenced on 7 September, a week after I had taken over. My past experience of these areas had taught me that authority must not only exist but must be seen and be effective. In Manipur government was conspicuous by its absence.

The central government particularly Rajesh Pilot, MOS, was firmly of the opinion that the situation cannot be retrieved unless president's rule is imposed. He was keen to do so immediately after I took over. Two or three days after I had taken over he sent an aircraft and requested me to come to Delhi to discuss the situation. I observed the courtesy of going to Delhi but was firm in my opinion that we should help the state government to handle the situation and recommend imposition of president's rule only as a last resort. I also told him that it will be possible for me to fully assess the situation after I had toured the districts. I conveyed this to the HM and the home secretary also.

It took the better part of two weeks to tour all the districts and see things for myself. Travelling by road I could meet maximum number of people and see conditions first hand. Both the government and administration were conspicuous by their absence and anger against their apathy was all too visible. Their absence and lack of action in most fields was visible not only in areas of violence but even in most peaceful areas. In the areas of recent violence both Nagas and Kukis were equally affected and equally ignored. Action to mitigate their suffering was confined to areas in Senapati district and hills around the valley. Nobody visited the inaccessible areas in Ukhrul, Chandel and Tamenglong districts. My most disturbing experience was in Tamei in Tamenglong and in Khopum Valley in Bishenpur district. In Khopum Valley the old Chachar Road from Loktak side had become non-existent, we had to walk 6 km to reach the other end of the road and transport had to be sent via NH 53 to meet us. In Tamei area people had huddled into areas considered safe with no food or shelter. All in all it was an eye-opener and a most disturbing experience. In Khopum and areas of Tamenglong there were places which even the DC had not visited in ten years. In Khopum the government project of a dam and buildings for the staff were lying vacant and unused, we probably were its first and only occupants. Citrus fruits rot in the Khopum Valley in thousands of tons every year as it cannot be taken out of the area or processed. Abandonment both by default and design seemed to be the government's policy. The outcome of the tour could be summed up simply by saying that I came to know of the real ground situation in all aspects and our total achievement was to make people aware that the government contrary to popular belief actually exists. I was one face of it, possibly known to some of them from earlier days.

I sent my detailed report to the president with copies under a DO letter to the prime minister and the home minister, as is the custom, on 5 October 1993. A copy of my report is attached as Appendix A to this Chapter. My report also included the situation in Nagaland as the Naga insurgency in the hill areas of Manipur is an extension of it. It was also relevant as I had been forewarned that I will be given additional charge of Nagaland. I was categorical and minced no words to expose the politico-insurgent nexus, which had come about in Nagaland and Manipur and this parallel industry had throttled development and economic activity. I also brought out that fighting insurgency at the ground level and trying to douse the fires of ethnic conflict would not succeed unless this nexus was broken. I named people in the government including ministers. It was a conscious decision on my part and I struck to my opinion in spite of all pressures. It created quite a stir in Delhi. While some felt that truth had to be faced, others under pressure of party loyalty and political pressure wanted me to be taken to task for accusing ministers of the party which had sent me as governor. After three months of dilly dallying the prime minister decided to bite the bullet and my report was accepted and president's rule was imposed on 31 December 1993. On imposition of the president's rule, I issued a message on 1 January 1994 which is given in Appendix B of this Chapter. During this period there were a number of pressures from different quarters but I refused to compromise or change anything. The urgency of four months earlier followed by three months of inaction did not help the situation, although it helped me to know the situation better both in Manipur and Nagaland. I took over additional charge of Nagaland on 2 October 1993. A clear advantage of the delay was that it gave me time to think and plan the course of action in each field and I was fully ready when asked to take over. I had already started intervening in the law and order field where I felt my intervention would help in dealing with the situation and everyone accepted it. Once my report was tabled on the floor of the Lok Sabha it was in the public domain. The opposition took the government to task for its failure to handle the situation and the debate on it was well covered by the national press. The local press in Manipur and Nagaland serialized my report with endorsement of its truth, which created a sort of political upheaval. Some of the affected leaders particularly the Deputy CM Rishang Keishing openly abused the central leaders for accepting the report and wanted legal action taken against me. He consulted a number of legal luminaries in Delhi, who told him that since the GOI had accepted the report, a complaint can only be filed against the central government.

As this stage it will be interesting to recapture an incident concerning 12 Naga MLAs. Toward the last week of December 1993, intelligence reports indicated that 12 Naga MLAs belonging to Congress (I), MPP and Janata Dal have been asked by the NSCN (IM) to resign by 31 December 1993. It was also reported that A.S. Arthur, vice-president of Manipur Congress Committee (I) and an ex-Thanghkhul MLA along with R.V. Shirang, president of the Poumei Naga Union, have been sent by Rishang Keishing, the deputy CM, to negotiate with them in Dimapur. Although I was not sure of the authenticity of the report, I informally passed the information to MHA and apprised them that the resignation of the 12 Naga MLAs may destabilize the ministry completely. Having apprised them of the situation, I followed it up with a brief one para report to the president on 31 December 1993 with a request for imposition of the president's rule. This in a way further confirmed the involvement of Rishang and others with the underground. To catch them red handed, I asked the Nagaland police to arrest Arthur and Shirang when the meeting takes place in Dimapur. The meeting was held with V.S. Atem, Self-Styled (SS), C-in-C of NSCN (IM), Khayao, (SS) home minister and Puni (SS) Kilonsar (minister) at Hotel Fantasy in Dimapur on 31 December 1993. The Nagaland police missed them but they were arrested by 30 Assam Rifles on 5 January 1994 on their way back along with a number of unlicensed and prohibited weapons. During their interrogation they confessed that they had gone to negotiate with the NSCN(IM). Later in his belated letter to me Arthur pleaded that he wanted to apprise me of the meeting but could not get through to me on telephone. I checked up and found it to be untrue. Consequent to the arrest of Arthur, Rishang Keishing and the Naga MLAs came to see me along with a resolution signed by them on 8 January 1994, saying that they had sent Arthur and Shirang to negotiate with NSCN(IM) as they considered the latter, 'asking them to resign as an ultimatum and a threat, apart it being an unconstitutional and undemocratic demand'. Therefore dialogue with NSCN became indispensable.

The delegation of Arthur and Shirang managed to settle the issue successfully.

Having listened to them, I asked them that even if I accept their good intentions, was it not incumbent on them as a minister and elected MLAs not to negotiate with the underground as they represented the government. Moreover, why did they not inform the CM or me of the threat and what they wanted to do. They had no answer. Having been caught, the façade was only to get Arthur off the hook. I had known of both Rishang and Arthur's links with the underground since the 1980s, when Rishang was the CM and Arthur the Secretary of Nagaland Assembly. I also wonder if the informal information passed to MHA by me or through information received by their own channels instigated the government to declare president's rule on 31 December 1993. Arthur's letter and the memorandum signed by the 12 Naga MLAs are attached as Appendices C and D respectively at the end of this Chapter.

Another sidelight of the above episode was that when I returned after one of my routine visits to Nagaland, I saw IB sleuths moving around Raj Bhavan to check its security. When I asked Angou my secretary as to what this was in aid of, he told me that IB has got a report that some Naga politicians have approached the NSCN(IM) in Dimapur that I am anti-Naga and therefore I should be eliminated. I told Angou to call the IB officer and tell him to stop all this activity and come to my office. When the officer came he explained to me that the report is high grade so they have been ordered to see how security at the Raj Bhavan can be reinforced. I thanked him for his concern and told him that he had done his duty by telling me, now he could leave Raj Bhavan immediately. He was a bit non-plussed. To put him at ease I told him that when NSCN(IM) takes a decision to eliminate me, I will be the first to come to know of it, even before him. I told him I have done nothing wrong so why should they try to kill me. After a week, the same officer came to see me and said NSCN(IM) in their meeting took a decision that I am equally harsh with Kukis and Meiteis so they have nothing against me. Later many friends in Nagaland told me that the episode was true as was the decision of the NSCN(IM).

The presidential proclamation and notification for the imposition of president's rule was received late at night on 31 December when most officials were in the officers club for the New Year's party. The chief secretary rang me up and asked me if I wanted to see him or issue any instructions. I told him a few hours will not make any difference and that he should enjoy the party and meet me at 0900 hours on 1 January 1994. I had had four months' time and was fully prepared for the situation in all fields and what needed to be done. I knew I had a year's time during the president's rule and what was possible during this period in each field. Based on this I had carried out a detailed assessment and drawn out a priority of work schedule. I had taken two basic decisions, one that I will function as a governor in council so that I could provide transparency in government functioning by associating public men and best-suited personnel while taking decisions on matters of public interest and concern. It will also help in ensuring that policy decisions taken during president's rule could not be swept aside easily by the popular government later as public will be aware of it. Secondly, to ensure coordinated and cohesive functioning of the administration to have only two advisors, one on the administrative and security side and second to deal with planning and development. The former would be Goswami the chief secretary who would also act as advisor and for the planning and development a person who knows the environment in the north-east. I had also divided portfolios amongst them based on the above framework.

On 1 January 1994, when the chief secretary met me I gave him a hand-written division of responsibilities amongst the advisors and asked for his suggestions and views, he made some good suggestions and I modified the list. We asked Delhi for a second advisor. I left it entirely to the then Home Secretary N.N. Vohra, whose judgment I respected and who was most supportive throughout my tenure. He selected P.P. Srivastava who turned out to be a very good choice. He arrived the next day. During my first meeting with the advisors, I gave them a draft copy of my directive to the administration and SF. It contained my assessment of situation in all fields and laid down the policy framework and goals to be achieved. I asked for suggestions to be given within a week. We finalized the directive within three days and issued it to all. In the directive there were different annexures for the administration, the police and SF and each was issued only the annexure relevant to them. I considered it prudent to do so as apart from their separate tasks and goals to be achieved, it included a critique of their functioning and performance and the areas to be improved. It was the first time that such a directive was issued and I wonder if a similar directive has ever been issued since. This became the policy framework and check sheet for all our future work. The establishment was to some extent overawed by the situation and government functionaries both in Manipur and Nagaland and even at the centre talked of only law and order and nothing else seemed to matter to them. While the law and order situation was bad but I knew that it was neither the total problem nor the only one, it was just one of the problems. There were a number of issues of concern to the public, which needed as much attention. For instance, the perception that unless the law and order situation was under control very little of anything else is possible. Having lived with and handled such situations I knew how fallacious this was. Everything needs to be attended to as even a little bit in each field contributes and helps in other fields. So I made it clear to the advisors and the officials that we will undertake all activities possible in all fields which will help in mitigating people's hardships.

SITUATION AND RESPONSE

It will not be possible to cover all activities undertaken during the president's rule, I shall confine myself to briefly covering the major areas. It will be logical to start with a mention of the political situation. There was a state of total political drift due to manipulation for power by different groups and individuals within the government resulting in lack of direction and guidance to the administration. Some unscrupulous elements were even using the government machinery and administration as an extension of their political design and authority and furtherance of insurgent agenda with common motives. The politico-insurgent nexus was well established and provided impetus to extremist activities, fuelling ethnic divide and Naga-Kuki clashes and incapacitating administration and law enforcement agencies, that had resulted in erosion of government authority, instability and alienation of the people. While insurgency in the hills had developed its ethnic and political roots, communal riots between Pangals and Meitei had added further turmoil in the valley where ME activities remained unabated. Insurgencies in Manipur and Nagaland are fuelled by the above politico-insurgent nexus since mid-1980s and all economic and developmental activities are throttled to feed this parallel industry. It was therefore vital that this nexus is not only exposed but also made ineffective as fighting insurgency solely at the ground level in the law and order field will only mean ignoring the major dimension of the malaise. Insurgency in the state was mostly criminalized, all underground and extremist organizations were deeply engaged in extortions and illegal collection of money, kidnapping for ransom and selective killings to terrorize. Departmental heads effected cuts on behalf of extremists, the going rate was 2 per cent per month, underground were nominating contractors for work contracts, who deposited a percentage of the contract amount with the insurgents. Transport operators plying both on NH 39 and 53 paid monthly or yearly taxes against formal receipts given by these insurgents. Traders paid regularly to ME through middlemen based on income assessed by ME. Some traders found it to be more profitable to be middlemen as it fetched them 20 per cent of collections. This was in addition to the lucrative trade of drug trafficking and smuggling of forest produce and gun running. Kidnappings was a major area of concern and in spite of our best efforts people were reluctant to report and seek help. Investigations revealed that relatives of some politicians were acting as negotiators for release. The Poana Bazar traders were reluctant to lose patronage and favour of the politicians and through them of the insurgents and ME. It served double purpose of political patronage for profit and safety. The state had abdicated and insurgents and ME were the authority.

In view of the above, I decided to sideline these elements and totally deactivate and degrade them. The vital need of public contact by the government was fulfilled by activating community's social and traditional institutions and citizenry at large. This paid us handsome dividends both in terms of public participation and responses. This also became our motivation and strength. Having apprised the prime minister during my first meeting with him after the imposition of president's rule and having included the framework of our policy and activities in my directive, I never felt the necessity to consult the centre and went ahead to implement what was planned.

In the insurgency and the law and order field, I re-established the well tried out system of clear-cut areas of responsibility of the SF, the police and the PMF. The valley was entirely the responsibility of the police and PMF under civil control. The hills were the responsibility of the Army and Assam Rifles with the GOC and Inspector IGAR looking after their areas. New areas in the hill districts of Tamenglong and Chandel districts, which had become active after three decades were brought under security cover and CI grids were established with the induction of additional Army and PMF. In areas under civil control policing was entirely under Manipur police. I appointed Bimol Chandra Singh and Roman Kumar Singh, both Manipuri officers, as IG Law and Order and DIG of greater Imphal. Having done so I left them to do their job but kept a tight supervision. Both of them produced good results.

Apart from the ongoing Naga and Meitei insurgencies, the Naga-Kuki conflict and ethnic divide was my main concern. The issue was made more complex due to its meshing with the political agenda of each community's politicians and that of the ethnic insurgent groups, which provided impetus to violence and ethnic divide. The challenge was re-establishment of hundreds of years of peaceful co-existence and the land management system within the Kukis themselves and between the Nagas and Kukis where the latter were the tenants. This was opposed by the politicians, Kuki chiefs, ethnic insurgent organizations and politicians, who were trying to create captive political contingencies and areas of influence particularly in Churachandpur and Chandel districts where majority of the Kuki refugees (out of a total of 6,800 families) had taken shelter. I was not willing for them to become the Kashmiri Pandits of Manipur. Having witnessed Punjab and J&K, two diverse sides of a similar story, I was determined not to repeat it. I had learnt from Jagmohan's mistakes. Both population and capital flight if not reversed immediately tends to become permanent. I visited each and every refugee camp of Kukis and a few Naga ones who had been displaced and made it clear to them that unless they returned to their original areas the government would give them no relief and help for resettlement. I explained to them that we could do everything for them but could not recreate the lost land. I also explained to them that the politician's and insurgent's agenda was political and that of influence and they will drop them once their purpose is achieved. The message went home and it had the desired effect. They returned to their areas, government provided security and helped in their resettlement by providing housing material worth Rs. 9,000 to each family, implements, rations and technical help. The entire implementation of rehabilitation was by self-help with government compensating in kind for labour. The entire relief and rehabilitation operations were handled by community and youth organizations under government supervision. Standing crops were harvested by original owners under government protection. We re-established the government's authority and domain and traditional systems between the communities. It took our major attention, effort and time and even we were surprised by the success of our efforts. It contributed substantially to improvement in law and order and healing of the wounds. By March 1994, 2,500 families had been settled back in their original locations and by July the process was completed just as monsoons descended.

During my tours and visits and while dealing with insurgency situation in the hills, the high level of mismanagement of the state security and police apparatus came to light. Politicians of all the three communities had managed that the district police and Manipur Rifles (armed police) located in their areas was entirely manned by its own ethnic community and they acted in a partisan and parochial fashion during the Naga-Kuki conflict. The situation was the worst in Ukhrul in Naga inhabited areas and in Churachandpur in Kuki dominated areas. The IPS cadre officers from outside Manipur were only spectators and totally subservient. Reorientation and remanning of police while handling insurgency and ethnic conflict was a major challenge. After removing ineffective and compromised officers, we managed to reorganize, re-orientate and reshuffle the police force. In this the new DGP Mishra, Bimol

Chandra Singh and Roman Kumar Singh were of great help.

One of the most disturbing element of the environment was that people had developed a negative mindset and had lost faith in the government and its instruments. They were tired of listening to sermons and promises and wanted action and results. Although it made the situation worse but in a way it helped me to decide and follow a proactive policy. Action with peoples participation and transparency became our beacon and watch-word. It was easier said than done. It started off small but gained strength and momentum as we showed results and generated hope and promise by our actions. I firmly believe that government has to be seen, working and effective to gain people's confidence and respect.

OPEN AND NEW FACE OF THE GOVERNMENT

In this regard the first opportunity came on 26 January 1994, Republic Day. An event normally celebrated by a parade in a highly guarded police stadium attended by ministers, dignitaries, officials, and some invited public. I decided to utilize the opportunity to display the new and open face of the government. We had to prepare for it. I had told the administration and SF that I will take the salute in the open in front of Kangla Fort's main gate. The parade will start from the police stadium, march through the main street to Kangla Fort and after I had taken the salute it will march through Paona Bazar and then return through the town to the police stadium. We invited the public of the entire Imphal town for the parade. I asked all schools, volunteer organizations of all communities and the youth clubs to participate. To get this participation I invited the youth club presidents and Meira Paibies (torch bearers) and asked for their cooperation. Apart from the security forces and police, there were over 20 youth clubs, schools and about a dozen social organizations. Initially when it started from the Police stadium there were very few persons and that too watching from half open windows but by the time it reached Kangla Fort more people had come and were clapping. Finally when it was passing through Paona Bazar people came out openly and clapped. Initially inquisitiveness and later a different and open Republic

Day drew people. We had won a moral victory and the insurgents and ME were on the backfoot. The local media and vernacular Manipur papers welcomed the change and posed the question, what next? After I left, the government reverted back to the old practice of holding the Republic Day parade and 15 August Independence Day celebrations in the protected police stadium. It is so even to-day.

Like any place where the government is corrupt, people develop the feeling that nothing can be achieved unless you pay for it or someone will do a favour looking for something in return. Manipur was no exception. The situation is made worse if there is no transparency and people just don't know what is happening. In addition the disturbed environment and security psychosis further helps in sweeping corruption and wrong deeds under the carpet away from public eye. In this regard probably Manipur is the worst in our country. Both types of corruption, major and petty, are found in abundance and are practised openly and in a blatant fashion. The common man is affected both directly by the petty and by the major or higher corruption mainly indirectly. This is one of the prime reasons for people's alienation and for the negative mindset. One of most publically talked about manifestations of this phenomenon is admission to professional colleges and other higher educational institutions. The admissions to the Regional Medical college were due, the Manipuri press outlined graphically the past corrupt record of the government as to how in spite of the façade of a competitive examination, not only undeserving candidates lower in order of merit got admission, in addition some candidates who had not even appeared but were relatives of ministers and high officials were admitted. Deserving candidates in the merit list were left high and dry. It ended up by saying that it was a challenge to the governor and his government during the president's rule. Without reacting to it, we decided to take up the challenge. I gave the responsibility to P.P. Srivastava and asked him to visit UPSC in Delhi, find the details of their system and implement it. We followed the entire system, changing of index numbers, seating arrangement, paper setting and production, invigilation and supervision. We followed the complete methodology of paper correction and result compilation. After I was briefed and I had seen the arrangements I added one additional precaution that the professors setting the papers will be chosen at the last minute, taken to the government guesthouse where they will set the papers and papers will be in the custody of the advisor and only run through the printing two hours before commencement of each paper. After the examination the papers will be brought to the government guesthouse, corrected without interruption day and night and the results compiled. The procedure was repeated for each paper. The examiners/papersetters stayed in the guesthouse till examination was completed, results compiled and announced. The advisor and the entire staff handling the examination also stayed at the guesthouse along with the examiners. When results were declared, one minister's son, one IG's son and a local newspaper editor's relative did not make it to the merit list. The local media went gaga over the results and not only complimented me, the advisor and all who made it possible but in addition the message for Manipur was, 'it can be done'.

DEVELOPMENT WITH PARTICIPATION

In the developmental field both planning and implementation had been distorted for political and personal gains by people in power. Bureaucracy with a few exceptions not only succumbed to political pressure but actively connived for mutual benefits. Grandiose schemes carved out and approved by Delhi had little relevance to the ground realities and were mostly unrelated to public needs and even unknown to them, however, these acted as easy money churners. A canal was dug from the base of Maphao hills with no dam in existence, it existed on paper only with the sole purpose of garnering the compensation money, which in turn became yet another cause of Naga-Kuki conflict as militants on both sides wanted the spoils. It left both the Naga-Kuki villagers homeless and jobless. Similar was the fate of Khopum Valley. Money was spent on non-existent roads and bridges. Worse was the fate of district plans, which were formulated on dictates of local politicians and most beneficiaries of rural development schemes were people nominated by politicians. Villagers and village councils/panchayats were denied access and sidelined.

Having assessed the ground situation during my visits to most of the areas, I in consultation with the advisors and heads of departments concerned decided to foreclose non-beneficial and non-viable projects. Monitoring teams were organized to verify on ground construction work on both roads and buildings and only after verification payments were made. Simultaneously useful works which had been abandoned such as Nambul River bypass channel, improvement of its banks, dredging to prevent flooding and water supply schemes to new areas, increase in storage capacity were revived. New schemes like the Lotak Lake catchment area scheme to improve the ecology and environment, availability of electricity, health and sanitation, improvement of NH 39 and 53, and revamping the district plans was the priority. Emphasis was laid on employment generating schemes which received priority. I visited each district and revived the district planning and publically announced allocations to various heads. Village councils and panchayats were empowered to decide schemes in their areas and decide on beneficiaries for the rural development schemes. I also announced that if government functionaries or insurgents take away money then I will stop all development in the district concerned and give it where it can be better utilized. It generated people's involvement and participation and helped us to meet our targets. It was most heartening to see people close to Muivah's village guarding explosives so that the road which was lying incomplete for a decade could be completed. Even the insurgents who were present in Ukhrul when I spoke to the public did not create obstructions for fear of people's resentment.

One of the most heartening experiences of generating public participation was clearance of encroachments on Nambul River in Imphal town to implement the anti-flooding scheme. I did not want the government to be seen to be acting independently on its own but instead on behalf of the people. I had a meeting with all the youth club functionaries in Imphal. There were over 50 clubs, one in each *lekei* (street). I told them that to prevent flooding of Imphal town and to implement the Nambul River scheme, I will only do it if people wanted it and for which they had to remove all the encroachments. I told them I was quite comfortable in Raj Bhawan and I was not affected, they would be the beneficiaries of the scheme. After 48 hours they came back and promised to remove all encroachments voluntarily. All encroachments were removed within a week except two commercial buildings, one belonging to a minister and other to an IG of police and a few guesthouses constructed by the *imam* of the mosque who was the recipient of rent from them. The newspapers reported the people are with the governor and have removed all encroachments and work on strengthening of bunds, the bypass channel and dredging had started. They wanted to see what was done with these buildings. I gave a statement that as the upholder of law in the state I would do it legally. Owners of the two commercial buildings filed a case against the eviction orders of the government and obtained a stay. We fought the case and got the stay vacated and then bulldozed the buildings. In the case of guesthouses constructed by the *imam* I asked for the help of Halim Choudhry, a retired deputy commissioner, to ask the *imam* to remove the guesthouses which were not part of the mosque complex, failing which these would be forcibly removed. While this approach through Halim and other prominent Pangal citizens was being made, the *imam* contacted Maulana Madni a firebrand Muslim MP, who went and spoke to the Home Minister Chavan. He rang me up to say that he did not want another episode like the Babri Masjid in the east. I told him to relax as I knew what I was doing and requested him to tell Maulana Madni, that if he came to Imphal he will be arrested and sent back with an escort. Knowing the futility of resistance and the advice given by Halim Chaudhry and other senior Pangals better sense prevailed. The *imam* removed the encroachments voluntarily. The public fervor was so great that people started removing all encroachments in other towns voluntarily which greatly facilitated our work on roads and bunds in all other towns like Bishenpur, Chandel, Thobal, Moirang and Jaribam. Maira Pabis and youth clubs in the valley and Naga, Kuki youth and other tribal institutions joined in the venture in the hills. The spirit was contagious and we used it to the fullest. It was an exhilarating experience. Public participation is essential to give correct orientation to development and for transparency. We achieved most of our goals. The end result was that 1994 was declared the year of development due to public pressure in spite of reluctance of the politicians even after I had left. Some of the salient details of work done are given in Appendix E at the end of this Chapter.

The other area of concern was the increasing unemployment, particularly amongst the educated youth. Over a period of time I realized that unless development and economic activity generates employment, their long-term effect is decreased. Manipur had 26.5 per cent unemployment amongst its economically active people. The main reason for it was low investments in the last 30 years and hence low infrastructure development. Large-scale unemployment amongst the educated youth is one of the main reasons for social tensions and law and order problems. After discussion with the advisors, some qualified public men, academicians and the planning department, we drafted a comprehensive package to improve infrastructure and create opportunities for self-employment. It had two parts, a list of projects of short-term gestation of Rs. 136.37 crore for immediate benefits, and part two of the package with an estimated cost of Rs. 876.57 crore for projects of infrastructure development. While part one of short-term projects was to be completed within a period of two years, the projects in part two were to spill over to the Ninth Plan. The package would have created additional employment of 146 lakh mandays in the first year. It was discussed and presented to Pranab Mukherjee, the Dy. Chairman of Planning Commission and Commerce Minister. He was greatly appreciative of the effort and promised to help. I do not know what happened after I left.

To prevent extortions and illegal collections by the insurgents and to reduce bulk availability of cash with the government departments, we introduced the scheme for payment of salaries of class III employees through banks. The modalities were worked out in consultation with the banks. To implement the scheme they demanded a levy of surcharge on the bank accounts of the drawing and disbursing officers of Rs. 10 per cheque issued by the District Development Officer (DDO) to each employee. The scheme was to be launched on 1 March 1994 but got deferred to June till we got instructions issued by the Ministry of Finance (Banking Division) on my intervention.

There was also the problem of net credit flow, which had declined since 1991. In most sectors banks had failed to fulfil targets set under the Annual Credit Plan (ACP) of the state deposit, the government share in the form of subsidies or grants provided to the banks. Matters got worse by ineffective presence and funding of branches in the outlying areas. This remained a constraint throughout due to unsettled conditions.

We also took up gradual liberalization of the Restricted Area Permit both in terms of areas that could be visited and delegation of powers for issue to the Resident Commissioner. Similarly, distinction between individual tourists and group tourists put the small groups at a disadvantage. The delay factor both in its issue and intimation to the state of Protected Area Permit (PAPS) issued by MHA was a source of embarrassment as it was mostly received after the due date. We also asked for clearance of NH 53 for entry by tourists.

Trading is a major economic activity in most of the north-eastern states and particularly in border states. After hectic effort an MOU on border trade was signed with Myanmar during my tenure. It had great potential economically and for employment generation. However, it can only fructify if value addition and benefits came to people of Manipur. For this there was need to give fillip to local finished goods as trading in raw materials and finished goods from outside will be beneficial to mostly non-Manipuris. For this there was need to enhance the cottage industries like weaving, citrus processing, clean industries like electronics and watch making and enhance bicycle assembly capacity in its factory. Within the means available we also decided to enhance the spindle capacity of the weaving factory. The need for scientific and technological orientation to education and establishment of ITIs was a primary requirement. This was included in our plans. Cross-border trading has a vast potential for employment in services like hospitability, secretarial services, finance and currency, transportation and communication including automation. Local youth could only benefit if they were trained. Bulk of trading in the north-east has been in the hands of outsiders, Marwaris, Bengalis, Punjabis and Tamils after they were thrown out from Myanmar. With the aim of preparing Manipuri youth, I started an orientation course of 250 educated Manipur youth in various disciplines. There was a lot of enthusiasm. I had mentally earmarked with the advisors the abandoned Imphal hotel owned by the government as a trading centre and a hub of these activities. It was most disheartening to learn that the popular government abandoned the idea after I left and Marwaris and others were once again in the forefront.

REVAMPING THE ADMINISTRATION

On the administrative side our main challenge was to re-orientate the administration to its original ethos of public service. I knew that changing people around hardly makes any sense unless there is a reason for it. So deviating from the norms of president's rule or any change in government. I made no change in appointments and responsibility but told everyone to perform to their best capacity. Once tasks were given they performed well and we had a reasonably efficient set up. According to my assessment they performed to 40 per cent of their expected capacity and it reached its peak after six months when it came up to 60 per cent in most cases. I had to remove one Manipuri officer in the education department for high level of corruption in the blackboard scheme implementation and one IG Police for similar reasons. It had the desired result. It will be morally incorrect if I do not acknowledge the support of the Prime Minister Narasimha Rao, Rajesh Pilot and particularly of the then Home Secretary N.N. Vohra, who understood the intricate and complex dimensions of the job I was doing and it was their unstinting support which made it possible. It will be no exaggeration to say that they got into the spirit of things and joined in our enthusiasm. Narasimha Rao told me that he wanted Manipur to be a model state in the north-east.

One of the most troublesome area of concern was the absence of lower level officers from the districts. When I went deep into it, I found that there was a sword hanging on their head. While there was a ban on filling vacancies but in most cases in the same vacancy there were two people employed on temporary basis one by the minister and other by the bureaucrat head of the department. Extensions were given six monthly or yearly for which the minister and head of department had to be compensated. These officers were mostly present in Imphal following their extensions rather than working. Similar was the case with the muster roll of employees, quite a few of them were fictitious. Efforts to get rid of some absentee employees led to litigation and courts ruling them as quasi-permanent and some would have qualified even as permanent. I was not interested in getting rid of them, I was interested in getting them to work. After prolonged deliberation and consultation we decided to take a view on their future. Most of the officers and even one advisor was against any action in that direction. They probably knew the approaches being made in Delhi, a bit of it later. I overruled the dissent and we took a very pragmatic and workable decision, which was welcomed by almost all the affected personnel. We decided that the personnel who qualified as per terms and conditions of service when they were recruited/joined and who had acceptable performance should be declared regular and those who did not meet the criteria should be considered for lower grade/jobs or continue as temporary. This had the desired effect and people joined and stayed in their jobs as they were no longer dependent on favour of ministers and the bureaucracy. Ministers who were under suspended animation went to Delhi to complain to the prime minister that what I was doing amounted to crossing the limit as I was hitting their livelihood (*hamare pet par laat mar raha hai*), they had a substantial amount coming to them monthly from the temporary employees.

Our success in what we achieved was due to our teamwork in which the chief secretary and advisors Goswami and Srivastava and Rashmi, Jarnail Singh from the administration, Bimol Chandra and Roman Kumar from the police, Maj Gen. Chopra from the Army, just to name a few contributed immensely.

While a good deal of attention had been paid to the Naga insurgency and happenings in Nagaland and the hill areas of Manipur and later Cachar Hills due to increasing influence of the Naga insurgents, the same cannot be said of Manipur and the Meiteis, in spite of eruption of the Meitei insurgency in late 1970s and its ongoing aftermath. I felt that it required equal if not more attention. Meiteis consider themselves as more advanced, closer to the national mainstream and with a fine sense of art and culture. Their antagonism, growth of Meitei sub-nationalism and its transformation into insurgency with secessionist overtones are the result of their contemporary experience. Issues of the manner of merger of the state with the Indian union, delay in grant of statehood, gifting of Kabaw Valley and waiver of its compensation and non-recognition of Manipuri language with a literary history of 2,000 years under the VIIIth Schedule till as late as 1992 were perceived as severe blows to the Meitei psyche. This was encouraged by antagonism against privileges granted to tribals in education and coupled with the jobs, alienation of their fertile land under the Manipur Land and Revenue Regulation, resulting in economic deprivation of primarily agricultural Meitei society. This was further fuelled by rampant corruption, unemployment and monolith nature of the society resulting in violent outburst and demands for dissociation from Indian-ness. Being conscious of these sentiments I ensured that while encouraging Meiteis there should be no discrimination against the hill people both Nagas and Kukis.

I attended Meitei festivals as I did the Naga and Kuki ones and encouraged arts and music both at the Jawaharlal Academy of Fine Arts and excellent dramas on different themes by Ratan Thiyam, a world renowned Manipuri playwright and director. I encouraged their love for sports. We had an international polo tournament in March 1994 in which 23 foreign participants took part and also conducted the National Football Tournament. I encouraged the participation of the Manipur contingent in the 3rd National Games in Maharashtra. They did exceedingly well by winning 13 gold, 11 silver and 18 bronze medals and were placed 9th. It was a small contingent, which could participate in only about 50 per cent of the events. I was thrilled by their performance and put in a bid for the National Games to be held in Manipur in 1996. We started preparations in real earnest for these with the help of the Sports Authority of India, the Indian Olympic Association and the Sports Ministry. But the politicians drawing huge sums of money under MP's and MLA's development fund were a terrible disappointment. There was delay in holding the games after I left but they did take place. I strongly feel that the potential of Meiteis, Nagas and Kukis need to be exploited for constructive activities.

As stated above Meiteis had and probably still have a sense of relative deprivation and denial compared to the hill people. It was very evident in services and in some government departments. Based on an independent study they were included in the OBC list in 1994, providing some satisfaction. Similarly, the sensitive and emotive issue of foreigners or outsiders had been going on since 1980 and it had assumed dimensions of a political football. No popular government has displayed the capacity to deal with the problem. The issue came up again due to Kuki infiltration from Myanmar and during the Naga-Kuki conflict it became a cause for agitation for the All Manipur Students Union (AMSU). Their delegation came and met me. I told Mohi Lal, president of AMSU, that I will act as per the Constitution and no Indian citizen from anywhere will be harassed. Any foreigners identified and located will be expatriated. I gave AMSU access to census reports past and present and told them to help the government to locate foreigners. We located and identified some Bangladeshi migrants in Jaribam and some Myanmar Kukis in Chandel, after verification they were pushed back across the border. With sincere efforts an agreement was signed by the chief secretary with AMSU in November 1994. Chavan, the home minister, rang me up and asked me as to how an agreement can be signed without his knowledge. I told him I am here to solve problems and not create them. I do not require centre's sanction for legitimate decisions. With good faith we can solve all problems and give legitimate satisfaction to public.

The Raj Bhawan was declared an open house and became a hub of all activities and resembled a war office. My secretary R.K. Angosana Singh and later Nikhilesh Jha, ADC Brojen and PS Machindran were almost run off their feet but they coped with the situation admirably. The household staff under Neelamani met huge demands of tea and biscuits at all hours of the day and night smilingly. While we planned in Raj Bhawan but the problems and implementation of decisions to resolve them were outside and that is where we spent most of the time.

The Japanese invasion of India in the north-east is little known outside the military circles and even amongst the armed forces it is more in the context of military history and confined to the Battle of Imphal and DC Hill in Kohima. But to those of us who have served in the north-east and particularly in Manipur and Nagaland its ground realities extend beyond these two battles and the cemeteries in Kohima and Imphal. Moirang, Red Hill and INA Memorial at Moirang are testimony to the sacrifice of the British, Indian, Japanese and INA soldiers. It can only be understood by a soldier and a nationalist of the independence struggle for their own reasons. I had been a regular visitor to these and other landmarks in Manipur and Nagaland. So when the Japanese Embassy approached the Government of India and I was asked to look into it, I was very happy. I told them to identify a suitable area for a memorial to the dead. I was further enthused when they told me that the memorial will be in memory of all dead from both sides, the Japanese, INA soldiers and the British and Indian soldiers. Finally, I suggested to them the area of Red Hill where the Japanese had fought a major battle with very high casualties, this was also where their advance on the Moirang axis was halted. It was on the Moirang-Imphal Road and a befitting site. After visiting the site they liked it immensely and they wanted to start work soon to commemorate the fiftieth anniversary of the event. I gave the sanction to what had been lying unattended in the bureaucratic labyrinth between Delhi and Imphal. We had a joint Indo-Japanese memorial service at the site, Maibam Lokpa Ching (Red Hill) 2926 on 21 March and I inaugurated the memorial on 7 October 1994 just at the base of the feature near the road in the presence of the Japanese cultural minister and their ambassador. The function at the Japanese memorial was most dignified, simple and genuine. There were flags of India, Japan, the Union Jack and a simple tricolour representing INA. After a short Buddhist prayer in Japanese, I inaugurated the memorial with a short speech which was followed by the Japanese minister's speech thanking the GOI and the Manipur government. In the evening the Japanese hosted an 'at home' where the local dignitaries were invited. I attended the function for a short while.

The occasion was also to be commemorated by the British by holding memorial functions at the Kohima and Imphal cemeteries, elaborate instruction for which had been issued by the Government of India including provision of guards of honour by the Assam Rifles. I received a formal invitation for the functions both at Kohima and Imphal, I decided to attend the function at Imphal only because of my schedule of work. As stated above, I had also received a request from the Japanese ambassador to inaugurate the Japanese memorial to the dead for which apart from the ambassador and his staff a senior minister of Japanese cabinet was to attend. The

British function in Kohima was a day earlier. After the function in Kohima some people from the British Embassy along with the BBC team went and contacted some disgruntled sympathizers of Phizo and recorded their unhappiness with the GOI and thus portraying support to the cause of dissidents and insurgents. When I got the report at night, I told the PRO to warn the concerned people and convey my unhappiness to the High Commissioner and that I will not be attending their function at Imphal.

Consequent to my decision in the afternoon, I received a request from the British High Commissioner to call on me. I invited him for tea. During the meeting I told the High Commissioner that the act of his embassy staff and BBC team was not only un-diplomatic but also in total disregard to the hospitality extended. He told me that he will look into it. I sent a report to the GOI. The BBC team came to interview me the next day, I curtly told them that their lack of manners towards their hosts was most appalling. This incident reminded me of our bureaucratic mindset. When in Delhi, a secretary in the MEA will not see an African diplomat at the appointed time and make him wait but rush to receive a Western diplomat. We still have a colonial hangover!

In the security field, one of the main challenges internally was revamping the police, particularly the Manipur Rifles which had got totally politicized. The Ukhrul battalion was manned entirely by Thangkhuls and the Churachandpur by the Kukis, these virtually became the private armies of Rishang and Doungal. The others two were infected but to a much lesser degree. We adopted a slow and deliberate policy of shifting the units and reinducting fresh blood of all communities. We held DPCs and promoted deserving people. In this the new DGP Mishra was very ably assisted by IG Bimol Chandra and DIG Roman Kumar. It met with stiff opposition but we managed to succeed.

Happenings in Nagaland influence events in Manipur and vice versa due to deep antagonism between the hills and the plains and Nagas and non-Nagas particularly when it is a question of Manipur's territorial integrity. Both the state government and the centre mostly tend to remain as spectators. In September 1994, Vamuzo the leader of the opposition in the Nagaland assembly tabled a private member's resolution demanding merger of Naga inhabited areas in Arunachal Pradesh, Assam, Manipur and Myanmar in Nagaland. I heard about it, after I had handed over charge, but still I spoke to Jamir and Rajesh Pilot of the quite unnecessary and provocative nature of this move. It may have had some effect as it was ultimately resolved into a reiteration of the resolution passed by the Nagaland Assembly on the same lines in 1977. All political parties and AMSU condemned the resolution and inspite of high tensions no serious untoward incident took place. This happened when there was a Congress (I) government at the centre and in Nagaland.

INTER-STATE FUNCTIONING

After the North Eastern Council meeting in Shillong in February 1994, the home minister held a meeting of CMs on security. I attended the meeting as there was president's rule in Manipur. The home minister mooted the idea that they (MHA) will coordinate all intelligence and anti-insurgent operations, through a controlling set up to be established in Shillong. Everyone accepted it. When I saw no one reacting to this quite unnecessary imposition by the centre, I decided to intervene. I explained to the HM that I was only temporarily dealing with it but I do feel that the CM is the master of all in the state and should also be accountable, as such he cannot be directed by the centre as law and order is a state subject. As regard the mechanism for coordination, it can be established by mutual consent. Hearing this, Hiteshwar Saikia, the then CM, agreed with me and subject to agreement of other CM's if they would like to discuss the issue under me and establish the *modus operandi*. The HM asked the other CMs, they all agreed. I requested Saikia if we could hold the meeting in Guwahati as it was central, he agreed. I held the meeting of all CMs in the next week. As is usual all the CMs brought their chief secretaries and DGPs with them. Saikia brought K.P.S. Gill in addition, who was already in Guwahati in connection with the induction of Punjab Police Commandos in Assam, which thankfully never took place. I told them that the discussion was between the seven of us and no one else would attend. I was frank and told them that security should be considered above and beyond politics as human lives are involved. After a very fruitful discussion, we decided the framework for intelligence coordination and sharing, cross-border operations to be coordinated at the DM and SP levels of border districts along with the SF commanders deployed in the area. The requirement of additional communication links and the level of its manning and finally the frequency and level of liaison meetings were also decided. After the meeting all the CMs asked me to brief their chief secretaries and DGPs. I agreed to do so and fixed a mutually agreed date during the next week. I prepared a note for the HM and the home secretary and was in the process of dispatching it, when I got a call from Rajesh Pilot, MOS that he was holding a meeting for the same purpose. I expressed my inability to attend and immediately after that I rang the home minister to tell him that I am backing out as two people cannot handle the same problem or situation because it creates confusion and duplication. This was a perpetual problem that we had with the MHA. Between Chavan, home minister and Pilot, MOS, there were always divergent views and on the line of action to be taken. I raised the issue with the PM during my next visit, he told me to deal with him directly and keep the home secretary in the loop. Not to antagonize anyone, I always made it a point to share the salient information with both the HM and MOS, it amounted to a bit of storytelling. After this I always saw the PM and discussed things with him and with Vohra before or afterwards. Discussions with him were always most useful.

NAGALAND

I took over the additional charge of Nagaland in October 1993 as I had been told earlier. A gist of the prevailing situation in Nagaland had been included in my report of 5 October 1993. My report clearly brought about the areas of influence of the rival factions of the NSCN and the violent clashes amongst them to increase their areas of dominance. I had also brought out the political dissidence within the ruling Congress and the ties of different political dispensations with the rival factions of the insurgents and its implications for the overall situation in Manipur and Nagaland and the ongoing Naga Kuki conflict. I gave a clear indication of the expanding areas of violence and conflict with their inter-ethnic and inter-tribal dimensions. The CM S.C. Jamir, most other ministers and politicians including the leader of the opposition Vamuzo and along with many of the officials were personally known to me. I was on home ground, so to say.

Having decided to adopt a proactive stance in Manipur I decided to follow a similar approach within the constitutional parameters. Most people in Nagaland knowing me expected the same. To start off I asked for a security briefing from the DGP and the corps commander and the IGAR. The defining features of which were similar to Manipur. The factional fights between the warring NSCN factions (IM) and (K) appeared to be of no concern to the security forces and similar was the case with the incidents of Naga-Kuki violence which was tolerated and accepted within certain parameters. I discussed the situation in detail and warned them that any insurgent activity which disturbs peace is their responsibility and violence in any form is not acceptable. I found the DGP Chaman Lal to be most forthright and frank in his views, which was most welcome. The partisan handling of the confrontation between NSCN factions and Naga-Kuki conflict was evident and I agreed with Chaman Lal that both were our areas of concern. The sad part of the situation was that security forces including the Army not only let the situation escalate but were partisan in handling the situation and thus played into the hands of the local political players. This at times even led to inaction or delayed action resulting in serious casualties, of which two commanding officers of a MLI battalion one after another were the sad victims, in a short period of time.

As in Manipur I decided to visit each district but kept my visits to short durations and only to the district headquarters and the troubled areas. I paid particular attention to state of communications, health and hygiene, civic facilities and availability of rations and consumer goods. The state of affairs varied from satisfactory to appalling. In places the pay and allowances of the medical and para-medical staff amounted to almost over a lakh per month but they did not get medicines worth even a few thousands. Towns had no system of garbage collection or disposal, sanitation was non-existent and water supply totally inadequate. After each visit I wrote a detailed letter to the CM asking for a feedback on the action taken. It was resented but resulted in some action. Whenever I dictated such a letter to my SPA, it was termed as a missile, later on I learnt that it became a standard joke between my secretary Bano Jamir and her husband Alamtamshi Jamir who was the secretary to the CM. Before sending the letter she would ring up her husband and tell him that a missile had been launched and was on the way.

I was very careful in not interfering with the government's functioning but never hesitated in asking the CM or a minister or any secretary to explain things to me, if I found anything wrong or amiss. This acted as a deterrent and kept everybody on guard. Two areas of law and order and financial utilization were where I had special powers under Article 371A sub-clauses (b) and (c) of the Constitution. I never hesitated in reviewing any situation, seeking explanation and where necessary admonishing of authorities was concerned but I always had an open mind and was receptive to suggestions and explanations.

On the issue of financial mismanagement and impropriety I regularly reported these in my monthly governor's reports, which I was told had a salutary effect.

During my visits to various parts of Nagaland I got a very positive response from people and lower level government officials. Similar was the response from Nagas and Kukis in Peren when I visited them during the Naga-Kuki confrontation, which was most heartening. Like Manipur, I kept an open house and met everyone who had a problem.

I handed over additional charge of Nagaland when O.P. Srivastava was appointed as the full-time governor in August 1994. There was a story attached to the appointment of a full-time governor and termination of my additional charge, which was widely circulated in the local press. The CM S.C. Jamir approached the centre asking for a full-time governor as in other states. However, the actual story in circulation was that he complained to his friends in the Congress that the present governor is sitting on top of him and not letting him function. It was alleged that he gave Rs. 25 lakh each to four members of the party to help in my removal. While three of them promised to help, the fourth after keeping the money said that he will keep quiet as the governor is doing a good job, neither will he speak in his favour nor against him. A lot of it was covered in the local press which was never denied and contradicted by anyone in the government, so when I was asked by a journalist if it was true. I had to keep a straight face and replied that I did not know.

DISMAL STATE OF GOVERNMENT APPARATUS

No discussion of that period of Nagaland can be complete without touching on the issues of extortion, looting of government money and corruption. The worst aspect of it was its tolerance and this has only increased since and made the state a hostage to it. Both the NSCN factions were having a field day in their areas of influence and domination. NSCN(IM) was dominant in Dimapur, Peren, Kohima, in South Wokha, Zunheboto and areas of Jessami and Phek along the northern boundary with Manipur, while NSCN (K) had its sway in North Wokha, North Zunheboto, Mokokchung, Tuensang and Mon districts. Two treasuries were looted of Rs. 30 lakh in Mokokchung district and there were numerous instances of both sides collecting Letter of Credit (LOC) and encashing them. There were also a large number of cases when contractors were appointed as nominated by the insurgents. With the passage of time these were not only tolerated but became the norm. Same was the case with extortions. Political and insurgent agenda were totally concurrent and showed all the signs of collusion. Mokokchung town was under NSCN(K) and Dimapur under NSCN(IM) control with full connivance of politicians and officials. There were two major cases of looting of weapons from the home guard detachment at the mini secretariat and from 1 Nagaland Armed Police armoury. There were household stories of political bigwigs helping the insurgents.

While law and order were subjects of most discussions and conversations but the context was only in relation to who defies with greater immunity. The depth to which this had sunk was illustrated by the classic case of Khyaho Huray, (SS) Finance Secretary of NSCN (IM), who was arrested on 27 January 1994 under the National Security Act of 1980. His detention was confirmed by the Advisory Board in March 1994 and promulgated by the Home Commissioner on 15 April. On 11 April R. Hungyo, president of the Thangkhul Ho Ho, Nagaland moved an application to the CM for his release. The CM sent a personal letter to the Advocate General at Guwahati, who gave his opinion within a day and Khyaho Huray's release orders were given and executed the second day. Such efficiency was unheard of from the government. The Security Forces opposed his release and gave an ultimatum of cessation of operations. When I reached Kohima on 20 April, I gave a bit of my mind to the CM and admonished the Advocate General. I sent a report to the home minister and clearly conveyed that such happenings sent a wrong signal to the government functionaries and demoralizes them. I was also unhappy with the corps commander for ordering cessation of operations and ticked him off for it. Till today I am not sure whether this was part of the drama enacted in connivance with the CM. While I believe there was some discussion on my report but no action was taken as the state government was a Congress one.

A major part of the deteriorating security environment was due to move out of the 8 Mountain Division which had looked after Nagaland and Manipur. They had established themselves in the hearts and minds of the people after decades of service there. Tribals take a lot of time to establish and give trust, which is missing today. This was the question I was asked both in Nagaland and Manipur followed by remarks conveying we don't know the new people and they don't know us. If the Army had need for troops, they could have taken any division from the east or even for that matter all the troops under 8 Mountain Division but let the headquarters stay as the expertise and traditions built over the years are imbibed in the headquarters, they also ensure that these are followed, as units keep changing. The Inspector General Assam Rifles (IGAR) headquarters with bulk of troops under him being Assam Rifles, a paramilitary force, does not give the IGAR the same authority as the GOC which took years to establish. There is no denying the fact that AR are excellent troops and the IGAR was an excellent officer from my regiment who had done well in

Sri Lanka and was decorated there. There is so much in a name and tradition that wherever I went it was, '*the GOC is back*'. The problem was compounded with a deactivated corps commander on top. Tolerance of compromises and living with the situation had even eroded the security system. Chasing and coaxing is no substitute for a cohesive and motivated set up. Two ambushes in Mokokchung resulting in killing of two COs was most disturbing. The only redeeming feature was an honest, upright and professional DGP in Chaman Lal, who also escaped an ambush. He was highly respected by the locals, who felt a great sense of remorse and were not convinced that it was the insurgents. Quite a few in the higher echelons of the government did not like this upright officer. It goes to his credit that he continued to perform his duty honestly under most adverse conditions. He had my full trust and respect.

BLATANT CORRUPTION AT THE HIGHEST LEVEL

The Congress (I) government at that time in Nagaland was installed after elections on 15 February 1993 after ten months of president's rule. The central government was considerate to their own government in the state to give Rs. 91.93 crore as ways and means advance to start it off with a zero deficit. The Assembly passed a 789 crore budget in July 1993 and the state government asked for an additional Rs. 310 crore in March 1994. In addition the state government borrowed Rs. 30 crore from Peerless General Finance and Investment Company at 18 per cent interest. In spite of this the opening deficit for 1994-5 was Rs. 85 crore. Moreover Rs. 36 crore received as royalty from ONGC was not reflected, which in itself was a huge bone of contention in Nagaland as according to the opposition and general public opinion it amounted to giving away its natural resources. The total amount was Rs. 1,215 crore and the 1994-5 budget estimates were 910 crore. What was most blatant was that out of the earmarked budget police and some other department salaries had not been paid, which included the Nagaland Armed Police battalion then operating in the UP foothills. I ordered the salaries of police and other government employees to be paid. No earmarked money was given for the district plans (Rs. 21 crore), rural development (Rs. 11 crore) and no money was given for medicines to the Medical Department. Instead the Doctor's Association had alleged that Steel furniture worth Rs. 5 crore was bought out of their funds. What was most blatant mismanagement of finance was that special LOC were issued worth Rs. 10 crore. According to my estimate Rs. 365 crore had been siphoned off in the month of March. I was in a position to compare it with Manipur and what astounded me was that Nagaland with one-third less population and area had persistently one-third or even more budget allocations. Appeasement was at its best. Manipur budget for 1993-4 was Rs. 534 crore with a deficit of Rs. 39.10 crore and for the year 1994-5 the projections were in the region of Rs. 550 crore. I called both the CM and the FM and asked for their explanation, which was most unsatisfactory. I wrote to the HM giving all the details and also spoke to the PM. It had the desired effect and the CM was taken to task. Ultimately it also resulted in the CM further intensifying his efforts for the additional charge of Nagaland being taken away from me which I have covered earlier. The issue of blatant corruption in the north-east and particularly in Nagaland has its peculiar dynamics. I shall cover it in greater detail later.

On assuming charge in Nagaland, I asked the Army ADC posted with the Governor of Nagaland a few details about the happenings and about the Raj Bhavan which should have been common knowledge. He was hesitant and told me that the Governor of Assam, who was looking after Nagaland before I took over, used to bring his own ADC, who acted not only as his aide, but also as secretary and dealt with everything. I learnt that the ADC was so powerful that the chief secretary and all other government officials not only held him in awe but did his bidding on everything. A few months later the same ADC was in the news in Guwahati as he reported a theft of over Rs. 5 lakh from his house. Nobody asked him as to how he had got this money and why it was lying in his house. Just as it caught the public eye, it was hushed up. This news led to some talking by people and one could easily surmise that he was part of the corrupt system and one of its conduits, that is why the extra power. It could not have been without the governor's knowledge.

NEGOTIATIONS WITH THE UNDERGROUND

The question of talks with the underground was mooted even during my time and I was told to look into it. An NSCN(IM) emissary from Nepal visited me. I told him that as a constitutional head, I cannot indulge in negotiations but in my individual capacity and since I know the place and people, I am prepared to listen. After a long preamble, the essence of what he conveyed to me was that one, they are more powerful, have better weapons and are better trained than ever. Two, they have international recognition in the United Nations Indigenous People Organisation—an un-official forum. Three, there will be no talks within the Indian Constitution and fourthly they want a free Nagaland including Naga inhabited areas in other states. I told him that they are living under an illusion as by challenging India's might they would get nothing. We can continue to fight and afford to lose lives, they will get dissipated in the bargain. As regards international recognition, it certainly is nowhere near that of Jammu & Kashmir and even that does not worry us. On the question of free Nagaland and no talks within the Indian Constitution, I told him that they were being naïve and I totally rejected it due to my position. I dismissed him by saying that we had nothing to talk. As he was leaving I told him the only people suffering are the Nagas and it is all their doing. Later when the first approach was made by Rajesh Pilot in 1995 resulting in the current negotiations, I was asked by someone in the PMO as to what I thought of it. I told them that since you have decided so why ask me. However, since you have asked for my opinion, I can only say that you should be clear of what to do if it succeeds or how to handle the situation if you fail. Since then 15 years have passed and except for the negotiators having a free house, telephone, car, other perks and free foreign travel there is no progress. Everyone has developed a stake in *status quo*. A few years back the civil society represented by Naga Ho Ho, Mothers Organization and the church were keen on peace and an end to the strife, they were called by NSCN(IM), 30 of them to Bangkok and told to shut up and to do as they were told. The people who have the maximum stake are put on the sidelines, the only actors are NSCN, now both factions, and the politicians, who have a common agenda of power.

You have a situation that we are running a democracy in Nagaland by agreement and connivance of insurgents and politicians in power, who support each other and the Government of India is the resource provider. Democracy, state and the people's will are all subverted. Altogether a fine way to run a democracy!

The bottom line is that there are no signs that differences between the Naga faction NSCN(IM), NSCN(K), NCC with its factions and NFG can be resolved. Due to tribal affiliations, no group is likely to accept the total domination of others politically. Naga leaders in power, while conniving with the insurgents for power, will not shed or share the same with people as both have vested interest in insurgency for power and financial gains. Most of the insurgent groups only influence the law and order field by exploiting state failure to remove deprivation of people. Our actions should be oriented towards people and not the ultras and the conniving politician. You cannot ever achieve peace this way, it can only lead to a catastrophe.

NEW CHALLENGES

In the contemporary period not only in Manipur and Nagaland but in the entire north-east the factors of ethnic resurgence and divide, corruption and development of a negative mindset towards the establishment and the central authorities is adding to the already volatile and unstable environment in the region. It is therefore essential that we understand the dynamics of these developments as dealing with these is the biggest challenge to governance.

Ethnic Resurgence in the North-East

In the overall context, the ethnic factor is central and has become omnipresent, particularly in the hill areas due to the closed nature of the societies there, where an outsider even if a neighbour is a suspect. To win over their trust and credibility are essential.

Ethnic consciousness in the plains is due to tribal ethnic assertion in their areas and the threat posed by the immigrants. It influences politics and generates or acts as a catalyst for conflicts. It is central to security, economic development and the crucial and the central issue of territory and land. It is a stabilizing factor at the individual, village and community level but causes instability within the states and at the regional level.

Its dynamics are based on inbuilt distinctions between ethnic groups since the British period, which differentiated between the hills and plains and followed different approaches to politics, administration and development for different areas. Unfortunately, we followed similar policies and the situation is further compounded by fractured political boundaries with no relationship to territories inhabited by ethnic communities.

In recent years the political elite and insurgents have exploited ethnic sensitivities and vulnerabilities in pursuance of power and increasing areas of influence. The main reason is electoral politics and the dubious role community leaders have played in creating fear psychosis to create exclusive constituencies where they can dominate land, commerce and community social and economic life for their own selfish ends. Similar is the motivation for insurgents. Their articulation is based on hatred and denial towards other communities. Nagas, Kukis and Meities in Manipur and Nagaland had lived together for centuries. Ethnic mobilization automatically poses a threat to adversaries.

Indigenous divide poses the biggest challenge to peace and harmony in the north-east and in most cases, as ethnic assertion can be equated with a case of culture submerged and recovered, over accentuated in its recovery. When we talk of multiculturalism, it is not just about song and dance but rights and power sharing. In the north-east it is now a case of cultural/ethnic divide combined with material inequality, a hot recipe for ethnic politics and mobilization.

My experience in the north-east has shown that ethnic politics is difficult to manage and explosive if mismanaged. The problem of ethnicity relates largely to deprivation and failure of governance, both actual and perceived, it is also where the solution lies.

Corruption

Corruption is a national phenomenon and no region is free from the evil. But in the north-east it has its own peculiar autonomy and character, resulting in debasement of the entire society.

North-east like some other areas is resource deficient and the bulk of finance comes from the centre. During the last decade of the last century, net devolution to the north-east was Rs. 51,000 crore. Orissa with the same population and being more backward got only Rs. 25,000 crore. In spite of this north-east is still dissatisfied and alienated. The reason is corruption, which is not only depriving the people of the benefits of development but also feeding insurgency.

Corruption related to money and resources provided by the centre does not involve a sense of guilt, moral or legal, attached to it as it is Indian money, therefore, not relevant. There is no public concern as the elite who is doing the taking is ours. A similar atitude prevails about insurgents taking it. Allied with it is the feeling that outsiders should not judge us, it is our affairs as our people are involved. The elite strata of politicians, bureaucrats, community and insurgents have conveyed to the community that no guilt is attached to stealing from the Government of India. Civil society is divided and fragmented along ethnic and parochial lines. If you raise the question that it denies the people fruits of development, they say Government of India is to blame and it is their problem.

The second issue is control of resources and economic activity—communities who are the real owners have lost control to the elite, who are averse to any rational exploitation by outsiders but siphon off this wealth for their own use. The same is the case of all developmental projects, which are sub-let to benami subcontractors by the local elite. This not only denies opportunity to genuine entrepreneurs but also adds to corruption.

In a closed society divided into small ethnic groups, electoral politics and corruption has affected all. Government resources are primarily used to gain and retain power. It has worked to the double advantage of the insurgents as due to denial of developmental benefits, people feel alienated and become vulnerable to insurgents' rhetoric and it becomes their support and resource base.

In the north-east financial packages and concessions are unlikely to achieve results, unless ethos of systematic utilization of funds is established and there is a monitoring mechanism.

The Negative Mindset

Our lack of understanding of the north-east and its people with their distinct and divergent perspectives and ethos combined with isolation has drawn negative responses. The barrier of isolation extends beyond the physical to the cultural, social and economic field. Of these physical isolation impinges on the minds of the people the most as it results in social and economic hardship and harassment. Cumulative effect of all this has resulted in a deep negative mindset amongst the people of the north-east.

This negative mindset has its roots in the contemporary experience of the people of the north-east. It extends from treatment meted out to CMs of states and response to the common man, who are looked upon as foreigners in their own country.

The negative mindset is reinforced by high level of corruption and political manipulation, which have left people disillusioned and helpless.

Both the people of the north-east and the establishment have developed a siege mentality, which is more mental than physical and they are not prepared to break out if it. It was the single most formidable obstacle I encountered in Manipur. The leadership of the north-east is to be equally blamed for it as they have developed a stake in perpetuating it to pass the blame for their failures to Delhi. It is a two-way deficit of understanding. While the country must assist the north-east to realize its full potential and avail of opportunities within and around it, on its part the north-east must assert itself to be an equal partner and contribute to Indian growth.

THE ARMED FORCES SPECIAL POWERS ACT

The Armed Forces Special Powers Act (AFSPA) has turned out to be Manipur's most prolonged and lasting plank for agitation and it reached its climax after Manorama's tragic death in July 2004. The Justice Reddy Commission has not been able to resolve the issue and government is in a state of indecision. I had enforced that law in the 1980s at the height of Meitie insurgency and later supervised its enforcement during my tenure as governor in 1990s. In a disturbed environment there would always be aberrations but acts of omissions and particularly commission should not be tolerated. There has to be constant monitoring of its implementation and mechanism for it has to be established by the security forces themselves. A public liaison cell was established by me in M Sector Headquarters, where anyone and everyone could walk in to seek information about arrests and status of those incarcerated and information of those killed in encounters. Those found innocent were released to Meira Paibis or other credible social organizations. Transparency and accountability go hand in hand. The law is as good or as bad as its application and depends on institutional safeguards within the police, PMF and the Army. (See *Indian Express,* 24 August 2004—write up reproduced in Appendix F.)

Before ending the narration of my stay in Manipur and Nagaland I feel morally obliged to acknowledge the support and help that I got from the Prime Minister Narasimha Rao, Rajesh Pilot and most of all from N.N. Vohra, the then home secretary. I always benefited by discussing the problems with Narasimha Rao, his understanding of India and each part of it was masterly in all its dimensions of geography, history, people and their culture. I doubt if any other political leader of present generation can match it. During discussions with him the minute I uttered a sentence, he knew why, in which context and the reason for it. In the initial stages, like all other politicians, he did not think much of president's rule and always considered it as an interlude. It was meant to look after security and let things carry on. When he received a copy of my directive and I briefed him on what I wanted to do in each field, he felt intrigued, and as things progressed in all fields of security, economic development, resettlement of refugees, health, education and civic spheres, he became more enthusiastic. He accepted my contention that if intentions are honest and one was willing to implement, both the president's rule and popular government can succeed. In September 1994, he told me that he wanted Manipur to be a model state for the north-east. He was upset and unhappy when I resigned. A month after my return I went to see him, he was very gracious and told me that I made a mistake and left the job half done. But he appreciated my point of view that having done and achieved what I had, I could not lose my credibility with the people of Manipur. I told him I will do it again given the circumstances. Once you had discussed a problem with him, when you asked him what is to be done, he always told you, '*aap ja ke dekh lo*' (you decide). This is what he told me when I saw him before leaving for Manipur. I had a free hand and never asked for any clearance or direction.

Rajesh Pilot was young, a doer and always in a hurry. He was dynamic, sincere and had a tinge of services orientation to resolve problems and did not tolerate and live with problems. He was an achiever and man of the masses. He kept in touch with me even after I had resigned. I felt sad that a dynamic political career was cut short so tragically. When I went for his last rites, I could not believe he was no more.

N.N. Vohra and I got acquainted in Punjab in 1985, when I took over the corps in Jalandhar and later when he came to MOD as additional secretary. It was a bit sudden when I was called from a vacation in Ranikhet and told to go to Manipur. I was similarly sounded about Punjab immediately after retirement so it was not a surprise in the real sense. But in the latter case it did not happen due to change of government. In this instance I was given no choice. Within the same day I met the prime minister, who wanted me to leave the next day, with great difficulty I got four days. After the formalities, it was really the briefing by Vohra that I got to know as to how bad the situation was. He told me that I will get all the help and support. This was absolutely true as long as he was the home secretary. During this period we developed a lasting friendship and understanding of each other. He is a thorough professional, with varied and wide experience of administration, legal and constitutional matters. His dedication and thoroughness are an object lesson for younger people. Later I enjoyed working with him on the Internal Security Committee in 2001. His handling of the aftermath of the Amarnath Yatra agitation as Governor of Jammu & Kashmir is a tribute to his professional sagacity.

THE RESIGNATION

To a lot of people it is a mystery as to why I resigned as Governor of Manipur. I feel the requirement to put forth the truth, not so much to defend my action but to raise issues based on it on the role and functioning of the governors in general. The role of governors in disturbed states like Manipur requires looking into as the number of states considered disturbed is increasing. Constitutionally as governor in Manipur I had hardly any active role to play when a popular government was in power. I could only observe and report to the Centre. In Nagaland constitutionally under Article 371 I had a role to advise and even intervene in matters relating to law and order and finances. As explained at the beginning of this chapter, the circumstance under which I took over as governor demanded a proactive stance even when an elected government was in power as I could not be a spectator to inaction when hundreds of lives were being lost. However, I made sure that the elected government was given full opportunity to redeem the situation before I recommended president's rule not as a viable option but the only one left. In my report to the president for the month of August 1994 in the early part of second six months of the president's rule. I had recommended that we should hold elections during the president's rule in December 1994 as the term of the current assembly was expiring on 15 February 1995 and the assembly which was under suspended animation should be dissolved. This I felt would be politically most fair and appropriate. However, if the central cabinet was of a different opinion then it was their prerogative, in which case I had recommended that the president's rule should be revoked at least a few months earlier as installing a popular government just on the eve of elections will not be credible. I had also made my stand clear during one of my visits to Delhi, well before December 1994 when the president's rule was to expire. Throughout the period from August to November 1994 during all my discussions in Delhi at all levels I was given the impression that they were not in favour of a popular government returning to power and disrupt the smooth way things were proceedings. Some even went to the extent of saying that Manipur has never had it so good and president's rule should continue and if required could be reimposed again. I even attended a meeting chaired by the prime minister and attended by CMs of Bihar, Orissa and some other states where elections were due and the

Chief Election Commissioner T.N. Sheshan was present to discuss the state of preparation including updating of electoral rolls and progress on ID cards. With this background I was a bit surprised when no indications of elections came till beginning of December and was totally taken aback when on 13 December I was told that president's rule will be revoked and a popular government installed. The residual life of the assembly was less than two months. My response was, it is the centre's decision and I would abide by it and observe the constitutional norms and maintain the credibility of institutions. I called the presidents of all political parties and told them that it had been decided that a popular government will be installed and all have the right to stake their claim as the earlier coalition and its political equations may have undergone a change.

Next day both the Congress and MPP staked their claim to form the government. To be fair and to ensure that everything was above board, I asked them to bring their supporters to the Convention Hall in Raj Bhawan, where each MLA will be identified and his affiliation recorded by the secretary of the assembly in my presence. This was done in a very open and congenial manner, which was most democratic. The Congress (I) and its supporters had a tally of 37 and others 23. I announced the results and R.K. Ranbir Singh, president of MPP, and Congress both accepted the result and thanked me for the very fair and friendly manner in which it was conducted. From the sudden and secretive manner in which the decision to revoke president's rule and install a popular government was taken everyone knew that it was entirely motivated by political expediency and primarily influenced by the perception that you had to be in power to get elected. Congress had a head start as just before the decision was officially communicated Santosh Mohan Deb and P.M. Syed MOS (erstwhile speaker) had already arrived in Imphal to collect their flock and ensure majority. Be that as it may I was determined to implement the decision in the most credible fashion. Once Congress(I) majority was confirmed I told their president Radhabinod Singh that I would like to swear in the ministry that evening itself. Santosh Mohan Deb and Syed along with Radhabinod Singh came to see me immediately afterwards and told me that Rishang Keishing has been elected as the leader and he alone should be sworn in today, the rest of the ministry can be sworn in later. I suggested to them that considering the present environment in Manipur it would be more prudent to have at least one Meitei and one Kuki minister sworn in along with the CM. They appreciated my suggestion and I swore in four ministers that evening on 13 December itself. After the swearing in as per protocol the CM along with the ministers and accompanied by the two central ministers called on me. After congratulating them I asked the CM as to how much time he would require to face the assembly and seek a vote of confidence. He told me three to four days were sufficient as has been the practice in the state. I told him to take a week. During the discussion one of them mentioned that they would be going to Delhi to get the high command's approval for the expansion of the ministry, which may take a day or so. I told him to take another couple of days and we all agreed that the assembly should be called on 23 December before the Christmas holidays and a vote of confidence taken. Deb and Syed thanked me for being most fair and correct.

Four days passed but there was no request from the CM asking me to call the assembly session. I asked my secretary Jha to ring up the CM and remind him. In response to my Secretary's call I received a letter from the CM requesting me to issue the proclamation to call the suspended assembly. I issued the proclamation and suggested to the CM that the governor's address should be short and simple to say that the government intended to continue the present policies and programmes till the elections. They sent a draft for my approval on the same lines, which I approved and it was printed. While these activities as per the laid down constitutional norms were going on, disturbing news of strong arm methods being used to intimidate and browbeat the opposition started coming in. I received news that the speaker had locked himself in his chambers in the assembly and attempts were made to set it on fire. There were other news of intimidating opposition MLAs and violence perpetuated by the ruling party activists. After waiting for two days I spoke to the CM asking him to put an end to this violent political confrontation. I also later called the chief secretary (new incumbent Sethi) and the

DGP and told them if they fail to control the violence I would take them to task in spite of the popular government being in power. Politically the confrontation continued and the speaker became equally adamant. The speaker continued to feed his side of the story, the local press was having a field day. Two days before the assembly was to meet the CM came to see me and asked me for ten days postponement or minimum up to 28 December for the assembly session. After listening to him patiently, I told him that I could not agree to his request of postponing the assembly as it was done with his concurrence and I had even given him more time than he had asked for. Moreover, there is no change in the situation even as it prevailed before imposition of president's rule. The case of the debarred MLAs was still pending with the Guwahati High Court as was the case against the speaker. In the meantime the government had distributed the governor's address to all the MLAs including the opposition.

On 22 December I got calls from both Santosh Mohan Deb and Syed requesting me to give more time to the CM. They were most apologetic as they knew that I had been most liberal and fair but as party men they had to help their CM. I refused them most politely. Later in the day I was rung up by the HM asking for the same which I refused. He rang up twice more during the day and my response was the same. He rang up the fourth time at night at about 9 p.m. and told me that the PM wanted me to give more time to the CM to prove his majority in the house. I told him the answer is still no and he can convey the same to the PM. He told me to ring up the PM and speak to him. I told him that I have no reason to ring up the PM and if he rings me up my answer will be the same. Finally, before ending the conversation I told him that if they wanted these dirty things to be done, they better find someone else as I would not be a party to it. After this conversation I thought about the whole episode and took the decision to resign. There were two thoughts upper most in my mind, which convinced me that it was the right decision. First and foremost was that my credibility both as the constitutional head and as a person who had done the right things and stood by what was right could not be compromised along with the fact that my credibility with the people of Manipur was sacrosanct. Secondly, as a constitutional head I could not be in conflict with the central government, which will do no good to either. Having taken the decision, I dictated my resignation to the president and faxed it to the President's Secretariat, the PM and the HM. It was the simplest and easiest draft I did, 'Respected President, I have the honour to resign as Governor of Manipur with immediate effect. Regards'. Simultaneously, I wrote to the speaker informing him that I have resigned as governor and it may be appropriate for him to await the appointment of a new incumbent and his installation. I was rung up by the Secretary to the President Murari and Ahuja from MHA requesting me not to precipitate matters. I thanked both of them for their kind consideration but politely told them that I will not change my decision. On hearing this Ahuja asked me to fax a handwritten letter of resignation as per the laid down procedure. Without a second thought, I faxed my handwritten resignation letter.

I understand that the speaker decided to call the assembly as per the proclamation and took the governor's address as read as it had already been circulated to all. For this a precedent existed in West Bengal when the Governor Dharam Vira's address, which had been distributed was taken as read. The government of Rishang Keishing was defeated in the assembly but it continued. The centre asked O.N. Srivastava, Governor of Nagaland, to fly to Imphal and take over. I understand that initially he resisted quoting that he was still overcoming the legacy left by Lt. Gen. Nayar as everyone in Nagaland quotes him. He was told by the home minister that he should proceed to Imphal otherwise he would lose his job. He accepted it but God and nature had destined otherwise. The weather gods poured all their fury on 23 December and neither could he come from Nagaland nor could the Chief Justice from Guwahati to swear him in. It also resulted in my not being able to leave on 23 December as planned. Srivastava was sworn in on 24 December afternoon. He revoked the speaker's decision and called the assembly session on 9 January 1995 for a trial of strength. The decision of the new Governor Srivastava to revoke the speaker's decision and reconvene the assembly when the government stood defeated was adversely commented upon both by the constitutional experts and legal pandits. Politically, except for the Congress it was challenged by all opposition parties at the centre and in the state. It captured the imagination of the media in Manipur, in the region and at the national level for quite some time. I leave it to the constitutional and legal experts to judge. However, I have the satisfaction that I acted in a constitutionally correct and credible manner. As is usual the news of the north-east, even of most violent nature, remains on the sidelines but in this case national press highlighted the news fairly well.

Somehow the word of my resignation leaked out, probably some of the staff from Raj Bhavan did it. I started getting a large number of visitors from all walks of life, most of them were upset and some were even annoyed with me. There were politicians from all parties, prominent citizens, community leaders, journalists and youth and student leaders. Some went to the extent of saying that they won't let me go, of these the youth and students led by Mohi Lal, the president of the AMSU were most vocal. They had planned a Manipur *bandh* and a *rasta roko* to prevent me from going to the airport. I felt alarmed at these reports as knowing that Manipur, irrespective of the cause, thrives on agitation. I made a public announcement saying that it was my personal decision and if the people of Manipur have any regard and affection for me and if they feel I have done some good for them then any agitation will undo what we have achieved. I also asked journalists and student leaders to convey my request. A day's delay due to bad weather helped and I was happy to learn that my departure would be peaceful. I was given state honours when I left and the entire cabinet, opposition politicians and a lot of public were present on the route to the airport and at the airport. I was touched by their affection and good will.

To my mind the entire episode raises issues beyond the constitutional and legal parameters. While it is accepted that governors in our context are political appointees and are expected to do the bidding of the government in power at the centre, their constitutional duty demands that not only constitutional and legal propriety is observed in the political arena, in addition they have a moral and humane duty to ensure that the rule of law is enforced and public interest guarded. It becomes a critical issue in the disturbed environment like the one prevailing in Manipur where people's interest and rights are the victims of political expediency, a main cause of their deprivation. The second issue is that hardly any professional with appropriate capability and inclination are considered for these appointments unless there is a crisis. Once they are appointed they require freedom of action to resolve situations. I was given this latitude till electoral expediency dictated otherwise. Imposition of such decisions dictated by political expediency can only result in either the incumbent succumbing to these pressures or quitting.

The third issue and certainly not the last is the apparent trend in recent years when a person or persons close to political power centres can influence appointment of a certain stream of bureaucracy and hailing from a particular area. The recent trend of appointing a large number of intelligence and police officers from the south on such appointments are an indicator of it. Track record of such appointees has been that of handymen. They hardly move out of Raj Bhawan, are worried about their personal security and have no public contact. They commemorate their tenures by renovation of the Raj Bhawan, producing coffee table books and gaining favour with authorities in Delhi. It noticeably leaves an adverse impression on the people of the state.

While passing though Calcutta, I was accosted by the local as well as the national press including correspondents of *Sunday*, *Frontline* and other magazines. I confined my comments to the facts of my resignation in Manipur and avoided passing any judgement. The local press was critical of both the Centre and the local leadership and commended my principled stand. The Manipur press also called me an upholder of democracy and not a decorative piece. The Nagaland press called my successor as 'helpless'. Editorials in *Telegraph* (25 December) and *Statesman* of 26 December, Calcutta depicted the shambles in Manipur realistically under the same caption. Even the *Hindu* from Madras (13 January 1995) made a pointed comment on the situation in Manipur and called installation of a popular government and not holding elections as a wrong decision. *Frontline* of 13 January called it a tragic-comedy, 'while central rule was withdrawn and a Congress(I) government installed, armed legislators charged with defection threatened to shoot the speaker and burn the assembly'. *Sunday* (1-7 January 1995) called it 'The Mess in Manipur: Rishang Keishing Government Loses Trial of Strength but Remains in Power'. Some papers in Manipur and Nagaland carried on the tirade up to August 1995 and the topic remains a point of criticism, whenever central government does anything against local sentiment.

On return to Delhi I was contacted by a number of journalists covering the north-east for interviews but I was not inclined, although I interacted with them informally after lectures and discussions at the USI and India International Centre. H. Khogan Singh, a young Manipuri journalist working for the *Hindustan Times*, was most insistent and ultimately I gave in to his persistence. A copy of his article published in *Hindustan Times* of 13 February 1995 is attached as Appendix 'G' in this Chapter. Some of my most memorable moments spent in Manipur were working with the youth and we developed a close understanding and attachment. It is out of this sentiment that I am attaching AMSU president's letter to me on the eve of my departure as Appendix H in this Chapter.

A few weeks after I returned to Delhi, George Fernandes rang me up and told me that he was sending Mrs Jaya Jeitley and a MP from his party to consult me. He apologized for not coming himself due to some other urgent work. An hour later they both arrived and after pleasantries told me that Janata Dal MLAs have been bought over by Rishang. They wanted my advice as to what to do. I told them that there is nothing they can do. After a cup of tea as they were leaving, in a lighter vein I told them, if they wanted their MLAs back, they have to buy them back at a higher price. I told them that they were confronting the ghost of Manipur.

I feel greatly rewarded by the affection and confidence of the people of Manipur, when ten years after I had left Manipur, during the most unusual protest of women in nude after Manorama's death at the Kangla Fort in August 2004, their leader Thokchem Ramini or Ima (Mother) said, 'they should see how Lt. Gen. V.K. Nayar performed his duty as a General in the 1980s and as Governor in 1990s. During his time things were better as he listened to our argument'. ('Mother's Courage', *Times of India*, New Delhi, 10 August 2004—attached as Appendix I in this chapter). Thank you, Ima.

APPENDIX A

EXTRACTS FROM GOVERNOR, MANIPUR'S SPECIAL REPORT TO THE PRESIDENT OF INDIA, DATED 5 OCTOBER 1993

In my opinion, in the conditions prevailing in Manipur at present, the real issue is not of the change in leadership or of alternatives but to find an end to periodic manipulations for power by different groups or individuals, as this has resulted in lack of political direction to the government and guidance to the administration. It has also given opportunity to unscrupulous amongst them on the behest of insurgents to use the government machinery and administration as an extension of their political authority, thereby strengthening anti-national sentiments.

The above state of affairs has resulted in total political drift, instability and alienation from the people. It has severely affected the already weak administration and resulted in serious erosion of the government's authority. The present coalition government is only superficially together, entirely motivated by the common interest to stay in power.

All shades of political and public opinion are unanimous in the view that the present coalition government is incapable of handling the situation. If any, the continuation of the present ministry will provide an impetus to the extremist activities, fuelling of Naga-Kuki clashes and further incapacitate the administration and law enforcement agencies.

LAW AND ORDER SITUATION

The situation in the five hill districts of the state is grave and it has the potential of getting out of control, both due to insurgent activities and Naga-Kuki conflict. The Naga-Kuki conflict is an extension of NSCN(IM) design for domination and ethnic complexion to it has been injected by the leaders of both the communities to further their political ends. Imphal valley is under full sway of the Meitei extremists. Their links with factions of the hill insurgents portends ill for Imphal Town and its outlying areas due to its mixed population.

HILL AREAS

NSCN(IM) and its sympathizers and collaborators over the past few months have surreptitiously revived and propagated successfully the old theme of south Nagaland by exploiting the sentiment of Naga identity and interest. In this, Rishang Keishing, Dy CM, Marung Makunga, Minister of State and A.S. Arthur, ex-MLA (all of Congress-I) have played a dubious role with the help of over ground front organisations of United Naga Council, Tangkhul Long and tribal student and youth organizations. A combination of Naga inhabited areas of four of the five hill districts of Ukhrul, Chandel, Senapati and Tamenglong. In real terms it is the domination of NSCN(IM) and Tangkhuls.

Killings by NSCN(IM) have increased to over 150 during 1993 so far, compared to 20 in 1991 and 30 in 1992, excluding mass killing of 300 Kuki men, women and children and 80 villages have been burnt.

NSCN(IM) cadre and weapon holdings have doubled during 1993, with two groups infiltrating in January and June, 1993 with approximately 200 sophisticated weapons. The capability is further augmented by approximately 2,000 Lim Guards, with 3,000 weapons purchased and recorded in the last one year, of which only 300 have been recovered by the security forces. They have further strengthened their links with the Meitei extremists, ULFA, HPC, the Myanmar insurgents and are actively supported by the DG Forces Intelligence of Bangladesh and ISI of Pakistan. They have reliable contacts for arms procurement in Thailand and other South-East Asian countries and established links for their transportation to camps in Bangladesh. NSCN(IM) participation in UNPO in July in Vienna has given them an opening to international forums and avenues for support.

The potential of the NSCN(IM) due to their unchecked dominance over the last two years in the hill areas, expanded cadre and well organized support of Lim Guards within Manipur has multiplied manifold. This has given them the ability to perpetrate violence of grave magnitude over the entire hill areas, with the ongoing Naga-Kuki conflict acting as a catalyst.

KUKIS

Kukis are dispersed in Senapati (Saikul and Sadar Hills), Ukhrul, Chandel, Churachandpur and Tamenglong districts. They are not so well organized and the recent threat from the Nagas/NSCN(IM) is the only unifying force and motivation for their identity as a tribe. Tussle between C. Doungel, finance minister and Holkhomang Haokip, power minister (both of Congress-S) and between Kuki National Assembly and Kuki Inpi, Manipur is being exploited by the CM and Rishang both, at the expense of the Kukis. Irrespective of which faction they belong to, they have no option but to depend on the government support.

Kuki underground organization, Kuki National Army (KNA), Kuki National Front (KNF) and Kuki Defence Force (KDF) in Manipur are extension of their parent bodies in Myanmar and are a divided house.

About 250 KNA/KDF cadres are suspected to be operating in Kuki-dominated areas of Manipur. They do not have the capacity to defend Kuki areas and, being fragmented, they can only perpetrate sporadic violence and thus escalate the Kuki-Naga conflict. Kukis have been demanding weapons to arm themselves against Nagas. I have forbidden it as it will escalate violence. This also imposes on security forces (SF) the added responsibility to protect Kukis in vulnerable areas.

The Kuki-Naga conflict is an extension of NSCN(IM) design to increase their domination, fight for control of NH 39 and Moreh for illegal resources borne out of smuggling of narcotics and contraband trade and to get major share of compensation of Rs 12.5 crore of Maphao Dam in Thoubal district.

VALLEY

Meitei extremists consisting of major factions of PLA, UNLF (two factions), Kangleipak Communist Party (KCP) and People's Revolutionary Party of Kangleipak (PREPAK) are all operating in Imphal Valley in a disjointed fashion. All have areas of interest in Imphal Town and Greater Imphal with PLA extending its area of operations to Thoubal and Bishnupur districts. Revolutionary Joint Committee (RJC), a front organization embracing PLA, PREPAK and KCP, is a recent development but no real co-ordination or understanding has come to notice. PLA supports NSCN(IM) primarily for weapons and factions of UNLF support NSCN(IM) and NSCN(K), and thereby their links with IBRF. Their main activities are extortion, kidnapping and façade of undertaking social reforms to pressurize government and discipline public. There has been steady escalation of killing by Meitei extremists—48 in 1991, 59 in 1992 and 70 in 1993 so far.

For the Meitei extremist insurgency is both an occupation and business and thereby control of activities in the valley to establish their writ, resulting in total erosion of government's authority, ineffective functioning of administration and law enforcement agencies. Meitei population, irrespective of status and position, are at present captive and subservient to the will of Meitei extremists, most pay taxes to the Meitei extremists and some actively support them.

COMMUNAL RIOTS

The Pangal (Manipuri Muslims)—Meitei communal riots in May 1993, in which 97 people were killed, of which 94 were Pangals, were totally out of character of the Imphal Valley. The dispute between Pangal arms smugglers and Meitei extremists could not have caused a communal flare up of such high magnitude. It was the handiwork of antisocial and criminal elements amongst the Meitei extremists in collusion with some politicians. At present the communal situation is well under control but the riots have left its ugly marks and Muslims feel insecure. There are reports that some Pangals have established links in Bangladesh and with ISI for weapons and other assistance. It is also reported that some have also joined RJC to provide protection to their community. In this regard the activities of the two new organizations, the Islamic Revolutionary Front and United Liberation Army, need to be kept under watch.

LAW AND ORDER

Rising insurgency, Naga-Kuki clashes and communal tensions have provided conducive environment and spurt to anti-social and criminal activities. Dacoities and murders have shown a marked upward trend, which has added to the problems of the police. Moreover, judiciary by and large is partisan and adopts the path of least resistance due to fear and involvement. Effective policing, so essential under the prevailing conditions, is lacking due to political interference. While resources are a constraint, but lack of correct orientation and motivation of the police force are the main drawbacks. Need to re-establish the rule of law by effective policing, without interference, is a prime requirement.

Situation in the valley is ripe for explosion and dealing with the Meitei extremists effectively is essential to re-establish government's authority and prevent communal and tribal-Meitei clashes due to mixed population in Imphal Town.

HMARS

Hmar pockets in Churachandpur, Tipaimukh area, in adjoining north Mizoram and south Cachar are under the sway of Hmar People's Convention (HPC). With HPC links with NSCN(IM), they are a vital link for passage of men and material. Therefore, control of these areas so far left free is vital for overall counter NSCN(IM) and Meitei extremists measures.

HAPPENINGS IN NAGALAND

NSCN(IM) has established their dominance in south Nagaland in Dimapur, Peren and Kohima in Kohima district, South Wokha, Zunheboto, Phek and Jessami area all along northern boundary of Manipur. NSCN(K) influence is confined to North Wokha, North Zunheboto, Mokokchung, Tuensang and Mon districts. Recent clashes between NSCN(K) and NSCN(IM) during July and August 1993 clearly indicate that struggle to bring more areas under their dominance has commenced and escalation of violence in both Nagaland and Manipur is likely to be widely spread.

Shri S.C. Jamir, the present CM, is firmly in saddle but has tribal and political dissidence with Hokishe Sema and the Semas. Although Chisi and Holohen, both Sema ministers in his government, are with him, they have Sema interest at heart. AOs, Konyahs and Phoms support S.C. Jamir and are firmly aligned will the NSCN(K), whereas Semas, Angamis and other southern tribes are aligned with the NSCN(IM). NNC influence and NFG capability are minimal. Vamuzo, the Leader of the Opposition, is under pressure and has already visited Rishang in Manipur in the last week of August. He may for political expediency and survival of NFG group exercise his option to join NSCN(IM). If this happens, then NSCN(IM) will be further strengthened and both dissidence and violence in Nagaland will further escalate.

Overall implications of the current situation in Manipur and Nagaland in the short term are that areas of violent conflict and unrest have widened to the entire hill areas of Manipur, with fallout in Imphal Valley and in Nagaland to central, southern Nagaland and western Nagaland bordering Manipur in the south. In the long-term, it will escalate Naga-Kuki conflict and has possibility of Meitei-Tribal conflict in Manipur and inter-tribal conflicts in Nagaland.

The above state of intense insurgency and internal disorder is due to lack of political stability and will, lack of an overall perception and monitoring of the worsening situation by the state government and security forces.

APPENDIX B

Lt.Gen. V.K. Nayar, PVSM, SM (Retd.)

RAJ BHAVAN
IMPHAL

January 1, 1994.

MESSAGE

The deteriorating law and order situation in Manipur, resulting in wanton killings and suffering to the people, disruption of public life and resultant constraints on economic activity and developmental work has forced the Central Government to impose President's Rule in the State.

It will be the endeavour of the Administration under me to restore peace, provide security to the people and undertake developmental work and welfare measures for the well being of the people. The Government will deal firmly with all disruptive elements irrespective of their political, ethnic and communal affiliation. The Administration will be impartial, sensitive and responsive to the people's needs. Special efforts will be made to overcome inadequacies in basic infrastructure like roads, public distribution system, transportation, health and community development.

Security Forces will operate with full freedom against anti-national and disruptive elements within the bounds of the law and will be totally impartial.

Our doors will be open to all who want to work for peace and well being of the people of Manipur.

Jai Hind.

V K Nayar

(Lt.Gen. V.K. Nayar, Retd.)

Lt. Gen. V.K. Nayar, PVSM, SM (Retd.)
GOVERNOR OF MANIPUR

RAJ BHAVAN
IMPHAL
January 1, 1994.

MESSAGE

The deteriorating law and order situation in Manipur, resulting in wanton killings and suffering to the people, disruption of public life and resultant constraints on economic activity and developmental work has forced the Central Government to impose President's Rule in the State.

It will be the endeavour of the Administration under me to restore peace, provide security to the people and undertake developmental work and welfare measures for the well being of the people. The Government will deal firmly with all disruptive elements irrespective of their political, ethnic and communal affiliation. The Administration will be impartial, sensitive and responsive to the people's needs. Special efforts will be made to overcome inadequacies in basic infrastructure like roads, public distribution system, transportation, health and community development.

Security Forces will operate with full freedom against anti-national and disruptive elements within the bounds of the law and will be totally impartial.

Our doors will be open to all who want to work for peace and well being of the people of Manipur.

Jai Hind.

(Lt.Gen. V.K. Nayar, Retd.)

APPENDIX C

A. S. ARTHUR,
Vice President MPCC [I]

Poumai Colony,
Imphal—795001
Tele : 225247

..18.1. 19 94

To Gen. V.K. Nayar(Retd)
HE The Governor of Manipur,
Raj Bhavan,
Imphal.

Sir,

I shall be so grateful if I could kindly be given some time to meet you at anytime as may be convenient to the Governor.

Yours sincerely,

(A.S. Arthur)

Enclosed two sheets.

A. S. ARTHUR
Vice President MPCC [I]

Poumai Colony,
Imphal—795001
Tele : 225247

18. 1. 1994

To Gen. V.K. Nayar (Retd)
HE The Governor of Manipur,
Raj Bhavan,
Imphal.

Sir,

I shall be so grateful if I could kindly be given some time to meet you at anytime as may be convenient to the Governor.

Enclosed two sheets

Yours sincerely,

(A.S. Arthur)

' **CONFIDENTIAL** '

A. S. ARTHUR,
Vice President MPCC [I]

Poumai Colony,
Imphal—795001
Tele : 225247

13.1. 1994

From Nagaland(Kohima) I arrive Imphal on 31.12.93 and I decided that before I meet anyone, I would meet HE The Governor to apprise him of the situation of the meeting at Dimapur. So around or a little after 7:30 a.m., I rang up the G's residence disclosing my identity and a female's voice received(I thought the G's daughter). I was informed that the Governor was on a morning walk in the garden and that "I can ring up after five minutes."

After about 20 or 25 minutes, I rang again and the same voice replied(received the phone). I was again informed that the Governor was in the bath and that " I can ring up after five minutes".

Just around 8:30 or so when I again rang up, one male voice received the phone. I told him that I would wish to speak to the Governor. He replied, " you can't talk to the Governor now, ring up after 10:00 am." I had a number of New Year's programme including the Church Service at 10 am and so I had not been able to ring up again.

Writing to the Governor asking for interview takes time and so even though it is never my practice to contact the Governor on Phone, I had ventured to try to speak because of urgency of the case.

During interrogation, I was asked whether I

A.S. ARTHUR
Vice President MPCC[I]

Confidential

Poumai Colony,
Imphal-795001
Tele : 225247

13.1.1994

From Nagaland (Kohima) I arrive Imphal on 31.12.93 and I decided that before I meet anyone, I would meet HE The Governor to apprise him of the situation of the meeting at Dimapur. So around or a little after 7:30 a.m., I rang up the G's residence disclosing my identity and a female's voice received (I thought the G's daughter). I was informed that the Governor was on a morning walk in the garden and that I can ring up after five minutes.

After about 20 or 25 minutes, I rang again and the same voice replied (received the phone) I was again informed that the Governor was in the bath and that 'I can ring up after five minutes.'

Just around 8:30 or so when I again rang up, one male voice received the phone. I told him that I would wish to speak to the Governor. He replied, 'you can't talk to the Governor now, ring up after 10:00 am'. I had a number of New Year's programme including the Church Service at 10 a.m. and so I had not been able to ring up again.

Writing to the Governor asking for interview takes time and so even though it is never my practice to contact the Governor on Phone, I had ventured to try to speak because of urgency of the case.

During interrogation, I was asked whether I

A. S. ARTHUR,
Vice President MPCC [I]

- 2 -

Poumai Colony,
Imphal—795001
Tele : 225247

.. .. 19

informed the Governor about the talk with the undefgrounds My replywas no. Because I feel it not necessary to drag in the name of the Head of Sate and also Head of Government at present for a case against me.

(A.S. Arthur) 13/1/94

informed the Governor about the talk with the undergrounds. My reply was no. Because I feel it not necessary to drag in the name of the Head of state and also Head of Government at present for a case against me.

(A.S. Arthur)

APPENDIX D

Proceedings of 12 (twelve) Naga M.L.As meeting held on 8th Jan. 1994 at the residence of Shri Rishang Keishing and adopted the following resolutions.

MEMBERS PRESENT.

1. Rishang Keishing
2. B.D. Behring
3. Daisin Pamei
4. L.S. John
5. S. Lorho
6. ~~W. Morung Makunga~~
7. K.S. Benjamin Banee
8. Ng. Luikang
9. Gaikhangam
10. Hangmila Shaiza
11. Somi Shimray
12. I.D. Dijuanang

The meeting discussed about the arrest of Shri A.S. Arthur, Ex-MLA and Vice President, MPCC(I) and Shri R.V. Shirang, President, Poumai Naga Union on 5th Jan. 1994 by 30 A.R. for having a dialogue with NSCN leaders relating to their letter to Naga MLAs of Manipur to quit from membership on or before 31st Dec. 1993. The letter being an ultimatum and a threat, also it being an unconstitutional and undemocratic action an urgent dialogue with NSCN leaders became indispensable and a delegation including Shri A.S. Arthur and Shri R.V. Shirang was arranged to settle the issue which they succesfully accomplished. The meeting affirmed and justified the action so taken by the delegation and strongly consider it a step inthe right direction to bridge the communication gap between the overgrounds and the undergrounds and to help defuse the on-going ethnic trouble and restore normalcy in the State.

The arrest of Sarvashri Arthur and Shirang is quite unjustified and strongly condemned. Their immediate and unconditional release from police custody is demanded.

The arrest of Sarvashri Arthur and Shirang is quite unjustified and strongly condemned. Their immediate and unconditional release from police custody is demanded.

Further the Naga MLAs decided to meet His Excellency, the Governor to apprise the situation and remove any misgivings.

K.S. Benjamin Banee, Recording Secy.

Proceedings of 12 (twelve) Naga M.L.As meeting held on 8th Jan. 1994 at the residence of Shri Rishang Keishing and adopted the following resolutions.

MEMBERS PRESENT.

1. Rishang Keishing	2. B.D. Behring
3. Daisin Pamei	4. L.S. John
5. S. Lorho	6. W. Morung Makunga
7. K.S. Benjamin Banee	8. Ng. Luikang
9. Gaikhangam	10. Hangmila Shaiza
11. Somi Shimray	12. I.D. Dijuanang

The meeting discussed about the arrest of Shri A.S. Arthur, Ex-MLA and Vice President, MPCC(I) and Shri R.V. Shirang, President, Poumei Naga Union on 5th Jan. 1994 by 30 A.R. for having a dialogue with NSCN leaders relating to their letter to Naga MLAs of Manipur to quit from membership on or before 31st Dec. 1993. The letter being an ultimatum and a threat, also it being an unconstitutional and undemocratic action an urgent dialogue with NSCN leaders became indispensable and a delegation including Shri A.S. Arthur and Shri R.V. Shirang was arranged to settle the issue which they successfully accomplished. The meeting affirmed and justified the action so taken by the delegation and strongly consider it a step in the right direction to bridge the communication gap between the overgrounds and the undergrounds and to help defuse the on-going ethnic trouble and restore normalcy in the State.

The arrest of Sarvashri Arthur and Shirang is quite unjustified and strongly condemned. Their immediate and unconditional release from police custody is demanded.

Further the Naga MLAs decided to meet His Excellency, the Governor to apprise the situation and remove any misgivings.

K.S. Benjamin, Recording Secy.

APPENDIX E

MANIPUR–1994: A YEAR OF DEVELOPMENT

The Year 1994 passes into the history and will not appear before us again in the cycle of life. What remains is the memory only, what left for the people of the State is the fruits of the seeds, sown during the eventful year-1994.

1994 has witnessed unfortunate and unwanted violent incidents arising out of ethnic clashes and insurgency movement in the State and yet, a lot has been done on developmental front— to beautify the capital city, to improve road communication, power, water supply and health facilities. In fact, the year has witnessed remarkable progress in various sectors. Apart from the counter-insurgency measures and the efforts to control the ethnic conflict, the Government has taken up massive and co-ordinated developmental activities both in the hill and valley districts of the State. Short and long term measures were taken up for bringing about a new and changed outlook of the State and also to meet the genuine and long felt desire of the people and to redress their grievances. Restructuring of administration has ensured the credibility and effectiveness of the State machinery. In order to ensure that the policies and programmes taken up are effective and that they are in conformity with the objectives laid, the Government had a thorough review on the progress of implementation of all important schemes, the priority and thrust areas adopted as well as functioning of the implementing Departments. The development schemes of important Departments have been reprioritised giving first priority to the schemes which are likely to complete early so that benefits start flowing early for completion of schemes yielding 'maximum benefit to the maximum people'.

THE FIRST TASK

The first task before the Government was to undertake relief measures for rehabilitation of those people who became victims of Naga-Kuki ethnic clashes.

* Massive rehabilitation measures taken up
* Over 2190 house-holds resettled.
* Elaborate measures taken up to control ethnic conflict.

BEAUTIFICATION OF IMPHAL CITY

In order to have an attractive and a new out look of Imphal city—the capital of the State, a Master Plan for beautification of the city has been taken up and works for beautification of the city have been intensified.

* Bir Tikendrajit Park renovated.
* Beautification of Kangla Moat Phase I & II completed.
* Uripok Kangchup Road, from Maharani bridge to Naoremthong bridge covered by street lighting with Son Lamps.
* Naga Mapal road lighted.
* Improvement work for Shri Shri Govindaji Road and its adjoining areas started.
* Traffic Island near Palace Gate almost completed.
* Widening and strenghening of Naga Mapai Road and Uripok Road taken up.
* Wire netting on the sides of Naga Nallah to prevent dumping of rubbish and garbages inside the Nallah started.
* Open Air Theatre of Jawaharlal Nehru Dance Academy improved.
* Gandhi Ghat on the bank of Nambul River at Uripok developed and inaugurated on the 2nd October.
* 8 Market sheds constructed in a record time (starting from March and completing in May) at Chakri Kom and to the eastern side of District and Session Court as a part of the drive to cleanse the congested market places and also to give proper accommodation to roadside women vendors of Khwairamband Bazar.
* A 10 seated 'Pay and Use' toilet complex made available to public at Laxmi bazar.
* All encroachments along Nambul River banks from Iroisemba to Hiyangthang evicted and river bed dredged out over a stretch of 6 kms to a depth of 4 metres.
* To make regular flow of traffic, a traffic island developed at the crossing of the ring road of Lamphelpat areas.
* At the Palace Ground, auditorium, art gallery, artists workshop-cum-dormitory and open air theatre being constructed and for this filling of earth done.
* After construction of a diversion channel of Nambul River just adjacent to Hump Bridge, and arc bridge also started construction over the diversion channel.

  Works for beautification of other areas/towns/ market have also been given due attention and intensified.
* Construction of Lamlong Bazar Market sheds consisting of 2 triple sheds and 5 twin sheds having a capacity of accommodating 272 women vendors completed.
* Construction of Heijingang Bazar consisting of 15 shops and 2 twin sheds completed.

* Construction of the southern side of the Shopping Complex at Porompat already completed and that of the northern side is in full swing.
* The two storeyed Shopping Complex has 142 shops. Restaurant, godown, post office and women vendor sheds being constructed within the Complex.
* A 10 seated 'Pay and Use' toilet complex taken up at Singjamei market.
* Encroachers at Kakching Bazar removed.
* Construction of playground at Senapati District Hqrs. completed.
* Nambul River dredged over a stretch of 6 kms. to a depth of 4 metres.

LOKTAK LAKE-MANIPUR'S RARE ASSET— ITS PRESERVATION

Keeping in view the important role of the Loktak lake in the economy of the State and also the deteriorating condition in ecology and environment, due attention has been given in the development of Loktak and also in the protection of ecology and environment. A new approach known as 'Attachment Area Approach' has been introduced and under this, efforts and implementation of schemes of soil conservation have been concentrated in certain important compact areas so that there should be definite impact.

* A total quantity of 4.32 lac cubic metres of silt and clay dredged out from the lake during the first 9 months of the year 1994.
* 2000 ha. afforestation by Forest Deptt. and 60 ha. each by Horticulture and Agriculture Department taken up to control Jhum, reduce soil erosion and improve the economy of the local people.
* Encroachment in the lake periphery near Ningthoukhong along Moirang—Sendra Road and Nambul River got vacated. Encroachment in the lake between Moirang and Thamnapokpi removed.
* 2 km. of the lake shoreline near Nngthoukhong and Moirang raised above flood level.
* Sendra Road widened.

RURAL DEVELOPMENT

Various measures have been introduced to create a tangible income earning asset for the villagers and also to control shifting cultivation and to wear away the people from shifting cultivation.

* 'Area Development Approach' scheme introduced.
* 'Own your Orchard' scheme taken up in Kachani area of Ukhrul district and Thanlon—Tipaimukh belt of Churachandpur district and it will be extended in Mao area of Senapati district.
* 'Satellite Tea Gardens' scheme prepared.

* Resettlement of 688 floating fisherman started at an estimated cost of Rs. 232 lakhs.
* Under IRDP, 4197 families (46.72 %) benefited.
* 58.59 % of target of employment generation achieved under JRY.
* Under EAS, out of the total fund of Rs. 1485 lakhs for 22 hill Blocks, Rs. 1022 lakhs spent primarily on upgradation of rural infrastructure.

HEALTH AND FAMILY WELFARE

Concerted efforts have been made to move towards the goal of providing health care for all by the turn of the century as stipulated in the National Health Policy. To take health care services at the door-step, establishment of essential infrastructure was given due priority.

* Construction of 24 PHSCs and 4 PHCs completed.
* Five 300 MA X-Ray machines installed at five Community Health Centres at Sagolmang, Thoubal, Yairipok, Nambol and Bishnupur.
* One 500 M4 X-Ray machine installed at J.N. Hospital, Imphal.
* Expansion of J.N. Hospital taken up. Construction of the overtop floor started and this will add more than 100 beds.
* Construction of Central Sterile Supply Department Block completed and with this availability of sterilised materials round the clock will be better ensured.
* 62 Low cost Sub-Centre/Dispensary buildings constructed under EAS.
* In Family Planning percentage of Sterilization, IUC and C.C. User made significant improvement over the last year.
* Under Universal Immunisation Programme, more than 100% of the target in T.T., D.P.T., O.P.V. and B.C.G. achieved.

WATER SUPPLY AND SANITATION

Keeping in view the importance of safe drinking water and proper sanitation system for healthy living due attention has also been given in this sector. Achievement made during the first 8 months of 1994 are as follows:

* Maximised production capacity from 8 mgd to 11.00 mgd for Imphal Water Supply.
* Opened a grievance redressal cell for nonavailability of water by dividing the city area into 10 zones during semi-drought period.
* Water supply extended to two towns of Lamsang and Yairipok line benefiting a population of around 6,000 heads.
* Laid 4630 m length of pipeline facilitating 4 Municipal areas of Thoubal town.

* Completed construction of 5962 m length pucca drain and 7149 m length of katcha drain (resectioning).
* 104 Tube wells bored in different villages/ habitations.
* Completed 31 nos. of low cost latrines.
* 195 Habitations with a population of 0.89 lakh covered under Rural Water Supply.
* The State has taken up construction of low cost latrine in the Minimum Needs Programme and Central Rural Sanitation Programme. Under the Programme, 1533 units constructed benefiting 0.08 lakh population.

POWER

Manipur does not have its own power generation and is totally dependent on North Eastern Grid for its power supply. The State's authorised share of power from the North Eastern Grid is only 42 MW against the peak demand of 60 MW. There is, therefore, a power shortage of about 30 per cent.

* Two 33/11 KV Sub-Station at Keishampat and Lamphel each having 5 MVA capacity completed and commissioned on 30.4.94.
* Stringing of 30 KM of 33 KV line between Rengpang and Tamenglong and 1 MVA, 33/11 KV Sub-Station at Tamenglong completed and changed on 5.8.94.
* The 1st unit of Gelnel Micro Hydel Project (2 × 200 KV) put on trial run and benefited 300 consumers. The 2nd unit also put on trial run and benefited 500 consumers.
* 132/33 KV Sub-Station at Kakching and 50 KM of 132 KV line between Yaingangpokpi and Kakching almost completed.
* Work on 132 Sub-Station at Karong and Churachandpur along with its associated transmission line in full swing.

ROADS AND BUILDINGS

The State Public Works Department paid due attention for improving the existing roads in the valley as well as in the hill areas. The State highways from Pallel to Chandel, Churachandpur to Singhat, Chandrakhong to Kasom Khullen, Ukhrul to Somdal etc. are worth mentioning. Shingling of 3 km. Inter Village Road from Japhou Bazar to Monsang Pantha has been completed under Employment Assurance Scheme of Chandel District. The National Highway No. 39 from Tangjeng to Moreh has also been improved.

* Widening and strengthening of a number of roads in the Imphal City area have been taken up.
* Special attention given in the works relating to Beautification of Imphal City.
* 34.5 km of premix carpeting completed.

* Tolloi—Mahadev Road made jeepable.
* Work onimportant buildings namely addition of 100 beds capacity at J.N. Hospital, District & Session Judge Court, Imphal; Directorate Complex at Lamphelpat, VIP Gallery of Khuman Lampak Stadium, Education Directorate, Open Air Theatre (4000 seat capacity) progressing well.
* Construction/Repairing of school buildings accorded priority.

IRRIGATION & FLOOD CONTROLS

* Under Irrigation & Flood Control Sector, the Khuga Multi-purpose Project costing about Rs. 3 crores is being targetted for completion during the 8th Plan.
* Water supply component of the project nearing completion (targetting for commissioning in December 1994).
* The Singda Project which has been lingering since 1975 being expedited for completion by Decmber 1994. Two mgd of water made available for Imphal city in October. Additional 2 mgd would be made available in November 1994. Completion in all respects by December 1994.
* Construction of Left Canal System of Thoubal Dam Project from RD 13.939 to 24.418 km along with 6 km long distributeries 10 nos. of outlets. 2 Drainage systems one at Lousipat and another at Poiroupat almost completed.

Removal of hill spurs in respect of Dolaithabi Barrage completed to the extent of 20 % and construction of residential and non-residential buildings completed to the extent of 60 %.

DEVELOPMENT SOCIETY

* As a land mark in the history of implementation of schemes with people participation, the MDS constructed 8 km long irrigation canal at Kakching Wairi Awang Loukon.

FOOD AND CIVIL SUPPLIES

* 5688 mts. of PDS rice procured from FCI and distributed 6057 mts. under Public
* Distribution System during January to August 1994.
* 5859 mts. of Levy sugar procured from FCI and distributed 5906 mts.
* Procured 8146 mts. of wheat and distributed 6776 mts.
* 3.34 Lac Ration Cards distributed.

INDUSTRIES

* 860 Persons selected for undergoing training in various Centres under

different trades of Small Scale, Handloom and Handicraft Industries during January to August 1994.

* 7 Courses of Entrepreneurship Development Programmes conducted covering 225 trainees.
* Seed Margin Money paid to 158 industrial units.
* Under Handloom Industries 114 ex-trainees benefited under the scheme of Follow up Programme to Ex-trainees.
* 327 Weavers benefited under Target Group Approach Scheme.
* Rs. 30 lakhs sanctioned under Individual Workshed Scheme to 570 weavers as Central share.
* Under Thrift Fund Scheme Rs. 1.28 lakhs sanctioned and benefited 1425 weavers as Central share.
* Under Margin Money for Destitute Weavers. Rs. 8 lakhs sanctioned and benefited 16 units.
* Under SEEUY Scheme, 840 beneficiaries selected and composite loan proposal forwarded to Schedule Banks.
* Under PMRY, 213 persons selected out of the total beneficiaries of 220. Rs. 94.45 lakhs released to 145 beneficiaries. Action for identification of a target of 900 beneficiaries for 1994-5 under process.

FIGHTING AGAINST DRUG

The Government has taken keen interest to check the drug trafficking and drug abuse in Manipur. Police have alerted in the Indo-Myanmar border to prevent the inflow of drugs into Manipur. A huge amount of contraband Ganja and intoxicated drugs were consigned into flames by the Governor of Manipur on June 27 this year in Imphal. More than 18,000 kgs. of Ganja, 2 lac 35 thousand Ganja plants, 1,900 phensedyle bottles, 42 grams of heroin and a few grams of opium were destroyed.

BORDER TRADE

To open border trade between India and Myanmar, the State Government also took much interest in the matter. The three day sectoral meeting was held at State Guest House in Imphal from 07th to 09th March. Mr. U. Aung Thein, Director General of Home Affairs, Myanmar led the 20 member delegation of Myanmar. Shri H.V. Goswami, the Chief Secretary of Manipur led the 30 member delegation of India.

A NEW MANIPUR

In short, the year 1994 has witnessed significant progress in various sectors. With the efforts made in 1994 a new Manipur is on the threshold. A new and a changed Manipur will be the gift of the year 1994 to the people of Manipur.

With the passing of the year 1994, let hatred and violence be disappeared from the soil of Manipur. Let peace, love and friendship be sprinkled on the soil of the State, by the year 1995.

P. Bharat Singh, IAS
Director (Publicity), Manipur.

APPENDIX F

DON'T CONDEMN THE LAW, ATTACK ITS IMPLEMENTATION

> The Armed Forces Special Powers Act like POTA is as good or bad as its application and depends on institutional safeguards within the police, paramilitary forces or Army
>
> AFSPA has been there since 1980. At height of Meitei insurgency, there were aberrations, but few. The reason: strict monitoring. A liaison cell existed where anyone could walk in, enquire about arrests.

Manipur has a history of high degree of political instability and mis-governance, even compared to the rest of the North-East, combined with widespread deprivation and frustration. Each community—the Meiteis, the Nagas and the Kukis—has their own complaints. Similarly, Manipur has an abundance of emotive issues the local politicians can manipulate. Those who are unaware of these deep rooted grievances are ill-suited to handle the current tense situation.

Distorted vision and lack of understanding in the last decade has added to Manipuris misery. Peace talks with the NSCN (IM) without a political framework, left entirely to bureaucratic and Intelligence officers, has made the issue of territorial integrity another controversial issue. The obsession with Nagalim (Greater Nagaland) has become a handy tool for politicians, civil groups and for Meitei extremists who want to exploit public sentiment and add to divisions among communities. It has sidetracked real issues of governance and development. For state politicians, such ploys are handy to cover up their failings. Manipur's economy is crippled, unemployment has increased, lack of water, electricity, health care and HIV/AIDS epidemic have added to anger and alienation.

The tragic death of Manorama at the hands of Assam Rifles on July 11 justifiably adds to peoples' anger and revives past ghosts of Heirangoithong, RMC (Regional Medical College) and Malom shootouts, with Irom Sharmila fasting since 2000.

Similarly, in the hills, ghosts of Oinam and Sajouba lie buried to be revived to exploit public anger. Justice must be done in Manorama's case and truth made public at the earliest. Governance and real issues of public interest can no longer be wished away, as it will only add to anger and frustration.

Turning to the Armed Forces Special Power Act (AFSPA), is the law itself defective or is its application and management at fault? The law has been operative since 1980. Admittedly, at the height of Meitei insurgency, there were aberration and some violent ones but these were few in number. It is a similar story in the hill areas affected by the Naga insurgency. The reason for this was strict monitoring and institutional mechanisms established by the Army itself, so that it stood forth as transparent and easily accessible to the public. A public liaison cell was established in 'M' Sector Headquarters, where anyone was free to walk in and enquire about arrests and status of those incarcerated. Those arrested but found innocent were released to the Meira Paibis or other social organisations in police presence (a permanent police officer was present at 'M' Sector), similar was the case in the hills where village authorities were co-opted. All those suspected of being UG (underground) activists or their helpers were handed over to the police within reasonable time as the law demanded. Interrogations were carried out at designated centres at formation level and in remote areas even at unit level.

The AFSPA, like POTA, is as good or bad as the manner of its application and institutional safeguards within the police, paramilitary forces or Army. Security forces are part of the establishment and they cannot be left alone to handle situations, with no action whatsoever being taken on the part of other instruments of state. The Army acts best and most efficiently when it is supported by the civilian structure; it cannot be expected to accomplish tasks far beyond its own capabilities.

The insurgency environment in the entire North-East has changed. In Manipur, it is a criminalized industry run by a nexus of politicians, insurgents and bureaucrats, with the state providing the capital, which is shared around for mutual benefit and to perpetuate the same power structure. Similarly, insurgent factions and politicians are hand in glove to ferment ethnic conflicts and exploit public anger. You cannot expect the Army to fight insurgency on the ground, yet leave the nexus that feeds it untouched.

In the recent situation, both the Governor and Chief Minister were absent from Manipur and away in Delhi, leaving nobody to interact with the agitators or take strong action to defuse the situation. Very cleverly, Chief Minister Ibobi Singh, like some of his predecessors, joined his voice to populist sentiments and threatened to pass a resolution against the AFSPA, thus confronting the Centre with a full-blown crisis. Is this not a case of the civilian state abdicating its responsibility? It is absolutely correct for the Centre to insist that the AFSPA will stay but now, what about putting in place mechanisms for safeguards against its misuse?

The Central Government's consultations with all constituents of the UPA, the Opposition and the establishment of a committee on Manipur are a typically bureaucratic reflex reaction, it is a political short-cut. Politicians bungle and then expect the Army to sort out the subsequent mess, at the same time refusing to provide the armed forces with the support of effective social and political structures. While Manipur burns, the experts gather in yet another dialogue of the deaf.

Indian Express,
24 August 2004

Lt. Gen. *V.K. Nayar (retd) served in the North-East and is also the former Governor of Manipur and Nagaland*

APPENDIX G

A CHIN-UP GENERAL

Occupants of Raj Bhawans are rarely known to be assertive. But Lt Gen (Retd) V.K. Nayar, the former Manipur Governor, refused to fit into the usual mould, says **H. Khogen Singh**.

When in August 1993, Lt. Gen. V.K. Nayar (Retd), a former Army Commander, was pulled out of retirement and made the Governor of Manipur, it passed off almost as a non-event. After all, his predecessor, Chintamani Panigrahi, a Congressman of Mrs Gandhi's era, had a none-too-distinguished tenure.

In any case, Governors have come to acquire the image of constitutional figureheads who dance to New Delhi's tunes. Occupants of Raj Bhawans can never be their individual selves, let alone be assertive, because most of them get their jobs by dint of the 'rehabilitation grant' doled out by the Centre.

But, Gen. Nayar proved that he was a Governor with a difference. In his one-and-a-half year tenure, he never let his voice be stifled by the Central rulers who have little knowledge of the North-East.

That he was not a rubber stamp Governor was proved again on the night of December 22 last year when 'a certain Home Minister' widely believed to be P.M. Sayeed, telephoned Gen. Nayar and asked him to postpone the scheduled trial of strength of the Rishang Keishing Ministry from December 23 to December 28. The former Governor, rather than acquiesce to the diktat, promptly faxed his resignation letter.

'It was not a spur of the moment decision. I resigned because I did not want to compromise', Gen. Nayar reportedly told newsmen in Calcutta on his way home to the Capital after an eventful stint in the gubernatorial office. Clearly, New Delhi had not bargained for this chest-out, chin-up ex-General to openly defy its commands.

The public reaction to Gen Nayar's resignation was spontaneous with several organisations calling for a bandh as a mark of protest. They saw in his exit the hand of the Centre which was bent upon foisting a popular Government. And a popular Government was the last thing the public wanted, for, the spell of President's Rule under Gen. Nayar had done a world of good to the State.

Although the bandh never took place, primarily due to Gen. Nayar's Opposition to the plan, the fact that such a move did take place testified to his popularity. No Governor, or for that matter, no official had ever earned so much goodwill of the people. This is significant, especially so in a State where non-Manipuris are generally unwelcome and are derogatorily known as 'mayangs' (meaning outsiders).

Of course, Gen. Nayar had his detractors, but they were mostly officials who had either been suspended, transferred or had earned his wrath for being corrupt. Politicians were another breed who, on Gen. Nayar's resignation, must have reacted with glee.

'Now that I am gone, I am sure things will come back to square one and all the good work will be undone,' he says. 'But, President's Rule is not the solution to the problems of the State.'

In fact, contrary to the popular perception that he was against lifting of President's Rule, Gen Nayar had always advocated restoration of a popular Ministry. 'I had advised the Centre in July 1994 itself to hold elections in the State by the end of the year,' he recalls. 'They agreed to the suggestion, but never did anything. Had they heeded my advice, perhaps the Centre wouldn't have had to so hastily lifted President's Rule and all that drama over the vote of confidence would have been avoided.'

He, however, admitted that he would have liked President's Rule to continue so that he had more time to give shape to his developmental plans. 'If I had one more year, I would have put Manipur on the road to economic prosperity,' he says.

Blaming the political leadership for the ills of the State, Gen. Nayar does not hide his anathema for the current crop of politicians. 'All of them are self-seekers who are only bothered about themselves and not the State,' he says. He, instead, pins his hopes on the never generation of politicians.

The future of Manipur lies with the younger politicians. Most of them have been educated outside the State and are more intelligent than the present politicians. The forthcoming elections (on February 16 and February 19) is the right opportunity for the people to throw out the older lot," he says bluntly. "But if the same old faces are re-elected, then I think the people of Manipur deserve what they have been getting all these years," Gen. Nayar adds.

Ominously for Manipur, the former Governor, who had commanded the 8 Mountain Division that is engaged in fighting insurgency in the North-East, sees no end to the Kuki-Naga ethnic clashes that have rocked the State for the past two years. Without naming Chief Minister Rishang Keishing, a Naga, and former Finance Minister C. Doungel, a Kuki, Gen. Nayar says that unless the instigators of the violence were tackled, the tangle will remain unsolved.

Gen. Nayar also sees no end to the insurgency in the State as long as it is seen purely as a law and order problem. 'There has to be a multi-pronged strategy to fight insurgency. And on this score, the first priority should be to bring about all-round development in the State,' he says.

A look at some of the indicators of development clearly brings out the level of progress in Manipur. As per the index of the relative development of infrastructure for 1991-2, Manipur lags behind the all India level by 22 per cent. The density of roads per 100 sq km is only 26.33 km as against an all India average of 47.24 km.

An analysis of the State's Gross Domestic Product of the last seven years shows that the share of industrial output, which was 7.01 per cent in 1984-5, has steadily declined to 3.09 per cent in 1991-2. This implies that the State has not fared well in the manufacturing sector.

Besides the lack of development, the State is bedevilled by a high rate of unemployment, especially among the educated. At present, the unemployment rate is 26.5 per cent, which is very high. But what is even more worrisome is that since 1991, the annual rate of increase in unemployment has consistently been 10 per cent or more.

To tackle unemployment, one of the main causes of insurgency in the State, Gen. Nayar advises generation of self-employment. He feels that the education system in Manipur is flawed and not geared towards this—there are hardly any vocational training institutes here.

Gen. Nayar also blames politicians for not consolidating the gains of the army's battle with insurgents; "When I was commanding the mountain division (from 1981 to 1983), we had all but made Ukhrul (district) free of insurgents. The State Government should have picked up from where we left and consolidated the gains. But, Ukhrul is again on the boil and for this I blame the politicians belonging to that area.

The former Governor, however, ends on an optimistic note and said that the situation was not beyond redemption. 'I managed to bring about a lot of development with whatever resources and manpower at my disposal.'

The former Governor claims that in a Budget of Rs 570 crore, he had even managed to show a surplus of Rs 7 crore whereas Nagaland, a State one-third the size of Manipur and with a population also one-third that of Manipur, had asked for over Rs 1,000 crore. 'This only shows that if there is sincerity of purpose, one can bring about development in the State', he concludes.

The Hindustan Times
13 February 1995

APPENDIX H

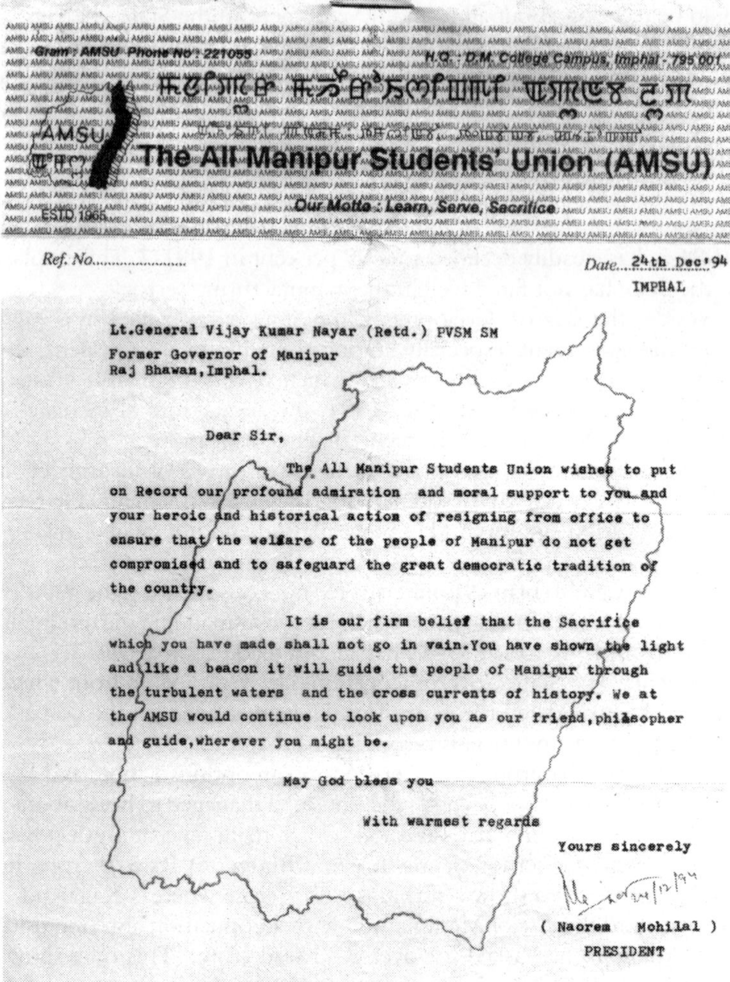

Gram : AMSU Phone No : 221055

H.Q. : D.M. College Campus, Imphal - 795 001

The All Manipur Students' Union (AMSU)

ESTD 1965

Our Motto : Learn, Serve, Sacrifice

Ref. No.......................

Date...24th Dec'94
IMPHAL

Lt.General Vijay Kumar Nayar (Retd.) PVSM SM
Former Governor of Manipur
Raj Bhawan, Imphal.

Dear Sir,

The All Manipur Students Union wishes to put on Record our profound admiration and moral support to you and your heroic and historical action of resigning from office to ensure that the welfare of the people of Manipur do not get compromised and to safeguard the great democratic tradition of the country.

It is our firm belief that the Sacrifice which you have made shall not go in vain. You have shown the light and like a beacon it will guide the people of Manipur through the turbulent waters and the cross currents of history. We at the AMSU would continue to look upon you as our friend, philosopher and guide, wherever you might be.

May God bless you

With warmest regards

Yours sincerely

(Naorem Mohilal)
PRESIDENT

Date 24th Dec. '94
IMPHAl

Lt.General Vijay Kumar Nayar (Retd.) PVSM SM
Former Governor of Manipur
Raj Bhawan, Imphal.

Dear Sir,

The All Manipur Students Union wishes to put on Record our profound admiration and moral support to you and your heroic and historical action of resigning from office to ensure that the welfare of the people of Manipur do not get compromised and to safeguard the great democratic tradition of the country.

It is our firm belief that the sacrifice which you have made shall not go in vain. You have shown the light and like a beacon it will guide the people of Manipur through the turbulent waters and the cross currents of history. We at the AMSU would continue to look upon you as our friend, philosopher and guide, wherever you might be.

May God bless you

With warmest regards

Yours sincerely

(Naorem Mohilal)
President
The All Manipur Students Union (AMSU)

APPENDIX J

MOTHER COURAGE

Imphal: **Thokchom Ramani** or Ima (mother) Ramani, 75, has studied only upto class two. But her's is a powerful voice that has always articulated the concerns of Manipuri civil society. She was the inspiration for the 12 women who shook the conscience of the nation by staging a naked protest in Imphal to highlight army atrocities. Ramani, general secretary of the All-Manipur Women Social Reformation and Development Samaj, tells **Oinam Sunil** that Manipuris will agitate until the AFSP Act is repealed:

What prompted you to take the extreme step of staging a naked protest in front of Assam Rifles headquarter at Kangla Fort?

We saw how a 32-year-old girl, Thangjam Manorama Devi, was killed by Assam Rifles personnel. We decided to teach the army a lesson and tell them that enough is enough. We chose to show our anger with such extreme form of protest. I am old now and nearing death. I told my colleagues; Let us do something to end the excesses.

What is your next step?

We will continue the agitation till the Armed Forces (Special Powers) Act is repealed from the state. Our chief Minister is weak and cannot take a decision. Now, we will try to involve the wives of politicians and bureaucrats in the agitation. The Centre should also know that people are fed up with this Act as the security forces are killing innocents instead of targeting militants. They should understand the pulse of the people and their sentiments.

But, the Act was imposed to curb militancy?

We do not oppose when the army takes on militants. But, they should not target unarmed people. As far as women are concerned, we have been victims for the last 24 years. There are numerous cases of rape by security forces. We cannot tolerate all these any more. If we don't do something now, what will be the future of our sons and daughters? We are ready to die now to save our children.

How long have you been fighting?

Since 1980, Manipuri women are in the forefront of the agitation against the Act. First, we fought alcoholism as it was destroying our social fabric. We had formed the All Manipur Women Social Reformation and Development Samaj in 1975. It was registered in 1978. Then, when the AFSP Act came, we saw many innocents being killed by security forces. The killing of popular dramatist Jogendra Pebia, and others like Kangujam Loken and Chanam Chaoba, have pained us a lot. As the men were being harassed, we, women, decided to lead the fight and tell the police and the army not to touch innocents.

But, the Act has been upheld by the SC?

Initially, we thought it will get better when the Supreme Court made issuance of arrest memo as mandatory for armed forces while apprehending any individual. The court also said the army should hand over the apprehended person to the nearest police station within 24 hours. But, the killings continued even after the issuance of arrest memos. See the case of Manorama. She was picked up from her house on July 10 by Assam Rifles. An arrest memo saying nothing was found from her house was also issued. Next day, they killed her and gave fake charges.

Have you lost trust in the army?

We have no trust in them after the recent episode. Officers should understand the ground reality and stop abusing our basic rights. They should see how Lt. General (Retd) V. K. Nayar performed his duty as General in the 1980s and as governor in the 1990s. During his time, things were better as he listened to our arguments. Army should understand that our children never told us when they joined the underground.

Security forces allege that women 'meira paibis' (torch bearers) are instigated by militants and many of them are their (militants') relatives?

I have three sons and three daughters. And, none of them is a militant. But, I am fighting the security forces' excesses. They cannot just blame us like that. They should, instead, correct themselves. Yes, till today, my children have not joined the ranks of militants, but if the abuse of human rights continues, I cannot say anything about my grandchildren. I cannot guarantee that they will not take to the jungles.

Will you wait till August 15 to see what the government does?

The chief minister has set August 15 as the deadline for repealing the Act. We are eagerly waiting for the outcome. If he fails, Manipur will burn as people cannot accept anything other than a repeal of the Act.

But, the Centre seems to be of the view that it will be difficult to handle insurgency without the Act.

They should first lift the Act and see themselves whether the situation has worsened or not. Then, they can assess the situation again. But, the Act must go first. Insurgency has only increased ever since the Act was imposed in 1980. Human right abuses by security forces have also increased after that. Last year, a girl committed suicide in Jiribam after she was allegedly raped by army troops. Army never revealed the findings of the court of inquiry. Another woman was raped in front of her own son. A woman was raped at Matai village of Imphal East district two years back in front of her own husband. How long shall we tolerate such a thing?

The Times of India,
10 August 2004

CHAPTER 9

Reflection on Conflicts and their Management: Approach to Security and Some Issues of Governance

In my book *Low Intensity Conflicts in India*[1] I covered the background, status and military aspects of the proxy war in J&K, insurgencies in the north-east and terrorism in the Punjab. Later I followed it by an analytical study of the socio-political, ethnic, religious and economic dynamics of the conflict areas of the north-east and J&K along with its historical and geographical imperatives for the Centre For Policy Research, which was published under the title, *Crossing the Frontiers of Conflict in the North East and J and K: From Real Politik to Ideal Politik.*[2] It also had a chapter on 'Drugs and Arms Linkages: Its Cross Border Nexus and Internal Security'. Here I want to cover only contemporary issues and their dynamics. I shall first cover the ethnic conflict in Sri Lanka mainly in the context of IPKF operations based on my visit and study in very broad terms.

ETHNIC CONFLICT IN SRI LANKA AND IPKF OPERATIONS

I have made a mention of Sri Lanka in Chapters 5 and 6 earlier. It will therefore be appropriate for me to record my impressions. My first association with it was while I was commanding the brigade group in Trivandrum. Those days Janatha Vimukti Peramuna (JVP) was at its most violent and aggressive high. During that period the Colombo Conference was taking place and PM Indira Gandhi was to attend it. A certain garbled version of a task for a rescue operation if required was given to me verbally by Lt. Gen. O.P.

Malhotra the then Army Commander. For this in addition to my brigade group 4 Para was earmarked for an airborne operation to be mounted ex-Bangalore and was placed under my command on arrival. With these broad directions, I planned to use 4 Para in an air borne role in the initial phase and one of my Madras battalions to land by sea. I planned to jump with the para battalion or reach by air. I was to be given my detailed instructions once the final decision was taken. I requested FOC-in-C Southern Naval Area (now command) Vice-Admiral R.L. Pereira (later CNS) for some landing craft to be positioned at Tuticorin port for training. He had received no orders but after checking up with Naval Headquarters, he moved the entire fleet of Landing Ship Transport (LST) available to Tuticorin, where the Madras battalion was already waiting and their training started. I spent two days with them and then spoke to CO of 4 Para Lt. Col. J.B. Bhada, who was an old officer of 2 Para and was for some time my 2IC also. We tied up details as much as we could in the light of very general and broad orders. We were fully geared up and waiting after training at our launch pads at Bangalore and Tuticorin. After a week we were asked to stand down. I never knew the details of the so-called rescue mission but it was a good experience to plan under such circumstance, what really came out was that one should familiarize oneself with likely target areas, terrain and whatever one knows about the situation and keep on thinking and discussing with one's juniors who have to do the task. This leads to developing common thinking and mental preparation, which helps when the task is known. Similarly, training with LSTs helped troops gain confidence and familiarization with procedures so that troops can concentrate on the task and do not get bogged down by details of procedures and drills for launching and disembarkation when the task is allotted.

The second exposure to Sri Lanka was when Gen. Krishna Rao, just a month before his retirement in July 1983, asked me and Brig. Narsiman to get familiar with the terrain and political situation in Sri Lanka and along with it keep an eye on developments in Tamil Nadu. Broadly speaking the focus was on the conflict between the LTTE and the Sri Lankan Army. It will not be prudent to give any further details, in any case we had no involvement at this stage. His orders were that it was to be between the two of us and the Chief.

When we asked him if Air Force and Navy are to be consulted or taken into confidence, he clarified not as yet. His last discussion with us was on the morning of the day he retired. Then DGMO Lt. Gen. Sommana and Gen. Vaidya were also present. He asked us to brief Gen. Vaidya in detail that very day. Both I and Narsiman did not go to Palam airfield to see off Gen. Krishna Rao, we took his leave in the Operations Room itself and got ready to brief the new Chief. Gen. Vaidya after seeing off Gen. Krishna Rao came straight back to the operations room and we briefed him on Sri Lanka. After this discussion Sri Lanka became a bit of a open house with both the Air Force and Navy participating but as far as the contingency reviews and planning was concerned we kept it confined to both of us only. In the initial stages we did not even have updated large-scale maps of Sri Lanka. By the time I left in July 1985, we had very detailed working knowledge of Sri Lanka and were well prepared for any contingency.

While in command of the Corps in Jalandhar, I heard of the Army involvement in operation 'Pawan'. Since I had nothing to do with it except my earlier mental involvement I got a bit perturbed when I learnt that we had suddenly changed our stance from that of a friend of LTTE to that of an adversary. When I checked up as to who was involved, to my utter dismay I found they had people handling it who had no experience of handling such situations. After thinking about it for a day, I decided to ring up Gen. Sundarjee, who had taken over as the Chief. I told him that I am not offering any opinion as I do not know the situation but I felt that some of the GOCs of the divisions involved were not suited. I suggested two of my tried brigade commanders, now Maj. Gens. Ramesh Kulkarni and S.C. Sardeshpande, I even offered myself as the overall commander. He discussed the situation very briefly and noted the names I gave him. He thanked me for offering my services but in view of my seniority and likely promotion he told me he will keep it in mind. Within months of the commencement of operation Pawan all three of my Para Commando (Cdo) battalions 1, 9 and 10 Para Cdos, and 4 Para and 5 Para were fully involved. Five out of nine battalions of my Regiment (The Parachute Regiment), whose Col I was, were involved and in the thick of it. A month later my reserve brigade in the corps was also moved to Sri Lanka. After a couple of months I requested permission from Gen. Sundarjee to visit Sri Lanka to see the battalions of my Regiment and the brigade from my corps. He did not agree to it and turned town my repeated requests later on as well. He was probably upset when Maj. Gen. Chibber, GOC of a division under me and Col of the Jat Regiment, after visiting 17 Jat, which had suffered heavy casualties, was very agitated and told him that the casualties were totally a result of bad planning as the advance party itself was inducted into the operations instead of doing familiarization as was the norm. Gen. Sundarjee was further upset when I defended my GOC and told him that operations being planned and executed on the direction of the so-called core group consisting of the VCOAS Lt. Gen. Rodrigues and MO directorate were unrealistic. I realized that I will not be given permission to visit Sri Lanka as part of the core group and he felt I will be critical. I asked him during his farewell visit again and he gave the permission knowing that the next Chief is likely to do so.

I visited Sri Lanka a month later and spent over a week there during which I visited and spent time with all my battalions and the units of the brigade from my corps. In addition I visited all the formations deployed in Sri Lanka and a number of CRPF battalions who had served under me in Manipur and Nagaland. Few details of the visits are important as it gave me an insight into the happenings. All my para commando battalions were carrying out operations against LTTE in the Vavunia jungles, so I landed in the brigade just outside the jungles, whose officiating brigade commander was Col. Sharma who had been my GSO-1 Training in Jalandhar. He briefed me in detail and after finding out the location of my para battalions in the jungles, I decided to land in the jungle on locations indicated by them. I also asked them if they required any ammunition, water or rations which I could bring. I spent the entire day doing landings in different locations in the jungle and meeting most of the columns. I made a total of eight heli landings and returned after dark. I did that for two consecutive days. On the second day I left for the division commanded by Maj. Gen. J.N. Goel from my regiment in whose area 4 Para was deployed. After we took off the weather packed up and for some time we lost our way, till looking at the map we decided to follow the railway line and branched off to the airstrip where the division headquarters was located. When we landed it was almost dark and seeing us Gen. Goel felt very relieved. I told him that there was no cause for worry as we had enough fuel and I am used to flying in bad weather. He told me that I had a very narrow escape as after I took off from Col. Sharma's location, the LTTE infiltrated and blew up the other helicopter parked there. It could have been mine. After that I visited the divisions commanded by Maj. Gens. Sardeshpande, Jameel Mahmood and Ashok Mehta. I got detailed briefing from them. After spending a night each with 4 and 5 Para I returned to Chennai (Madras). I had detailed discussions with the GOC IPKF Lt. Gen. A.S. Kalkat, a friend since Staff College days, who was kind enough to share his thoughts with me. Later during a dinner arranged by Lt. Gen. Kalkat I met N. Ram of the *Hindu* who shared his thoughts on Sri Lanka and on GOI changing stance on LTTE. It was most informative and useful but I refrained from expressing any opinion.

On return to Delhi I met Gen. V.N. Sharma, the new Chief, and he asked me as to what I felt about Sri Lanka. Since I knew him well and we had been together in the MO directorate and later as army commanders, and as he was aware of my stance on these issues I decided to be frank but not critical in a derogatory way.

I started by telling him that I know only as much about our aim in Sri Lanka as Gen. Sundarjee told us during the briefing at the Army Training Conference in Bhatinda in November 1987. Which was quite general and broad based and it was difficult for me to discern it clearly. The key element has been that our stance changed from totally a pro-Tamil and LTTE to totally anti-LTTE which was most confusing even for me, to say nothing of the troops and the Tamil population. I am not so much questioning the validity but the confusion needed to be cleared. The basic question that troops at the ground level faced from the Tamil population of the northern and eastern provinces was, 'Is IPKF for us or against us'. There was no clarity on this either in the minds of our troops or the Tamil population. I told the Chief that now that he is the Chief, I hope the aim of the GOI and what we are trying to achieve in Sri Lanka are clear. The second major issue was that the so-called core group in Delhi took all the decisions, both long-term and on day-to-day operations, but the responsibility rested with the commanders in Sri Lanka. The Southern Army Commander who should have been overall in-charge was gradually sidelined and the core group, essentially the Chief and VCOAS, dealt directly with GOC IPKF. This disrupted the entire command structure at the top level and created confusion as people responsible for planning and decision-making were far removed from the battle scene. Moreover, it resulted in a very impersonal approach to commanders and troops in the battlefield. Even the IPKF Headquarters in Madras was on the wrong side of the sea right till the end. This had a very adverse fallout as the pressures generated by the demanding Core Group in Delhi detached from the battlefield reality was passed right down to troops, this should have been contained at the level of the IPKF Headquarters in the absence of the Command Headquarters. This did not happen as IPKF Headquarters considered itself to be part of the core group rather than the commander of troops in Sri Lanka. This pressure resulted in troops being launched unprepared, hastily and with total disregard to ground realities, a prime example of it was launching of an advance party of 17 Jats, which had just arrived, into operations totally unprepared, which could hardly be called professional, it took the battalion time to recover. Both Gen. Sundarjee and VCOAS then Lt. Gen. Rodriques had no experience of this type of warfare. As regard the command structure we broke it up even at the formation level, a number of battalions did not fight under their own brigade commanders as was the case at the divisional levels. Very often failures of higher command were blamed on troops, the most often talked about topic in Delhi was that our troops were not trained to fight in built-up area. It is my conviction that any infantry battalion given the time for orientation and preparation can deal with not only built-up area but any terrain and adversary. It is a command responsibility to launch troops after adequate orientation and preparation, even in an emergency and if they lack capability in any field, the commanders should build it up as we go along. Launching troops unprepared and in a disoriented fashion is nothing but command failure. The fact that IPKF performed in spite of these handicaps is a tribute to our junior commanders and troops.

The bigger question was what was our aim in Sri Lanka? Was it to protect the Sri Lankan Tamils interest as was indicated by the initial messy air drop of rations followed by parleys with Prabhakaran or was it as later events indicated to preserve the integrity of Sri Lanka. Both aims although appear to be conflicting are not in reality so. Our methodology made sure that we failed in both. To achieve both required diplomatic arm-twisting of both parties with threat of armed intervention lurking in the background but not to be used unless everything had failed. We tried to be high and mighty first with one party and then with the other. It was a political, diplomatic and military fiasco. My doubts that Delhi was not alive to the ground realities were further reinforced when I visited the CRPF battalions near Jaffna and later when I met their DIG Prasad at Madras, who had served under me in Nagaland. During our discussion he told me that before the start of the hostilities when Prabhakaran was a friend and welcome guest at the division headquarters near Jaffna, which he often visited under a white flag, he not only met the GOC but also the Army Commander Lt. Gen. Depinder Singh during his visits. While all this was happening, Prabhakaran was secretly getting ready for the showdown, he was fortifying the Jaffna fort and laying mines and wire obstacle obstacles. He was well prepared when we blew the whistle. This is a startling case of not only intelligence failure but of our government functioning in a manner where the left hand does not know what the right hand is doing, how else can you explain that Prabhakaran overnight from a favoured friend became an enemy.

The Sri Lankan episode will not be complete without mentioning that as a follow-up of my views to the Chief on the command and control during the Army Commanders Conference in 1988, I raised the issue again. I asked the new Southern Army Commander as to how could he let the IPKF in his command be taking orders directly from Delhi and he just remained the provider of logistic support. He had no explanation, I could not help in saying that if any one tried it with me, I would have resigned. The statement caused hurt like all truth does.

RETROSPECTION

The above broad-based narrative is based on what I saw on the ground and learnt during my visit and discussions with five battalion commanders from my regiment, battalion commanders of reserve brigade from my old corps, almost all brigade and divisional commanders and finally my detailed discussion with the GOC IPKF and N. Ram of the *Hindu*. With the above background I made it a point to read almost everything written about the Sri Lankan situation and IPKF operations. I feel that the most honest and realistic account of it has been recorded in his book, *Assignment Jaffna*[3] by Lt. Gen. S.C. Sardeshpande, UYSM, AVSM (Retd). Based on it, I wish to record some of my key observations and views on what I consider to be the core issues. It is particularly important as this was our first projection of power outside the country and in a well-known area of our interest in the neighbourhood, where we had been intimately involved with one or other aspect of the problem.

Lack of strategic discernment both at the national and services level was all too evident, there was no clear formulation of our national aim at the political level and thereby a clear military strategy directed to achieve it was missing. The Indo-Sri Lanka Accord (ISLA) could possibly be considered as the guiding formulation. The main points of the accord were to preserve the unity of Sri Lanka and its multi-ethnic society and ensure integrity of the Tamil-speaking peoples areas. Both the governments had agreed that to achieve it, the establishment of a North-Eastern Provincial Council (NEPC) and holding of elections to the Provincial Council (PC) were essential. The Government of India had also agreed to extend military assistance to Sri Lanka if asked to implement the provisions of the accord. The Government of India was deemed to be the guarantor of the agreement. The annexure to para 6 of ISLA gave IPKF on the invitation of the Sri Lankan president, added responsibility to underwrite the resolution and provide full-fledged military support beyond peacekeeping. Such a mandate required clear cut political directive with priorities not only to fulfil requirements of the accord but also to safeguard Indian and Sri Lankan Tamil interests. A critical analysis of the above would reveal that requirements were not only conflicting but fulfilment of some clauses would negate others. Confusion and dichotomy was bound to happen. What made it worse was that the core group sitting in Delhi was dictating orientation of military operations based on their perceptions at any given point of time. Further confusion resulted due to the lopsided command and control set up, whereby GOC

IPKF was more a henchman of the core group in Delhi than the field commander in command of troops. In the absence of a clear-cut strategy and CI philosophy, the fact that we achieved remarkable results is a tribute to our divisional and brigade commanders in the field and the units who implemented local initiatives both in the strategic and tactical arena. There cannot be a greater tribute to the Indian Infantry and its leaders.

On the contrary, the LTTE had a clear-cut aim of Elam and were determined to achieve it. Their strategy against IPKF was not to defeat it but to wear it down over a period of time, while retaining their bases intact and keep the Tamil population subjugated and under control, if required even by killing and destruction of their homestead. The Srilankan Army was mainly confined to their bases. There was no overall discernment at the strategic level of LTTE's intentions, plans and tactics. These after initial setbacks were effectively countered by the local initiatives at the formation level. It was also at the tactical level that the formation and the units discovered the methodology and innovative tactics of the LTTE and adopted countermeasures against it. Of special significance is the girded improvised explosive devices (IED) network for protection of their bases, Jaffna and other towns. IEDs were an art with the LTTE and a challenge to IPKF which it met with credit.

COMMAND AND CONTROL

The directing headquarter was the Army Headquarters, where all planning and coordination was done. The Force Headquarter at Madras though placed under HQ Southern Command dealt directly with Army Headquarter on all operational matters, while HQ Southern Command was responsible for logistics only. Although the Southern Army Commander was the Overall Force Commander (OFC) but all operational planning and execution was done by GOC IPKF who was also nominally designated Deputy OFC. While there may have been cooperation and interaction amongst the services, MOD, MEA, MHA, I&B ministry, intelligence agencies and Indian High Commissioner and a hoard of other agencies but hardly anything of consequence was ever conveyed to the formation commanders in the field. The requirements of the commanders in the field of psychological operations, civic action and similar local requirements of great value to them were never taken into consideration. The OFC tried to push the headquarter/ IPKF into Sri Lanka when the situation escalated but the Army Headquarters negated it. The structure itself lent to discord and perceptions and functioning.

While the higher leadership were all attuned to a short war, the commanders at the ground level knew they were in for a long haul of CI operations. Lack of experience of the core group that I have highlighted earlier in my analysis was a constraint which never got resolved. Ultimately it resulted in failure of higher political and army leadership to inspire. The troops performed well in spite of the political imperatives and urgency dictated by it.

In two and a half years in Sri Lanka, IPKF saw more than 100 units participating in operations as a result of normal turnover. Of the 10 GOCs of the four divisions deployed in Sri Lanka, only one was an artillery officer, the rest being Infantrymen. Of more than 40 brigadiers who went through operations in Sri Lanka as brigade commanders and Deputy GOCs of divisions only one was from the Armoured Corps and one from Engineers (both were deputy GOCs), the rest were infantrymen. Engineers came very close to Infantry in most of its domain. Sappers performed admirably in most spheres including those of Infantry. Artillery though small in numbers, mostly deployed in troops and the Air Observation Posts did well under pressure and coordinated naval guns, air defence (AD) guns, armed helicopters and mechanized elements when in action. Signals did a marvellous job of ingenious structuring, engineering and routing of communications. Services, particularly ASC, and Ordnance did an excellent job of adjusting to the intense environment, looked after their own protection and delivered the requirement of forward troops under their own steam.[4]

I would like to end by quoting what Lt. Gen. Sardeshpande said

> it is the system that has been becoming over the years, callous, cynical and moribund. Views and visits of senior generals and their interaction with field commander and troops did little to inspire us as subordinates provided little worthwhile guidance and clarified little as to what the whole game plan was about. Everybody lived and thought from one day to the

next. Our wait for pearls of wisdom remained endless! What increasingly showed up instead was the political eye and bluster of GOC IPKF, the tentativeness and uncertainty of the Army Commander above him and the Army Chief's loquaciousness which did little to change systematic incongruities and tackle the hidden rot, in all those two years and more of our military adventure.[5]

ANALYSES: IPKF OPERATIONS

In the absence of a known official government or even services reviews of the IPKF operations in Sri Lanka, it is left to individuals to express their opinion. It becomes all the more important in the absence of an authentic review. I therefore have no hesitation in giving my opinion based on my experience and study. The task of the IPKF was a politico-military task set out in ISLA's framework. To achieve it, LTTE the dominant Tamil group, had to be brought to the negotiating table by dialogue, coercion or even by force. Equally the Sri Lankan government (SLG) had to be diplomatically and politically forced to give concessions to create the necessary atmosphere and climate of trust. Holding of elections to provincial council (PC) was a part of the process and not an end in itself. Elections had to be fully representative for which LTTE or its representation was essential. With our experience of the 1983 elections in Assam, we should not have indulged in an unrepresentative farce of elections. While we had the responsibility to underwrite the accord, we were equally responsible for getting the Tamils their just due. Military action was to lead to both parties (LTTE and SLG) to come to political negotiations. Confinement of Sri Lankan Security Forces (SLSF) to their locations was to minimize conflict and violence. While the IPKF largely succeeded in its military aim to subdue LTTE and to create a reasonable assurance in the minds of the Tamilian civil population that a ceasefire would be in order. Our failure to use political and diplomatic pressure resulted in LTTE entering into negotiation with SLG which nullified ISLA and our efforts. What was worse was our not so glorious exit, unwanted by both of whom we had gone to help.

While the services can feel satisfied in performing the task fairly well considering the political ambiguity and lack of strategic discernment and supportive action in the diplomatic field, the ISLA was a flawed accord with no clear-cut strategic and political aim, resulting in lack of direction and bad implementation. What made it worse was that our efforts beyond the military field did not respond to situation on the ground and stance of the contending parties. In short there was no political management of the conflict throughout as has also been our experience internally. In spite of all the criticism this was a maiden and unique experience for the country and the services. Which could be most useful if we decide to learn from it. You cannot be a powerful nation without participating in such ventures but to succeed it requires clear national and strategic aim and will to achieve it.

THE NORTH-EAST REVISITED

The present situation in the north-east has two major negative undercurrents, one of crisis of credibility and an equally strong one of a deeply negative mindset amongst its people. It is due to the unresolved issues of the past with new sustaining dimensions resulting from people's frustration. The cumulative effect of these is a high degree of socio-political unrest and economic stagnation, which continue to fuel agitations and conflicts. The continued politicization of the issue of migration has not only made its resolution difficult but also politically inexpedient, resulting in disruption in the agricultural and labour fields and alienation of land has become a critical issue. With limited and undeveloped economic base, denial of resources for development has resulted in frustration and a sense of deprivation. Corruption, bad financial management and absence of monitoring have disintegrated administration and the economic structure. Central aid is both the sustenance and mainstay of corruption, its allocations are guided by political clout and expediency. Extortions and denial of resources are the ugly fall-outs of the central government's policy of pumping in money when under pressure and to meet the ends of political expediency. In such a pervading atmosphere of corruption, money and muscle power and violence, both the politicians and insurgents are motivated by gains centring around money and power. Insurgency in the north-east has become an industry in which main and only motive is profit for people in power and both ballot and bullet are the instruments. The politician, bureaucrat and insurgent nexus is well established for mutual benefit.

The nexus has perpetuated ethnic divide and conflict to further their agenda. Since 1990, instigation and sponsorship of ethnic conflicts by the insurgent groups in connivance with the parochial politician is all too evident as it helps in consolidating power and influence to the advantage of both. The Naga insurgent groups' demand for extension of ceasefire or of historical claims to Naga inhabited areas outside Nagaland (south Nagaland or Nagalim) is limited to extension of power and influence and land and territory and not to the well-being of Nagas as a community as none of the tribes gain from it. Both the insurgents and the political articulation are based on hate and denial to other communities. The insurgents and the politicians have dismembered community institutions and divided homogeneous communities, which had lived together sharing land and its resources.

The negative mindset is the outcome of our ignorance and lack of understanding of the north-east and has its foundations on the contemporary experience of the people of the area, of these corruption and political manipulation and bad politics are the ugliest facets. The ignorance of the central government has also been responsible for misjudgement and many wrong decisions resulting in distrust, ill will and hostility. The handling of the extension of ceasefire with the NSCN(IM) to areas of Manipur, Assam and Arunachal Pradesh is a prime example, which led to bloodshed in Manipur and resentment and violence in other areas. Our ignorance and lack of sensitivity was further exposed by a similar lack of response during the Manipuri women's naked demonstration after Manorama's death in 2004 at Kangla Fort. There is a siege mentality and lack of will to break it both by the people and the local leadership is resulting in perpetuating this mindset. Neither the central initiatives have helped in overcoming it. To do so we need to look beyond electoral politics and conflicts.

Our lack of understanding over the past is also highlighted by the fact that while insurgent groups have responded to changing environment internally in the politico-social field and externally in the geostrategic field, we are caught in a mindset of *status quo*. This is clearly brought out by insurgents shifting their bases from the east to west and back to eastern borders in Myanmar on the formation of Bangladesh. They also reacted to changes after the death of Mujibur Rehman in 1975 and recently on the return of Sheikh Hasina to power. Internally, insurgents have learnt by experience that control of population and subversion accompanied by planned acts of violence and terror are rewarding at minimum cost. Their greater emphasis on exploiting ethnic ties to influence events in the social, cultural and economic fields and shifting support base from rural to urban areas as urbanization increases for resources and influence is a testimony to it. Due to our inability to respond to changing situations, it has resulted in a reactive event to event response. In the absence of knowledgeable political handling the field is left to bureaucracy and intelligence agencies, who have a *status quo* mindset and perpetrate it.

The present situation in the north-east generally and particularly in Manipur and Nagaland is a very apt example of all parties developing a stake in the *status quo*. Continuing the ceasefire and negotiation with Naga factions for the last 15 years with no tangible progress or end in view. The so-called no hostilities and peace is illusionary as extortions have increased and people have given up hope. It is the people who have the biggest stake in peace and they have been sidelined. The only actors are the insurgent factions, the politicians both local and central with common agenda of power and money.

A critical analysis in various spheres all point to a failure in governance and more than anything else its absence which is more worrisome to the people and is their main concern. Their cry is, we have had enough of the so-called democracy, let us have some governance. Special areas of attention are to establish the credibility and legitimacy of the state, implementation of schemes to remove people's deprivation, manage disparities, to deal with ethnic sensitivities and divide and to secure the environment. The credibility of the government can only be established by a pragmatic and implementable policy, institutional approach and a transparent implementation with people's participation and positive responses from people.

WHAT IS MISSING IN KASHMIR

A lot has been written on Kashmir and everyone has an opinion on it. The Government of India has had and still has a number of interlocutors, the previous ones' were mostly from the bureaucracy and the intelligence set up. In addition it has a number of committees and commissions advising it on various aspects. Within Jammu & Kashmir Valley each political party has its own agenda, various shades of dissidents and moderates have their views and agenda. The Indo-Pak dimensions of the problem further confuse the situation. The Government of India's initiatives become prey to one or the other dissident element, which results in a bureaucratic *status quo* mindset. The situation simmers on and responses become event and crisis based. In such a situation I feel we need to get down to the basics. Since Kashmir Valley is the centre of attention, I shall primarily confine to it. Some of these elements have been lingering in my mind since 1997, it will be therefore relevant to record their inception along with these.

Normally, visits to Kashmir end up in listening to different elements of the establishment, the security forces and other available Kashmiri leadership. We try and generally widen this interaction by talking to journalists. During one of my many visits to the valley in 1997. Events since then have proved that real issues confronting us remain the same. I was determined to find out what was in the minds of the dissidents and the so-called anti-establishment elements as I thought that with the situation improving time was ripe for it. Much to the annoyance of the establishment, I managed to meet some of them through common friends and well-meaning journalists. I also took the opportunity to meet community leaders in the north and south of Kashmir. Of these the views of Yasin Malik of JKLF both as a militant and dissident are of relevance. Similarly, the views of Mian Basheer (the Gujar leader), whose son Mian Altaf was a minister in Farooq Abdullah's cabinet, as a community leader and as an inactive but well-informed political leader are relevant. These to my mind represent some of the key elements.

Meeting with Yasin Malik was a bit of a cloak and dagger affair and took place after a lot of persuasion as the suspicion of a retired army officer and a former governor were genuine. I met his representative at the tourist centre and was driven in his red Maruti into the interior of Srinagar's Masooma area and then on foot through *galis* till I reached an innocuous house. I was offered Kahwa and told that Yasin Sahib would come soon. During the journey and while waiting I did have a feeling of apprehension of it being a trap. However, Yasin Malik arrived escorted by two persons. He appeared to me an angry but genuine person. He believes in Azadi and has never changed his stance. He also believes in the integrity of the state of Jammu & Kashmir and has a totally secular outlook. From our discussion two issues stand out in my memory, one regarding militancy itself. He emphasized the changing face of militancy and its increasing Islamic and pro-Pakistani dimensions. He attributed it to a total lack of politico strategic vision of the Indian leadership. He maintained that JKLF was pro-Azadi and not pro-Pakistan, its dismemberment resulted in the entire Kashmiri struggle and militancy passing into the hands of pro-Pak Tanzeems. As a professional I could not disagree with him as signs of it were already emerging and later years proved it beyond doubt.

On the issues of talks and negotiations, he was all for it but had a long tale of woes and said lack of trust was the main hurdle. In this regard he mentioned the denial of visa by the Government of India to him and his colleagues to Pakistan Occupied Kashmir (POK) and again to Nepal to meet Azad Kashmir leaders. He also narrated to me as to how the Government of India having invited Kashmiri dissident leaders to Delhi, when asked by the press, Chavan the then home minister told them that they (dissident leaders) have come to Delhi as they had lost their relevance. It was an act totally lacking in trust and of political one upmanship. He was firmly of the opinion that the Government of India does not trust Kashmiris and Kashmiris do not trust the Government of India. Mistrust is the bane of political or any dialogue or negotiations. I agree with Yasin Malik and having experienced the dealings of our political leaders, particularly late Chavan, I can vouch for it. Unless we can overcome this mistrust and talk openly and sincerely, progress in resolving the Kashmir imbroglio will be tardy and unsuccessful in spite of all the concessions. If you want to establish trust then we should deal with dissidents directly and confront them with what one can offer and what one cannot and hear them out. Dealings through intelligence operators and bureaucrats, who have a mindset biased by past experiences and prejudices can never establish trust. Moreover they do not have a clear mandate to discuss the real core issues.

My discussions with Mian Basheer were wide ranging and I used him as a sounding board to some of the things I had picked up in different parts of the valley and in some ways he reinforced them. He was emphatic in emphasizing two aspects. First that while the general standard of living and well-being of Kashmiris has improved but a sense of being deprived persists. To illustrate his point, he mentioned that Kashmiris no longer go as labourers to Punjab, Himachal Pradesh and rest of northern India to work in saw mills or as porters at bus stands and railway stations. He felt that in spite of all the money Government of India has pumped in, the lack of essential amenities like water, electricity, schools and hospitals irks the common man and militancy has added to it. The feeling of frustration of not being able to lead a normal life due to militancy has further aggravated it and is being exploited both by the politicians and the dissidents. It is an environmental fallout but needs to be recognized. The other issue he raised was of recognition, which centres around lack of knowledge, response and ultimately affects governance. He put it simply and said that leaders come from Delhi, talk to ministers, bureaucrats, police and army officers but nobody talks to us, the people and the community leaders. He said it is a change since the days of Nehru and Gandhi leadership. Nehru knew all of us, he passed it to his daughter Mrs. Indira Gandhi and the mother passed to it onto the son Rajiv Gandhi, so they knew us and the people. The present leaders do not know us and do not know what people want or feel. Similar feelings with and without dissident overtones were expressed by villagers in the north and south of Kashmir. At the core was a feeling of neglect resulting in frustration and anger, easy situation for exploitation.[6]

On return to Delhi, I conveyed the gist of my observations to N.N. Vohra, the then principal secretary to the PM, I.K. Gujral. He felt that I should meet the PM and arranged it also. He had to go abroad for talks with Naga leaders and also on some other errands. I was rung up twice by the officials in the PMO regarding the postponement of my meeting with the PM, when I informed them of my scheduled departure for New Zealand to be with our daughter. A few days later I was told of the third postponement and asking me to postpone my departure. I told the PMO representative that I was not interested in meeting the PM and left for New Zealand. Later in 1999, when I.K. Gujral was no longer the PM, I met him during our visit to Bangladesh. He complained to me about not meeting him. My reply was simple, you wanted something from me, so you should have made sure of it. I also told him that if you ring up a politician, his and his subordinates' first thought is what does he want from us. I did not want anything from you, so I did not pursue. I have narrated this only to illustrate as to how much interest our political leaders have in real issues which matter to people and the nation.

The vital issue of trust has been our singular failure in dealing with human problems. People's sufferings and their sense of want/dissidence can to a large extent be mitigated by meeting people, listening to them with understanding. There cannot be a better example of it then the Reconciliation Commission in South Africa after years of apartheid. Unfortunately, our politicians are steeped in politics of expediency and power and to establish trust appears beyond them so far. However, they must realize that without it you cannot win over people irrespective of all other pretences. In Manipur and Nagaland both as GOC and later as governor, I listened to people, talked frankly and told them what I will do and what I won't. This helped me to establish trust and gain their confidence, cooperation and participation in all I did. We need to establish trust with people of Kashmir.

The important issue of knowing people at the grassroot level and their feelings and wants was the hallmark of our earlier leaders who participated in the independence struggle. They knew people, communities, met and recognized them and thus motivated them, gained their confidence and following. The current leadership is dependent on bureaucracy and establishment and has no link with the people. You cannot deal with human beings and their problem through local political leaders, bureaucracy and establishment. Their orientation is to politics, power, money. Listening to people and understanding issues only can resolve issues, not politicking. Their interest in real issues is illustrated by Gujral's attitude that I mentioned above.

The above break and distancing from people also results in bad governance. Our economic and development plans are the product of economists with total lack of knowledge of area and its people and without their participation and involvement. While the Rangaraj Committee on the economic wants of people and its package will be of help but it will fail to touch the Kashmiris. Railway and other infrastructure is essential but so is the ABC dimensions[7] as outlined in my book, *Low Intensity Conflicts in India*. To the common man, availability of civic facilities and response to his daily needs is essential under all circumstances. These are (*aab*, bijli, communication, distribution, education, fire for people's warmth and an amelioration of these, *ghar* or shelter and health) at the grassroot level. The failure of administration at the local level to meet the people's basic requirements is the main cause of their frustration. Political dialogues and handouts cannot replace real governance and political sincerity and trust.

The recognition of the above truths is essential to resolve the Kashmir tangle. Will we do it!

SOME ISSUES OF GOVERNANCE IN THE NORTH-EAST AND JAMMU & KASHMIR

In South Asia there is a crisis in nation building and governance, irrespective of the system adopted by different nations after gaining independence. Some in India believe that the British parliamentary system which we adopted has failed as it only permits people to elect their representatives but does not assure their participation in decision-making. They feel there is a need for a new system and constitution. I am aware of the studies done by eminent scholars on problems of governance in the South Asian Countries (Bangladesh, India, Nepal, Pakistan and Sri Lanka) and on common problems of governance in South Asia. Having gone through these over a period of time and having had the opportunity to be involved in governance in some of our disturbed areas, I am firmly of the opinion that our major failure has been in not working the system as both the Constitution and the system permit doing the right and legitimate things. We have subverted and distorted the system in its implementation. It is therefore imperative that we restore the system and work it as the constitution and law of the land demands it. It is not the system but its mismanagement and wilful distortion, which are at fault. The main reason for it is bad politics.

Before dealing with issues of governance specific to the north-east and J&K, it will be relevant to touch upon certain common issues relevant to the country as a whole. Due to constraints of space I shall confine myself to the major ones only.

In a democracy political power is the undisputed master both in principle and practice, therefore the key elements of governance are political will and intention, a clearly defined and credible policy based on correct inputs and an efficient and responsive machinery. However, in our case political will and perceptions are confined primarily to win elections and electoral politics are the main occupation of politicians and political parties. This has led to political expediency overriding all other considerations thereby subversion of the government machinery and utilization of resources to gain, retain and consolidate power.

This has also led to centralization of authority and lack of transparency. Permissiveness in government functioning is evident by its adverse fallout in most fields of government activity and is the main cause of corruption. The root cause of permissiveness is political expediency as political perceptions are entirely dictated by electoral politics. The element of permissiveness and divisions that have emerged in the society have affected governance and the very governability of the society. What people are asking for is justice, instead political leadership offers them appeasement. This had deepened the divisions in the society along caste, religious and ethnic lines. Religion should be the affair of individual and the community and not of the political process. The use of religion for political and electoral gains should be constitutionally and legally prohibited.

The North-East

In the north-east our flawed policies based on sentiment and rhetoric have created a mess of governance. While geography and history should provide insight into the area, its people and their diverse culture, traditions and distinctive social and political evolution. But our policies after independence should have been based on emerging geopolitical and security imperatives and need for social and economic integration of the area with the rest of the country. Instead we adopted Elwin's philosophy and in the 1950 Constitution, North Eastern Frontier Agency (NEFA) was restored to the governor as an agent of the centre. Adoption of Elwin's theory, 'while acknowledging the need not to let matters drift in Tribal areas or just not take interest in them, we should at the same time avoid over administering these areas and in particular sending too many people in tribal areas. It is in between these two positions that we have to function'.[8] This was perpetuation of the British policy of exclusiveness and division and further isolated the people of the north-east and created hurdles for integration. We failed to meet the middle ground, while legislating measures to safeguard their tradition, culture and customs, we have failed to provide them real autonomy in their own affairs and economic independence or sustainability, without which political autonomy is meaningless.

The core of most of the ills and negative manifestations in the north-east lies in the creation of the states itself as a measure of political expediency. They do not have economic viability to sustain their administrative and non-development expenditure. Neither much thought and planning has gone into developing their basic strength in agriculture, horticulture and hydel power with the result that their dependence on central grants grew and any change in this was agitated against as anti-north-east. This dependence on political and financial dispensation has grown and become a ploy for the local political leaders, who have developed a vested interest in it and are its main beneficiaries. This has resulted in a total disincentive for generating local revenue and exploiting internal resources. It has also resulted in a narrow and a negative mindset, wherein interaction within the north-eastern states and with the rest of India got constrained thus stalling economic activity and development. The north-east has to integrate within itself as much with the rest of the country.

Our policies have resulted in structural conflicts and defects in the system of governance. The extension of the Sixth Schedule to the hills has not helped. While on one hand, it has created multiple layers of administration, on the other hand, it has divided people on ethnic lines and clamour by other smaller groups to obtain a separate and similar status has increased. It has also led to ethnic parochialism and provided the local elite opportunity to exploit ethnic sensitivities. This is accompanied by a perceptible change in the functioning of the administration of the states in north-east since 1970. The emphasis has shifted from administration with involvement by the old Indian Frontier Administrative Service (IFAS) cadre to that of white collar bureaucratic one of the IAS cadre. Local officers over subscribe to the cadre, who are empanelled based on ethnic and political patronage. At the district level there is multiplicity of functioning between Autonomous District Councils (ADC)/panchayats, local MLAs, district administration and state departments, all wanting control over financial allocations. State finance commissions are not functioning or not permitted to function and there is no financial management and allocations based on prioritized needs and requirements. To revive the administration, reintroduction of the old Indian Frontier Administration Service (IFAS) cadre in the hill states is particularly necessary. It is further discussed in greater detail under J&K.

The traditional institutions have been made defunct and new (modern) institutions are non-functional. A comparative study of the Sixth Schedule and Panchayati Raj Institutions (PRI) under the 73rd and urban ones under the 74th Amendment need to form the grassroot level framework, with traditional institutions and nomenclatures incorporated. The new PRI system has better institutional structure for self-governance due to better demarcated operational area, adequate authority and resources to manage its affairs, provided the state finance commissions function properly. ADC has greater dependence on the state and on political patronage. The PRIs are elective at all levels and it caters to all segments of the society. This is supported by the findings of an independent study carried out in Mizoram.[9]

The issue of immigrants or foreigners as they are called in the north-east is a major challenge for governance as unabated trans-border migration has altered the demographic profile of Tripura and is threatening to change that of Assam and other states of the north-east. It raises strong feelings amongst the people, particularly in Assam, at the same time it is highly politicized. Failure to implement the Assam Accord of 1985 and conflicting stands on the now defunct, 'Illegal Migrants (Determination by Tribunals) Act 1983' had further confused the issue and made the situation volatile. All well-meaning people have a reason to be satisfied that it has been struck down by the Supreme Court. There is a need for realism in tackling the issues, border fences and strict border regimes alone will fail to restrain it. We need a clear cut policy. First of all there has to be a firm commitment of all political parties to the cut-off date of 25 March 1971 as agreed in the Assam Accord. Any dilution of it under the garb of discussion on indigenous people should be done away and Foreigners Act of 1952 as applicable to rest of India should be enforced. We also need to realize that trade related issues and labour movements in the region will be a major requirement in the liberalized economic environment. This will require a well thought out immigration and naturalization policy. There is an urgent need for identification cards for Indian citizens and updating of the citizen's register after due verification. Similarly, there is need for work permits for immigrant labourers to control and regulate the labour inflow. These should be preferably on a group basis with proper sponsorship. There is need to take a holistic look at the issues of the Foreigners Act, identification cards for Indian citizens, work permits for migrant labourers and setting up of an immigration and naturalization regime like the one in the USA. This could possibly be done by a national commission. There are clear indications that economic interdependence, free flow of trade and commerce and workforce will be the hallmark of future regional cooperation. Thereafter growth and well-being of Bangladesh along with the north-east is vital for the stability of the region.

No discussion of the north-east and governance can be complete without examining its economic maze. Mainstream thinking that large-scale development and financial assistance from the centre will overcome the feeling of neglect, discontent and insurgency, is fallacious. First of all we must dispel the myth that the north-east is tribal and backward. Mizoram, Nagaland,

Meghalaya and Arunachal Pradesh are tribal and all dispensation to them as tribals is justified. The truth is that the tribals in the north-east are more advanced and literate compared to tribals in the rest of India. The tribal population is only 27 per cent and this one-fourth of the population owns two-third of the land.[10] The concept of Autonomous District Councils (ADCs) has failed to protect their interest due to politicization and corruption. While land is denied on the pretext of protecting their interest for all economic activity but alienation of tribal land has taken place by their own elite.[11] It has also resulted in political and bureaucratic feudalism.[12] Logical inference should be that the north-east is not totally tribal or backward. North-east is labour deficient and it is labour from Bangladesh, Nepal and other parts of India which is sustaining both agricultural and non-agricultural economic activities. This is also the reason for failure of labour-intensive schemes. The choice is either we permit free movement of labour from within India or invite continuous influx from Bangladesh.

In the last decade there has been serious discussionon converting the locational disadvantage into an asset because of globalization. The 'Look East' policy is unlikely to fructify unless states in the north-east and their political leadership clean up their act and stop turning a blind eye to illegal trade and extortions on NH 39 and 53 and regain control. In this context north-east needs to meet the basic requirements of economic liberalization and dynamics of a market economy. An essential part of this will be improvement of infrastructure and flow of investments which depend on political and economic stability, a secure environment and level and quality of administration.

The north-east is an interesting study in negotiations for political solution of conflicts ending in various failed and defunct accords. The Mizo Accord of 1986 has lasted and is a success, it also presents a best case scenario. The same cannot be said of the current prolonged negotiations and ceasefire with the various Naga factions. There is a sea change in the situation, attitude of the insurgents and what makes it worse is the fragmentation of the society, the polity and insurgencies itself. Civil society has been sidelined and focus is on politicians and insurgents, for both it is a power game. We need to focus on the people. Considering the nature of conflicts, the paradigms of conflict resolution and management relevant to the situation in the north-east are 'Ideal Politics' and a cooperative approach. The prevalent environment in the country on the other hand is of 'Real Politics' and a competitive one at that. This needs to change.

The north-east is rampant with corruption, maladministration and ethnic parochialism, which is keeping it isolated and divided from within and from the outside world. Of this physical isolation and division within are the cause of economic and social harassment. To break this isolation, first the north-east must break the physical barriers by better connectivity within and with the outside. Similarly, the north-east must first integrate within before it can look outwards with confidence.

Jammu & Kashmir

There has been a tendency amongst our policy planners to examine the J&K situation primarily in the Indo-Pak context and equate the state of J&K with the Kashmir Valley. This tends to distort the problem. J&K is a multi-ethnic, multi-religion and multi-lingual state, in which different communities and different areas have different political and socio-economic perspectives and aspirations. We need to realize it that our failure to do so will result in resentment of one or the other. We have had agitations in Ladakh earlier and the recent ones in J&K Valley are indicative of it. While Pakistan will always remain a factor in resolving the problem and we should be conscious of it but internal dynamics are equally important and is the key to governance. I shall thereafter confine to these.

The period from 1953 to 1989 can be summed up as one of political ineptness and expediency, rigged elections, corruption and alienation resulting in militancy and insurgency. Trust was the biggest casualty. However, the three elections since then have presented changed political dispensation and the legitimacy and fairness of the system has been re-established to a large extent.

J&K has a good record of land and administrative reforms under the J&K Agrarian Reforms Act of 1976 and establishment of the 'Single Line Administration (SLA)' borrowed from the administrative set-up in erstwhile NEFA and replicated in the administrative structure in Ladakh as far back as 1975 during Sheikh Abdullah's second tenure. Under this dispensation the administration in all the districts was reorganized with all field departments of the district under the effective administrative and financial control of the DC, who in addition to his regulatory functions of district magistrate and district collector was the District Development Commissioner (DDC) designate. The planning of all development schemes, allocation of resources and location of district institutions was decided and supervised by the District Development Board (DDB). The board had a number of elected representatives in addition to officials representing important departments at the district level. It was headed by the DDC. The state cabinet was mandated to visit each district once a year to review development and the functioning of SLA. Since these meetings were always chaired by the CM, so it had the support and approval of the cabinet. Some changes in the SLA were brought about in 1993 but the structure remained intact in essence. However, on return of the popular government in 1996, the government nominated each of its ministers as chairman of one of the district DDB and instructions were passed to select plans and works, particularly related to the Department of Rural Development. PWD and PHE department at the choice of the ruling party MLA of the district. Both these changes totally politicized both development and the institution of DDB, it also resulted in allocation or denial of funds based on political affiliation of the MLA. The SLA in its original form was the most effective tool to bring about socio-economic betterment of the people. The need is to restore the SLA to its original status.

J&K Panchayat Act of 1989, which replaced the Act of 1958 was essentially in line with the provision of the 73rd Amendment applicable to rest of the country. It envisages a three-tier system of planning and development at village panchayats, Block Development Councils and District Planning and Development Boards. These will comprise mostly elected representatives and government officials. Provision also exists for devolution and earmarking of financial resources and administrative powers to these units. Panchayat elections were held in 2001 after a gap of 25 years, repeated again in 2011 with success. Effective funding of panchayats and SLA will mitigate people's sense of deprivation to a large extent at the grassroot level. The need to remove political interference and state government officials' pressure is essential for successful functioning of these institutions.

It is estimated that there are over 1.5 lakh (estimate of 2003) unemployed youth. Both the centre and state government's efforts to provide employment in defence services, paramilitary forces and police (including Special Police Officers) cannot meet the requirement. The state sector is totally saturated, there are over 4 lakh government and public sector job holders and over half a lakh of casual and work charge employees. With awareness and literacy every educated person's expectations have risen. The situation is made worse due to lack of entrepreneurial skills and initiatives and reluctances of youth to search for job opportunities outside which is slowly being redeemed. There is an urgent need for a strategy for income generating activities and training of youth for self employment.

The Pahari belt in Kashmir from Uri to Tilel opposite POK requires special attention and dispensation under the Border Areas Development Scheme. The area is inhabited by communities of different ethnic and language groups, who have no commonality with the Valley Kashmiris except religion. There is a sense of neglect and deprivation amongst them which requires sustained and deliberate responses specially in terms of education (opening of schools), health, animal husbandry and civic amenities like water, electricity, hygiene and sanitation.

Introduction of railways into the valley specially when the link to Udhampur is completed will go a long way to bring people closer economically and socially and lead towards greater integration. However, more important is the connectivity within the state. The road infrastructure is old and inadequate, there is urgent need for upgradation. This should be a priority task both from the security and development point of view.

The other area of concern is the dismal state of power availability, which in spite of the vast potential is an area of irritation particularly during winter. J&K has one of the lowest power consumption in the country, it only consumes 9.1 kw/hr compared to Haryana which consumes 5238 kw/hr per capita. J&K has

9 per cent of the total hydel potential of the country of which only 2 per cent has been tapped. The river basins of Chenab, Jhelum and Indus have a potential of 12,000 MW, against the total requirement of 700 MW in the last plan which would have increased to almost 1000 MW by now. Of the combined capacity of Mahura, lower Jhelum, Salal and Chennai of 400 MW, only 200 MW is available as lower Jhelum capacity of 100 MW reduces to 30 MW during winter and only 80 MW from Salal phase I comes to J&K, the rest is fed to the National Northern Grid. Uri Hydel project with a capacity of 500 MW was completed but is not fully available due to inadequate transmission lines. Jammu-Srinagar power line is still to be completed.

In spite of emphasis on social services, the result have been nowhere commensurate to the money spent on these. A clear example is the education system, the low literacy rate is a testimony to it. Same is true of health services. Generally it is also true of other services. The need in the services is to consolidate before expansion, this is also true of infrastructure. You can only increase the level of satisfaction if services are available and is of satisfactory standard. Similarly, in spite of all ill effects of military, it has in a way broken the isolation of the Kashmiris as the Kashmiri traders were forced to move out as did the youth for education to different corners of the country. However, this phenomenon was entirely due to compulsion and private initiative. There has been no major effort either by the state or the central government to encourage this. In a way it has integrated the Kashmir economy with the rest of the country and opening of trade with Pakistan will further improve economic and social ties and make people look beyond the political arena. We need to encourage it.

While there had been substantial improvement in the standard of living in J&K preceding the 1987 elections, the poverty line had declined to 16.3 per cent[13] and per capita income rose to Rs. 3,344,[14] the sixth highest in the country but in the perception of the Kashmiris it did not benefit them in real terms. This reflects the psychological barrier which can only be bridged by overcoming the past policies of political manipulations and generating trust. These are in the political domain and needs to be addressed as the key factor to overcome alienation. Can we do it?

Like the north-east there is a lack of administrative leadership at the divisional and district level. Officers hardly move out or visit areas and leave execution to the lowest level, who fail to deliver both due to lack of capability and supervision. As in the north-east, there is a need to reintroduce the Indian Frontier Administrative Service (IFAS) Officers who should be drawn from volunteers from the middle level from defence services, paramilitary and police as well as volunteers from amongst the IAS and other central services.

No discourse on J&K can be complete without discussing the core issue of autonomy. The perceptions on this vary from region to region. It will be logical to first discuss the regional autonomy within J&K first, for what you cannot give and share with your own constituent parts within the state asking for it for the state will only repeat the past experience of opposition from within. The regional imbalances need to be addressed. The Glancy Commission of 1931, Gajendra Gadkhar Commission in 1967 and Sikri Commission of 1978 had all made recommendations to remove these. The provinces of J&K should have proportionate representation in the Cabinet and the Dy CM should be from Jammu. Ethnic, linguistic and religious minorities must have seats reserved for them in the legislature. Ladakh Autonomous Council should be strengthened and given administrative and financial autonomy.

The outright rejection of autonomy to the state was a mistake by the NDA government. In my opinion the Six-point Indira-Shiekh Abdullah Pact of 1975 should act as a base for further negotiations. It preserves the sanctity of Article 370 and protects state's interests without compromising the sovereignty and territorial integrity of the country. It is also in keeping with the federal structure as provided in the Constitution and recommended by the Sarkaria Commission.

Policy implementation, rejuvenating the administration, implementation of economic programmes and security management are all part of governance. Without effective and good governance neither we will be able to secure the environment nor implement our policies to remove people's deprivation. Special area of concern for governance both in J&K and the north-east are the establishment of the credibility and legitimacy of the state and its institutions. It can only be done by a pragmatic and implementable policy, institutionalized approach and a transparent and sincere implementation by credible people. While resolving and managing conflicting perceptions is primarily in the political field, implementation of solutions in a just and fair fashion is part of governance.

TERRORISM

Wrong priorities and ignoring the basics came to the forefront as a sad commentary during the 26/11 Bombay attack by the Pakistani *jehadis*. It showed the Indian State and its police forces as inadequate professionals and in very poor light. Rhetoric and misdirected anger clouded our responses. The threat from terrorism requires a long-term response at the strategic level, with the tactical battles being fought by the intelligence agencies and police, fitting into the overall strategic framework. Unfortunately most responses have been at the tactical level and protective in nature. This is due to public pressure and to meet the ends of political expediency. The delay in response to the Bombay terrorist attack in November 2008 was due to lack of anticipation in spite of warning, resulting in disjointed responses at the local level and delay in decision-making in Delhi. There was hardly any justification in waiting for the National Security Guard (NSG) from Delhi. There was enough police to tackle the terrorists at the Chhatrapati Shivaji Railway Station (two terrorists), Cama Hospital and Leopold Café areas. The terrorists at the Israeli Kasabat, Nariman House, Taj Mahal Hotal and Oberoi Trident could have been tackled by the Naval Commandos assisted by the Army. What was lacking was overall command and leadership. The total casualties were 183 killed (including 22 foreigners and 20 security personnel) and 239 persons including 23 foreigners were injured. The casualties could have been reduced by prompt action. The NSG arrived only on the morning of 27 November and started blasting everything in their way. I consider this along with Operation Blue Star as the worst slur on our special forces. The display of our helplessness was made more vivid and a bit comical by the intense and hoarse rhetorics of Barkha Dutt of NDTV and other television reporters in competition. The sight of army cordon and naval commandos lying in wait on television was pathetic. Action and not static display was required. The entire operation took 60 hours, a sorry reflection of our response capability and efficiency, which was made worse by high casualties. The situation can best be described as a state of paralysis marked by indecision, inaction and a total absence of leadership.

The augmentation of the NSG and its pre-location in major cities in different zones of the country can only result in better reaction after the terrorists have struck, provided it is close to its location but it cannot prevent it. Moreover, terrorists will strike where and when they can succeed. Nagpur will make as much news as Bangalore or Calcutta.

Having said so, the need is for a dispassionate review of what has been done and what needs to be done. For doing so, we must discern the nature and dimensions of the threat. Terrorism in our context is primarily Islamic and Pakistan sponsored. The security situation in Pakistan is that it is battling Talibans within for its own survival. There is a high probability of Pakistan carrying out adjustments with Afghan Talibans to protect its interests in Afghanistan while subduing the indigenous Talibans within its frontier areas. Simultaneously, Pakistan will continue to tolerate, accommodate and even encourage Lashkar-e-Toiba (LET) and other *jihadi* groups with anti-India and Kashmir-centric orientation and preserve these as its instruments of anti-India policy. There is also a religious dimension to it as Talibans are Deobandis whereas LET and anti-India *jihadi* groups are of Salafi orientation with greater affinity and tolerance for Pakistan's Islamic government. The likely American exit starting 2011 will affect both Afghanistan and Pakistan and will have a fallout in the region. However, it is the LET and other *jihadi* groups which will continue to be a constant threat to India irrespective of the situation in Afghanistan. The threat to us is constant, long-term and potent. We should not be unduly influenced by the American or Western perception of terrorism to them and the world at large. Moreover, we cannot afford to lose sight of the fact that whenever under pressure Pakistan can always raise the ante to divert attention of her people.

The fight against terrorism requires pursuing both the protective and preventive strategies concurrently while protective measures are essential to give the public a sense of security and minimize damage. These measures are rightly in the public domain. But prevention is the cutting edge of our fight against terrorism. It requires silent domination of the suspected or vulnerable areas and personnel through continuous surveillance and intelligence. This should be followed by well-directed small-scale covert operations to eliminate terrorist operators, supporters and disrupting and breaking their network. The key to success is laborious intelligence gathering, analysis, understanding of terrorist group's organization, methods, capability, psychology and motivation and penetrating their network. It is a job of application which requires dedicated work and devotion. Special operations in this domain require a small force, highly trained and kept away from the public eye. These operations should completely be out of the public domain. We have the capability but lack thinking and implementation of capability. For success teamwork between the special terrorist cells in the special branches and Anti-Terrorist Squad (ATS) of the state police and central agencies is essential. Unless state police are up to it, central agencies on their own cannot succeed. Raising the National Investigating Agency (NIA) would be of limited help. The need is to overcome the flaws of our federal system and empowering the IB, as dealing with terrorism and investigation cannot be separated from intelligence. IB and other central agencies and forces should develop the art of functioning intimately with the state agencies. It is a joint venture with both as equal partners and nobody superior or subordinate. It requires political wisdom and will, at both the centre and state levels. Can we do it?

We seem to be following the USA to a large extent in recasting our security framework, which could be good in parts and unsuitable in other areas. The newly mooted controversial Counter Terrorism Centre proposed by the MHA is opposed by the states and needs review. Our environment, societical structure and ethos are different. State intrusion and resentment against it has surfaced in certain areas. Similarly state trying to protect itself rather than the people is all too visible, particularly in the urban centres. There is also a need for balance between security and cost, particularly in a devleoping country like ours. Most of these issues have been brought out by Fareed Zakaria in his article, 'Terrorism's

Greatest Victory is Curtailing of Freedom' in *Newsweek*[15] in 2010. Commenting on the nine year period since 9/11, he acknowledges that while Osama Bin Laden's terror network has been unable to launch a serious attack on any high value target in USA or Europe but it has inspired a large number of local *jihadis*. Today Al-Qaeda's hope is to find a troubled young man, who has been radicalized over the internet and teach him to stuff his underwear with explosives. He also concludes that in recent times the USA has been right about the evil design/intentions of its adversaries but vastly exaggerated its strength. In the 1980s when America thought Soviet Union was expanding its power and influence, it was on the verge of economic and political bankruptcy. Similarly, in the 1990s, USA thought Saddam Hussain had a nuclear arsenal. In fact, his factories could barely make soap. The error this time is more damaging. 11 September 2001 was a shock to the American psyche and the American system. As a result, they overreacted.

The arcticle also projects the finding of a *Washington Post* reporting project, 'Top Secret America'. Dana Priest and William Ashim spent two years gathering information how 9/11 really changed America. The highlights of their findings are:

- Since 11 September 2001, America has created or reconfigured at least 263 organizations to tackle some aspect of the war on terrorism.
- Money spent on intelligence has risen 250 per cent to US $75 billion (which is the official figure), which is a gross underestimation. The actual may be US $103 billion. Which is more than what the rest of the world spends put together.
- Thirty-three new building complexes have been built for intelligence bureaucracies alone, occupying 1.5 million sq.m—the equal of three Pentagons.
- Eight km south-east of the White House, the largest government site in 50 years is being built at the cost of US $3.4 billion to house the largest bureaucracy after the Pentagon for Department of Home Security, which has a workforce of 2,30,000.
- Some 30,000 people are now employed to listen to phone conversations and other communications in America.

- The new system produces 50,000 reports a year, 136 a day, which of course means, few are ever read.

The list goes on and on. Yet no one in army intelligence noticed that Maj. Nidal Malik Hasan had been making a series of threats at the Walter Reed Army Medical Centre. Similarly, the father of the Nigerian Christmas bomber reported his son's radicalism to the US Embassy, but it got lost in the vast security maze.

The above should be an eye-opener for our security planners. Escalation in number and type of organizations is no panacea for efficiency. It only confuses the issue and dilutes the purpose. I have already said this earlier with regard to the PMF. Without making full use of the existing organizations with due reorientation, creating new bureaucracies will not give the desired results. If anything in India's case inter-agency turf war will create greater confusion. I hope the message is clear to 'Top Secret India'.

LEFT WING EXTREMISM (LWE)

In the last decade LWE has grown both in its dimensions and territorially and has been termed as the biggest threat to our internal security. The casualties in real numbers are over 7,000 and the proportion of CPO and LWE casualties has multiplied unfavourably. After the Dantewada massacre of April 2010 which left 76 security personnel dead, it appeared that the state and the police forces were on the backfoot. The only success story has been that of the Grey Hounds of Andhra Pradesh. It was so even in 2001 when I visited some of these areas as a member of the Internal Security Task Force with N.N. Vohra. My memory of what a district collector told us during our interaction with the administration and the people is still fresh. He told us that Naxalites or Maoists were doing what we (administration) should be doing. While it is true to a large extent but the context has changed. The LWE having established their writ, like all power wielders, have developed a stake in perpetrating it and people have become a pawn in this game. They (LWE) instead of working for people are denying them a say in their affairs, have taken on themselves the onus to represent and decide for people and thus become arbitrators of their fate. Denial of benefits offered by the government unless it suits their design, fits into their scheme of things and is part of their strategy. Denial and deprivation are their main weapons and they thrive on people's sense of deprivation and alienation from the government. A game which should be all familiar to our politicians. The challenge to the state is clear and LWE must be put down firmly with effective armed response, at the same time the government needs to change its ways to become an effective instrument to satisfy people's legitimate needs and deliver. We have let the problem escalate by inaction. The need is for a holistic approach and sustained action in all fields.

You can only deal with people's deprivation if you know its causes and understand its nature and magnitude. The affected base areas are forested tracts of central and peninsular India, mostly inhabited by tribals, who have been denied their traditional rights of access to and usage of forest produce, which has been their sustenance. Enactment of recent legislation to give jungle dwelling tribals greater access and use of its produce is a late but welcome step. However, its diligent implementation only can retrieve the situation. There is also a co-relation between areas with coal, forest and mineral resources. Industrialization and exploitation of these areas may economically be justifiable but no value benefits have come to the inhabitants and has left them marginalized. What is worse is that it has in addition led to their displacement in large numbers (almost 40 per cent). Their plight is even worse than that of the SCs and OBCs, they are the worst sufferers of the relative deprivation syndrome. Some modern sociologists (like Durga Mitra) have argued that LWE is a direct growth of the failure of the state to effect comprehensive penetration and control of the forest areas. This is a Western and a theoretical view. In our case while it is true that there has been no effective administrative penetration but there has been bureaucratic and contractor control of the forests, which gives no benefits to its dependent inhabitants either way. In such a scenario no bureaucratic planning and delivery system can work or schemes fructify. The need is for grassroot level planning and implementation with people participation under supervision of dedicated administrators imbibed in the culture of the old Indian Frontier Administrative Service. The key to success is correct identification and vigorous implementation with people's participation. Raising and creation of a police organization similar to the Border Roads Organisation (BRO) is yet another case of making wrong choices and lopsided priority. For such an organization to function properly, the area has to be first secured, otherwise effort will be diverted to their protection and they would not be able to function. On the contrary it will provide the Naxalites another soft target. The need is for local small-scale efforts in secured areas as a start.

In the security field broadly speaking there can be two approaches, one to eliminate LWE by armed action and alternately secure the environment against LWE thus rendering them ineffective. The former will be an unending battle as the breeding ground of LWE will remain untouched with people's deprivation persisting. The second course will be more prudent, slow and painful but effective in the long run. It will also eliminate extremists as we go on securing the environment. It will be a sustained battle by the CPOs and police to secure the area and become effective. Effectiveness and security are integral to each other, you cannot have one without the other. Our approach to achieve security has to be holistic, embracing all aspects of people's life. To achieve it the area has to be dominated by permanent physical presence. Considering terrain and vastness of the area, the deployment should be in armed police battalions with the command and control elements present with the units. The police culture of deployment by sub-units or companies with senior officers (up to commandants) away and out of their areas of deployment and responsibility resting on the local SP will not work. The need is to secure an area and enlarge control beyond it, till a grid is established. It helps in domination, mutual support and coordination. An armed police culture like the one in insurgency areas under the Army needs to be developed. Most CPOs who have operated in these areas with the army are familiar with it. As areas are secured, administration expands into these areas and carries out functions for welfare of the people providing food, health care, education and civic services and undertakes developmental work in cooperation with the people. Only such a holistic approach can succeed.

The challenge both in the security and administrative field is to shed the colonial culture of superiority over the subjects. Instead they should behave and function like public servants. LWE like all complex problems needs simple down to earth solutions and a people-oriented and humane approach.

CONFLICT RESOLUTION AND MANAGEMENT

Conflict resolution and efficient conflict management requires a holistic approach incorporating political, socio-economic and law and order aspects. The overall policy framework for conflict resolution provides the long-term strategic orientation and within these parameters conflict management deals with the tactical aspects in all spheres at the ground level. Such a policy framework helps in creating synergy between the various organs of the state. Conflict is a dynamic process and all factors which contribute, effect and interact with it are relevant to the conflict environment. Being a dynamic process, it comprises phases of initiation, escalation, controlled maintenance, abetment and termination or resolution. When parties to a conflict employ competitive means of dealing with the situation, they pursue their perception of mutually incompatible goals of physically damaging each other or eliminating each other physically and psychologically. Our approach to conflicts has been primarily competitive and therefore essentially confined to the law and order field.

The basic paradigms relevant to conflict resolution and management are 'Real Politik' and 'Ideal Politik', these are poles apart, the basic difference is one of nature and nurture. While one makes the best of a negative situation, the other emphasizes the changeability of the situation. These also are the foundations of the two approaches to conflict, competitive and cooperative. Conflict as a process should be handled so that real politik driven competitiveness can be replaced by an ideal politik based process of conflict resolution. For details of 'Conflict Management and Resolutions' refer to this author's study published in *Akrosh*, January 2000, vol. 3, no. 6 and his books referred above.

COMMAND STRUCTURE

Unified command at all levels is essential to coordinate political, economic, social and military actions. The activities in each field are complementary and supportive; disjointed efforts in any field imposes constraints or nullifies action in other fields. This can only be achieved by a unified command structure. Proper tasking and goals have to be laid as progress is made and their achievement monitored. There are no short cuts in counter-insurgency, and actions once started in any field must be taken to their logical fulfilment.

In a CI environment at the tactical level there is operationally no distinction between command and control. CI operations are most mobile, opportunities are fleeting and come after long and patient waiting and intelligence building. The entire exercise is attendant with heavy protective and surveillance duties. The command has to be direct and execution immediate. Formation commander's feel of the area, backed by formulation and constant updating of the overall picture provide flexibility and anticipatory capability for actions. All units including the Central Police (CPOs) are tactically deployed in a formation area of responsibility. The need is therefore for all to be under the operational command of the formation commander responsible for the area. Units continue to be commanded by their own officers. Both functions cannot be diluted without paying a heavy price. These functions cannot be exercised by a security advisor or a unified headquarter, neither can they be divided.

Based on years of experience of CI operations in the north-east, an effective and functional command and control structure had been established. The essence of it was that all Army and CPO units (AR, BSF, CRPF and even Armed Police units of state inducted in the area) employed on CI duties were under the operational command of the GOC of the area. The CPOs performing duties for state administration were under civil control. This can only ensure unity of command and execution and accountability. It worked both in the 1980s when I was GOC and later in the 1990s during my tenure as governor.

Today *inter se* seniority within the CPO and desire of the CPO hierarchy to control their forces without command responsibility and accountability, has resulted in varying perceptions between the Army and CPOs deployed in the area or even between CPOs, isolated functioning and lack of accountability. It has also resulted in CPO unit commanders exercising command by remote control, they are never seen with troops even during crisis. The ingrained police culture is the bane.

INTELLIGENCE: A VITAL FUNCTION OF COMMAND IN AN INSURGENCY AND TERRORISM ENVIRONMENT

Commanders who function in the field through established staff channels and procedures hardly influence situations and add to the burden and fatigue of troops. This is particularly true in insurgency and terrorism areas, where there is no identifiable enemy or opponent and physical objectives to capture. Therefore a commander's perception based on the feel of the situation combined with intelligence is essential for planning and conduct of successful operations. Commanders develop the former by experience based at the grassroot level, in-depth knowledge of the area, its people and problems and understanding of the contemporary situation. To refine, discard and/or reinforce elements of it good and up to date intelligence is vital. It is the sum total of the discerning analysis of these elements which forms the basis of planning. This also provides the necessary flexibility and mobility which is the key to success in such an environment. Therefore intelligence becomes an important function of command and cannot be left in the domain of staff activity. Commanders need to orientate and dedicate themselves to this important function of command.

The intelligence requirements can broadly be divided into two basic well-known categories of strategic or long-term and tactical. While the first category is essential for background confirmation and to identify the overall dimensions of the problem for long-term planning, the latter is essential as actionable intelligence at the ground level. By and large most of the intelligence agencies are able to provide reasonable strategic and allied nature of inputs which is reasonably or even well collated and presented but at times it is not timely, particularly when security forces move into the area initially due to late deployment of resources by the intelligence agencies. However, the main concern of the security forces is actionable intelligence. It has been generally the experience of the security forces that intelligence agencies have failed to provide hard actionable intelligence in time based on which operations can be planned and action initiated. Most of the successes of the security forces has been based on intelligence collected by the security forces themselves as a follow-up of chance encounters. The only intelligence agency which has been able to provide hard actionable inputs has been the local special branch, when manned by dedicated and high calibre staff. It is therefore essential that security forces' own intelligence agencies establish close and intimate relationship with the Special Branch for sharing intelligence, perceptions and assessments for mutual benefit of both.

The reason why intelligence agencies have not been able to provide hard actionable intelligence is because requirements as perceived by their controlling hierarchy and actual one are divergent and therefore tasking is not related to requirements of the security forces. This results in lack of orientation, accountability and field-work required for tactical Intelligence. Normally, they get away by general assessments in long drawn out reports which are readily accepted by their superiors, who do not have intimate knowledge of the area and its requirements. They require a complete reorientation and are to be made accountable to the local authorities. There is also a problem of multitude of intelligence agencies operating in an area without proper tasking by any one local head, who could task them and coordinate their activities. In my opinion all intelligence agencies except those integral to security forces deployed and the local special branch should come under a local head of intelligence, who could then task them for specific intelligence based on their charter, role and capability. At present limited resources of dubious authenticity are feeding all intelligence agencies with no hard intelligence worth the while.

One of the key areas requiring attention to improve intelligence is language. We must accept that the local terrorists/insurgents/militants have strong bonds with their own ethnic community or tribe, which makes the task of penetrating it and obtaining information, to say nothing of intelligence of the underground, very difficult due to the in-built defensive mechanism, which dictates that a stool pigeon and his family are vulnerable to severe reprisals. This results in sources of dubious reliability. In order to gain the confidence of the locals and gain access, knowledge of the local language is vital and a must for functioning in these areas.

Taking an overall view, we have adequate intelligence resources, if the effort, resources and capabilities are pooled and tasked in a coordinated fashion. Similarly, financial and material resources are dissipated due to uncoordinated utilization and segmented creation of assets resulting in dissipation of effort without any gainful results. Similarly, our counter propaganda should be organized at the state level with the help of a special cell, to wean away misguided local miscreants and establish the credibility of the state. Credibility is a key factor in this regard in such an environment and can only be built based on true and sincere projection. Selection of personnel for these areas should be a judicious and healthy mix of people with knowledge of the area of outsiders and locals. This requires long-term planning and implementation. We have been in these areas for a long period of three to five decades but no worthwhile network or base has been established. Intelligence agents should not be permitted to live a static and domesticated life in sensitive areas as they became security conscious and their functioning is adversely affected.

COUNTER-INSURGENCY AND TERRORISM

It has been the experience of most people who have handled conflict situations of terrorism, insurgency and now proxy war that once the situation has been brought under control and the retrogression phase sets in, efforts to consolidate our gains and bring in normalcy do not fructify. This is primarily due to lack of understanding of the LIC phenomenon in general and how to handle the retrogression phase of it in particular. A few thoughts on it based on our contemporary experience would be in order.

Counter-insurgency includes all measures to frustrate insurgency with minimum overt action. The principles are equally applicable to subversion, terrorism and proxy war with variations in emphasis and modifications related to each situation. The aim is to nullify the elements on which insurgency strives. Counter-insurgency starts with political structure, responsive civil administration and a cohesive security apparatus (includes paramilitary, police, intelligence, the armed forces and a judicial system geared up to meet the requirements). This must be supported by economic infrastructure (material resources, finances, transport, communications, public distribution system and civic services set up), informational and propaganda set up and diplomatic effort to gain recognition and support to our efforts and cause. It also includes population and resources control, civic action, psychological operations, political and administrative measures and larger socio-economic reforms. It thus includes both preventive and remedial measures to control, contain and defeat insurgency.

APPROACH TO SECURITY MANAGEMENT

Our approach to security management should be in keeping with the overall strategy of 'ideal politick' and the cooperative approach. Keeping these in mind I consider security and effectiveness along with securing the environment and control of the area as the key result areas for efficient conflict management which in the long run would contribute to conflict resolution.

Security and Effectiveness

Security and effectiveness are the Key Result Areas for the administration and security forces. Security embraces all aspects of public life and it should be understood and implemented in all its connotations of physical, economic, social, ethnic and religious security. Similarly, effectiveness not only means physical effectiveness, in addition it encompasses positive contribution by the government and all its instruments to the economic, religious, cultural and social well-being of the people. The guiding principle in securing the environment is that you cannot be secure unless you are effective. In any disturbed environment, physical security and effectiveness are the foundation on which action in other fields are built up, it cannot be otherwise.

Securing the environment is the whole canvas in which anti-insurgent operations are only a part. By carrying out anti-insurgent operations, you are only fulfilling a part of the overall task of securing the environment. Foundations of securing the environment and all military operations are laid by controlling the areas.

Control of the Area

Control of the area of responsibility of one's command is the key to success in the insurgency environment. Without control neither can one gather intelligence, nor can anti-insurgent operations by security forces and counter measures by administration be successful. The word 'control' should not be understood in its restricted or defensive sense; it really means total domination of the area, whereby security forces and administration provide protection to the population, are aware of all happenings and can predict and forestall or influence events in every field of activity. The essence of control can be summed up as 'Nothing can happen in the area without our knowledge and without we being aware of it in time to counter and influence it'. This largely contributes to the physical isolation of the insurgents and in creating a secure environment.

Political Management of the Conflicts

Any discussion on conflict resolution and conflict management and retrogression phase of counter-insurgency would clearly demarcate the pivotal and vital role of political will and political management. Most advanced nations have developed effective systems of management of their external and internal security problems and political management is part and parcel of their security systems. Unfortunately in most developing countries this is lacking, essentially due to a lack of a strategic culture, India is no exception. In India, we have a Cabinet Committee for Security which is charged with deliberating on security and foreign affairs. But in spite of the fact that most of the key cabinet ministers (PM, HM, DM, FM) are part of this committee, the political management of our security problems is tardy and disjointed. Political management of these problems within the parameters defined by national interest is essential, if political will has to manifest. This management should be by the government for which an organization within the framework of Cabinet Committee for

Security be instituted in keeping with the democratic norms and chairman of the NSC should be part of this committee to provide the unbiased inputs.

The issue of political management of conflicts is vital, to provide consistency and political guidelines for conflict management in the absence of which law and order dimensions of conflicts is tackled in isolation and there is no coordination between efforts of security forces to improve law and order situation and other measures in the economic, social, cultural, ethnic and religious fields. But most of all lack of sound political management (based on national interest) leads to political expediency and distortion or even conflict between the political establishments and other agencies, particularly the security forces. It is therefore vital that the Cabinet Committee for Security with the assistance of the National Security Council undertakes this responsibility totally divorced from party politics. Then only the political will manifests, which is the vital key for conflict resolution and efficient conflict management.

THE MISSING CIVIL FACE OF COUNTER-INSURGENCY

The unified headquarters both in its constitution and functioning represents the military or the law and order facet and primarily deals with security and operations. The all important civil face is missing. The civil face must be predominant and visible at all levels from top to bottom. Conflict resolution and management requires a holistic approach incorporating political, socio-economic and law and order aspects. The overall policy framework at the apex level provides the long-term strategic orientation and within these parameters, conflict management deals with tactical aspects in all spheres at the ground level. This creates synergy between the organs of the state (the political leadership, bureaucracy and the security forces).

During our deliberations of the Special Task Force on Internal Security of which I was a member, we noticed that there was a proliferation of central police forces at the cost of the state police. State civil police supported by the special branch are vital for handling any situation including insurgency situation particularly in urban areas. It is the cutting edge and needs to be rejuvenated and reinforced. The other area of concern is the deactivation of the state administration and particularly the police as soon as the situation deteriorates and Army is called in. This becomes counter-productive in the long run. Policing and police operations can best be performed by the police. I found Manipur and Nagaland police to be efficient and effective provided they are commanded well and well directed.

NOTES

1. Lt. Gen. V.K. Nayar, *Low Intensity Conflicts in India*, United Service Institution, New Delhi, 2000.
2. *Crossing the Frontiers of Conflict in the North East at Jammu and Kashmir: From Real Politik to Ideal Politik*, published under the auspices of the Center for Policy Research, New Delhi, Shipra Publications.
3. Lt. Gen. S.C. Sardeshpande, *Assignment Jaffna*, Lancer Publishers, New Delhi, 1992.
4. Ibid., pp. 139, 140.
5. Ibid., p.157 and back cover.
6. Author's interview with Yasin Malik and Mian Basheer also recorded in n. 2 above, pp. 260-3.
7. n.1 under the title, *The Winning Game*, pp. 82-4.
8. V. Elwin, *A Philosophy of NEFA*, 1959.
9. n. 2, pp. 141-53.
10. Gulshan Sachdeva, *Economy of the North East: Present Conditions and Future Possibilities*, Konark Publication, New Delhi, 2000, pp. 69-78.
11. B.N. Bardoloi, 'Land Alienation Among Tribals of North East India: Problems and Policies', *IASSI Quarterly*, vol. 12, nos. 3 and 4, 1994, pp. 17-48; M.N. Karma, 'The Agrarian Scene', *Seminar*, no. 366, February 1990, pp. 30-8.
12. B.K. Roy Burman, *Land and Forest Rights*, pp. 25-9.
13. *Statistical Outline of India*, 1989-90, Tata Services Ltd., 1989, p. 27.
14. Ibid.
15. Article titled 'Terrorism's Greatest Victory is Curtailing Freedom', by Fareed Zakaria in *Newsweek* as reproduced in *New Zealand Herald* of 11 September 2010.

CHAPTER 10

Looking Within to See Beyond

Each event generates its own thought or thoughts singly or collectively. One normally gets a chance to express most of them but some remain stored in the mind, even get catalogued and when recalled, come up as a coherent whole. I have expressed the most relevant ones in the previous chapters. However, out of those left out, I wish to share the important ones. Before doing so, I wish to acknowledge a self-imposed restraint on retirement, I took a vow never to give public expression to any opinion which may appear to be detrimental to the army's or nation's interest. I also decided never to give any advice unless asked for. As I sincerely maintain and believe that we have had our opportunity while in service to do our bit and later incumbents are equally or more capable to deal with their responsibilities. Moreover, they are accountable as we were. However, the events of the past decade and responses to some of these by the army and the government have raised questions which need to be addressed. Naturally, my main focus will be the Army and nation and its security. I can only do so at the systemic level and in the overall context.

IMAGE OF THE ARMY

Even discounting the human tendency to consider that our times were better, by and large the feeling in the informed circles both within the service and outside it is that the leadership in the army is not up to the desired standard. Similarly, the image of the army in the public eye has come down considerably. This is in spite of the fact that the professional competence at all levels from the ranks to the highest level has gone up and compares very favourably with the best armies in the world. Our army's competence is well acknowledged both at home and abroad. Their performance in the

Kargil War, in proxy wars in Jammu & Kashmir and insurgencies in the north-east has been of a very high order. But the professional conduct of some senior officers came under a cloud during the Kargil War and in some instances in J&K and the north-east. The decline is in the qualities of head and heart. There have been a number of incidents of questionable conduct amongst senior officers, even at the highest level. These should be brought out in the open, enquired into and the guilty punished irrespective of their rank and status. This is imperative for the greater good of the service and its high image.

The nation and public at large had always held the services, particularly the army in high esteem and treated it as a symbol of moral uprightness, honesty and free of misdemeanors. The army has been also considered as the last bastion of hope and succour in crisis. This has been in spite of the fact that in nations around us their armies have played a dictatorial role and subjugated the civil society and suppressed democracy. The Indian Army has time and again proved to be an effective instrument of democracy and is totally apolitical. These public perceptions and expectations are based on its long experience of over six decades after Independence. The decline has been gradual but discernible over a period of time but it has reached such a low ebb in recent years that it has become a cause of concern to the public and also within the services itself.

One of the major controversies in recent decades in the operational and professional field came up during the Pakistan intrusions in Kargil area in 1999. It was at a time when the proxy war sponsored by Pakistan had been fully contained and J&K was well on its way to normalcy. However, there were definite indications of militancy developing its Islamic orientation for sustenance and to further Pak designs. The failure to discern Pakistan's design during the Kargil intrusions in 1999 was bad enough professionally for the higher echelons of the army at the division and corps level, in the intelligence field and strategically at command, Army Headquarters and at the national level. But worse was the cover up, denial and blame being passed to lower levels for it. Before the Kargil intrusions the proxy war had changed its complexion and orientation to that of Islamic and Pro-Pak dimensions, with ISI controlling its direction and conduct. Expansion of Muslim-dominated areas and targetting of non-Muslim population was its manifestation on the ground. With nuclearization of the subcontinent, in Pakistan's perception nuclear parity had minimized the chances of a major conventional war and the world had got used to the ongoing proxy war. To raise the ante and to rejuvenate attention to J&K, a sizeable intrusion across LOC was ideal as insurgency does not convey the same effect as heightened military activity across a disputed border inhabited predominantly by Muslims. It was a counter to Siachen.[1] Our junior leaders up to battalion level and brigade and divisional commanders did us proud to evict the intruders against all odds and from most formidable positions by July defying most professional estimates by months. Their valour, grit and performance has few equals. But the same cannot be said about the higher commanders. I have highlighted the above incident as junior officers (Brigade Commanders and COs) blamed for the failure to detect the intrusions were absolved of it by the Armed Forces Tribunal in 2009 and their honour restored.

Apart from the controversy, there were definite signs of lack of trust between the junior leadership, brigade and below and the higher echelons of leadership. It also brought into focus the failure of the higher leadership to acknowledge the ground realities and give the required professional and moral support to junior commanders in the field. There had been simmerings of this for quite some time in J&K and in the north-east. Omissions and at times failures in the profession of arms are hazards which will always pose a challenge, the leadership should accept it and overcome it. Failure to do so is the real failure. It is not an issue of professional competence but of moral courage, so vital for leadership. Another aspect of the failure of higher leadership has been that they have failed to address the issue of the cost that army has had to pay for political and administrative failures over a period of time, which continue unabated. The feeling that the army was being used to retrieve the situation from the mess made by the politicians and the bureaucrats was palpable amongst the junior officers at the ground level for quite some time. The higher leadership failed to address it and take up with the political leadership if necessary to make an issue of it. I told this to George Fernandes, the then defence minister, in 1998 but none of our senior leaders of the time did that. I always did so while in service. You cannot adopt the attitude that it is not our job or concern. We have suffered enough for others' mistakes.

Like our national leaders, the leadership in the army is also imbibing a culture of superficiality. Such a trend in the profession of arms is most undesirable. Image building has become an occupation of some of our senior service officers. This is both a professional and cultural degradation as we are not in the business of advertising and selling any product, neither are we competing for market access or domination with any one as in the corporate world. Our image, was and would continue to be sustained by what we achieve in spite of difficulties and even at the risk of our lives. Ultimately our image as leaders of men essentially pertains to the men we command, who never judge their leaders by what they pretend or profess but by what they actually are and expect them to be one with them. This is the real image we should strive for, men only respect such leaders even if they have shortcomings and even fail at times but who own it up. Trust can only be sustained by such leadership.

The most worrisome aspect in recent years has been the army coming into adverse media and national radar due to its senior officers indulging in corrupt practices and the tendency to cover it up. While corruption may be a national phenomenon but the services should be the exception and not the trend followers. Moreover, if a number of senior officers indulge in corrupt and permissive practices, it not only affects the juniors, encourages some others to indulge too and those who even unwillingly participate in its execution lose respect for the seniors. Unlike other organizations army functions as one cohesive team, whose foundation is laid on comradeship, mutual trust and respect and faith in seniors, which cements its structure. Any kink and break in it weakens the structure. Similarly, leadership in the army is different from corporate and civil services or any other organization which depends on management skills and techniques. In spite of the best management techniques and operational research and its application, it still requires personal leadership to take a person to his death, the ultimate motivating force is trust and faith in the leader and loyalty to the *izzat* of the

Paltan. Apart from societal, social and environmental changes there has been dilution and distortion of the systems within the army which has made it vulnerable to these pressures thus eroding its resilience and moral fibre.

SYSTEMIC FAILURES

We inherited very sound systems and traditions from the British Indian Army, which we modified and improved to fit into our democratic system and meet our emerging requirements. The regimental system which we adopted from the British has stood us in good stead and has been the mainstay of our resilience and reason for excellent performance during testing times. The same was the case with our management of the officer cadre in the formative years after Independence. However, the system which had functioned efficiently for over 40 years was interfered with and distorted without valid reasons or requirement in the 1980s. Of this one of the major casualty has been the system of selection of officers for higher ranks and appointments and the entire system of cadre management has been distorted under various circumstantial and parochial pressures since the mid 1980s. It has therefore become imperative to examine on priority the changes made in this period, which in spite of severe criticism have not been rectified. As I have said earlier I can only do so at the systemic level and in the overall context.

Talk of any aspect of officer management, the first factor that draws attention is the quality of the recruits. The officer cadre like its ranks is drawn from the cross-section of its society and across the country. A higher proportion of northern Indians is primarily due to its traditional background, however, with the passage of time there is increasing representation of all regions. There is also a slow and gradual increase in the number of JCO and OR children and the so-called 'lower segments' of the society. This is a healthy sign and should be encouraged as they pass the same competitive examinations and tests. Moreover, the standard of all round development amongst them is comparable to any average middle class family and it is good for tradition building. The number of sons of army officers keeps fluctuating but it has a fair representation. It is often said that the better qualified youth go to the corporate sector, IAS and IPS and very few come to the defence services. But this has been the case since independence or even earlier. Moreover, defence service requirements are different. While we require well educated youth but not necessarily scholars, who are robustly healthy and with greater orientation to the outdoors and for adventure. Later training moulds them to our requirement. This category of youth is available in large numbers in our vast society, we also have a traditional reservoir in communities across the country. This is not an area of concern. However, the shortfall in intake persists and our efforts have so far failed. We have primarily confined to modern methods of advertisements and publicity. This needs to be supplemented in flesh and blood with distinguished and decorated officers visiting schools, colleges and universities with help from formations located in the area. The AG needs to give this aspect a serious thought.

The other factor which has a bearing on the quality of intake is the initial training and grooming. It is done mainly at the two institutions, the NDA at Khadakvasla, for which the intake is after school leaving at 10+2. The second is for the older lot after graduation into the IMA at Dehra Dun. Earlier it was after 10th class for the former and school leaving certificate for the latter. The NDA cadets have a training period of four years, of which they do the last year at the IMA. The training for direct entry into IMA is one and a half years, earlier it was two years. Due to age, education and exposure, the level of maturity is different. While those coming directly from IMA are more mature and have a better all round development, the NDA entrants tend to be less mature and due to regimentation at a young age they develop an attitude of old hands at soldiery, a gung ho attitude, in few cases they even display immaturity. By and large the impression within the service is that comparatively the direct entry cadets are more mature, balanced and steadier in their disposition and demeanour. They also develop traits connected to sobriety to a greater extent. There is a need to examine whether early regimentation of young minds is better or worse for the service. SS through OTA and IMA are comparative of the higher age group as are the NCC inductees. Their personalities and basic traits are already developed on joining.

Some fit well after training and orientation and others consider it only as occupation for livelihood. We need to modify their selection for regular commission. I recommend that in addition to their reports they need to go through a selection process at the selection centres for which SSBs need to institute special tests. Their selection should be based on a combination of SSB recommendations and reports. In the overall context we need to consider if there is a need for changing the mode of initial selection and training for regular commission intake. My personal preference will be greater reliance on direct entry after graduation through IMA.

A connected issue is the deficiency of over 11,000 officers which naturally get reflected essentially at the junior levels at the company/sub-unit and unit levels, which is the cutting edge. While there is decline in the intake but the problem is compounded by the additional aggravating factors of upgradation of ranks and poor management. We add to our own problems by creating unproductive assets in the shape of new formation headquarters and organizations, which take away officers on staff as formation commanders do not accept any deficiencies and shortfall, which ultimately gets reflected in the units. The upgradations of ranks and raising of new headquarters and organizations have taken place without any major accretions in combat units of teeth arms. Time scale promotion to Lt. Col. rank had added further to the confusion, it has not only upset the organizational and command structure at the unit level, which is the cutting edge but has also added to the syndrome of people with rank with no equivalent responsibility. While still recovering from it, the government has decided to extend the provision of timescale promotions to colonel's rank with a qualifying service of 26 years provided there is no vigilance bar. It is also rumored that this may further be extended to the brigadier's rank. This is bound to create greater confusion and adversely impact the army's functioning. Such measures are the outcome of the bureaucratic and inexperienced mindset.

The systemic changes based on personal whims and fancies and motivated by parochial interests combined with ill-conceived upgradations of ranks has disrupted the functional structure of the army and caused decline in the higher and middle level leadership in the army. This has adversely affected the right type of leadership emerging out of the available officers. We inherited the system, organizational structure, tradition and value system of the erstwhile British Indian Army. Over a period of time the army and its leadership adjusted well and imbibed the functioning as an instrument of democratic nation. The credit fully goes to our founding military leaders like Cariappa, Thimayya and Sam Bahadur. The backbone of the adopted system were the regimental system at the ground level and the time tested system of General Cadre for leadership at the middle and higher levels. The regimental system is still functional at the unit and regiment level with few aberrations due to upgradations in rank structure and additional burden of providing men and officers for the RR and other specialized forces without any accretion in strength to make up for it. It continues to be our mainstay and prime reason for Indian Army's resilience and ability to deliver in crisis in spite of omissions and failures at higher levels.

The General Cadre officers provided the leadership at the middle and higher level, who manned key command and staff appointment at the middle and higher level. This cadre primarily consisted of selected officers from the two combat arms of the Armoured Corps and Infantry, with selected high calibre officers from supporting arms of the Artillery, Engineers and Signals who were inducted into General Cadre at the brigadier's level after they had successfully commanded an equivalent formation (brigade) in their own arm with distinction. This is well illustrated by the fact that the number of Chiefs, Army and Corps Commanders who rose to these ranks after joining the General Cadre. Some of the finest commanders and leaders have been from supporting arms and their genius is fully recognized. It is not these officers which are a cause for concern as they will find their place in the Army. It is the average officer of various arms and services for whom careful selection has to be made before they are entrusted with leadership role in an environment for which they lack training, experience, culture and ethos.

In the late 1970s, Army Headquarters formed a committee under Lt. Gen. R.D. Hira, PVSM, MVC, who was my Army Commander, to examine the existing system to assess whether it fulfilled the interests of the Army and ensured a fair deal to the officers. It was clearly laid down that service interest was to be paramount in all its considerations. To this date a lot of us are at a loss as to what instigated this study. The fact that a gunner chief had ordered it raises a suspicion, which is reinforced by subsequent events and the fact that gunners have been the main beneficiaries of the distortion of the system. General Hira was asked to select his team for the study. He consulted Maj. Gen. S.C. Sinha, me and Brig. D.K. Sen, his then Chief of Staff (COS), Brigadier General Staff (BGS) and Brigadier in-charge Administration (Brig. i/c Adm.). We suggested to him that he should not take any current or ex-Military Secretary's (MS) Branch officer as they might justify the existing system. Although we felt that the system by and large has worked well and could be compared to the best in the armies of the world and the focus should be on better management and implementation. After discussion, Lt. Gen. K. Balaram, the then GOC 33 Corps, was selected to assist Gen. Hira and other officers were to be nominated based on further requirements. The first meeting was held at the Command Headquarters in Lucknow at which I was present. During this meeting we went through the directive of the Army Headquarters and the terms of references. At the end Gen. Balaram was asked to work out the approach and discuss it with the Army Commander in Delhi after a couple of weeks, where he will be attending the Army Commander's Conference. The meeting took place during the second biannual Army Commander's Conference in 1979, to which I had accompanied Gen. Hira. Gen. Hira gave me a chart given by Gen. Balaram, which he could not fully understand due to lack of time during the conference. He asked me to go through it and brief him. The chart was titled 'Flowchart', without a legend or an explanatory note. It took me some time to decipher and break it down. It was as dubious as simple. It depicted based on strength of officers in Major's rank, a proportionate rank structure from Major to Lt. General rank in each arm and service. The proposition showed total disregard to army's organizational structure and operational requirement. In essence it disregarded the directive and terms of reference set out by the Army Headquarters. Its implications went even beyond fitting a square peg into a round hole. I explained it to Gen. Hira, he was equally upset and his reaction can be summed up as, 'How can this be and how will Army function?' I am not aware of what instructions he gave to Gen. Balaram as after the Conference Gen. Hira proceeded on leave to the UK and on return he was posted to the Southern Command.

The Hira Committee report was published, sometime in the middle of 1980 and when we went through it at the Command Headquarters, we found that Gen. Balaram had largely succeeded in his design. I can only attribute it to either of the two factors or possibly both. Gen. Hira was a commander in his mental make-up and was not fond of deliberate application or meticulous discernment and hard work associated with completed staff work. He fully trusted his staff and subordinates as I had found working with him. He was due for retirement and may have lost interest or had been given verbal directions unknown to us, which were dictating the thrust of the study. We found that Gen. Balaram had introduced the idea of proportionate promotions in the garb of removing disparities. There was a strong dissenting note from Maj. Gen. S.K. Malhotra of the Madras Regiment, the only other General Cadre permanent member of the study group. The study group had also selectively employed few other General Cadre officers on secondary issues like promotion of low medical category officers and views of heads of supporting arms and services were given prominence. Gen. W.A.G. Pinto the new Army Commander held a detailed discussion at the Command Headquarters and with formation commanders and it was decided to strongly counter the study group's recommendations as these were detrimental to the interest of the Army and loaded in favour of supporting arms and services. I prepared the paper and after further discussion and refinement it was sent to Gen. Krishna Rao and Gen. S.P. Malhotra, Western and Northern Army Commanders, Gen. Sethna, VCOAS and the AG, Gen. M.L. Chibber. They put up a joint front and the report was rejected much to the disappointment of Gen. Balaram and the parochial elements of supporting arms and services. I still possess the paper written by me.

It is important to put across the issues raised in the above paper as their validity is all the more relevant in view of what has happened since then as we shall see later. The major issues raised in the paper were the cadre management, the selection system, manning of key appointments at Army Headquarters and other higher formations and concept of MS pool appointments and its management. The study group had ignored the key clauses of the directive given to them, which was to examine the present system to assess whether it fulfilled the interest of the service and ensured a fair deal to officers. It was clearly laid down that service interest was to be paramount in all its considerations. It also ignored the organizational structure of the army and operational imperatives and over emphasized the interest of officers and displayed an extremely favourable bias in favour of supporting arms and services. It took a simplistic and a totally mathematical view of equality rather than equitable opportunity detriment to the fighting efficiency and functional aspects of the service. Shifting of emphasis from equitable to equal opportunity totally distorted the study group's approach to cadre management. It totally ignored the fact that combat arms of Infantry and Armoured Corps face the brunt of the war, casualties and risks, which is not peculiar to army alone. Its sister services, the Air Force and Navy have their GD (P) and Executive branch, who also have primacy due to their similar role. The environment of combat arms is oriented to decision-making under stress and danger and in crisis situations in battles, the same is not true of supporting arms and services. There are different environmental variables in respect of each arm and service, in which officers get ingrained, with distinct culture and influencing factors. These mould the attitude of the officers and give them different orientation based on their experience. *Combat arms of infantry and armour develop the habit of decision-making while in direct contact with the enemy and lead men into battle in direct physical contact with the enemy. While supporting arms, officers and men have a more detached exposure to battle and are in an advisory capacity. These dictate the quality of leadership and its orientation.*

The study group ignored the organizational structure of the army for cadre management and reworked the cadre for each arm and service on proportionate basis, when the only aspect which required deliberation was the military secretary's pool appointments. Even for these guidelines existed, which included Qualitative Requirements (QR) for each appointment and the arm and service best suited to provide the officer along with the merit of the officer. Instead the study group derived the total number of ranks from major to general and worked out a mathematical cadre structure for each arm and service based upon its strength at major's ranks. It went to the extent of recommending that Director Staff Duties (DSD) should examine and modify the organizations within arms and services to accommodate this proportional pattern which was most ridiculous. The logic could not be turned on its head upside down more blatantly. The study group also expressed a rather unusual view that senior officers of arms and services were capable of taking decisions on all arms problems because some of them had the benefit of attending a few all arms courses. They failed to realize or deliberately ignored the fact that exposure to all arms training courses for these officers was to enable them to understand the functioning of all arms so that they can utilize the resources of their arms or service in support of their formation in the most efficient manner. This was to come up again to the detriment of the army when the two stream concept was introduced by Gen. Sundarjee.

Unfortunately these ideas continued to ferment in the parochial minds of the supporting arms and services. After Gen. Sundarjee took over as COAS in 1985 the idea of improving the career prospects of officers was again mooted, Gen. Balaram was then the AG and was very close to him. The government sanctioned additional vacancies to improve the career prospects of all ranks. The cadre review resulted in upgradation of a fair number of command appointments and corresponding staff ones. The upgradation of unit commanders from lieutenant colonel to colonels was noteworthy as it benefitted most middle level officers both on command and staff. The spread was throughout the army in all arms and services. This resulted somewhat due to necessity but equally by connivance in diluting the QR for filling critical staff and some extra regimental and instructional appointments. It particularly upset the well established structure of staff as well as command appointments in static formations like areas and sub-areas. The opportunity was seized by the supporting arms and services and it started the gradual process towards proportional promotions in total disregard to operational and organizational requirements. General Sundarjee's favourites in supporting arms and services who had served with him took full advantage to further their interests. Dilution of army's structure and operational norms took place in two ways, one by upgradation which upset the functional rank structure and secondly by change of promotional parameters and dilution of the QR of appointments. To compound the officer management problem Gen. Sundarjee introduced the two stream concept of promoting officers to Maj. Gen. and Lt. Gen. 'Command and Staff' and 'Staff only' purportedly to overcome the management problem of filling-up a large number of upgraded appointments but its real motivation was to induct favourites from non-general cadre list of officers of supporting arms and services into senior key appointments as is brought out later. The two stream concept was flawed both in its concept and implementation. It failed to recognize that our reporting system was primarily based on command performance and did not have adequate inputs for suitability of officers for staff only. The qualitative requirement for, command and staff stream laid down was that an officer must have a minimum of two above average reports each on command assignment in present and previous rank with 100 per cent recommendations for promotion on command from all reporting officers. For staff only, a minimum of two high to above average reports on each command appointment in present and previous rank with at least 75 per cent recommendations for command from all reporting officers. It was totally subjective. This resulted in total disadvantage to general cadre officers as they lost their seniority for promotion and non-general cadre officers gained as they got promotion before their batch in their own arm and service. They also considered themselves at par with the general cadre officers in staff only stream. Moreover, a non-general cadre officer could return to his own arm or service for promotion but general cadre officer in staff stream lost his original seniority and served one year less. It had greater opportunity for yes men and play safe type of officers. Adhocism came to the forefront as there was no distinction of staff appointments tenable by command and staff stream and staff stream only. This resulted in officers without command experience posted as GOC areas and staff only stream officers as COS corps, which required command experience. All this tended to make the staff stream as second class citizens. I as

GOC of a corps at that time wrote against it but had no success with Gen. Sundarjee and his coterie. I again took it up with the next Chief. Gen. Sharma as Western Army Commander and he was agreeable to review it. The two stream concept was adversely commented upon by retired senior officers and the media. Even the law ministry considered it bad in law. General Sundarjee was able to push it through due to his influence with the then Minister of State for Defence Arun Singh. Even then he could only succeed for ranks of major general and lieutenant general only and did not have his way at lower level due to opposition from within the army, MOD and MOL.

The overall effect of the division of officers in the above two streams was that it further diluted the general cadre and opened senior staff appointments to supporting arms and later even services to accommodate Gen. Sundarjee's favourites. Staff stream was used to induct non-general cadre officers into senior staff appointments till then held by general cadre officers, this included principal staff officers at Army Headquarters. The overall impact was that general cadre officers going for command of corps and commands were denied the experience of higher staff and lower calibre officers and unqualified officers from supporting arms and services with no experience of middle and higher level of command and of formation functioning occupied senior staff appointments including PSOs at Army Headquarters. The army lost both ways. To further aggravate the problem a time bar of minimum of two year's for army commanders was introduced, which implied that you had to have a minimum of four year's service left to be given command of a corps. While it had merit to provide continuity at higher levels of command but putting all these changes together in a short period of time resulted in upsetting army's functioning, structure and management of officer cadre which became a victim of adhocism. How the army and few of us opposed to it survived is a miracle. The worst effect of it was that you could play favourites in reporting, selection and promotions. The worst sufferers were the original general cadre officers of the Armoured Corps and Infantry, the backbone of the army. The level of favouritism can be judged that for the first time the army had an ASC officer as MS, non-general cadre officers as QMG, MGO and Additional

Director General Financial planning, and army created one time three additional VCOAS posts all at the same time to accommodate favourites.

It also resulted in officers of supporting arms and services who spent most of their service in peace stations with little or no exposure to high altitude, insurgency, proxy war and enjoy the comfort of depth areas during war were equated with people, who spent most of their service in field and operational area and who actually fought.

The dilution and distortion of the system was further effected and become a victim of parochial design under the three artillery chiefs during the period 1991 to 2010. The system of proportional promotion was fully cemented to the advantage of its main beneficiaries—the larger number of artillery officers amongst the supporting arms and services. It delayed promotions by almost two years for officers of Armoured Corps and Infantry compared to officers of supporting arms and services. Promotions in ASC, EME were fastest, which in some case even resulted in denial of promotions to combat arms (Armoured Corps and Infantry) due to delay.

The cumulative effect of these changes since 1980 is shorter command tenures at the brigade, division and corps levels. The current tenure of corps commanders is down to one year. Short tenures have resulted in a compulsiveness to prove oneself, which really amounts to doing what is visible, would be noticed and liked/approved by the superior at the cost of real training and improving the operational efficiency of the formation. In a proxy war and insurgency situation it results in pushing troops to produce results rather than planning and achieving sustained operational targets over a period of time. In a war situation like Kargil it results in avoidable casualties and witch hunting. In short the aim is to earn a good report for further advancement ignoring privation or unwarranted pressure on troops. It has encouraged sycophancy and permissive obedience to unfair and at times unlawful orders and demands of superiors. Operationally it distorts priorities and results in higher casualties. This trend started during the IPKF operations in Sri Lanka in 1985 and has since surfaced to some extent in J&K and north-east. Realizing that short tenures at unit command levels had resulted in a somewhat similar syndrome as at higher levels, the unit commanders tenure has been increased to two and half years. But the distortion of short tenures at higher levels would result in even greater pressure on units as unit commander will be subjected to urgency of two or in some cases even three brigade and division commanders trying to prove themselves. The need is to restore viable tenures at all levels, which can only be achieved by reverting to the old system period of the 1980s. This is discussed in the succeeding paras.

Time scale promotions are currently given upto a Colonel's rank and these officers are mostly employed in junior appointments. With re-employment now being opened upto a Brigadier's rank, these officers would be mostly employed in Command, Army Headquarters and may even go down to a corps in junior appointments. Additional officers in both the senior ranks can neither contribute much nor would it commensurate with their age, rank and prestige. It can only add to the confusion and disrupt the functional system and lower efficiency.

The army's officer management problems are further compounded by the bureaucratic sops to appease the army as done recently under the Ajai Vikram Singh Committee report. It has further recommended escalation in rank structure to improve career prospects. I hope army refuses to accept any more escalation in ranks as while a joint secretary may sit and work as a desk officer without disturbing the system, army cannot have red tabs doing a captain's or a major's job. It will be a kind of *band, bajaa, baraat* syndrome. Rank structure must fulfil requirements of operational and functional structure of the army. While in civil services you can divide functioning into sub-subjects, you cannot divide command and responsibility in the army. It will make the services dysfunctional. Is that the intention?

The only remedy I can think of is to restore the disturbed balance between the organizational structure and operational parameters on the one hand and the requirement to improve career prospects of officers on the other. The present system has disturbed the organizational structure by distorting the functional rank structure particularly at the combat unit level and field formations of brigade and divisions and the corresponding staff appointments.

To ease the management problem between command and staff appointments QR of operational staff appointments, which were diluted, need to be restored keeping in view the upgraded rank structure. It should be done over a period of time and we should restore the old parity between command and staff appointments with QRs with old compatibility.

The need to restore professional balance between command and staff appointments at higher levels is even greater along with return to the old general cadre system, which is imperative. However, while doing so, we have to recognize that supporting arms and services have a fair and equitable share of additional vacancies on staff and ERE compatible with their capability and experience within the organizational structure and upgraded ranks with a pragmatic QR to fill these. The above two measures once implemented will restore the necessary balance and tenures will become longer and help in efficiency.

The question of better prospects for all ranks and relief for other ranks on superannuation at younger age can be achieved to a very large extent by lateral induction into paramilitary forces and delinking pay from rank. The logic of delinking pay from rank has been accepted by most armies of advanced and even middle world countries. The logic is irrefutable as with age your domestic responsibilities increase, which has little to do with your professional advancement. Also the service conditions of services are entirely different and peculiar compared to that of civil services. Linking their pay and other emoluments with them has completely distorted both the equation and functioning and denied them just compensation and reward for their hard conditions. The battle for status is the bane of our nation and comes at a huge price. A separate pay commission for the services is not only justified but also essential.

DECLINE IN VALUES AND SOME UNHEALTHY TRENDS

The changed environment the world over and in the country has eroded moral values and ethics. The irony is that while people realize that deterioration in the core values has adversely affected the nation, the leadership has failed to arrest the slide and restore balance. Most social upheavals are in more ways than one the result of it. Irrespective of it, the army and services as an organization cannot let these be compromised as it not only is eroding its capability but is also blunting the only efficient and functional instrument left in the nation. The core values of the army are enshrined in the IMA motto. The credo of IMA is:

The safety, honour and welfare of your country come first, always and every time. The honour, welfare and comfort of the men you command come next. Your own ease, comfort and safety come last, always and every time.

Due to the disturbed internal and external environment, army's involvement has increased manifold and it is likely to be so in the foreseeable future. Lack of a strategic vision and policy at the national level has resulted in responses generating primarily in the crisis management realm, which generates greater pressure on the army. This demands greater anticipatory forward planning by the higher commanders to minimize its effect. Unfortunately, since the days of Operation Blue Star and IPKF we have been caught unawares and thus succumbing to these pressures. What is worse is that instead of resisting these and minimizing their effect by containing these, there has been a marked tendency to pass it down to the junior commanders and troops. These at times may be unavoidable, in such cases it is imperative that the pressure generated by such events is contained at the appropriate levels of higher command. It also mandates the higher command to pursue the desired objectives in a most professional manner and not succumb to political pressure or immediate demands of the situation. The bigger the crisis, greater the need for professionalism. Our failure to resist these pressures and to compromise on professionalism due to exigencies of the situation is bound to result in junior commanders and troops becoming unsure and even suspicious of motives of higher commanders and political leadership. It has also resulted in higher casualties both during Operation Blue Star and IPKF operations in Sri Lanka. In recent years these tendencies were discernible to some extent in J&K and in few areas of the North-East. In J&K a sense of disillusionment was palpable amongst the junior commanders and the troops irrespective of the colour of uniform. The question lurking in the minds of unit and lower commanders is, 'We had brought the situation under control and when we return next time it is again bad, why are we suffering for the mistakes and incompetence of others?' It is not a good sign. The political leadership and administration need to do their bit. I have conveyed it to senior commanders and political leadership a number of times. But they are too busy with their own affairs to pay serious attention to it.

In the very recent past like the government in the aftermath of 2G and other scams the services too have also shown marked tendency of playing safe and hedging decision-making. While the government and the bureaucracy can get away for some time at least by resorting to the ploy of group of ministers and committee of secretaries, which has been the hallmark of its functioning recently, the services cannot afford any such luxury as they can only delay decisions on operational and procurement issues at a cost. Which is bound to effect its capability and effectiveness. As a matter of fact such circumstances necessitate greater goading of the bureaucracy and the government to get them moving. The other unhealthy tendency of recent origin is that senior officers want to leave a mark, mostly not in a substantive way, but in a visible and superficial manner by laying foundation stones, installing statues, renaming roads and other landmarks in military stations and cantonments. In one case it has gone to the ridiculous extent of even naming different tees on a golf course and other sports venues. This may probably be due to short command tenures, earlier when we had full tenures of command at all levels the emphasis was on improving capability of one's command, welfare of men under you and sustaining military traditions and ethos. I wonder if it is only the short tenures responsible for this or a much deeper malaise of a cultural change and degradation in the services ethos.

DUPLICATION AND MULTIPLICITY IN ORGANIZATIONS RESULTING IN UNPRODUCTIVITY

The trend of duplicating functions and creating unproductive assets is all prevailing in the nation. For every new activity or function in the government a new department or even a ministry is created without redeploying redundant manpower and assets. It is particularly prominent in the developmental and planning fields. Some similar trends are visible in the Army Headquarters in the strategic planning, logistics and training areas. We raised a perspective planning cell in the MO directorate in the mid-1980s, later on we upgraded it to a full-fledged directorate, which led to its redundancy to a large extent as it could not be privy to operational plans. Perspective planning in essence is an extension of functions of MO directorate and Directorate of Operational Logistics, a cell in each would have met the requirement.

It is in the training field that multiplicity exists to a larger extent. When the College of Combat was raised to enlarge the training scope to include an HC wing, it was fully justified. The Faculty of Studies in the College of Combat was to provide not only faculty support in terms of training manuals for the Junior, Senior and HC courses but also to update doctrines and improve strategic thinking and culture as it was felt that the DMT was too occupied with current training activities and with looking after the training institutions in the army. While the new system was still finding its feet and had just got into a productive mode, we decided to raise a Training Command. It started functioning and did some useful work in the doctrinal field. The army then started a Centre for Land and Air Warfare Studies outside the Army's organizational structure but supported by the army. Not to be left out the other two services raised similar setups outside the services but supported by them. The Air Force has the Centre for Air Power Studies and the Navy has National Maritime Foundation under the Naval Foundation. While jointness in modern times is a major requirement we have proceeded in achieving it in a haphazard fashion. Instead of instituting the CDS system, we have gone only a small way by having integrated defence staff under a so-called Chairman Chiefs of Staff Committee, which is neither here nor there. Chief of Integrated Defence Staff have also done their bit to raise a Centre for Joint Warfare Studies. Due to this multiplicity both the aims and efforts of these institutions are diffused and nobody seems to be doing what they should be doing. All this while United Service Institution of India of over 142 years standing is available and capable of doing a lot more than them, having all the expertise available. The Institute of Defence Studies and Analysis under the MOD has turned into another white elephant and job provider for some retired bureaucrats and a few service personnel of lower ranks.

Since the Kargil War in 1999, some of our responses in the operational field have resulted in new headquarters and other unproductive assets being created at the cost of improving our cutting edge. Raising and induction of a Corps Headquarters into Ladakh across Zojila has resulted in more mouths to feed, maintain and sustain these without corresponding increase in troops. I view the raising of the South Western Command in the same light as there has been no accretion in troop levels. Today, if any, the span of command has increased geographically and strategically due to better air mobility, communications including IT and infrastructure. Moreover division of problem at the operational level results in disjointed responses, higher commanders bearing down on lower formation commanders and worst of all lack of flexibility at the theatre level. The recent announcement in January 2011 of raising of a Strategic Forces Command further add to escalation and confusion and may constrain flexibility further.

Army is short changed in manpower, arms, equipment and latest technology. We must demand what we require to be effective and strive constantly to achieve it. It has always been an uphill battle but this needs to be waged constantly and should be the prime concern of army and other Service Headquarters. Having said so, there is a natural corollary to it which we can ill afford to ignore. With resource constraints and our ever increasing commitments, we can ill afford the luxury of unproductive and low priority assets. These trends of multiplicity and creating unproductive assets need to be examined not only in services but in the entire nation.

STYLE AND SUBSTANCE IMBALANCE

Lastly, army had always maintained a fine balance between style and substance. Tradition and style in the army were an outcome of service requirements of discipline, steadfastness and *esprit-de-corps*. Ceremonial parades, ceremonies connected with battle honours, of past valour, courage and professional achievements. There was a substantial social side of army traditions based on camaraderie, which centred around its social institutions for the men and officers. Officers' interaction with men was formal on parade and informal off parade. Informal or social interaction was as intense and centred around sports, ***durbars***, ***langars***, ***bara khanas***, visit to lines and keeping a tab on men's welfare including those of their families. Unfortunately, in recent years style has not only become superficial, straying from tradition and imbibing greater corporate five star culture but also overlooking army professionalism and getting preference over substantial work and effort. This has led to disorientation and wrong type of officers being nurtured. In professional seminars and discussions, more time and effort is spent on inaugurations, get up, décor and menu rather than the main purpose and the objective of the discussion and its professional contents. Similarly, inviting politicians and other dignitaries to regimental functions decreases its value and divests from the main purpose of regimental interaction and catching up. Similarly, welfare activities for men and their families should be totally or mostly oriented towards them. While raising money and resources for these is legitimate but this legitimacy should be sustained only by legitimate means and efforts. There must not be exhibitionist displays to show and impress outsiders but to actual welfare. In this regard the Army Wives Welfare activities need to be re-orientated. In the overall context there is an urgent need to restore the balance between style and substance both in terms of its nature and professional and traditional orientation.

I made a passing reference to the professional pressures generated by short tenures of command. In the same context it will be relevant to point out that while it is the desire of all commanders to achieve maximum operational efficiency of their command in keeping with their competence and experience, in doing so they must not overlook the human factor. In my opinion a very important element of this human aspect is a happy and satisfied rank and file. Unless professionalism and efficiency is backed by a happy, contented and motivated man, it will not draw that extra effort, which goes to win battles. It is a happy and satisfied man who fights well. Overburdened and tired men succumb under pressure. The second part of the IMA dictum about the men is founded on it.

A NATION IN DISCONNECT

There can be no doubt that our economic growth and progress in all fields like science and technology, services sector, industry and even in communications has been very impressive and could be the envy of most developing nations. Along with China and Brazil we are considered as the future economic giants. I as an Indian take pride in these achievements. I spend some months abroad in New Zealand with my daughter and travel quite a bit, one feels a sense of pride when people respect and recognize you as a part of an upcoming nation, it feels good to be noticed. However, this receives a jolt as most of the coverage in the international media is of disasters, rail accidents and darker side of the common man's misery. This truth hits you deeper each time you return home, and pride and the feel-good factor takes a backseat. Progress has not touched the common man and neither has he got a sense of well-being or feel-good. I cannot claim to be a common man in the real sense of the word but I am one in more than one sense. The level of frustration that I feel in daily life has gone up and I feel a sense of void and absence of good feeling in areas of interest in the common domain which all of us share.

In the last decade or may be a bit more, the effort that I spend on daily chores of living and surviving has increased from a low of 15 to 40-50 per cent in different areas, even after discounting the age factor. This is in spite of the fact that I live in a good area where civic services by Indian standards are good and responsive. But as a human being you cannot live in isolation, as you feel and are affected by your environment. Leaving aside major issues like the Nithari murders and threat to life and property which are becoming more frequent, there is a perpetual disconnect between reality and what you hear from institutions of governance. People have stopped believing in the establishment and started fending for themselves individually or collectively, whether it is water, power, civic services and even in matters of health, hygiene and education. It cannot be in all areas and for all, so the common man suffers.

You move out of Noida, irrespective of the direction of your entry to Delhi, all the roads have potholes which have widened over the years, the surface is uneven, there are diggings on one or both sides of the road, most work is done during peak traffic hours in the day. While roads are hardly repaired, the dividers, iron railings or fencing are constantly changed. Solid real stone on dividers and pavements since pre-Independence days are replaced with cement cast low quality ones, which will last one monsoon or two at the most. If you travel to different parts of Delhi, which I often do, you find fencings uprooted from one area is put in another area. When you ask the labour to confirm, they laugh and tell you they do it all the time. Is it to provide employment or to make money on material both ways or an exercise in the fine art of hoodwinking? While the commuter is left to fend for himself in increasing misery. In most countries all road repairs are done at night and in diversions with traffic guides for major works are the norms. The above state of affairs discounts the works taken up for Commonwealth Games in October 2010. I often joked with people that in Delhi or surrounding areas, you can just put a yellow board with CWG and start digging anywhere and nobody will question you. Delhi today is: *yeh khuda, woh khuda aur wahan khuda—jahan dekho khuda hi khuda* (This digging, that digging, these diggings—wherever you look digging is all you see).

I travel in the comfort of my car and avoid peak hours but delays due to heavy rush of traffic have become irksome. For a job or an outing of two to three hours you spend as much time on road. The plight of the common man travelling in a crowded public transport is much worse, he hangs on for his dear life and each ride is a survival exercise. Metro Rail has made life a bit easier for travel to areas connected by it, even they are overcrowded during peak hours with sitting not possible for half the travellers. Increasing traffic with restricted road capacity, made worse by thoughtless traffic experiments like the BRT has added to the misery and danger. Buses are a law onto themselves with overtaking and double driving abreast, everyone has to watch out for one self. Police just stand and twiddle their thumbs. After each catastrophe and uproar they get active but instead of more vigilant traffic management, there is a spate of fines on law-abiding citizens for suspected marginal infringements. Most South-East Asian countries are doing better. Have we given up?

The debate on sealing, removal of unauthorized constructions and master plans are unknown to the common man. The result will be a mess either way. The battle between the Municipal Corporation, Delhi state and the centre has added to the mess, the one upmanship can only result in further disaster. It has all the hallmarks of the twin evils of money and power. It is hard to believe that our leaders lack normal civic sense, we were taught this in schools and at home. So why this mess and why is the bureaucracy toeing the line. It can only be power or money or both. The need is not for a debate or more examination by a new committee or more legislation but for a sensible doer. One may disagree with Jagmohan or the likes of him but only such action can redeem the situation.

The common man is feeling insecure in all spheres of his life, security of life for self and family, job and hardships of daily life. Confining oneself to physical aspects only, security is entirely oriented to government, its institutions and managers, the common man does not figure in its planning parameters. However, it is its physical implementation and manner which gives a sense of harassment and annoyance to the common man and even people like me who understand its nuances. Apart from this it adds to the sense of insecurity of the common people. It has done nothing to make communities feel secure, with some targeted for having bad elements amongst them. In some ways these measures have become symbols of state interference and in few cases of repression. We should try and make people secure. Nothing is more hurting for the common man than to find that mass scale death of innocent public becomes a victim of political gimmickry.

We as a nation are very competent in producing planning documents, some are termed as vision documents, some are government sponsored and others by different think-tanks. The recent one by government on revamping the higher education system is an example. These normally aim at what India could be and not should be. They miss the reality of India wholly or in parts. Vision for India requires understanding of India with its diverse culture, history, geography, people and their attitudes, beliefs and perceptions. Then only you can chalk out a course for each distinct entity and bind it with the cultural and historical common experience of Indianness. Only such an effort can make people feel a part is theirs as others have a part. A vision propagated but not recognized cannot be implemented. All such formulations have political overtones which should relate to people and not to an agenda entirely political in nature. A key element of such formulation should be that it does not divide communities, instead help them to recognize each other and bring them together. Sachar Committee Report on Muslims and some of the earlier reports on SC and ST have not paid dividends. How wisely the Muslim leaders at Lucknow snubbed the report after its publication. Society is waking up to its exploitation. Similarly, seminars and conclaves on such issues organized by media or corporate organizations at the behest of politicians neither make India shining nor better. People organizing these and participating in them are the main beneficiaries. The same, to some extent can be said of our much publicized grandiose schemes for poverty alleviation and for the disadvantaged sections of society. These are bigger with thousands of crores allocated but fail to achieve the desired results due to lack of will and capacity to implement, as these are primarily confined to gaining political objectives. Instead these have resulted in more corruption.

Some time back it was interesting to read as to how the intellectual elite has succumbed to political pressure irrespective of their orientation to the left, right or centre. They may be loyal to their political mentors but are they true to their convictions. Delhi abounds in think-tanks, they are overflowing with funds and gain legitimacy by inviting public figures, particularly politicians in power. There is a crisis in morality and honesty which the intellectual community can and should provide. This can only happen if they do their duty as intellectuals and not seek patronage.

India is functioning at two levels, one at political, bureaucratic and corporate level and other at the grassroot or functional level, which is mostly dysfunctional. There is a total disconnect between these two. The higher level is oblivious to reality at the lower levels. You pick-up any issue and there is disconnect of what is seen, perceived or propagated at the decision-making level and the actual reality. Happenings like the Amarnath issue in J&K and Nandigram and in other Naxal areas are the manifestations of this. Nobody wants to remove or overcome the dichotomy or narrow the gap, on the contrary you have Mamata Banerjee and Medha Patkar who thrive on it. My mind goes back to a national interest article by Shekhar Gupta titled, 'Our Defeat Enshrined', in the *Indian Express* of 9 August 2008, where he aptly describes the Indian political class collectively snatching a defeat which should have been Pakistan's, 'When J&K was at peace, Pakistan and separatists were frustrated, then came the Congress and the BJP'. What is worse is that some in the political class like Mamata Banerjee mock the common man's suffering by calling the Maoist attack on railways with large number of deaths as a political conspiracy. It is not only dangerously irresponsible but amounts to waging political battle over the dead. The disconnect cannot be more visible. Political governance needs to address the disconnect between political vision and perception and reality.

The disconnect was most vivid during the preparation of the recently held Commonwealth Games, when instead of it being the glory of the games, it was a gory tale with a bloody price. In September before the games, the city resembled an enormous ghost building site with venues, roads and surrounding areas muddy and murky due to the anger of the rain gods. We already had over 1,50,000 homeless and with evictions during the preparation of the games the number became officially double. Dalits were worst hit not only by evictions but the money earmarked for Dalit homes was used for the games. The fate of the street vendors was no better as they were removed. They have always been an attraction for the tourists and part of our culture and economic structure at the local level, over 8,000 of them were removed from 25 markets near the games venues. The state of disconnect was blatantly illustrative by the CAG's report on the Commonwealth Games. It manifests shameless display of moral, economic and social degeneration.

NOTE

1. I had highlighted these changing dimensions of insurgency in a lecture at the USI in 1998, Excerpted text is published in July-September 1998 issue of the *USI Journal*.

CHAPTER 11

Post Script: Break Down in Civil-Military Relations

During my lecture on Civil-Military Relations at the Lal Bahadur Shastri Academy of Administration in October 2008, there was a great temptation to examine the subject in the domestic Indian context due to the then ongoing face-off between the services and the government on the Sixth Pay Commission's award implementation. However, I felt it more prudent and appropriate to take an overall and macro view of the subject due to India's emerging position in the world order. Based on my study of practices the world over and developments in Civil-Military Relations since Second World War, I highlighted the great need for democratic governance of defence and security and need for strategic thinking due to globalization. The gist of my observations during the lecture based on my study and experience of Civil-Military Relations at all levels are given in Chapter 7 under the heading, 'Flawed Structure and Civil-Military Relations'. However, my conclusions, related to the domestic environment were not included in the above episode. Seeing the current state of Civil-Military Relations which I shall discuss later, these have a relevance and are reproduced below:

(a) The recent impasse about the implementation of the Sixth Pay Commission for Armed Forces reflects the current state of Civil-Military Relations and in a way it epitomizes what is wrong. There is lack of mutual trust. In my opinion things are heading for sad consequences and in this turf war there will be no victors only victims, the worst sufferer will be the nation. There is an urgent need for a change in the mindset.

(b) While bureaucracy since Independence may feel happy and satisfied to have helped national leaders in their unfounded fear of a powerful military and rejoice in their success in the down-gradation of the military's status and prestige, it had indirectly degraded national power and cohesiveness of its capability. In spite of it, military has remained apolitical and an effective national instrument.

(c) On the sidelines of this known turf war there has been a further silent subversion of the system (including the bureaucracy) by the intelligence agencies who have exploited the hunger for power of our political elite as well as their fear of losing to gain direct access to PMO and other power centres and thus wielding undue influence. Long tenures of B.N. Malik, S.F. Santook and the present security set-up should be an eye-opener. There are wheels within wheels in the power structure and the system has collapsed.

(d) Today we depend on the army and other services to bail us out of dirty situations resulting due to failures of others. What is worse, we take it for granted and refuse to give them their due. God help the nation when the military fails it.

The year 2012 marks the lowest ebb in the Civil-Military Relations with an open and direct confrontation between the Army Chief Gen. V.K. Singh and MOD and thereby the government. It had been building up over a number of years and the stand off in 2008 over the Sixth Pay Commission was the last open one before the big blow-up now. The issues and their nature have varied time to time but underlying these has been the mounting resentment in the services on being systematically sidelined on issues of national security and connected areas of direct concern to them. As I have brought out earlier in spite of various studies, the last one after the Kargil conflict by Arun Singh, the services remain cut-off from the decision-making, functioning of MOD and government's thinking and deliberations on national security. The current ongoing study under Naresh Chandra is unlikely to result in better or joint cohesive functioning. The MOD exists for the services and should be integrated with it, it is not above the services. In the changed security environment, challenges to the political and military leadership have increased and become more complex, which cannot be managed by bureaucratic procedures and ill informed decision makers. It mandates a cohesive and jointly crafted policy by the political and military leadership. The political elite should get over their fear of the military, which was encouraged and sustained by the bureaucracy to retain their hold. As I said earlier unlike Pakistan, legitimacy of the political authority has a traditional acceptance by the military in India. In spite of various provocations it remains apolitical, which was well demonstrated by a Kashmiri Pandit Chief, Gen. Raina, appointed by Mrs Gandhi, who refused army's association even in the slightest manner during the emergency in 1975. But military cannot tolerate bureaucratic control as bureaucracy is only another executive instrument.

The *Indian Express* of 4 April 2012 carried a front page main story of the move of two army units, a Para unit from Agra and a mechanized one from Hissar to the outskirts of Delhi on the night of 16/17 January 2012, the day Gen. V.K. Singh's petition was to be heard in the Supreme Court. The belated release of this information to the media was followed by a quick clarification by the MOD that although the move was not notified to them but they did not suspect any malafide motive. This was followed by news of the recall of the Defence Secretary Shashi Kant Sharma from Malaysia and MOD asking the Director General of Military Operations about the move of these two units. The contents of the news clearly indicate that it could only be passed by a person in the defence establishment and its belated release are indicative of a dubious motive and it could only be a motivated leak. Those who put it out and the media who projected it could not be termed ignorant and thus became partners in the conspiracy.

As indicated above by highlighting the government (MOD) point of view based on motivated leaks by it, some in the media became partners to the controversy. It should be apparent to even a layman that two units on their own could hardly stage a coup, when none of the field formations located in Delhi or near by were even alerted. Such malicious instigations deserve the most contemptuous condemnation. Event to event write-ups in the print media and frequent debates on the television channels brought both the issues and differing points of view in public domain and both the media and public opinion were divided. While the establishment, both political and bureaucratic, in spite of public pretences view it as a challenge to their authority. Public by and large view it as a badly handled sensitive issue by the political establishment. Within the services and amongst the retired fraternity the vast majority feels that what has happened was fermenting for a long time and it was high time that services stood up to the political and bureaucratic establishment for not only ignoring their sensitivities but treating them as any other department in the government. I cannot get over the feeling that majority of the media had either been muzzled or bought over as most of the coverage of the events had been one-sided and not fair. One only hopes that the episode plays out to the benefit of the country and both sides sit down and decide to work together, it certainly cannot be going back to the old methodology. So far the political leadership has neither displayed the understanding and sensitivity required. There can be no victors in such situations. I also feel most humbly that the honourable Supreme Court failed to do justice to the issue before them.

Without going into an event to event view of the standoff, a dispassionate broad consideration throws up the issue of corruption within the army and defence deals, which affect the preparedness and battle worthiness of the army. The corruption within the army has a serious adverse effect on the ethos, culture and its traditional code of conduct amongst the officer corps as gentlemen. Leaving aside his personal age issue Gen. V.K. Singh deserves credit for bringing out the issue of corruption within the army and dealing with it firmly and in the defence establishments outside. The confrontation between Gen. V.K. Singh and the government should be examined in the realm of principles and not events. According to me his linking up of his age issue with the major issue of corruption and Army's state of readiness was ill advised and diluted his principled fight against corruption. Gen. V.K. Singh has himself during an interview in Thiruvananthapuram on 8 May 2012 acknowledged that the age controversy could have been but avoided.

The age issue was the first one to appear in public domain when Gen. V.K. Singh filed his petition in the Supreme Court consequent to rejection of his statutory complaint by the MOD. The MOD responded only to the age issue and that too not only on the legal platform but in the media as well. The main issues raised by Gen.

V.K. Singh in his letters of September 2010 to the raksha mantri and in March 2011 to the prime minister on corruption in defence deals and particularly in the supply of Tatra trucks remained buried.

A dispassionate review of current cases of corruption within the army would reveal that these are primarily due to the dilution of the value system, increasing materialistic mind set and vaulting ambition amongst senior officers. Since days gone by, one of the traditions inherited by the army was the unwritten code of conduct that in addition to professional excellence expected of him, an officer was also a gentleman. The *Oxford Dictionary* defines a gentleman as 'a man of chivalrous instincts, fine feelings and good breeding'. The code of conduct is inculcated from the very beginning at the Indian Military Academy, where cadets are designated as Gentlemen Cadets. While any weakness or lapses in military and academic subjects could be condoned but any failing or even the minutest of a lapse in OLQ (officer like qualities) was never accepted or pardoned as such acts were deemed as conduct unbecoming of an officer and gentleman within the purview off the Army Act. I have given a few examples of it in the first chapter, a cadet was thrown out for cheating, a false statement or even back biting of another colleague. In recent years of economic liberalization, consumerism, commercialism and media explosion, army has deviated from its traditional cultural moorings, indulged in superficial image building, adopting corporate style and their five star culture and failed to cope with the disparity in lifestyles of the corporate class and elite including politicians. The above is equally matched with the low quality of our national leadership morally. As I have said earlier the balance between style and substance in the army is seriously disturbed and style has not only gained undue prominence but is largely divorced from service discipline, steadfastness and *esprit-de-corps*, which is founded on army and regimental traditions. In the olden days we earned much less than compared to a boxwala, businessman or a contractor but we were looked up to, admired and respected for our adherence to values. While we rode cycles, others in the family and friends outside rode motorcycles, scooters and some even cars. There was only one car in the entire brigade, that of the Brigade Commander. Messes and clubs had cycle stands and your esteem amongst your colleagues went up if you owned a cycle and not one on Rs. 10 per month on hire from the unit *bania*. We accepted hospitability only if we could repay. Everyone knew we had little money but we were respected and everyone trusted our word, for we were officers and gentlemen.

Short tenures at higher levels, dilution of command stream and demands of materialist and inflated lifestyles provide impetus to ambition beyond one's capability and getting into the so-called rat race. The Napoleonic dictum, 'Moral to the physical is three is to one', the qualities needed in battle, the soul aim of the soldier has been lost sight off. The blame lies entirely within the army. We were all taught that command was personal and its foundations were laid on personal example and conduct. Personal competence and conduct of commander and honour of the unit, regiment or formation you belonged to were sacrosanct. Lapses of juniors under you were dealt with compassion and were corrected and not only punished. People rarely went to court to seek legal redress as justice was dispensed at some level or the other within the army. We the older lot considered the establishment of the Armed Forces Tribunals as a slur on the army justice system and a cause for introspection. Does it imply a lack of confidence and faith in the system of military justice or is it a failure of the system due to weak moral fibre of the officer cadre. Today's commanders take undue recourse to military legal processes and threat of ACRs to exercise command rather than personal face-to-face command. Without resuscitation of the honour code, exercise of personal command and insisting on moral values, where guidance takes precedence over punishment and where setting a personal example of uprightness and impartiality will find its own reward in strengthening the *esprit-de-corps*. Having said so, I reiterate that senior officers involved in Adarsh and Sukhna scams must be punished to set an example. My generation owes a lot to people like late Lt. Generals M.L. Thapan and Inder Gill and others, whose conduct, guidance and propagation of the value system stood us and the army in good stead through out our careers and later life.

Before I express my views on defence procurements and corruption in defence deals, I must at the very outset acknowledge that I have no experience of dealing with the subject, I have only functional knowledge like any other senior officer. This probably enables me to take an overall view and not get involved in procedural wrangles. The subject of defence procurement has been a live one ever since the Bofors purchases in 1987. A number of retired officers who have dealt with the subject have written on defence procurement strategy. I have drawn heavily on my discussions with these officers, particularly with Lt. Gen. Chandrashekhar, PVSM, AVSM (Retd), former Vice-Chief of the Army Staff, whose book, *Arming the Defence Forces* (2004) and his various articles in defence journals and newspapers provided the latest updates on the subject till as late as March 2012. The subject was reviewed in detail in 2001 as part of Arun Singh Committee on defence, one of the committees after the Kargil Committee under late K. Subramanian. Later in 2005 Kelkar Committee made detailed recommendations with reference to self-reliance in defence preparedness. In spite of various reviews and committees our defence procurement policy has failed to meet defence requirements fully and in a timely fashion. There have always been serious shortages and services have had to function with antedated equipment and arms. Almost 70 per cent of our defence needs are met by imports, in spite of large defence infrastructure of Ordnance factories, Defence Public Sector Undertakings (PSUs) and Defence Research and Development Organisation (DRDO) research facilities. Self-reliance has only been a talking point with very little done to build capacity in the government and private sector. DRDO and Defence PSUs deserve full credit for development of integrated missile systems, EW systems and recently the Brahmos cruise missiles. But equally upsetting is the huge cost and time overruns in the case of MBT Arjun, WLR, Nag, AJT and Pinaka MBRL just to name a few. With the end of days of rupee payment for equipment/weapon purchases from USSR, the cost of acquiring weapon systems has increased manifold.

Our reliance on direct purchases, setting up of licensed production facilities and lack of investment in technology development and faulty and cumbersome procurement policies pursued by officials who are not trained to manage defence contracts has resulted in the current state of affairs. We have failed to follow and adopt technologies of reverse engineering or adopt joint production followed by countries like China, Israel, South

Africa and Brazil, who have become arms exporters. They have cemented their linkages with leading arms producing countries for guaranteed investments and technology transfers. Thus they have long terms stakes and incentives for successful technology transfers and production facilities.

Our procurement structure is coordinated by a high level council designated as Defence Acquisition Cell (DAC) headed by the Raksha Mantri, with the three Service Chiefs, the Defence Secretary, Secretary (DP&S), Secretary (DR&D) and Secretary Defence Finance as members. The procurement planning process is supposed to be under the overall guidance of this cell. Headquarters Integrated Defence Staff (IDS) in consultation with the Service Headquarters formulates the fifteen years perspective plan and five years services capital acquisition plan for approval of the DAC. However, in the absence of a Chief of Defence Staff (CDS), it really results in compilation of service plans as IDS has no authority to alter priorities laid by Service Headquarters. DAC decisions on procurement are in practice taken by Defence Procurement Board (DPB), Defence Production Board and Defence R&D Board respectively. DAC is never able to meet regularly so it depends on IDS, DPB for inputs, rather than giving them strategic direction and long- term perspectives. DPB takes all the 'buy' and 'buy and make' decisions, which creates bottlenecks and delays. A separate DPB for each service may hasten up the process but the question of inter- service priorities would still remain hanging. There is also a Special Secretary for capital acquisition with separate divisions of Land, Maritime, Air Force and a systems division, each under a Joint Secretary as Acquisition Manager, a technical manager, a Major General rank officer or equivalent from the other two services, along with a Financial Advisor Acquisition (FA Acquisition) who advises the special secretary on all financial matters. From the above structures it should be clear that MOD and its officers are the key players, who lack the expertise. Moreover, since the responsibility is shared by too many agencies, each one tends to shift responsibility. In contrast the Project Executive (PE) in UK has officers from the three services, the technocrats and civilian officers who work in close cooperation to plan and execute the entire procurement process. We need to create an integrated procurement agency, consisting of scientists, Defence Forces, management experts and dedicated administrators to plan defence policy, budget and weapon procurement and projects. There is a crying need for a CDS as without it the IDS is ineffective. Our system tends to delays in processing deals, lacks transparency and accountability and is prone to pressure. The enforcing authority can only be the political leadership, which should be decisive, open and transparent.

Without going in details of any defence deals, some of the recent ones have been brought out by Gen. V.K. Singh in his letter of 12 March 2012 to the prime minister and earlier brought to the notice of the raksha mantri in 2011. I shall only cover corruption in defence deals very broadly as I have no authentic knowledge of individual deals. The two past cases which are well known to the public are the Jeep purchases when V.K. Krishna Menon was our High Commissioner in UK and the other one in 1987 of the Bofors Gun purchase. It is the Bofors case which brought out the role of the middleman in defence deals. The crux of the problem is that no arms manufacturing country or consortium can afford to place their representatives in all the prospective buyer countries. So local representatives are normally selected and appointed. This goes for all goods, including consumer ones to be marketed, they appoint salesman on commission which is a legitimate reimbursement for their labour. The same is the case with the arms manufacturers/ dealers, who appoint local representatives in prospective buyer countries. The local representative should normally register himself and say what all companies he represents as there may be more that one concern that he represents. The local representative (or middleman) finds out the demand, locates the armament or equipment which meets the buyer's requirement and acts as a go between and lobbies and canvasses for the item to be sold. Once the deal and its terms are finalized by the company or country concerned he is given an agreed commission which is part of the contract. That is how the Nandas, Khannas and other arms dealers established themselves by understanding Indian requirements and locating the right sources. Apart from the commission there may have been other money/incentives to facilitate the deal. Whatever was taken by the politician or the bureaucrat was on the pretext of 'for the party'. The people involved in clinching the deal were known and in a manner there was an element of regulation in commissions/facilitation money as such and there was a fair amount of transparency. There was never any fiddling with the services recommendations, quality or prices. Price was a consideration when there was a substantial price difference in two comparable weapons or equipment, when services were consulted before finalization. However, it was in the 1980s that the middleman became an enigma and direct dealing with manufacturers was resorted to and the rumour was that whatever was gained should come to the political party direct and was not to be shared with any middleman or representative. Direct negotiations resulted in lack of transparency, deals shrouded in secrecy and in turn leading to corruption, compromises and delays. The system demanded that services be kept away and if someone raised a noise, to be bribed, silenced or ignored. This also lends to price escalation and compromises in quality of parts and spares. Tatra is an apt example of it. Because of secrecy in deals the competing parties go to court, resulting in delay and blacklisting of firms which again adds to delay and even compromising on quality.

As I have already said at the beginning that Gen. V.K. Singh's raising his age issue with the other major issue of corruption was ill advised and in my opinion diluted his stance from principles to events. However, having said so, the age controversy has brought out issues which cannot be wished away. The episode has brought out some systemic and procedural deviations in the selection of the senior ranks. I have discussed these in detail in a chapter earlier under the heading, 'Systemic Failures'. The reader would do well to refresh the above. I will therefore confine myself to the all important issue of selection of the Chief of the Army Staff.

The selection of the Chief of the Army Staff followed a well-defined system of the seniormost Army Commander in service at the time of the incumbent Chief's retirement taking over. There were exceptions in the case of Gen. G.G. Bewoor and Gen. Vaidya who superseded Gen. P.S. Bhagat and Gen. S.K. Sinha respectively. Normally two months before the incumbent Chief's retirement, dossiers of three seniormost Army Commanders were sent to the Cabinet Committee of Appointments. The retiring Chief was informally consulted by the Appointments Committee. By and large there were no dissensions or discussions even in the case of the above two supersessions, although there was always some talk for a period to discern the possible reasons. It will be pertinent to remind the reader of the distortions brought into the system by Gen. Sundarjee by having command and staff and staff only streams during the cadre review. Later the leeway provided by it was fully exploited by the three artillery chiefs, Rodrigues, Padmanabhan and Deepak Kapoor, by adopting the system of proportionate promotions to the maximum advantage of artillery officers, who are the main beneficiary of the distortion from the time tested General Cadre system. This also opened the system to manipulation for helping favourites to the disadvantage of the army and in total disregard to qualitative requirements of different appointments

During our service at times one felt a subdued feeling amongst some of the Sikh officers in the army that there existed a silent political reservation against having a Sikh Army Chief, while both in the Air Force and Navy it was acceptable. We the junior officers felt its vibration but there was never an expression of it, neither did it create any ill feeling amongst the officer class. Moreover, there was no supersession of any Sikh officer. The only possible exception was when Gen. Bewoor was given an extension of three months and Gen. Bhagat after retirement took over as chairman of the Damodar Valley Corporation and we all are aware of what a tremendous success he made of it. Everyone in the army felt that Gen. Bhagat was sidelined because he would have been a strong Chief, which probably was not acceptable to the government, particularly the bureaucracy, but there was never any communal element attributed to it. The same was our feeling on supersession of Gen. Sinha.

The issue of the COAS's selection was for the first time put in public domain beyond Army, MOD and government's purview, when Gen. J.J. Singh was to become the Chief. It is well known in Army circles that Gen. J.J. Singh, in spite of being the seniormost army commander, often talked within the army and to some in the retired fraternity that he may not become the army chief because he is a Sikh. This was well known and became the subject of talk in the army circles. His lobbying beyond the services is well known and covered by the media. The vocal part played by Tarlochan Singh, the then head of the Minorities Commission and other community adjuncts particularly in Punjab are well known and were highlighted by the media at that time. The PIL filed by retired Naval Chief Admiral Ramdas, ex-Maj M.G. Devasahayam, IAS (Retd), N. Gopalaswamy, ex-CEC and others although dismissed by the Supreme Court brought out the unsavory facts vividly. It is no one's case whether Gen. J.J. Singh deserved to be Chief or not but a tinge of communal element had been inducted and his subsequent actions even if not accepted officially are for all to see, certainly the army is aware of it. It is interesting that this happens at the time of the first Sikh prime minister. This was also the time when incidents of corruption in higher echelons of the army started becoming frequent and pronounced subject of talk within the army circles, there was mention of corruption and misdemeanour in the northern army. A situation to the liking of politician and bureaucracy as it is easy to deal with compromised individuals.

It is alleged that Gen. J.J. Singh when he was the Chief instituted a deep look down policy going right down to brigadier level to work out a likely line of succession, which his detractors term as Operation 'Moses'. This also finds mention in the PIL mentioned in the above paragraph. Even if one believed there was no such deep look down policy and operation Moses was an imaginative fabrication, but nobody can deny that there was talk of it in the army and promotions of some of the upcoming colleagues of then Brig. Bikram Singh, all brigadiers were scuttled. The PIL gives names. It is very rare that a Chief takes personal interest in the brigadiers promotions. The MOD's stance on the line of succession being disturbed if Gen. V.K. Singh's age was accepted as 1951 is dodgy. People do not become the COAS by succession but by selection. All this read together casts a doubt.

If there was a disparity in the age of Gen. V.K. Singh, why was it not resolved within the army as proposed by the Adjutant General, the official record keeper of officer's personal documentation. It is a strange coincidence that the issue was raised in 2006 when Gen. J.J. Singh was the Chief. Why did J.J. Singh not issue instructions to resolve it within the army with intimation to Gen. V.K. Singh in writing, when throughout his career he had shown his DOB as

1951. It is also questionable as to why MOD got involved with date of birth issue and one of its directors issued instructions to the army to record Gen. V.K. Singh's DOB as 1950. Connivances at various levels including the MOD can only be the motivating factor. To my mind Gen. V.K. Singh has erred in judgement by trusting the two Chiefs J.J. Singh and Deepak Kapoor thus weakening his stand. He should have taken it up in 2006 itself through a statutory complaint. The judgment of the Supreme Court had put the onus on MOD to take a fresh look on Gen. V.K. Singh's statutory complaint as ministry had withdrawn its rejection of it, which it failed to. The feeling within the army is totally with Gen. V.K. Singh as he stood up and exposed corruption both within and outside the army. He will certainly be remembered with respect and pride on this account. As to whether he will be a 'footnote' as contended by Shekhar Gupta in his article quoted below, will entirely depend on how Gen. V.K. Singh upholds his dignity and his actions post retirement. I hope he does not get carried away by personal ambitions. For public eminence is temporary and only moral standing lasts. So far his conduct in this respect has been disappointing and his hobnobbing with politicians and other public figures is indicative of his personal ambitions. This has considerally lowered his personal stature and is not at all in keeping with the dignity of the office of the Chief of the Army Staff he recently occupied.

As a soldier I always felt that old soldiers should just fade away but the failure of the government to resolve the issues in the last decade and particularly lack of sensitiveness to current standoff was a cause of serious hurt and anguish for us. I morally felt compelled to convey my feelings to the prime minister, who I felt should have taken things in hand. My letter to the prime minister is attached as Appendix A.

My good friend Shekhar Gupta in his article, 'With Prejudice', published in the *Indian Express* of 28 April 2012 has very ably, though in my opinion in a bit motivated vein, written about the valuable part Sikhs have played in wars against Pakistan. More than anyone else the army and people like me particularly take pride in it. However, his invoking Operation Blue Star and the part played by my two close colleagues in it, which according to him defeated Bhindranwala's bogey of discrimination against Sikhs was not only a bit out of context but sounded similar to government's lauding the loyalty of these officers to justify the operation. I have covered that in Chapter 6. His comments on the PIL filed by a group of prominent citizens and its dismissal by the Supreme Court, 'By giving communal twist to the naming of the next Army Chief, PIL tried to revive fears long buried until Apex Court threw it out', are refuted by M.G. Devasahayam, one of the litigants in his article 'With No Prejudice' published in the *Indian Express* of 19 May 2012. I would not like to enter into any controversy and, it is best left to the reader to decide. I agree with both of them that Manmohan Singh the prime minister for whom I have the highest regards can never be called communal. But what is worrisome is his silence throughout the episode which tends to give a wrong impression by default. Before I end I cannot help but feel compelled to record a disturbed feeling. So far only parochialism known in the army has been that of the regimental one, which is traditional and represents a soldier's pride in his regiment and paltan, the motivating force during battle and foundation of self-sacrifice. Any other parochialism needs to be curbed and nipped in the bud. Failure to do so will be costly for the army and the nation.

Finally, irrespective of all the justification from everyone, this episode is bound to have its after effect both within the army and on the Civil-Military Relations. Only wisdom and sensitivity will help in resolving the issues, this puts the onus on the political leadership to take the initiative.

I consider the entire episode a tragedy as Gen. V.K. Singh with his impeccable professional record and uprightness and A.K. Antony, the raksha mantri, well known for his honesty and clean image became adversaries rather than partners in resolving corruption and permissiveness in the services and the defence establishment.

APPENDIX A

LETTER TO PRIME MINISTER MANMOHAN SINGH

23 February 2012

Respected Prime Minister,

Most people, including myself, believe that old soldiers should just fade away. Ever since retiring from the Indian Army as the Western Army Commander and subsequently having served as the Governor of Manipur and Nagaland, I firmly held that we have had our innings and matters were best left to those who followed us. However, after giving it considerable thought, I take the liberty in all due respect of writing this 'open letter' to my prime minister for like hundreds and thousands of my brother officers—both retired and serving—I am deeply concerned about what today is talked about as the 'Age Controversy'!

In my book, leadership, be it in matters military or otherwise, is based on three simple principles—righteousness, decisiveness and fairness! All three of these seem to have been vitiated in this particular case. There is no doubt that all records, both in the MS and AGs branch, until 2006 clearly reflected 1951 as the Chief's date of birth. Based on an erroneous entry in the Army List, after the officer had already been cleared for the rank of Lieutenant General, first the MS branch records and then the AGs records were tampered with. To my mind and understanding, this is the simple crux of the issue and I fail to understand what sort of message has been given to the rank and file of the Indian Army by your government's inability to resolve this issue.

To hide behind the legal system—the retraction of the government's rejection of the Statutory Complaint frankly left the Chief's lawyers with no choice but to withdraw their petition—and for the media and your government to project this as a defeat for General V.K. Singh is indulging in theatrical politics. Like many of my brother officers, after the media blitz that reported on the Supreme Court's deliberations, I too felt that the Chief should immediately resign in protest. However, once the Order of the Honourable Court came out five days later—without any TV channel or newspaper reporting it—the shoe seems to be on the other foot. By not resigning and continuing with his job despite what was widely projected as a 'public humiliation', V.K. Singh has shown a degree of personal courage that makes me proud of the man and by extension, the Indian Army. Had he resigned, it would have been a petulant act. We must not forget that there is a lot more to the office of the COAS than just the age issue.

Today, Mr. Prime Minister, many would like to bury this issue and may accuse me of flogging a dead horse. However, it is my duty as an elder who has served my country to the best of my ability, to point out to you that once the smoke settles, you will be asked why you let this happen. In a system that is reeling from endless corruption charges, where many have learnt to bend with the wind, one man stood up for what he considered wrong. The 'system' may have closed in around him and in the short term, defeated him by denying him justice. But you, Mr. Prime Minister, are today being seen as the person who is not only shielding the perpetrators of this original crime, but also protecting the beneficiary of this blatant manipulation.

I have had the honour of interacting with you when you were the Finance Minister of our country. I have always found you to be a man who could quickly grasp the larger picture and resolutely follow your convictions. Since Independence, the civil-military equation in this country has evolved in its own unique way, perhaps creating certain imbalances which need to be looked at for like the 'age issue', these too cannot be wished away. In a fractured and fragmented country that came together in 1947 as the Union of India, I can say with great pride that the Indian Army managed to retain its secular and non-communal outlook. This has to be protected at all costs! In your watch, if all the lions were to get up and go, the wind will say, I told you so!

With regards.

LT. GENERAL V.K. NAYAR
PVSM, SM(Retd)

CHAPTER 12

Retirement, Readjustment, Fulfilment and Tragedy

On retirement we shifted to a small bungalow in Delhi Cantonment till our flat, which was on rent could be vacated and whitewashed. This was in spite of the fact that I had given a year's notice to the tenant. Life in the cantonment was hassle free but unsettled as the process of resettlement and readjustment could not start. Things got a bit complicated as in spite of our meticulous planning—some of our luggage got misplaced and some damaged during shifting. Moreover, we could not order any furniture till we had shifted and assessed the requirement. When I retired I did not possess any personal furniture, not even a bed to sleep on as after our initial experience of constant damage during our transfers we gave up the idea, moreover we felt that a house should be equipped to meet your and its requirement in terms of size, design and cost. My friends always pulled my leg that having spent the last five years of my service in Punjab, I did not even order a stick from Kartarpur. I always maintained that to be honest you have to pay the price for it, while in service one should refrain from making personal possessions and things.

The initial few month's inconvenience turned out to be a blessing in disguise as with the summer approaching, we decided to go to Ranikhet and on return in July we found Delhi still very sultry, humid and hot. Our flat on the first floor in Som Vihar facing Sangam Cinema became intolerable and unliveable for my wife who was a patient of acute migraine. While days were an agony due to heat, nights were disturbed due to noise and music from Sangam Cinema. Things were as bad for our servant Parsa Ram and our two dogs in one of the bed rooms, we had no servant quarters or covered garage. In spite of all the attractions of Delhi and its elite get up, we decided to look for a more liveable place. After a lot of scouting around Delhi, Gurgaon and Noida, we found the place which met our requirements in a spacious flat with open terraces, a small unit for servants and a garage in Sector 15A in Noida which we bought after disposing off our Som Vihar flat to another service officer. Once there, the process of resettlement went ahead, we hired two carpenters and saw everything made to our requirement. In less than a year the place became very comfortable and livable. Both me and my wife have never regretted the initial unsettled period as we built everything as we wanted and within our means. The process helped in readjustment and set the stage for enjoying small things of life for which you had no time earlier. We learnt that if you do things yourself, they are not only easier but also enjoyable, our later experience only reinforced it.

Before going any further, I must narrate another related experience. In the last year of my service I was given the honour to take the salute at the passing out parade at the IMA. During our short stay in Dehradun we went to see Lt. Gen. F.N. Billimoria's house in Vasant Vihar opposite the Forest Research Institute. We really liked the house, the colony and almost succumbed to his suggestion to settle down in Dehradun. With a lot of other friends there it was an attractive choice but after a chance encounter with some other senior retired officers at the IMA Golf Course later in the evening we changed our mind. After the game of golf I asked one of the elders as to how was life in Dehradun and what was their routine. He told me that after golf in the morning they have breakfast, do some household chores, primarily a visit to the market for daily requirements, which they never did in service but wives insisted that they do so now. Rest of the morning is spent in reading newspapers and if some issue agitates then write to the editor, it hardly matters if it is published or not. When I asked him about the social life and the activities at the Doon Club, he told me that the club had been taken over by tailors, shoemakers and petty businessmen and was no longer conducive for gentlemen. Social life was confined to a close circle of friends and relatives if any. Other veterans had more or less similar views, all in all it was a dreary peaceful life. I always felt that after retirement one still had a number of years of fruitful existence. One is mentally agile and physically fit to do things which one wanted to do and enjoy. I had a yearning for self-education and improvement and to write. I felt that in the quiet and laid back atmosphere of a place like Dehradun, I would not only feel retired but somewhat retarded. So the idea to adopt Dehradun as my home town was shelved and we decided on Delhi where I had been brought up and educated. This decision was further reinforced by the knowledge that it offered both physical and mental outlets of your choice, which you could pick and afford. The fact that both our families were in Delhi made it easier. We have never regretted it and enjoyed our years after retirement inspite of increasing un-liveability of Delhi and its stresses and strain. When people ask me as to how do I pass my time, I tell them 40 per cent of my time and effort is spent on survival and rest in what I wish to do and enjoy. Similarly, after our yearly sojourn in New Zealand with our daughter's family, when we return to India and she asks us as to how is life, we reply we are running to stay at the same place. In spite all this life goes on and various irksome harassments keep us going. One must learn to relax, enjoy and take life as it comes. Thank god we are in Delhi and still out of it.

Retirement is only another phase of life and it requires an attitudinal change more than anything else. Another Army Commander and a senior friend often complained that the people who used to run around you tend to ignore you after retirement. One day while playing golf he complained of the same. I asked him as to out of ten people that he came across that day, how many ignored him and how many acknowledged him. He replied only three wished him and the rest ignored him. I told him to be grateful for those three and ignore the other seven. My experience has been just the opposite, any one that I know and recognize, I wish them, preferably taking their name if I can recollect and I have never felt ignored. As a matter of fact I feel gratified that after so many years, so many people still know you and are so kind.

Two minor incidents within a short period of retirement are worth narrating as these taught me a lot and may be of help and interest to others. After we had shifted to our flat in Noida, a few months later our servant went home on leave. A few days later I was cleaning my car, when the caretaker of the guest house flat above us, an ex-servicemen from the Kumaon Regiment came running to me and said, *aap yeh kam kaise kar sakte hain, aap to general hai* (how can you do such work, you are a general), *laiye main gari saf kar deta hoon* (I will clean your car). I told him 'Pandit ji, "*yeh mera kam hai aur apna kam karne mein koi sharam nahi—aap ek din ya do din kar do ge, phir jab main iske liye kahunga—aap muh pher kar meri taraf nahi dekho ge*", (Pandit ji, this is my work and there is no shame in doing your own work. Moreover, you will do it for a couple of days and after that when time comes, you will look the other way). I do not want to be obliged or dependent on any one. Once people know they respect you and you become self-sufficient.

The second incident relates to a small work of putting up a swing on our terrace for my grandchildren. After the swing was installed I asked a painter to paint it in silver colour after giving it the anti-rust coat. He finished half the job of painting it with anti-rust paint and promising to complete the work next day left. He did not return for three days. After waiting for him for a day, I put on an old T-shirt and shorts and finished the anti-rust painting in a few hours. Next day I finished the silver painting of the swing and its beam. A day later the painter turned up, seeing the job has been completed he was very agitated and told me as to how I can get someone else to do the job. I told him that I found a sucker who did it for free and if he does not leave quietly I will throw him out. Apart from the fact that you are not dependent on others, doing your own work gives you contentment and happiness and you can plan and do things in time.

Retirement does not mean life and activities only centred around home and family, there are other things and interests which you have and should continue to develop. After a hectic professional life, you remain a professional in mind and heart and should continue to pursue it depending on your inclination and opportunities. In this regard I have had great satisfaction in being part of the United Service Institution, the Centre for Policy Research and Centre for North East Studies and Policy Research and the activities of some other think tanks. It keeps one mentally alert and involved and helps you to keep in touch with areas of your interest and you also make a cotribution. It is also essential that we pursue our leisure and social interests in the best manner suitable to us. Travel for pleasure and to keep in touch with relatives and friends is enjoyable and rejuvenating as reviving old memories are always a pleasant and learning experience.

In the services one misses a lot of family life and events. Retirement gives you the ideal opportunity to catch up and revive family ties. There is great fun in being together and there are enough occasions, reasons and excuses for it. Bigger the family, better the fun. Enlarged family circle ensures that. While it gives pleasure to the older, for the younger generation it is an excellent opportunity to know each other. The perception that the joint family system is breaking down and there is a dilution of family ties is correct to a large extent. We had experience of both and consider ourselves lucky for it being on the positive side. We saw how family ties dilute and its adverse effect on the elders particularly whenever we lived abroad. We always felt lucky like most Indians that our children still care so much for us, the affection and care that they bestow on us is most heartening. Most other local elders abroad envy us. Even at home in India in Delhi family get-togethers are mostly confined to occasions of celebrations and sadness. In the changed environment, the pace of life being what it is we cannot but accept it. We had a very telling and healthy experience of its flip side during the third year after my retirement. My younger brother had a sudden and serious cardiac attack one night, we rushed him to Kalawati Heart Clinic and after a few days he was shifted to AIIMS. He being a bachelor, was living alone therefore someone had to be present at the hospital all the time. We all brothers and sisters decided to share the duty. What was most heartening was that the children of the entire family, most of whom were working, volunteered to take on these duties on all the nights and holidays. This was entirely voluntarily arranged by them amongst themselves. Later on my brother stayed with us, with my other brother and sisters and all the children really looked after him. Ever since I have maintained that while the joint family system is breaking down but the jointness of the family ties is still strong and we need to nurture it. We had similar experiences later on a number of occasions.

Our most pleasurable and happy moments have been the time we spent with our grandchildren as they were growing up. It is a special bond which in a lot of ways is different from the parents and their children's bond and in spite of their growing up, it continues. It is a bond of love and full of understanding and compassion. My daughter's two girls grew up abroad and we had little opportunity to be with them, the elder one was the first grandchild so she will always have a special place for us. She left India when she was little but her return to us was always full of joy and fun. The younger one, born abroad, was a bundle of joy whenever they came to India or we visited them. My wife really doted on them. They have grown up to be young ladies but the bond persists. My son's twin boy and girl grew up in our presence and the contact was more intimate and lasting and is continuing, they are in their teens now. Once while driving the twins when they were four years old, I suddenly braked hard and shouted a Hindi abuse (*ullu ka patha*) as a cyclist suddenly crossed the road and could have died if I had not reacted quickly. A couple of months later while again taking them out for an ice cream, a similar incident occurred. Before I could respond my grandson shouted the same abuse out to the cyclist. When I asked him as to why he said that, he told me that anyone so stupid to cross the road like that could only be it. I learnt to be careful in what one utters in front of children specially grandchildren. Later while my son was posted at Khasa near Amritsar, one day my twin grandchildren rang me up to complain against the uncalled for scolding they got from their mother and what was worse that their father supported it. I told them to put their parents on the line so that I could talk to them, they told me that they are ringing up from a STD booth and not from home, so that the parents don't know. I got a bit worried and told them not to go out like that. They told me not to worry as the STD booth was in the cantonment and close to the house. A few hours later I rang up my son and daughter-in-law enquiring as to why they had scolded the children. They both were intrigued as to how sitting in Noida we knew about it, both of them got a scolding from my wife. This bond is also very fruitful for the grandchildren to learn and experience new things as parents have less time, the grandparents have both the time and inclination. Both me and my wife and later me alone after her death have enjoyed this relationship fully.

Of all the living species, human being is the most understanding, intelligent, innovative, constructive and creative, at the same time most selfish, self-centred and possibly most destructive. While they solve problems, at the same time they create them and accentuate human suffering. Without sounding very philosophical, it has been my experience that most problems are creation of perception. We tend to think mostly what is best for us, without caring or worrying about what others feel or think. I got the best advice on this from a village elder in Manipur. After one of our operations in a Meitei village in the Imphal Valley, I was talking to some of the villagers and asked them if there were any problems. One of the elders came forward and after shaking my hand he told me that you must carry out operations but before imposing any restrictions on the villagers you must ask them how it affects them and for how long can they bear it as it might help both sides in doing their job better. This is equally true of day-to-day life, before taking a decision which affects others, we should visualize as to how it will affect them. It will help in a more pragmatic and better decision-making, which is accepted willingly. Being conscious of other's feelings is of utmost importance for all human relations.

The interlude in Manipur and its abrupt end resulted in yet another minor exercise in resettlement. My son Vicky who had just arrived two days earlier on leave to be with us took charge of the packing and everything fell into place quickly. He knew Manipur as he had done a stint with my battalion in the late 1980s. He asked me as to where we would like to stay for a week, while he gets our flat in Noida ready after a white-wash and fresh coat of paint as it had been locked up. I told him that I had already rung up Maj. Gen. Reddy, GOC of Delhi Area to put us up for a week in one of the Area Guest rooms. He had also promised to send a car to meet us at Palam airfield on arrival.

On arrival at Palam, we were received by the Resident Commissioner of Manipur and in spite of his insistence to stay at Manipur Bhavan, we went to the cantonment and stayed there. During this period Th Brojan Singh, my ADC from Manipur police, stayed in Delhi and constantly checked on our comfort and requirement if any, of which we had none. I thanked him and Minnie his wife for their consideration. My son Vicky and Shiva our faithful servant put the place in order in record time and we shifted to our home for the New Year. Shiva while with us in Manipur had very little to do except an odd chore for my wife and me. We all in the family appreciated the way he from a life of comfort and no work again took over all the responsibility of running the house as if the sojourn in Manipur had never happened. In Manipur I made Shiva complete his education to be able to either join the Army on which he was very keen or failing which pick-up a better job. I firmly believe that everyone looks forward to advancement and we should encourage it. A year after we returned, he joined my regiment and became a Naik in five years time. Unfortunately, we lost Shiva forever in 2005 during operations against insurgents in J&K. He will always remain a part of our lives. God bless his soul.

Life fell into the old routine in Delhi and I renewed my association with the United Service Institution of India and some other think-tanks. I spoke at the United Service Institution of India, India International Centre and few other places on the prevailing situation in the north-east with particular reference to Manipur and Nagaland. There were a number of questions on the situation and few on my resignation. Most of the questions related to my report of 5 October 1993 to the president and people appreciated my principled stand. The United Service Institution of India had just established a research centre and Maj. Gen. S.C. Sinha (Retd.), its Director, wanted me to be its head. I politely declined as the Deputy Director, Air Commodore N.B. Singh (Retd.) was already working on it. However, I conceded to their request to do a research project on 'Low Intensity Conflicts in India', which was published in 2000. My association with the USI continues till date and I enjoyed my close association with its new Director, Lt. Gen. Satish Nambiar, who extended its sphere of activities to expand the Research Centre into a full-fledged Centre for Strategic Studies and Simulation and in addition established a new Centre for Armed Forces Historical Research and a Centre for United Nations Peacekeeping Operations for training. Satish brought greater worldwide recognition to the Institution due to his personal competence, professionalism and eminence. Association with the USI gave me the opportunity to interact and be associated with both national and international experts and associations, in particular those of our neighbouring countries—Nepal, Sri Lanka, Bangladesh, Pakistan, Bhutan and

Egypt and South-East Asian Countries—Japan, Philippines, Malaysia and Thailand.

In February 1995, I was invited for a seminar on insurgency at the Centre for Policy Research, which was the start of my association with them. It lasted till 2005, when my wife's deteriorating health required my full attention. When I joined Centre for Policy Research, L.P. Singh was still alive and V.A. Pai Panandikar was the president and director. The faculty meetings were most incisive, lively, enthusiastic and frank and varied in terms of subjects, issues and participation. The faculty had experts in most disciplines and the centre was ever inviting people from outside to participate. The centre's interaction with prominent think tanks the world over was well established and there was mutual eagerness to visit and benefit from each other. I rarely missed a faculty meeting and benefitted from the knowledge and wisdom of others. It gave me the opportunity to visit most troubled areas in the country and Bangladesh and Myanmar, to see things first hand on ground. During my association with them, I did a research project on the historical, geographical, social, cultural and economic dimensions of conflicts in the north-east and J&K. The study also had a chapter on Drugs and Arms Linkages and their cross-border nexus. It was published as a book, entitled, *Beyond the Boundaries of Conflict: From Real Politik to Ideal Politik, in the North East and J&K*. In addition I contributed research papers on internal security as apart of other larger studies. I cherish my association with the Centre for Policy Research.

I joined the Centre for North East Studies and Policy, when it was established in 2000 by Pai Panandikar and Sanjoy Hazarika. We took a proactive stance on issues connected with peace and peace talks with the Naga underground and doused the fires of greater Nagaland (Nagalim), in Manipur, Arunachal Pradesh and Assam. We continue to contribute to the north-east in whatever manner it is possible but the lethargy of government institutions is the most discouraging factor. Over a number of years the centre's stance has deviated from its original objectives. Finding it difficult to adjust to it, I resigned at end of 2010. I shall continue to offer my services in whatever manner I can contribute.

As an aftermath of Kargil war in 1999, I joined N.N. Vohra on the task force on Internal Security in 2001. It was another very educative though in parts somewhat disturbing experience. We visited almost all states and all the troubled areas of the country and apart from official briefings, we interacted with a broad cross-section of intellectual elite, public men, administration and public at the grassroot level. In addition we had detailed briefings and interaction with intelligence agencies and defence and police forces at all levels. The briefings by various sections of the MHA and MO directorates were most useful. After a very fine briefing by the head of RAW, which was followed by an equally detailed briefing by the DIB, two issues bothered us. If all this was known to the government then why actions in spheres other than law and order field were missing. My impression was that government response is only confined to law and order, and lack of action to deal with the generic causes in the political, social and economic field was missing or ill directed, and was confirmed as our work progressed. Its effect was most telling in the internal security field. The question I asked all the heads of intelligence agencies and police forces was, whether further militarization will result in improving the situation. We discussed it at length, by and large the opinion was that unless all dimensions of the problem were addressed, action in the law and order field can only contain the problem for a time period. Our study also revealed that this has also resulted in escalation in the number and types of armed police forces without commensurate increase in efficiency and improvement in the internal security environment. There is an optimum level of militarization beyond which it becomes counter productive.

After a very detailed review and assessment of the situation based on all inputs including ground visits, the task force presented a very comprehensive assessment of the IS situation and what needs to be done. Some of the key recommendations were that the special branch, civil police and state armed police were required to be modernized, revamped and reinforced on priority as these are the cutting edge and front line of effective internal security response. These had not been looked into in most cases for over two decades and entire emphasis was on raising of central armed police battalions in CPOs. The second major recommendation was that the Central PMF like BSF and CRPF should first be employed in their primary role, void determined and additional units, if required raised over a period of time. The present employment of forces was contingency based as requirements arose. It was also recommended that CRPF should primarily be the IS Force with elements specifically earmarked for normal law and order and insurgency and terrorism situation. The latter has to be younger, trained for insurgency and terrorism environment and entirely oriented to its role. The above arrangement could also provide for inter change of personnel for rest and relief. Much to our disappointment and on the instigation of PMFs they raised additional CRPF, BSF and India Reserve armed police battalions. The requirements of state police were mostly ignored. What is worse, even the army raised additional RR battalions. We are still paying and shall continue to pay for our lopsided priorities and emphasis. Missing the basics resulted in a sad commentary during 26/11 Bombay raids and in Naxalite areas. I have covered these in the previous chapter.

My wife was an old patient of migraine and at times these attacks were so severe that they kept her confined to her room for a full day. Pain killers were a help but not always. Apart from this she did not have any health problems. She was a very lively person and full of zest for life and highly talented in more ways than one. She was a very fine and highly versatile singer and excelled in semi-classical vocal and *ghazals*. She was very house proud, loved keeping a good house at minimum cost without any splendorous frills. She was an excellent cook and loved entertaining, primarily confined to close friends and associates. She was a good organizer and genuine in her interest of regimental and service welfare but she never imposed on anyone. Often in the battalion she would spend time with families informally helping and understanding their problems. She carried this attitude with her even when I was Corps and Army Commander and participated in welfare activities and believed in constructive participation. 'Glimpses of India' in Jalandhar, a song and dance presentation of different regions and its people and 'Vasant Utsav' in Chandimandir are a tribute to her memory. I always depended on her to play her part as my wife both as a junior officer's wife and later as the senior lady. Even after retirement I left it entirely to her to deal and manage family affairs and dealing with relatives. In a way it came about naturally without effort as all my brothers and sisters and other family members responded to her in a very affectionate and intimate fashion. After I lost my father, she took charge of family affairs and to the younger ones in the family she was like a mother.

Life after retirement coasted along, till we discovered that she was suffering from diabetes and thyroid problems, which were kept under control by regular medication. A few tragedies in the family took their toll and affected her adversely and she became physically inactive gradually but no major danger to her health, least to say of life, was ever suspected. She was very happy to be at home and with the family. Our yearly trips to our daughter in New Zealand became a regular feature from 2001 onwards as did visits to our son in the army, wherever he was posted. On our daughter's insistence, we even applied for permanent resident's status, which was granted to us in 2007. During our daughter and granddaughters visit to us in the beginning of 2008, we took her for a routine check-up to the Armed Forces clinic in Noida. She was checked up both by the cardiologist and opthalmologist and found alright. On arrival back at home my daughter asked me to take my elder granddaughter to the People's Union for Civil Liberties office, where she was doing a research project and she would take her mother up to our flat. I must not have been away more than twenty minutes, when I returned I found the Kailash Hospital Cardiac van with doctors attending to my wife. She had a silent cardiac attack and being a diabetic never felt any pain and collapsed in my daughter's arms. A silent tragedy struck us on 8 February 2008, which left us stunned and helpless. Its gravity has left a void forever. She was always smiling and cheerful and never created a stir, she went the same way. God bless her soul and keep her spirit ever smiling and cheerful. We shall always miss her.

Life goes on and we are learning to cope with the loss. Events, occasions and memories connected with her have become a source of remembrance which me and my children never miss and always talk to each other irrespective of where we are. It helps. Both my daughter Ritu and son Vicky (Vikrant) are now more concerned about me, especially when I am alone in Noida. In spite of my knowingly not acknowledging it, they do a lot of monitoring through frequent telephone calls and through relatives and friends. This has eased a bit as time has passed but is still fairly regular. Their concern makes one wanted, loved and is a source of happiness and satisfaction.

Ritu married Virender Kapoor in 1984 and they moved to New Zealand in 1986 with their first child Megha when she was just one year old. They were blessed with a second daughter Ayesha four years later in 1989. Virender went as a consultant to a tourist consortium but a few years later set up his own business of manufacturing agricultural machinery. He started small but is now manufacturing heavy machinery like stone crushers of over 100 tons and seagoing barges. A few years back Virender was recognized as a young and upcoming enterpreneur by the New Zealand government and has further enhanced his status since. My daughter was working in the finance department of Tourism Auckland but took a break as the girls were growing up. She is currently a financial consultant with an MNC dealing with disaster management. Last year and the recent earthquake in February 2011 in Christ Church has kept her very busy and fully occupied. Megha after her graduation in Law and Commerce from Trinity College in Melbourne opted for her passion of fashion designing. She is now the Assistant Fashion Editor of *Vogue* in Sydney. Ayesha is a graduate in Bio-chemistry and is pursuing further studies in medicine.

Vikrant, my son, is a year younger to my daughter. He joined the Army in 1986 and is a Brigadier now. After commanding 7th Light Cavalry, a year's stint in an UN assignment in Congo, Deputy Brigade Commander in an Armoured Brigade in Rajasthan he is now commanding an Armoured Brigade. He is a graduate of the Defence Services Staff College. He did his infantry attachment with my battalion deployed in CI operations in Manipur and did GSO-2 of the CI Sector in Kupwara in Jammu & Kashmir. He married Rashmi in 1989 and were blessed with twin boy and girl, Adhiraj and Shagun in 1995. They are now in the 12th standard and are good in studies and sports. One feels blessed with such a family and thanks God for it everyday. We can never thank god enough for his blessing and good things that he gave us.

Index